Focus on GRAMMAR 2

FOURTH EDITION

Irene E. Schoenberg

ALWAYS LEARNING

PEARSON

Focus on Grammar 2: An Integrated Skills Approach, Fourth Edition

Copyright © 2012, 2006, 2000, 1994 by Pearson Education, Inc.

Pearson Education, 10 Bank Street, White Plains, NY 10606

Staff credits: The people who made up the *Focus on Grammar 2, Fourth Edition* team, representing editorial, production, design, and manufacturing, are Elizabeth Carlson, Tracey Cataldo, Aerin Csigay, Dave Dickey, Christine Edmonds, Nancy Flagmann, Ann France, Lise Minovitz, Barbara Perez, Robert Ruvo, Debbie Sistino, and Kim Steiner.

Cover image: Shutterstock.com
Text composition: ElectraGraphics, Inc.
Text font: New Aster

Library of Congress Cataloging-in-Publication Data

Schoenberg, Irene, 1946–
    Focus on grammar. 1: an integrated skills approach / Irene E. Schoenberg, Jay Maurer. — 3rd ed.
        p. cm.
    Includes index.
    ISBN 0-13-245591-9 — ISBN 0-13-254647-7 — ISBN 0-13-254648-5 — ISBN 0-13-254649-3 — ISBN 0-13-254650-7 1. English language—Textbooks for foreign speakers. 2. English language—Grammar—Problems, exercises, etc. I. Maurer, Jay. II. Title.
    PE1128.S3456824 2011
    428.2'4—dc22
                                                                                    2011014126

PEARSON LONGMAN ON THE **WEB**

Pearsonlongman.com offers online resources for teachers and students. Access our Companion Websites, our online catalog, and our local offices around the world.

Visit us at **pearsonlongman.com**.

Printed in the United States of America

ISBN 10: 0-13-254647-7
ISBN 13: 978-0-13-254647-8

11   16

ISBN 10: 0-13-211443-7 (with MyLab)
ISBN 13: 978-0-13-211443-1 (with MyLab)

4   16

CONTENTS

WELCOME TO *FOCUS ON GRAMMAR*

Now in a new edition, the popular five-level *Focus on Grammar* course continues to provide an integrated-skills approach to help students understand and practice English grammar. Centered on thematic instruction, *Focus on Grammar* combines controlled and communicative practice with critical thinking skills and ongoing assessment. Students gain the confidence they need to speak and write English accurately and fluently.

NEW for the FOURTH EDITION

VOCABULARY

Key vocabulary is highlighted, practiced, and recycled throughout the unit.

PRONUNCIATION

Now, in every unit, pronunciation points and activities help students improve spoken accuracy and fluency.

LISTENING

Expanded listening tasks allow students to develop a range of listening skills.

UPDATED CHARTS and NOTES

Target structures are presented in a clear, easy-to-read format.

NEW READINGS

High-interest readings, updated or completely new, in a variety of genres integrate grammar and vocabulary in natural contexts.

NEW UNIT REVIEWS

Students can check their understanding and monitor their progress after completing each unit.

MyFocusOnGrammarLab

An easy-to-use online learning and assessment program offers online homework and individualized instruction anywhere, anytime.

Teacher's Resource Pack   One compact resource includes:

THE TEACHER'S MANUAL: General Teaching Notes, Unit Teaching Notes, the Student Book Audioscript, and the Student Book Answer Key.

TEACHER'S RESOURCE DISC: Bound into the Resource Pack, this CD-ROM contains reproducible Placement, Part, and Unit Tests, as well as customizable Test-Generating Software. It also includes reproducible Internet Activities and PowerPoint® Grammar Presentations.

THE *FOCUS ON GRAMMAR* APPROACH

The new edition follows the same successful four-step approach of previous editions. The books provide an abundance of both controlled and communicative exercises so that students can bridge the gap between identifying grammatical structures and using them. The many communicative activities in each Student Book provide opportunities for critical thinking while enabling students to personalize what they have learned.

- **STEP 1: GRAMMAR IN CONTEXT** highlights the target structures in realistic contexts, such as conversations, magazine articles, and blog posts.
- **STEP 2: GRAMMAR PRESENTATION** presents the structures in clear and accessible grammar charts and notes with multiple examples of form and usage.
- **STEP 3: FOCUSED PRACTICE** provides numerous and varied controlled exercises for both the form and meaning of the new structures.
- **STEP 4: COMMUNICATION PRACTICE** includes listening and pronunciation and allows students to use the new structures freely and creatively in motivating, open-ended speaking and writing activities.

Recycling

Underpinning the scope and sequence of the *Focus on Grammar* series is the belief that students need to use target structures and vocabulary many times, in different contexts. New grammar and vocabulary are recycled throughout the book. Students have maximum exposure and become confident using the language in speech and in writing.

Assessment

Extensive testing informs instruction and allows teachers and students to measure progress.

- **Unit Reviews** at the end of every Student Book unit assess students' understanding of the grammar and allow students to monitor their own progress.
- Easy to administer and score, **Part and Unit Tests** provide teachers with a valid and reliable means to determine how well students know the material they are about to study and to assess students' mastery after they complete the material. These tests can be found on MyFocusOnGrammarLab, where they include immediate feedback and remediation, and as reproducible tests on the Teacher's Resource Disc.
- **Test-Generating Software** on the Teacher's Resource Disc includes a bank of *additional* test items teachers can use to create customized tests.
- A reproducible **Placement Test** on the Teacher's Resource Disc is designed to help teachers place students into one of the five levels of the *Focus on Grammar* course.

COMPONENTS

In addition to the Student Books, Teacher's Resource Packs, and MyLabs, the complete *Focus on Grammar* course includes:

Workbooks Contain additional contextualized exercises appropriate for self-study.

Audio Program Includes all of the listening and pronunciation exercises and opening passages from the Student Book. Some Student Books are packaged with the complete audio program (mp3 files). Alternatively, the audio program is available on a classroom set of CDs and on the MyLab.

THE *FOCUS ON GRAMMAR* UNIT

Focus on Grammar introduces grammar structures in the context of unified themes. All units follow a **four-step approach**, taking learners from grammar in context to communicative practice.

STEP 1 GRAMMAR IN CONTEXT

This section presents the target structure(s) in a natural context. As students read the **high-interest texts**, they encounter the form, meaning, and use of the grammar. **Before You Read** activities create interest and elicit students' knowledge about the topic. **After You Read** activities build students' reading vocabulary and comprehension.

Vocabulary exercises improve students' command of English. Vocabulary is **recycled** throughout the unit.

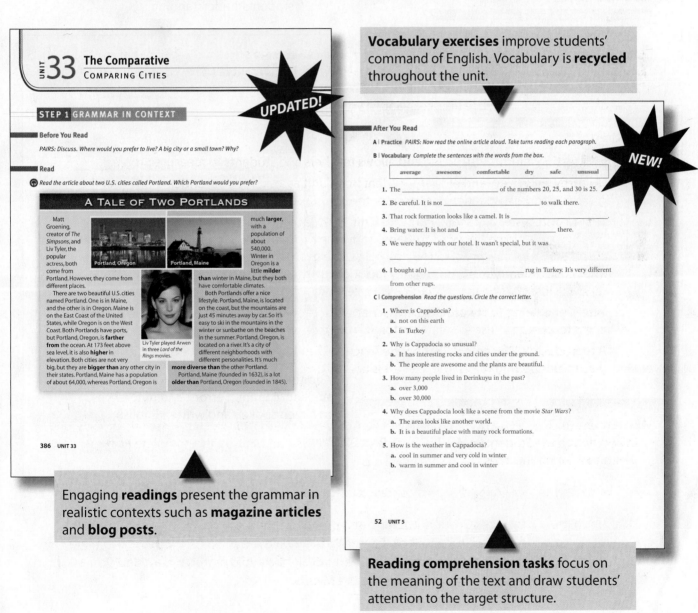

UNIT **33**
The Comparative
COMPARING CITIES

STEP 1 GRAMMAR IN CONTEXT

Before You Read

PAIRS: Discuss. Where would you prefer to live? A big city or a small town? Why?

Read

Read the article about two U.S. cities called Portland. Which Portland would you prefer?

A TALE OF TWO PORTLANDS

Matt Groening, creator of *The Simpsons*, and Liv Tyler, the popular actress, both come from Portland. However, they come from different places.

There are two beautiful U.S. cities named Portland. One is in Maine, and the other is in Oregon. Maine is on the East Coast of the United States, while Oregon is on the West Coast. Both Portlands have ports, but Portland, Oregon, is **farther from** the ocean. At 173 feet above sea level, it is also **higher** in elevation. Both cities are not very big, but they are **bigger than** any other city in their states. Portland, Maine has a population of about 64,000, whereas Portland, Oregon, is

Portland, Oregon   Portland, Maine

Liv Tyler played Arwen in three *Lord of the Rings* movies.

much **larger**, with a population of about 540,000. Winter in Oregon is a little **milder than** winter in Maine, but they both have comfortable climates.

Both Portlands offer a nice lifestyle. Portland, Maine, is located on the coast, but the mountains are just 45 minutes away by car. So it's easy to ski in the mountains in the winter or sunbathe on the beaches in the summer. Portland, Oregon, is located on a river. It's a city of different neighborhoods with different personalities. It's much **more diverse than** the other Portland. Portland, Maine (founded in 1632), is a lot **older than** Portland, Oregon (founded in 1845).

386 UNIT 33

After You Read

A | Practice *PAIRS: Now read the online article aloud. Take turns reading each paragraph.*

B | Vocabulary *Complete the sentences with the words from the box.*

average	awesome	comfortable	dry	safe	unusual

1. The _____ of the numbers 20, 25, and 30 is 25.
2. Be careful. It is not _____ to walk there.
3. That rock formation looks like a camel. It is _____.
4. Bring water. It is hot and _____ there.
5. We were happy with our hotel. It wasn't special, but it was
   _____.
6. I bought a(n) _____ rug in Turkey. It's very different from other rugs.

C | Comprehension *Read the questions. Circle the correct letter.*

1. Where is Cappadocia?
   a. not on this earth
   b. in Turkey
2. Why is Cappadocia so unusual?
   a. It has interesting rocks and cities under the ground.
   b. The people are awesome and the plants are beautiful.
3. How many people lived in Derinkuyu in the past?
   a. over 3,000
   b. over 30,000
4. Why does Cappadocia look like a scene from the movie *Star Wars*?
   a. The area looks like another world.
   b. It is a beautiful place with many rock formations.
5. How is the weather in Cappadocia?
   a. cool in summer and very cold in winter
   b. warm in summer and cool in winter

52   UNIT 5

Engaging **readings** present the grammar in realistic contexts such as **magazine articles** and **blog posts**.

Reading comprehension tasks focus on the meaning of the text and draw students' attention to the target structure.

This section gives students a comprehensive and explicit overview of the grammar with detailed **Grammar Charts** and **Grammar Notes** that present the form, meaning, and use of the structure(s).

Grammar Charts present the structure in a clear, easy-to-read format.

Grammar Notes give concise, simple **explanations** and **examples** to ensure students' understanding.

STEP 2 GRAMMAR PRESENTATION

THE SIMPLE PAST

Affirmative Statements (All Verbs Except *Be*)

Subject	Verb	
I	stayed	home.
We	went	

Affirmative Statements with *Be*

Subject	Verb	
I	was	at home.
We	were	

Negative Statements (All Verbs Except *Be*)

Subject	Did Not (Didn't)	Base Form of Verb	
I	did not	stay	with them.
We	didn't	go	

Negative Statements with *Be*

Subject	Verb	
I	was not	at work.
	wasn't	
We	were not	
	weren't	

Yes / No Questions (All Verbs Except *Be*)

Did	Subject	Base Form of Verb
Did	she	leave?
	they	

Yes / No Questions with *Be*

Was / Were	Subject	
Was	he	home last night?
Were	they	

Wh- Questions (All Verbs Except *Be*)

Wh- Word	Did	Subject	Base Form of Verb
When		you	arrive?
Where		he	work?
How	did	it	begin?
Why		he	leave?
Who(m)		they	help?

Wh- Questions with *Be*

Wh- Word	Past Form	Subject	
When		she	there?
Where	was	he	from?
How		his	tests?
Why	were	you	late?
Who(m)		they	with?

Wh- Questions About the Subject (All Verbs Except *Be*)

Wh- Word	Past Form	
Who	walked	to the station?
What	happened	to him?
How many people	waited	there?

Wh- Questions About the Subject with *Be*

Wh- Word	Past Form	
Who		his friend?
What	was	his last name?
How many people	were	there?

236 UNIT 21

GRAMMAR NOTES

1 Use **have to** and **must** to talk about things that are **necessary**. Both *have to* and *must* are followed by the base form of the verb. *Must* is stronger than *have to*.

USAGE NOTE: We usually use *have to* in speaking and informal writing.

BE CAREFUL! *Have to* is different from the verb *have*.

NOTE: The past of *must* and *have to* is *had to*.

- I **have to take** a test next week.
- Students **must take** a three-credit history course.
- I **have** a psychology class.
- I **have to read** 50 pages for this class.
- Last week I **had to buy** a lot of textbooks.

2 Use **don't have to** or **doesn't have to** when there is no necessity. You have a **choice**.

- I **don't have to sit** in the same seat every day. I can sit wherever I want.
- He **doesn't have to wear** a suit to work. He can wear a shirt and slacks.

3 **Must not** or the contraction **mustn't** means that you are **not allowed** to do something. You don't have a choice. You can't do it.

- You **must not take** scissors on a plane.

4 Do not repeat *must* or *have to* when you use two verbs or verb phrases with one subject.

- You **must take** a test and **write** a paper.
- He **has to work** and **study**.
  NOT: He must take a test and ~~must~~ write a paper.
  NOT: He has to work and ~~has to~~ study.

5 **BE CAREFUL!** Do not use *to* after *must*.

- He **must write** a report.
  NOT: He ~~must to~~ write a report.

6 **USAGE NOTE:** We rarely use *mustn't* in conversation except when talking to small children or telling rules. We use *can't* instead.

- Children, you **mustn't** cross the street when the signal is red.
- You can't park there.
  NOT: You ~~mustn't~~ park there.

REDESIGNED!

Additional **Notes** provide information about spelling, common errors, and differences between spoken and written English.

Controlled practice activities in this section lead students to master form, meaning, and use of the target grammar.

STEP 3 FOCUSED PRACTICE

EXERCISE 1: Discover the Grammar

Underline the simple present. Circle the present progressive. Underline twice all non-action verbs.

Raisa has a new phone with a lot of great features. She likes her phone a lot. Her phone keeps her in touch with her friends wherever she is. Right now Raisa is texting friends. They are making plans for the evening. She and her friends often text. They don't talk much on the phone. They also connect through Facebook®. Raisa often adds new friends to her site. Sometimes she doesn't know them very well. Raisa's mother, Olga, worries about that. Olga doesn't use social networks. She prefers to talk on the phone or connect through email.

EXERCISE 2: Simple Present; Non-Action Verbs; Present Progressive *(Grammar Notes 1–5)*

Complete the conversation with the words in parentheses. Use the simple present or present progressive. Use contractions when possible.

A: What _____*are*_____ you _____*doing*_____?
           1.   2. (do)

B: I _____ my messages. Look. That's my friend from high school.
     3. (check)

     She _____ three kids now. They _____ happy birthday to
         4. (have)   5. (sing)

     their father.

A: Oh. That's nice.

B: _____ you _____ social networking sites?
     6.   7. (use)

A: No, I _____. I _____ to email my friends. I _____
         8.   9. (prefer)   10. (think)

     it's more personal. Also, I _____ there are privacy features in social
         11. (know)

     networking sites, but I _____ about my privacy.
         12. (worry)

Discover the Grammar activities develop students' recognition and understanding of the target structure before they are asked to produce it.

A **variety of exercise types** engage students and guide them from recognition and understanding to accurate production of the grammar structures.

EXERCISE 4: Comparison of Adjectives   *(Grammar Notes 1–7)*

Complete the paragraph with the adjectives in parentheses. Use the comparative form.

You are choosing between two cities to live in, Los Angeles or Glendale. You aren't sure which is a _____*better*_____ choice. Los
                 1. (good)
Angeles is a much _____ city than Glendale, and it has all the problems of big
            2. (big)
cities. Los Angeles is _____ than
            3. (polluted)
Glendale, and traffic is _____.
            4. (bad)

Rodeo Drive, Los Angeles

The streets of downtown Los Angeles are

_____ too. However, Los Angeles is much _____ than Glendale.
5. (busy)   6. (exciting)

Los Angeles has a great night life. Glendale

is much _____ at night. Both
          7. (quiet)

cities have the same great climate. It's hard

to compare housing costs. Some parts of Los

Angeles are _____ than Glendale
         8. (more / expensive)

and other parts are _____. Both
         9. (less / expensive)

cities are close, so if you make a mistake, you

Bicycle trail, Glendale, California

can always move.

EXERCISE 5: Editing

Correct the sentences. There are seven mistakes. The first one is already corrected. Find and correct six more.

1. Our new apartment is ~~more~~ comfortable than our old one.
2. Florida is more hotter than Maine.
3. Oregon is far north than California.
4. A motorcycle is more fast than a bicycle.
5. Traffic at 8:00 A.M. is more heavy than traffic at 10:00 A.M.
6. The climate in Portland, Oregon, is mild than the climate in Anchorage, Alaska.
7. The location of Jake's apartment is more convenient than his sister.

An **Editing** exercise ends every Focused Practice section and teaches students to find and correct typical mistakes.

STEP 4 COMMUNICATION PRACTICE

This section provides practice with the structure in **listening** and **pronunciation** exercises as well as in communicative, open-ended **speaking** and **writing** activities that move students toward fluency.

Listening activities allow students to hear the grammar in natural contexts and to practice a range of listening skills.

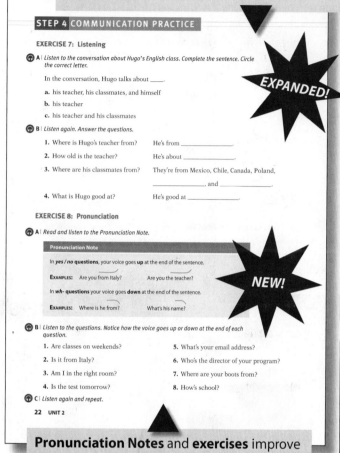

STEP 4 COMMUNICATION PRACTICE

EXERCISE 7: Listening

A | *Listen to the conversation about Hugo's English class. Complete the sentence. Circle the correct letter.*

In the conversation, Hugo talks about _____.

a. his teacher, his classmates, and himself
b. his teacher
c. his teacher and his classmates

B | *Listen again. Answer the questions.*

1. Where is Hugo's teacher from?   He's from _____.
2. How old is the teacher?   He's about _____.
3. Where are his classmates from?   They're from Mexico, Chile, Canada, Poland, _____, and _____.
4. What is Hugo good at?   He's good at _____.

EXERCISE 8: Pronunciation

A | *Read and listen to the Pronunciation Note.*

Pronunciation Note
In *yes / no questions*, your voice goes **up** at the end of the sentence.
EXAMPLES: Are you from Italy?   Are you the teacher?
In *wh-* **questions** your voice goes **down** at the end of the sentence.
EXAMPLES: Where is he from?   What's his name?

B | *Listen to the questions. Notice how the voice goes up or down at the end of each question.*

1. Are classes on weekends?
2. Is it from Italy?
3. Am I in the right room?
4. Is the test tomorrow?

5. What's your email address?
6. Who's the director of your program?
7. Where are your boots from?
8. How's school?

C | *Listen again and repeat.*

22 UNIT 2

EXPANDED!

NEW!

Pronunciation Notes and **exercises** improve students' spoken fluency and accuracy.

Speaking activities help students synthesize the grammar through discussions, debates, games, and problem-solving tasks, developing their fluency.

EXERCISE 8: Comparing Train Systems

PAIRS: Look at the information about the London Underground and the Moscow Metro. Together write as many comparative questions as you can. Ask other pairs your questions. Answer their questions. Then compare these subways to others you know.

    EXAMPLE: **A:** Is the Underground faster than the Moscow Metro?
               B: No, it isn't. It's slower.

	London Underground	Moscow Metro
Year opened	1863	1935
Length of tracks	250 miles (400 kilometers)	187.2 miles (301.2 kilometers)
Number of passengers each day	4 million	6.6 million
Hours of operation	5:30 A.M. to 1:15 A.M. (Fri. & Sat. closes at 2:00 A.M.)	5:30 A.M. to 1:00 A.M.
Cost of ride in euros	4 euros for shortest distance	26 rubles = .66 euro
Speed	20.5 mph (33 km / h)	25.82 mph (41.55 km / h)

EXERCISE 11: Writing

A | *Compare two ways of travel. Use at least three comparative adjectives.*

    EXAMPLE: Most cities have busses and trains, but in San Francisco some people also travel by trolley, and in Venice people sometimes travel by gondola. Both the trolley and the gondola are more fun than the bus or the train. The gondola is more romantic than the trolley, but the trolley is more exciting, especially when you're traveling down one of San Francisco's steep streets.

B | *Check your work. Use the Editing Checklist.*

Editing Checklist
Did you . . . ?
☐ use comparative adjectives correctly
☐ check your spelling

NEW!

Writing activities encourage students to produce meaningful writing that integrates the grammar structure.

An **Editing Checklist** teaches students to correct their mistakes and revise their work.

Unit Reviews give students the opportunity to check their understanding of the target structure. **Answers** at the back of the book allow students to monitor their own progress.

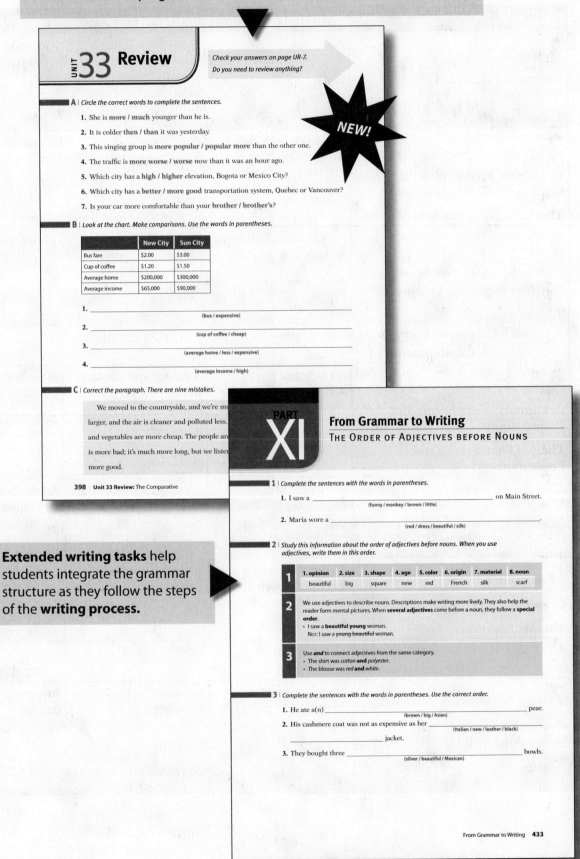

UNIT **33 Review**

Check your answers on page UR-7.
Do you need to review anything?

NEW!

A | *Circle the correct words to complete the sentences.*

1. She is **more / much** younger than he is.
2. It is colder **then / than** it was yesterday.
3. This singing group is **more popular / popular more** than the other one.
4. The traffic is **more worse / worse** now than it was an hour ago.
5. Which city has a **high / higher** elevation, Bogota or Mexico City?
6. Which city has a **better / more good** transportation system, Quebec or Vancouver?
7. Is your car more comfortable than your **brother / brother's**?

B | *Look at the chart. Make comparisons. Use the words in parentheses.*

	New City	Sun City
Bus fare	$2.00	$3.00
Cup of coffee	$1.20	$1.50
Average home	$200,000	$300,000
Average income	$65,000	$90,000

1. _____
   (bus / expensive)
2. _____
   (cup of coffee / cheap)
3. _____
   (average home / less / expensive)
4. _____
   (average income / high)

C | *Correct the paragraph. There are nine mistakes.*

We moved to the countryside, and we're m...
larger, and the air is cleaner and polluted less. ...
and vegetables are more cheap. The people ar...
is more bad; it's much more long, but we liste...
more good.

398 Unit 33 Review: The Comparative

PART **XI**

From Grammar to Writing
THE ORDER OF ADJECTIVES BEFORE NOUNS

1 | *Complete the sentences with the words in parentheses.*

1. I saw a _____ on Main Street.
   (funny / monkey / brown / little)
2. Maria wore a _____.
   (red / dress / beautiful / silk)

2 | *Study this information about the order of adjectives before nouns. When you use adjectives, write them in this order.*

1	1. opinion	2. size	3. shape	4. age	5. color	6. origin	7. material	8. noun
	beautiful	big	square	new	red	French	silk	scarf

2	We use adjectives to describe nouns. Descriptions make writing more lively. They also help the reader form mental pictures. When **several adjectives** come before a noun, they follow a **special order.** • I saw a **beautiful young** woman. NOT: I saw a ~~young beautiful~~ woman.

3	Use **and** to connect adjectives from the same category. • The shirt was *cotton* **and** *polyester.* • The blouse was *red* **and** *white.*

3 | *Complete the sentences with the words in parentheses. Use the correct order.*

1. He ate a(n) _____ pear.
   (brown / big / Asian)
2. His cashmere coat was not as expensive as her _____
   (Italian / new / leather / black)
   _____ jacket.
3. They bought three _____ bowls.
   (silver / beautiful / Mexican)

From Grammar to Writing **433**

Extended writing tasks help students integrate the grammar structure as they follow the steps of the **writing process.**

SCOPE AND SEQUENCE

UNIT	READING	WRITING	LISTENING
1 page 2 **Grammar:** Present of *Be*: Statements **Theme:** Famous People	An article: *Famous Couples*	Sentences about a famous person or talented friend or relative	Occupations and countries of famous people
2 page 13 **Grammar:** Present of *Be*: *Yes / No* Questions and *Wh-* Questions **Theme:** First Day of School	A conversation: *Arriving in Class*	Questions about a language school	A conversation about an English class
3 page 25 **Grammar:** Past of *Be*: Statements, *Yes / No* Questions, *Wh-* Questions **Theme:** First Jobs	An illustrated story: *A boy's first job*	An email to a friend about your weekend	Phone messages
PART I **From Grammar to Writing, page 36** **Capitalization**			
4 page 40 **Grammar:** Count Nouns and Proper Nouns **Theme:** Photographs and Photographers	An article: *A Photographer and a Photo*	A paragraph about a photo of a person you know	A conversation about a family gathering
5 page 51 **Grammar:** Descriptive Adjectives **Theme:** Cave Homes	An online article: Cappadocia, Turkey	A paragraph about an interesting place	A telephone conversation about a vacation
6 page 60 **Grammar:** Prepositions of Place **Theme:** Locations	An online posting and a conversation: *At the Museum*	An invitation to a party with directions	Locations of countries
PART II **From Grammar to Writing, page 70** **Connecting with *And* and *But***			
7 page 72 **Grammar:** Imperatives; Suggestions with *Let's, Why don't we . . . ?* **Theme:** Long Life	An online article: *Secrets to a Long Life*	An advertisement for a hotel in Ikaria, Greece	An advertisement for a spa

SPEAKING	PRONUNCIATION	VOCABULARY	
Pair Discussion: Occupations *Class Discussion*: Talented People	Tips for *he, she, he's,* and *she's*	athlete busy exciting	famous husband talented
Pair Activity: Asking and Answering Questions *Role Play*: Meeting at a Party	Rising intonation in *yes / no* questions Falling intonation in *wh-* questions	by the way excuse me on time	right room
Guided Conversation: Describing the Weather *Group Discussion*: The First Day of School	Extra pronounced syllable in negative forms of *be* Clipped /t/ sound in *wasn't, weren't*	a big deal boring busy	make money still
Game: Describing Things *Game*: Comparing Choices	Sound of plurals: /s/, /z/, /ɪz/	all over almost be born	holiday special striking
Group Discussion: Asking Questions about a Place	Syllable stress	average awesome comfortable	dry safe unusual
Game: Guessing Countries *Game*: Describing Locations	Stressed words for emphasis	appointment be free cafeteria	flight rest room sculpture
Pair Activity: Making Suggestions for You and Another Person *Pair Activity*: Giving Advice *Pair Activity*: Giving Directions	Linking sound in *don't + you*	advice dead island	nap pray secret

SPEAKING	PRONUNCIATION	VOCABULARY	
Pair Discussion: Likes and Dislikes *Group Discussion*: Clothing Customs of the World	Third person singular ending /s/, /z/, or /ɪz/	alone companies cute	middle school senior teenager
Pair Discussion: Comparing Habits and Personality *Game*: Find Someone Who . . . *Game*: What's in Your Backpack?	Linking sound in *does it* and *does he*	bother easygoing messy neat	outgoing private stay up wake up
Pair Survey: Sleeping Habits *Group Survey*: Sleeping Habits *Pair Activity*: Information Gap	Consonant clusters with /r/ and /l/	author guest nightmares	remember unfortunately
Pair Activity: Comparing Pictures of a Street *Game*: Tic Tac Toe	Homophones: *there, their,* and *they're*	amusement park attraction get away include	indoor international market one of a kind
Class Activity: Asking about Family Photos *Game*: Find Someone Who . . .	Ending sounds with possessives: /z/, /s/, /ɪz/	back composition grade	handwriting recognize
Game: Find Someone Who . . . *Game*: What Can Your Group Do?	Reduced vowel in *can* when followed by base form verb Stressed vowel in *can't*	be surprised genius intelligent	invent professor
Information Gap: Asking Questions about a Website	Vowel sounds /eɪ/ and /ɛ/	especially gain lose	overweight pound

SPEAKING	PRONUNCIATION	VOCABULARY	
Game: Describing a Classroom Photo	Unstressed *-ing* ending in the present progressive	competition extracurricular give up	top tough wealthy
Role Play: Talking about Movies *Pair Activity*: Describing Pictures for a Partner to Draw	Stressed final syllable in abbreviations	catch a cold classic cough	favorite fever scene
Pair Discussion: Guessing About People *Group Activity*: Survey	Intonation to express emotions	connect constantly improving	minor waterproof
Pair Discussion: Talking About your Weekend *Game*: Truths or Lies	Final sound with simple past verbs: /d/, /t/, or /ɪd/	bumpy canceled freezing	landed picked up
Group Activity: A Memory Game *Group Discussion*: A Wonderful and Terrible Day	Vowel sounds /æ/ and /ɛ/	appeared border lucky	shout suddenly terrible
Pair Discussion: Describing a Performance or Event	/dʒ/ and /y/ sounds	author be out mystery	play poem

SPEAKING	PRONUNCIATION	VOCABULARY	
Group Activity: A Quiz Show *Pair Discussion*: What Were You Like as a Child? *Information Gap*: Guess the Musician	/ɝ/ and /ɔ/ and the consonant cluster /kt/	admire be based on illustrated	noticed statue
Pair Discussion: Preferences *Game*: What Do I Do? *Pair Activity*: Problem Solving	Unstressed sound /əv/ in *of* Linking of consonant with *of*	avoids can't stand competitive	dress clothes personality predictable
Information Gap: Inventions	Stress on first syllable in compound nouns	accepted came up with comes after	invented rejected

Pair Discussion: Changes in Your Life	Reduced pronunciation of *going to* "gonna"	against announced be worth it	in my opinion increased tuition
Group Activity: Survey *Class Survey*: In the Future *Class Activity*: Making Predictions	Linking between subject pronoun and *will*	common disappear meal	spend time vegetarian
Pair Discussion: Describing Plans	Stress on numbers ending in *-ty* and *-teen*	commute entire flooding highways	mild predicted storm

Class Activity: Cooking Class Presentation *Group Discussion*: Your Favorite Restaurant	Schwa sound /ə/ in the indefinite article	atmosphere delicious main course	menu reservation service

UNIT	READING	WRITING	LISTENING
28 page 321 **Grammar:** *How much / How many*, Quantifiers, *Enough*, Adverbs of Frequency **Theme:** Desserts, Cooking, and Baking	A conversation: Desserts	A paragraph describing desserts	A conversation about a recipe
29 page 334 **Grammar:** *Too much / Too many*, *Too* + Adjective **Theme:** The Right Place to Live	An online article: Three U.S. cities	An email of complaint to a newspaper about an aspect of city life	A conversation about apartment rentals
PART IX From Grammar to Writing, page 344 **A Business Letter**			
30 page 348 **Grammar:** Advice: *Should, Ought to, Had better* **Theme:** Dos and Don'ts of the Business World	An online article: Global Business	A paragraph of advice to a businessperson about a culture that you know well	A conversation about travels to Japan
31 page 360 **Grammar:** Requests, Desires, and Offers: *Would you, Could you, Can you . . . ?, I'd like . . .* **Theme:** Neighbors	A message board: Problems with neighbors	Two email requests to neighbors	A telephone conversation between neighbors
32 page 370 **Grammar:** Necessity: *Have to, Don't Have to, Must, Mustn't* **Theme:** Rules at School	A conversation: Requirements for a history class	A paragraph about an elementary school where you grew up	Advice from a college counselor to a student
PART X From Grammar to Writing, page 382 **Expressing and Supporting an Opinion**			
33 page 386 **Grammar:** The Comparative **Theme:** Comparing Cities	An article: *A Tale of Two Portlands*	A paragraph comparing two ways to travel	A conversation about city improvements

SPEAKING	PRONUNCIATION	VOCABULARY	
Class Survey: Eating Habits *Information Gap*: Recipes *Group Presentation*: Desserts	/aʊ/ sound	in season ingredients neighborhood	prepare pretty good taste
Role Play: Living Situations *Group Discussion*: Describing Your City	/t/, /θ/, and /ð/ sounds	climate crime free time	housing pollution unemployment
Pair Discussion: Gift Giving *Group Discussion*: Body Language	Reduction of /t/ sound after *shouldn't* before a verb	business receptions confusion consider	customs insult
Group Survey: Making Requests *Role Play*: Making Polite Requests *Pair Activity*: Offering Invitations *Role Play*: Offering Invitations and Making Requests	Vowel sound /ʊ/ in *would*; Reduced forms of *would you* /wʊdʒə/ and *could you* /kʊdʒə/	be hurt go away lend me a hand	post a message selfish
Class Discussion: School Rules *Class Survey*: Preventing Cheating	Stress and unstress in *have to* or *has to*	average due final hard copy	midterm outline pass percent
Pair Activity: Comparing Train Systems *Pair Discussion*: Making Comparisons *Class Discussion*: Comparing Cities	Unstressed vowel in *than*	be located coast diverse mild	personality port sea level ski

SPEAKING	PRONUNCIATION	VOCABULARY	
Group Game: A Chain Story *Pair Discussion*: A Sports Event	Intonation to express emotions	applause appreciated audience facts	jokes polite seriously
Pair Activity: Describing Yourself *Class Survey*: Comparing Similarities	Unstressed vowel in *as . . . as*	I'm a loser I'm not going to make a fool of myself I'm not his type Making excuses No one can get a word in edgewise	
Group Survey: Animals	Unstressed *-est* syllable in superlatives	centimeter explorer extinct feathers	inch kilogram pound species

ABOUT THE AUTHOR

Irene E. Schoenberg has taught ESL for more than two decades at Hunter College's International English Language Institute and at Columbia University's American Language Program. Ms. Schoenberg holds a master's degree in TESOL from Columbia University. She has trained ESL and EFL teachers at Columbia University's Teachers College and at the New School University. She has given workshops and academic presentations at conferences, English language schools, and universities in Brazil, Chile, Dubai, El Salvador, Guatemala, Japan, Mexico, Nicaragua, Peru, Taiwan, Thailand, Vietnam, and throughout the United States.

Ms. Schoenberg is the author of *Talk about Trivia*; *Talk about Values*; *Speaking of Values 1: Conversation and Listening*; *Topics from A to Z*, Books 1 and 2; and *Focus on Grammar 2: An Integrated Skills Approach*. She is the co-author with Jay Maurer of the *True Colors* series and *Focus on Grammar 1: An Integrated Skills Approach*. She is one of the authors of *Future 1: English for Results* and *Future 3: English for Results*.

ACKNOWLEDGMENTS

I gratefully acknowledge the many reviewers for their suggestions and comments. There are many people at Pearson who have contributed to the development and production of this edition. I would like to thank them all, in particular:

- The people in production who helped carry the project through: **Rhea Banker** and especially **Robert Ruvo** for his indefatigable efforts.
- **Lise Minovitz**, the supervising editor, for her expert guidance and unflagging energy in keeping a very complex project on target.
- **Debbie Sistino**, the series director, who, in addition to managing the entire series, was always available to answer any of my questions.
- **Joanne Dresner** for her original vision and guidance of the *Focus on Grammar* series.
- My editors of the first three editions for helping to bring the books to fruition.
- **Ann France**, for her attractive new design, and **Aerin Csigay** and **Kim Steiner** for great photos that make the pages come alive.
- Above all, I'm most grateful to my editor **Kim Steiner**. Her dedication to the project, her brilliant solutions to problems, her creativity, her availability and her eye for detail, have made working on the revised edition a joy.
- Finally, I thank my family for their love and understanding: **Harris**, **Dan**, **Dahlia**, **Jonathan**, and **Olivia**.

REVIEWERS

We are grateful to the following reviewers for their many helpful comments:

Aida Aganagic, Seneca College, Toronto, Canada; **Aftab Ahmed**, American University of Sharjah, Sharjah, United Arab Emirates; **Todd Allen**, English Language Institute, Gainesville, FL; **Anthony Anderson**, University of Texas, Austin, TX; **Anna K. Andrade**, ASA Institute, New York, NY; **Bayda Asbridge**, Worcester State College, Worcester, MA; **Raquel Ashkenasi**, American Language Institute, La Jolla, CA; **James Bakker**, Mt. San Antonio College, Walnut, CA; **Kate Baldrige-Hale**, Harper College, Palatine, IL; **Leticia S. Banks**, ALCI-SDUSM, San Marcos, CA; **Aegina Barnes**, York College CUNY, Forest Hills, NY; **Sarah Barnhardt**, Community College of Baltimore County, Reisterstown, MD; **Kimberly Becker**, Nashville State Community College, Nashville, TN; **Holly Bell**, California State University, San Marcos, CA; **Anne Bliss**, University of Colorado, Boulder, CO; **Diana Booth**, Elgin Community College, Elgin, IL; **Barbara Boyer**, South Plainfield High School, South Plainfield, NJ; **Janna Brink**, Mt. San Antonio College, Walnut, CA; **AJ Brown**, Portland State University, Portland, OR; **Amanda Burgoyne**, Worcester State College, Worcester, MA; **Brenda Burlingame**, Independence High School, Charlotte, NC; **Sandra Byrd**, Shelby County High School and Kentucky State University, Shelbyville, KY; **Edward Carlstedt**, American University of Sharjah, Sharjah, United Arab Emirates; **Sean Cochran**, American Language Institute, Fullerton, CA; **Yanely Cordero**, Miami Dade College, Miami, FL; **Lin Cui**, William Rainey Harper College, Palatine, IL; **Sheila Detweiler**, College Lake County, Libertyville, IL; **Ann Duncan**, University of Texas, Austin, TX; **Debra Edell**, Merrill Middle School, Denver, CO; **Virginia Edwards**, Chandler-Gilbert Community College, Chandler, AZ; **Kenneth Fackler**, University of Tennessee, Martin, TN; **Jennifer Farnell**, American Language Program, Stamford, CT; **Allen P. Feiste**, Suwon University, Hwaseong, South Korea; **Mina Fowler**, Mt. San Antonio Community College, Rancho Cucamonga, CA; **Rosemary Franklin**, University of Cincinnati, Cincinnati, OH; **Christiane Galvani**, Texas Southern University, Sugar Land, TX; **Chester Gates**, Community College of Baltimore County, Baltimore, MD; **Luka Gavrilovic**, Quest Language Studies, Toronto, Canada; **Sally Gearhart**, Santa Rosa Community College, Santa Rosa, CA; **Shannon Gerrity**, James Lick Middle School, San Francisco, CA; **Jeanette Gerrity Gomez**, Prince George's Community College, Largo, MD; **Carlos Gonzalez**, Miami Dade College, Miami, FL; **Therese Gormley Hirmer**, University of Guelph, Guelph, Canada; **Sudeepa Gulati**, Long Beach City College, Long Beach, CA; **Anthony Halderman**, Cuesta College, San Luis Obispo, CA; **Ann A. Hall**, University of Texas, Austin, TX; **Cora Higgins**, Boston Academy of English, Boston, MA; **Michelle Hilton**, South Lane School District, Cottage Grove, OR; **Nicole Hines**, Troy University, Atlanta, GA; **Rosemary Hiruma**, American Language Institute, Long Beach, CA; **Harriet Hoffman**, University of Texas, Austin, TX; **Leah Holck**, Michigan State University, East Lansing, MI; **Christy Hunt**, English for Internationals, Roswell, GA; **Osmany Hurtado**, Miami Dade College, Miami, FL; **Isabel Innocenti**, Miami Dade College, Miami, FL; **Donna Janian**, Oxford Intensive School of English, Medford, MA; **Scott Jenison**, Antelope Valley College, Lancaster, CA; **Grace Kim**, Mt. San Antonio College, Diamond Bar, CA; **Brian King**, ELS Language Center, Chicago, IL; **Pam Kopitzke**, Modesto Junior College, Modesto, CA; **Elena Lattarulo**, American Language Institute, San Diego, CA; **Karen Lavaty**, Mt. San Antonio College, Glendora, CA; **JJ Lee-Gilbert**, Menlo-Atherton High School, Foster City, CA; **Ruth Luman**, Modesto Junior College, Modesto, CA; **Yvette Lyons**, Tarrant County College, Fort Worth, TX; **Janet Magnoni**, Diablo Valley College, Pleasant Hill, CA; **Meg Maher**, YWCA Princeton, Princeton, NJ; **Carmen Marquez-Rivera**, Curie Metropolitan High School, Chicago, IL; **Meredith Massey**, Prince George's Community College, Hyattsville, MD; **Linda Maynard**, Coastline Community College, Westminster, CA; **Eve Mazereeuw**, University of Guelph, Guelph, Canada; **Susanne McLaughlin**, Roosevelt University, Chicago, IL; **Madeline Medeiros**, Cuesta College, San Luis Obispo, CA; **Gioconda Melendez**, Miami Dade College, Miami, FL; **Marcia Menaker**, Passaic County Community College, Morris Plains, NJ; **Seabrook Mendoza**, Cal State San Marcos University, Wildomar, CA; **Anadalia Mendoza**, Felix Varela Senior High School, Miami, FL; **Charmaine Mergulhao**, Quest Language Studies, Toronto, Canada; **Dana Miho**, Mt. San Antonio College, San Jacinto, CA; **Sonia Nelson**, Centennial Middle School, Portland, OR; **Manuel Niebla**, Miami Dade College, Miami, FL; **Alice Nitta**, Leeward Community College, Pearl City, HI; **Gabriela Oliva**, Quest Language Studies, Toronto, Canada; **Sara Packer**, Portland State University, Portland, OR; **Lesley Painter**, New School, New York, NY; **Carlos Paz-Perez**, Miami Dade College, Miami, FL; **Ileana Perez**, Miami Dade College, Miami, FL; **Barbara Pogue**, Essex County College, Newark, NJ; **Phillips Potash**, University of Texas, Austin, TX; **Jada Pothina**, University of Texas, Austin, TX; **Ewa Pratt**, Des Moines Area Community College, Des Moines, IA; **Pedro Prentt**, Hudson County Community College, Jersey City, NJ; **Maida Purdy**, Miami Dade College, Miami, FL; **Dolores Quiles**, SUNY Ulster, Stone Ridge, NY; **Mark Rau**, American River College, Sacramento, CA; **Lynne Raxlen**, Seneca College, Toronto, Canada; **Lauren Rein**, English for Internationals, Sandy Springs, GA; **Diana Rivers**, NOCCCD, Cypress, CA; **Silvia Rodriguez**, Santa Ana College, Mission Viejo, CA; **Rolando Romero**, Miami Dade College, Miami, FL; **Pedro Rosabal**, Miami Dade College, Miami, FL; **Natalie Rublik**, University of Quebec, Chicoutimi, Quebec, Canada; **Matilde Sanchez**, Oxnard College, Oxnard, CA; **Therese Sarkis-Kruse**, Wilson Commencement, Rochester, NY; **Mike Sfiropoulos**, Palm Beach Community College, Boynton Beach, FL; **Amy Shearon**, Rice University, Houston, TX; **Sara Shore**, Modesto Junior College, Modesto, CA; **Patricia Silva**, Richard Daley College, Chicago, IL; **Stephanie Solomon**, Seattle Central Community College, Vashon, WA; **Roberta Steinberg**, Mount Ida College, Newton, MA; **Teresa Szymula**, Curie Metropolitan High School, Chicago, IL; **Hui-Lien Tang**, Jasper High School, Plano, TX; **Christine Tierney**, Houston Community College, Sugar Land, TX; **Ileana Torres**, Miami Dade College, Miami, FL; **Michelle Van Slyke**, Western Washington University, Bellingham, WA; **Melissa Villamil**, Houston Community College, Sugar Land, TX; **Elizabeth Wagenheim**, Prince George's Community College, Lago, MD; **Mark Wagner**, Worcester State College, Worcester, MA; **Angela Waigand**, American University of Sharjah, Sharjah, United Arab Emirates; **Merari Weber**, Metropolitan Skills Center, Los Angeles, CA; **Sonia Wei**, Seneca College, Toronto, Canada; and **Vicki Woodward**, Indiana University, Bloomington, IN.

Be: PRESENT AND PAST

Present of *Be*: Statements

FAMOUS PEOPLE

Before You Read

GROUPS: Name a young and famous person. Tell your group one thing about this person.

> **EXAMPLE:** Lionel Messi. He is a great soccer player.

Read

Read the article about the people in the photos.

Famous Couples

POP
Culture
News

They're young. They're rich. They're talented and famous. Who **are** they? Where **are** they from? What do they do?

The woman on the left **is** Carrie Underwood. She **is** from the United States. She's from the state of Oklahoma. Carrie **is** an American country singer. She **isn't** just a singer. She's also a pianist and a songwriter.

Carrie is married to Mike Fisher. He **is** also talented and famous. He **isn't** from the United States, and he **isn't** a singer. He's an athlete from Ottawa, Canada. Now he's an ice hockey player for the Nashville Predators. Carrie Underwood and Mike Fisher have homes in the United States and Canada.

Who **are** the people in the second photo? They're Gisele Bündchen and Tom Brady. Gisele **is** a supermodel. She's from Brazil, but she **is** famous all over the world. Her husband **is** Tom Brady. He **is** an American football player. He's from California. He plays quarterback for the New England Patriots.

The lives of these famous people **are** exciting. Their lives **aren't** easy. They **are** always very busy.

It's wonderful to be young and famous. Many young people want to be rich and famous. It takes talent, hard work, and good luck.

After You Read

A | Practice *PAIRS: Now read the article aloud. Take turns reading each paragraph.*

B | Vocabulary *Complete the sentences with the words from the box.*

athlete	busy	exciting	famous	husband	talented

1. Mike Fisher is Carrie Underwood's _____.

2. Carrie Underwood plays piano, sings, and writes music. She is very _____.

3. People know Gisele Bündchen all over the world. She is very _____.

4. Tom Brady is a great _____. He's a football player for the New England Patriots.

5. Brady works hard. He is _____ all the time.

6. Bündchen goes to many parties and travels to many interesting places. She has a(n) _____ life.

C | Comprehension *Complete the sentences. Circle the correct letter.*

1. Carrie Underwood is married to _____.
   a. Tom Brady   **b.** Mike Fisher

2. Underwood is a singer and _____.
   a. an athlete   **b.** a pianist

3. Underwood's husband is an _____.
   a. ice hockey player   **b.** actor

4. The New England Patriots are a _____.
   a. football team   **b.** talented player

5. Gisele Bündchen is a _____.
   a. supermodel   **b.** pianist

6. Bündchen is from _____.
   a. Canada   **b.** Brazil

7. Tom Brady is from _____.
   a. New England   **b.** California

8. To be rich and famous takes _____.
   a. time and money   **b.** hard work and good luck

PRESENT OF *BE*: STATEMENTS

Affirmative Statements

Singular			Plural		
Subject	*Be*		**Subject**	*Be*	
I	**am**		Masami and I We		
You	**are**		You and Josh You		students.
Mike He		talented.	Ivona and Juan They	**are**	
Carrie She	**is**		Seoul and London They		cities.
Hockey It		a sport			

Contractions				
I am	→	**I'm**	we are →	**we're**
you are →	**you're**		you are →	**you're**
he is →	**he's**		they are →	**they're**
she is →	**she's**			
it is →	**it's**			

Negative Statements

Singular	
Subject + *Be* / *Not*	
I **am not** **I'm not**	
You **are not** You**'re not** You **aren't**	from California.
He **is not** He**'s not** He **isn't**	
She **is not** She**'s not** She **isn't**	
It **is not** It**'s not** It **isn't**	new.

Plural	
Subject + *Be* / *Not*	
We **are not** We**'re not** We **aren't**	
You **are not** You**'re not** You **aren't**	in Brazil.
They **are not** They**'re not** They **aren't**	

GRAMMAR NOTES

1	The **present of be** has three forms: *am*, *is*, *are*.	• I **am** a student. • He **is** from Brazil. • They **are** famous.
2	Use the correct form of **be** + **not** to make a **negative statement**.	• I **am not** from Turkey. • It **is not** from Canada. • We **are not** famous.
3	Use **contractions** (short forms) in speaking and informal writing. There are two **negative contractions** for *is not* and *are not*.	• I**'m** from Mexico. • I**'m not** from Ecuador. • Mr. Crane**'s** from Los Angeles. • It**'s not** difficult. OR It **isn't** difficult. • We**'re not** single. OR We **aren't** single.
4	All **sentences** have a **subject** and a **verb**. **BE CAREFUL!** You cannot make a sentence without a subject. You cannot make a sentence without a verb.	SUBJECT VERB • **Gisele is** from Brazil. NOT: ~~Is from Brazil.~~ NOT: ~~Gisele from Brazil.~~
5	The **subject** is a noun or a pronoun. Subject pronouns (*I, you, he, she, it we, you, they*) replace subject nouns. **BE CAREFUL!** You cannot put a subject pronoun right after a subject noun.	SUBJECT NOUN • **Mike Fisher** is from Canada. SUBJECT PRONOUN • **He** is from Canada. NOT: ~~Fisher he~~ is from England.

STEP 3 FOCUSED PRACTICE

EXERCISE 1: Discover the Grammar

A | *Check (✓) the negative statements.*

   ✓ **1.** Carrie Underwood isn't single.

_____ **2.** Underwood is married to Mike Fisher.

_____ **3.** Fisher and Tom Brady are athletes.

_____ **4.** They aren't actors.

_____ **5.** I'm from Canada.

_____ **6.** I'm not from the United States.

B | *Look back at Part A. Underline the contractions.*

C | *Look back at sentences 1–3 in Part A. Change the subject nouns to subject pronouns.*

EXERCISE 2: Affirmative Statements

(Grammar Note 1)

Complete the sentences with **am, is,** *or* **are.**

1. Soccer _____is_____ popular all over the world.

2. Football _____is_____ popular in the United States.

3. Football and soccer _____are_____ different sports.

4. Tom Brady _____is_____ a great football player.

5. Lionel Messi _____is_____ a great soccer player.

6. I _____am_____ a football fan. I love football.

7. My cousins _____are_____ soccer fans. They love soccer.

EXERCISE 3: Affirmative and Negative Statements

(Grammar Notes 1–2)

Complete the sentences with **am, is,** *or* **are,** *and the word in parentheses.*

Parminder Nagra _____is_____
1.

a talented actor. She and Keira Knightley

_____are_____ the stars of the movie *Bend*
2.

It Like Beckham. It _____is_____ a comedy.
3.

In the movie, Nagra _____is_____ a young
4.

Indian girl in England. She _____is_____
5.

a good soccer player, and she loves soccer.

But her parents _____are_____ traditional. They _____are not_____ happy. They
6.   7. (not)

do not want her to play soccer. They say, "Soccer _____is not_____ for girls. Marriage
8. (not)

_____is_____ for girls. Look at your sister. Your sister _____is not_____ a soccer
9.   10. (not)

player, and she _____is_____ about to marry." Parminder says, "I _____am not_____
11.   12. (not)

my sister."

EXERCISE 4: Subject Pronouns and Contractions

(Grammar Notes 3, 5)

Change the underlined words. Change nouns to pronouns and write contractions of **be.**

1. Lionel Messi is from Argentina. ~~Messi is~~ a great soccer player. *(He's)*

2. Mr. Smith is a soccer fan. ~~Mr. Smith is~~ a football fan too. *(He)*

3. My partner and I are on a soccer team. ~~My partner and I are~~ not on a football team. *(We)*

4. Soccer is a great sport. ~~Soccer is~~ popular all over the world. *(It)*

5. Parminder Nagra and Halle Berry are actors. ~~Nagra and Berry are~~ talented. *(they)*

6. Ms. Brown is an English teacher. ~~Ms. Brown is~~ a supervisor too. *(He)*

7. Tennis and ping-pong are great sports. ~~Tennis and ping-pong are~~ exciting games. *(we they)*

EXERCISE 5: Affirmative and Negative Contractions

(Grammar Notes 1–4)

Write true sentences with the words in parentheses. Use the affirmative or negative. Use contractions when possible.

1. Lionel Messi is a soccer player. (He / popular all over the world)

   He's popular all over the world.

2. Soccer is a great game. (It / popular in my country)

   It's Popular im my country.

3. Rafael Nadal is a tennis player. (He / from Spain)

   He's from Spain.

4. Cristiano Ronaldo and David Beckham are famous. (They / talented soccer players)

   They are talented soccer Players.

5. (I / a student)

   I am a student.

6. (I / from London)

   I am from London.

7. (My friends and I / soccer fans)

   My friends and I are soccer fans.

8. (Soccer / my favorite sport)

   Soccer is my favorite sport.

EXERCISE 6: Editing

*Correct the paragraph. There are nine mistakes. The first mistake is already corrected.
Find and correct eight more.*

> My family ~~is~~ in Mexico. I ~~am~~ in Los Angeles. My father is a businessman,
> and my mother ~~is~~ a math teacher. Alessandra is my sister. She ~~is~~ an
> engineer. Marco is my brother. ~~He is~~ in the family business with my
> father. We ~~are~~ all soccer fans. Our favorite team is the Club de Fútbol
> Monterrey. Our team on TV very often. I call my family, and we ~~are~~ talk
> about the game on TV. They ~~are~~ far away, but thanks to email and cell
> phones, we ~~are~~ close.

STEP 4 COMMUNICATION PRACTICE

EXERCISE 7: Pronunciation

A | *Read and listen to the Pronunciation Note.*

Pronunciation Note

Some students confuse *he* and *she*. To pronounce *he* and *she* correctly, follow these
tips:

- **Smile** when you say *he* or *he's*.
- **Relax** your lips to say *she* or *she's*.

B | *Listen to the sentences. Check (✓) the correct box.*

	He's	She's
1.		✓
2.		
3.		
4.		
5.		
6.		

C | *Listen again and repeat.*

EXERCISE 8: Listening

A | *PAIRS: Look at the pictures. Do you know these talented people? Try to complete the chart with the words from the box. Follow the example answer.*

actor	Argentina	~~baseball player~~	England	ice skater	Korea	soccer player	Ukraine
actress	Barbados	Brazil	film director	~~Japan~~	singer	Taiwan	writer

	Hideki Matsui	Lionel Messi	Rihanna	Kim Yu-na
Name				
Occupation	*baseball player*			
Country of Origin	*Japan*			

	Rob Pattinson	Olga Kurylenko	Paulo Coehlo	Ang Lee
Name				
Occupation				
Country of Origin				

B | *Listen and write the correct occupation and country of origin for each person. Discuss your answers with your partner.*

EXAMPLE: A: Who is Hideki Matsui?
               B: He's a soccer player from Japan.
               A: He's from Japan, but he's not a soccer player. He's a baseball player.

C | *Listen again and check your answers.*

EXERCISE 9: Talking about Occupations

A | *PAIRS: Look at the occupations. Make a list of other occupations. Check (✓) your occupation and the occupations of your relatives and friends.*

_____   _____
_____   _____
_____   _____

☐ a nurse ☐ a stay-at-home mom or dad ☐ a doctor ☐ an athlete

☐ a plumber ☐ a writer ☐ an electrician ☐ a detective

☐ a lawyer ☐ a carpenter

B | *Talk about the occupations of your relatives and friends. Use the words from the box.*

boring	dangerous	difficult	exciting	interesting

EXAMPLE: **A:** My cousin is a detective. His job is dangerous, but it's interesting.
B: My uncle is a businessman. His job is difficult.

EXERCISE 10: Talking about Talented People

A | *PAIRS: Look at the list of qualities. Add four more qualities to the list.*

successful   funny   smart   hardworking

_____   _____   _____   _____

B | *Fill in the circles with information about a talented person you know. Then tell your partner.*

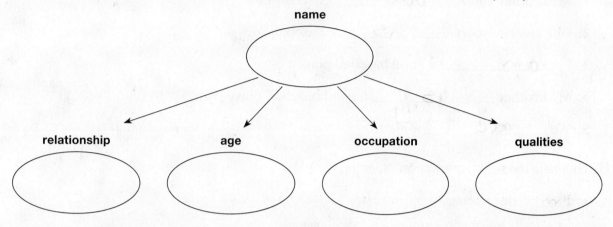

EXAMPLE: Noah is my brother. He's 19 years old. He's a baseball player and a musician. He's talented and hardworking. His dream is to be a great musician. Noah is not famous now. But one day everyone will know him.

EXERCISE 11: Writing

A | *Write four sentences about a famous person from Exercise 8 or a talented friend or relative. Give the person's name, country, and qualities. Add any information you know about the person. Use the present form of* **be.**

EXAMPLE: Hideki Matsui is a baseball player. He's from Japan. His nickname is "Godzilla." He's big and strong and talented.

B | *Check your work. Use the Editing Checklist.*

Editing Checklist
Did you . . . ? ☐ use the present form of **be** correctly ☐ use a subject and verb in each sentence ☐ check your spelling

A | *Complete the sentences. Use* **am, is,** *or* **are.**

1. My brother and I _____*are*_____ baseball fans.

2. Our favorite sport _____*is*_____ baseball.

3. I _____*am*_____ a good baseball player.

4. My brother _____*is*_____ a good baseball player too.

5. We _____*are*_____ athletes.

B | *Complete the sentences. Use* **'m, 's,** *or* **'re.**

1. I*'m* from Korea.

2. She *'s* from Brazil.

3. We *'re* in school in New York.

4. It *'s* a good school.

5. We *'re* happy to be here.

C | *Change the underlined words. Change nouns to pronouns and use contractions.*

1. *He*
   ~~Lionel Messi~~ is not in Argentina now.

2. *They*
   ~~Soccer and baseball~~ are exciting sports.

3. *We*
   ~~My partner and I~~ are not baseball fans.

4. *She*
   ~~Ms. Nagra~~ is the star of the movie *Bend It Like Beckham*.

D | *Correct the paragraph. There are six mistakes.*

My father and mother are from India, but they're in Canada now. My parents are doctors. My father ~~a~~ sports doctor, and my mother ~~she~~ is a foot doctor. My parents and I love sports. My father ~~are~~ *is* a soccer fan, and my mother *is* a baseball fan. I'm a soccer fan. My father and I ~~am~~ fans of Lionel Messi and Nuno Gomes. My sister ~~no~~ is good at sports. She's not a sports fan. She loves movies.

2 Present of *Be*: *Yes / No* Questions and *Wh-* Questions

FIRST DAY OF SCHOOL

STEP 1 GRAMMAR IN CONTEXT

Before You Read

A | *Talk to four students. Write their names in the chart. Ask them the question, "Are you always on time for _____?" Write* **Yes** *or* **No** *for each response.*

Are you always on time for these things?				
Student's name	School	Work	Dates	Parties

EXAMPLE: MARIA: Juan, are you always on time for school?
JUAN: Yes, I am.

B | *Report to the class.*

EXAMPLE: MARIA: Juan is always on time for school. Sekura is always on time for dates.

🎧 *It's the first day of an English class. Read the conversation.*

ARRIVING IN CLASS

LIDA KOZLOV: Excuse me. **Where's room 2?**

ALEX BROWN: It's right here, next to the office.

LIDA: Thanks. Uh . . . **are we late for class?**

ALEX: No, we're right on time.

LIDA: Whew! That's good. I hate to be late on the first day. **Is the teacher here?**

ALEX: Yes, he is.

LIDA: **How is he? Is he a good teacher?**

ALEX: I think he's very good. My name is Alex, by the way. **What's your name?**

LIDA: Lida.

ALEX: Nice to meet you. **Are you new here?**

LIDA: Yes, I am.

ALEX: Nice jacket.

LIDA: Thanks. It's from Italy.

ALEX: Oh, **are you from Italy?**

LIDA: No, I'm from Moscow. Hey, your English is so good! . . . **Where are you from?**

ALEX: I'm from Michigan.

LIDA: Michigan? But that's in the United States. **Are you in the right class?**

ALEX: Yes, I am.

LIDA: **Why are you here? Who are you?**

ALEX: I'm not a new student. I'm a new teacher. I'm your new teacher.

LIDA: Oh . . . !

After You Read

A | Practice *PAIRS: Read the conversation again aloud.*

B | Vocabulary *Complete the sentences with the words from the box. Remember to start sentences with a capital letter.*

by the way	excuse me	on time	right	room

1. _____, where's the elevator?

2. Your class is in _____ 102 next to the stairs.

3. Room 202 is _____ over there, near the elevator.

4. We're _____. We're not late or early.

5. Thanks for the coffee. _____, is the computer lab nearby?

C | Comprehension *Read the questions. Circle the correct letter.*

1. Are Lida and Alex on time for class?

   a. Yes, they are.   **b.** No, they're late.   **c.** They're early for class.

2. Where is Lida from?

   a. Italy   **b.** Michigan   **c.** Russia

3. Where is Michigan?

   a. in the United States **b.** in Mexico   **c.** in Italy

4. Are Lida and Alex students?

   a. He is, but she isn't. **b.** She is, but he isn't. **c.** Yes, they are.

5. What's the teacher's name?

   a. Lida Kozlov   **b.** Alex Brown   **c.** Alex Kozlov

6. What do you know is true? Alex is ___.

   a. not in the right class **b.** a good teacher   **c.** Lida's teacher

PRESENT OF *BE*: *YES / NO* QUESTIONS AND *WH-* QUESTIONS

Yes / No Questions Short Answers

Singular		
Be	Subject	
Am	I	
Are	you	
	he	in room 2?
Is	she	
	it	

Singular				
Yes		No		
	you **are**.		you**'re not**. you **aren't**.	
	I **am**.		I**'m not**.	
Yes,	he **is**.	No,	he**'s not**. he **isn't**.	
	she **is**.		she**'s not**. she **isn't**.	
	it **is**.		it**'s not**. it **isn't**.	

Plural		
Be	Subject	
	we	
Are	you	on time?
	they	

Plural			
Yes		No	
	you **are**.		you**'re not**. you **aren't**.
Yes,	we **are**.	No,	we**'re not**. we **aren't**.
	they **are**.		they**'re not**. they **aren't**.

Wh- Questions Short Answers Long Answers

Wh- Word	*Be*	Subject		Short Answers	Long Answers
Where		you	from?	Michigan.	I'm from Michigan.
Why	are		here?	I'm the teacher.	I'm here because I'm the teacher.
What		your	name?	Alex.	My name is Alex.
How	is	he?		Good.	He's a good teacher.
Who		she?		A student.	She's a student.

GRAMMAR NOTES

| 1 | Yes / no questions usually have a *yes* or *no* answer. | A: Is he a student?
B: **Yes**, he is. OR **No**, he isn't. |
| | **Wh- questions** ask for information. | A: **Who** is he?
B: He's the teacher. |

| 2 | Use **am**, **is**, or **are** before a subject in **yes / no questions**. | BE   SUBJECT
• **Am**   I   in English 2?
• **Is**   she   a student?
• **Are**   we   late? |

| 3 | We usually **answer yes / no questions** with short answers, but we can also give long answers.

BE CAREFUL! Do not use contractions in short answers with *yes*. | A: Are you a new student?
B: **Yes.** OR **Yes, I am.** OR **Yes, I am new.**

    NOT: Yes, ~~I'm.~~ |

| 4 | **Wh- questions** ask about the following:
Who → people
What → things
Where → places
When → time
How → in what way | • **Who** are they?
• **What** is in your bag?
• **Where** is our classroom?
• **When** is lunch?
• **How** is school? |
| | *Why* asks for a reason. We can give short or long answers. In long answers, use *because* before the reason. | A: **Why** are you late?
B: My bus was late. OR I'm late **because** my bus was late. |

| 5 | Use a **wh- word** before *is* or *are* in *wh-* questions. | WH- WORD   BE
• **What**   **is**   your name?
• **Where** **are** the books? |

| 6 | You can use **contractions** (short forms) with *wh-* words in speaking and informal writing.

We usually don't write the contraction with *are*. | • **Where's** the library?
• **When's** the class trip?

SPOKEN ONLY: Where're the kids? |

| 7 | We usually give short answers to *wh-* questions. We can also give long answers. | A: Where are you from?
B: **Mexico.** OR **I'm from Mexico.** |

| 8 | When we do not know the answer to a question, we say, "I don't know."

When someone asks a *yes / no* question that we think is true, we say, "Yes, I think so." If we think it is not true, we can say, "No, I don't think so." | A: Is the men's room nearby?
B: **I don't know.**

A: Is she in the library?
B: **Yes, I think so.** OR **No, I don't think so.** |

EXERCISE 1: Discover the Grammar

Look at the picture. Match the questions and answers.

_e_ **1.** Is the door open?		**a.** Yes, he is.
_c_ **2.** What time is it?		**b.** I don't know.
_a_ **3.** Is the teacher a man?		**c.** It's ten o'clock.
_h_ **4.** Are the students hungry?		**d.** Near the blackboard.
_f_ **5.** Is the woman at the door early?		**e.** No, it's not.
_b_ **6.** Is the woman at the door unhappy?		**f.** No, she's late.
_d_ **7.** Where is the teacher?		**g.** September.
_g_ **8.** What month is it?		**h.** Yes, I think so.

EXERCISE 2: *Yes / No* Questions

(Grammar Note 2)

Write **yes / no** *questions about the statements in parentheses.*

1. (Today is Friday.) _Is today Friday?_

2. (We are in the right building.) _Are we in the right building?_

3. (You are a new student.) _Are you a new student?_

4. (The teacher is from Canada.) _Where is the teacher from?_

5. (It's ten o'clock.) _What time is it?_

6. (They are new computers.) _Are they new computers?_

7. (Two students are absent today.) _Are two students absent today?_

8. (I'm in the right room.) _Am I in the right room?_

EXERCISE 3: Word Order of *Yes / No* Questions

(Grammar Notes 1–3)

Write **yes / no** *questions with the words in parentheses. Then write true short answers.*
Use contractions when possible. Use **yes / no**, *or* **I don't know**, *or* **I think so / I don't think so**.

1. (you / Are / usually early)

   A: _Are you usually early?_

   B: _Yes, I am. OR No, I'm not._

2. (your watch / fast / Is)

   A: _Is you watch fast?_

   B: _No, it is not_

3. (from Italy / your jacket / Is)

   A: _Is your jacket from Italy?_

   B: _No, it is not._

4. (your birthday / in the spring / Is)

   A: _Is your birthday in the spring?_

   B: _Yes, it is._

5. (your name / Is / easy to pronounce)

   A: _Is your name easy to pronounce?_

   B: _Yes, it is._

6. (different cities / Are / from / you and your classmates)

   A: _Are you and your classmates from different cities_

   B: _Yes, they are_

7. (busy / Are / your classmates / now)

   A: _Are your classmates busy now?_

   B: _Yes, they are._

EXERCISE 4: *Wh-* Questions

(Grammar Notes 1–4)

*Read the answers. Then write **wh-** questions with the words in parentheses.*

1. A: (Who) _Who's Alex Brown?_____

    B: Alex Brown is the teacher.

2. A: (Where) _____

    B: The computers are in room 304.

3. A: (What) _____

    B: Today's date is September 3.

4. A: (Why) _____

    B: We're late because we were in the wrong classroom.

5. A: (Why) _____

    B: She's the teacher because Alex isn't here today.

6. A: (How) _____

    B: My computer class is great.

EXERCISE 5: *Yes / No* Questions and *Wh-* Questions

(Grammar Notes 1–8)

A | *Read Alejandra's question on SmartGirl's blog. Write questions with the words in parentheses. Then write short answers.*

smartgirl.com

Alejandra Suarez
Hey SmartGirl,
I have a great boyfriend, Oscar. He's fun and intelligent. We're a good match. But there's one problem. He's always late. Always.
Why?
Alejandra

1. (Oscar / fun)

    A: _Is Oscar fun?_____

    B: _Yes, he is._____

2. (Oscar / smart)

    A: _____

    B: _____

3. (Alejandra and Oscar / a good pair)

    A: _____

    B: _____

4. (Who / always late)

    A: _____

    B: _____

B | *Now read SmartGirl's answer. Write* **yes** / **no** *questions. Use the words in parentheses. Then answer the questions with* **Yes, I think so, No, I don't think so,** *or* **I don't know.**

Smartgirl

Hey Alejandra,

OK, so your guy is great, but late. And you hate to wait. Why? Maybe he thinks, "I'm late. That means I'm important." Maybe he doesn't know it's a problem for you. He thinks it's no big deal. Tell him it is a big deal to you. Maybe he's just bad at planning his time. Try to help him.

Good luck.

SmartGirl

1. (Oscar / great)

    A: Is Oscar great?

    B: *I don't know.* _____

2. (Oscar / a bad boyfriend)

    A: _____

    B: _____

3. (Oscar / bad at planning time)

    A: _____

    B: _____

4. (Smartgirl's answer / good)

    A: _____

    B: _____

EXERCISE 6: Editing

Correct the conversations. There are nine mistakes. The first mistake is already corrected. Find and correct eight more.

1. A: Are you in the office?

    B: Yes, ~~I'm.~~ *I am*

2. A: Is easy?

    B: No, it's hard.

3. A: He Korean?

    B: No, he's isn't.

4. A: Excuse me. Where's the office?

    B: Yes, it's here.

5. A: Is this English 3?

    B: Yes, I think.

6. A: Is they in room 102?

    B: I don't know.

7. A: Where you from?

    B: I'm from Peru.

8. A: How your class is?

    B: It's very good.

9. A: What your nickname?

    B: Susie.

EXERCISE 7: Listening

A | *Listen to the conversation about Hugo's English class. Complete the sentence. Circle the correct letter.*

In the conversation, Hugo talks about _____.

a. his teacher, his classmates, and himself

b. his teacher

c. his teacher and his classmates

B | *Listen again. Answer the questions.*

1. Where is Hugo's teacher from?   He's from _____.

2. How old is the teacher?   He's about _____.

3. Where are his classmates from?   They're from Mexico, Chile, Canada, Poland,

    _____, and _____.

4. What is Hugo good at?   He's good at _____.

EXERCISE 8: Pronunciation

A | *Read and listen to the Pronunciation Note.*

Pronunciation Note
In *yes / no* **questions**, your voice goes **up** at the end of the sentence.
EXAMPLES: Are you from Italy?   Are you the teacher?
In *wh-* **questions**, your voice goes **down** at the end of the sentence.
EXAMPLES: Where is he from?   What's his name?

B | *Listen to the questions. Notice how the voice goes up or down at the end of each question.*

1. Are classes on weekends?

2. Is it from Italy?

3. Am I in the right room?

4. Is the test tomorrow?

5. What's your email address?

6. Who's the director of your program?

7. Where are your boots from?

8. How's school?

C | *Listen again and repeat.*

EXERCISE 9: Asking and Answering Questions

PAIRS: Look at Exercise 2 on page 18. Take turns. Ask your partner the questions. Use **yes / no** *short answers or* **I don't know, I think so,** *or* **I don't think so**.

EXERCISE 10: Role Play: Meeting at a Party

PAIRS: Imagine you and your partner are at a party. Give yourself a new name, a new country, and a new occupation. Introduce yourself to your partner.

EXAMPLE: **A:** Hi, I'm Eun Young.
B: Nice to meet you. I'm Ana. Are you from around here?
A: No, I'm from Korea. I'm here on business. What about you?

EXERCISE 11: Writing

A | *PAIRS: Read the ad for University Language School. Together write five* **wh-** *questions and five* **yes / no** *questions. Read your questions to other pairs. They close their books and answer your questions.*

LEARN ENGLISH AT ULS!

Register now for English classes at University Language School

Placement Test: Sept. 1 in Room 203

Classes begin September 8

phone: 989-870-3456
email : ULS@GreatSchools.com
University Language School   650 Elm Street, Long Beach, New York

Director: Jim Reilly

EXAMPLES: **A:** Where is ULS?
B: Who's the director?
A: Is ULS in Canada?

B | *Check your work. Use the Editing Checklist.*

Editing Checklist

Did you . . . ?
☐ use the correct word order for **yes / no** and **wh-** questions
☐ check your spelling

Check your answers on page UR-1.
Do you need to review anything?

A | Complete the questions. Circle the correct word or words.

1. A: **Where's / What's** the library?   B: In room 3.

2. A: **Who's / How's** your class?   B: It's great.

3. A: **What's / How's** your name?   B: Jin-Hee Lee.

4. A: **Is / Are** you from Seoul?   B: Yes, I am.

5. A: **Is / Are** it cold in Seoul now?   B: No, it isn't.

B | Complete the short answers.

1. A: Are you home?   B: Yes, _____.

2. A: Is your nickname JD?   B: No, _____.

3. A: Are they late?   B: No, _____.

4. A: Are we in the right room?   B: Yes, _____.

5. A: Am I late?   B: No, _____.

C | Write questions. Use the words in parentheses.

1. _____?
   (What / today's date)

2. _____?
   (Where / the men's room)

3. _____?
   (Why / he / absent)

4. _____?
   (When / your first class)

5. _____?
   (Who / your teacher)

D | Correct the questions. There are five mistakes.

1. She your teacher?

2. What your name?

3. Where your class?

4. Is Bob and Molly good friends?

5. Why you late?

STEP 1 GRAMMAR IN CONTEXT

Before You Read

A | *Look at the pictures on this page and page 26. Guess the story.*

B | *PAIRS: Discuss the questions.*

    1. What was your first job?

    2. Was it easy? Was it hard?

Read

Read the story about Hugo Rubio's first job.

I **was** 16 years old. It **was** my first job. I **was** a lifeguard at a swimming pool for the summer. I **was** happy to have a job.

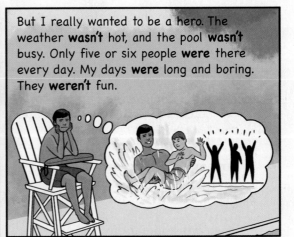

But I really wanted to be a hero. The weather **wasn't** hot, and the pool **wasn't** busy. Only five or six people **were** there every day. My days **were** long and boring. They **weren't** fun.

One day a woman slipped in the pool. I wanted to jump in to save her, but two guys **were** there before me.

They helped the woman, and they **were** the heroes.

(continued on next page)

Finally it **was** the last day of the season. The pool **was** crowded. More than 50 people **were** there.

A little boy fell in the pool. I jumped in and saved him.

It **wasn't** a big deal, but the little boy **was** the son of the mayor. The next day my picture **was** in the paper. I **was** a hero. It **was** exciting and fun.

Lifeguard Saves Mayor's Son

After You Read

A | Practice *PAIRS: Now read the story aloud. Take turns reading each paragraph.*

B | Vocabulary *Complete the sentences with the words from the box.*

a big deal	boring	busy	make money	still

1. I'm sorry. I don't have the report. I was very _____ last week.

2. I can't study full time. I need to work and _____.

3. I can work late today. It's not _____.

4. It's 11:00 P.M. Is he _____ at work?

5. Every day I do the same thing. My job is _____.

C | Comprehension *Answer the questions.*

1. What was Hugo's first job? _____

2. How old was he? _____

3. Was he a hero? _____

4. Was the job fun? Why or why not? _____

5. Was Hugo happy to be in the news? _____

PAST OF *BE*: AFFIRMATIVE STATEMENTS

Singular			
Subject	*Be*		Time Marker
I	was		
You	were	a student	last year.
He She	was		
It		busy	

Plural			
Subject	*Be*		Time Marker
We You They	were	in New York	two weeks ago.

PAST OF *BE*: NEGATIVE STATEMENTS

Singular			
Subject	*Be / Not*		Time Marker
I	was not wasn't		
You	were not weren't	at school	last night.
He She It	was not wasn't		

Plural			
Subject	*Be / Not*		Time Marker
We You They	were not weren't	at work	last week.

PAST OF *BE*: *YES / NO* QUESTIONS

Singular			
Be	Subject		Time Marker
Was	I		
Were	you	in the wrong room	yesterday?
Was	he she it		

Plural			
Be	Subject		Time Marker
Were	we you they	in the wrong building	last week?

SHORT ANSWERS

Singular					
Yes	Subject	*Be*	*No*	Subject	*Be*
	you	were.		you	weren't.
Yes,	I he she it	was.	No,	I he she it	wasn't.

Plural					
Yes	Subject	*Be*	*No*	Subject	*Be*
Yes,	you we they	were.	No,	you we they	weren't.

PAST OF *BE*: *WH-* QUESTIONS

Wh- word	Be		LONG ANSWERS
What		your first job?	I was a ticket taker at a movie theater.
Where		the movie theater?	In Jacksonville, Florida.
When	was	the last movie over last night?	The last movie was over at 1:00 A.M.
How		the movie?	It was pretty bad.
Why		it bad?	The acting was bad.
Who	were	the actors?	I'm not sure.

GRAMMAR NOTES

1	The **past of be** has two forms: **was** and **were**.	• She **was** at the airport. • They **were** late.
2	Use **was** or **were** + **not** to make **negative statements**.	• He **was not** at work. • They **were not** in class.
3	In informal writing and speaking, use the **contractions wasn't** and **weren't** in negative statements and negative short answers.	• He **wasn't** at an interview. • They **weren't** in class. • No, he **wasn't**. • No, they **weren't**.
4	To ask a **yes / no question**, put *was* or *were* before the subject. Use a **wh- word** before *was* or *were* in **wh- questions**.	BE SUBJECT • **Was** she at work? • **Were** you a server? • **How** was your day?
5	**Time markers** (*yesterday, last week, two days ago,* etc.) are usually at the end of statements. Time markers are sometimes at the beginning of statements. Time markers go at the end of a question.	• We **were** in Toronto **yesterday**. • **Yesterday** we **were** in Toronto. • **Was** he in Toronto **yesterday**?

EXERCISE 1: Discover the Grammar

Read about the first jobs of famous people. Then underline **was, wasn't, were,** *and* **weren't.**

A new job is exciting. A first job is very exciting. A first boss and a first paycheck are hard to forget. But a first job is not always the job of your dreams. Here are the first jobs of some famous people: Mick Jagger <u>wasn't</u> always a singer. As a teen he was an ice cream salesman. Ray Romano, the comedian, was a bank teller. Jennifer Aniston and Madonna weren't always stars. Before they were famous, they were servers in restaurants.

And Warren Beatty, the actor, was a rat catcher in a Virginia movie theater. So maybe you're not happy with your job today. Maybe it isn't the job you really want. Don't feel bad. Just keep looking.

EXERCISE 2: Questions and Answers   *(Grammar Notes 1–4)*

Complete the conversation. Use **was, wasn't, were,** *or* **weren't.**

A: _____*Were*_____ you at work yesterday?

B: No, I _____. I _____ at a job interview.
                    1.   **2.**

A: Oh? How _____ the interview?
                    3.

B: Good, I think.

A: _____ the questions hard?
           4.

B: Well, some _____ hard, but I _____ prepared.
                    5.   **6.**

A: Well, that sounds good. Good luck.

B: Thanks. It sounds like a good job. How _____ school?
                                                        7.

A: It _____ fun. I really like my classmates.
           8.

B: _____ you on time?
           9.

A: Yes, but my teacher _____ there. She was away. We had a substitute.
                                10.

EXERCISE 3: Affirmative and Negative Statements

Complete the sentences. Change the statements from the present to the past.

1. They are busy now. Last month _____ *they were busy* _____ too.

2. It's not sunny today. _____ *It wasn't sunny* _____ yesterday either.

3. My uncle, Jun, is in Seoul now. _____ last year too.

4. Today it's cold. Yesterday _____ too.

5. She's not in class this week. _____ last week.

6. He's at a job interview this morning. _____ yesterday morning too.

7. She's in the swimming pool now. She _____ last Wednesday too.

8. His phone is busy. It _____ yesterday evening too.

EXERCISE 4: Questions and Answers

(Grammar Notes 1–5)

Complete the conversation with the words in parentheses. Use the correct form of the past of **be.**

A: _____ *Was David at the party Friday night* _____?
   (David / be / at the party / Friday night)

B: _____.
   (No, he / not)

A: _____?
   (Where / he)

B: _____.
   (He / in Vancouver)

A: _____?
   (Why / he / in Vancouver)

B: _____.
   (He / there for work)

A: _____?
   (How / the weather / in Vancouver)

B: _____.
   (It / terrible)

A: _____?
   (the airport / closed)

B: _____.
   (No, but all the planes / late)

EXERCISE 5: Editing

Correct the email. There are five mistakes. The first mistake is already corrected. Find and correct four more.

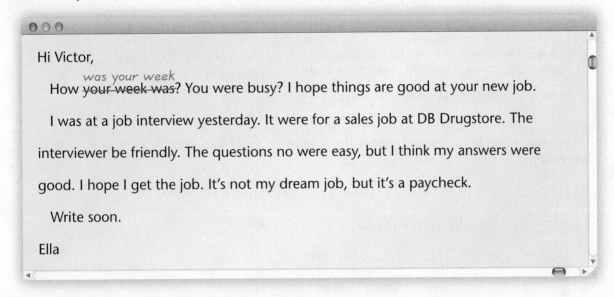

Hi Victor,

    How ~~your week was~~ *was your week*? You were busy? I hope things are good at your new job.

    I was at a job interview yesterday. It were for a sales job at DB Drugstore. The interviewer be friendly. The questions no were easy, but I think my answers were good. I hope I get the job. It's not my dream job, but it's a paycheck.

    Write soon.

Ella

STEP 4 COMMUNICATION PRACTICE

EXERCISE 6: Listening

A | *Listen to the phone messages. Who is each message from? Check (✓) the correct column.*

	Friend	Family	Business
Message 1	✓		
Message 2			
Message 3			
Message 4			
Message 5			

B | *Listen again. Complete the quotes. Write the correct words or numbers.*

Message 1. "How was the _____*interview?*_____"

Message 2. "The _____ was great. We _____ so happy to _____ Jay."

Message 3. "The _____ in Ottawa _____."

Message 4. "Please call me at _____."

Message 5. "We were _____ with Mona."

EXERCISE 7: Pronunciation

🎧 **A |** *Read and listen to the Pronunciation Note.*

Pronunciation Note
The **negative** form of *be* adds an **extra syllable**. The final sound of *wasn't* and *weren't* often sounds like / **n** / . We don't always hear the / **t** / . **EXAMPLES:**   was – **wasn't**   were – **weren't**

🎧 **B |** *Listen and repeat the sentences. Notice the pronunciation of* **was, wasn't, were,** *and* **weren't.**

1. It was a good interview. / It wasn't a good interview.

2. We were late. / We weren't late.

3. He was a server. / He wasn't a server.

4. I was an accountant. / I wasn't an accountant.

🎧 **C |** *Listen to the sentences. Which negative form do you hear? Check (✓) the correct box.*

	Was	Wasn't	Were	Weren't
1.		✓		
2.				
3.				
4.				
5.				

EXERCISE 8: Describing the Weather

A | *Study the words for weather.*

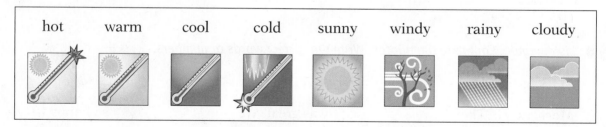

hot   warm   cool   cold   sunny   windy   rainy   cloudy

B | *PAIRS: Look at the chart below and choose a country. You are an airline flight attendant. A friend calls. Have a conversation about the weather in the country you are in. Take turns.*

A: Hello.

B: Maria? This is Bob. Where are you?

A: In _____.

B: How's the weather?

A: Well, today it's _____, but yesterday it was _____.

City	Yesterday	Today
Bangkok		
Beijing		
Budapest		
Istanbul		
Rio de Janeiro		
Seoul		
Vancouver		

EXERCISE 9: Talking about the First Day of School

*GROUPS: Each student says one true thing about the first day in school. Use **was**, **wasn't**, **were**, or **weren't** in each sentence. Continue as long as you can.*

EXAMPLES: **A:** It was warm and sunny on the first day of class.
B: I wasn't nervous.
C: Our class was exciting.

EXERCISE 10: Writing

A | *Write an email message to a friend. Tell about last weekend. Use contractions and the past and present of **be**.*

EXAMPLE:

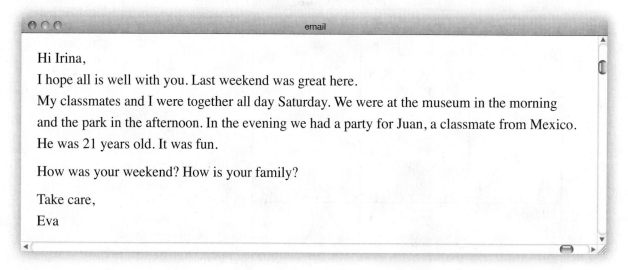

Hi Irina,

I hope all is well with you. Last weekend was great here.

My classmates and I were together all day Saturday. We were at the museum in the morning and the park in the afternoon. In the evening we had a party for Juan, a classmate from Mexico. He was 21 years old. It was fun.

How was your weekend? How is your family?

Take care,

Eva

B | *Check your work. Use the Editing Checklist.*

Editing Checklist

Did you . . . ?
☐ use the past of **be** correctly
☐ check your spelling

A | *Complete the questions. Use **was** or **were**.*

1. When _____ your interview?

2. Where _____ your interview?

3. _____ you nervous?

4. How _____ the questions?

5. _____ she at a job interview too?

B | *Match the questions and answers.*

_____ 1. How was the weather?   **a.** No, I wasn't.

_____ 2. Who was there?   **b.** Jon and Sri.

_____ 3. Were they home all evening?   **c.** Warm and sunny.

_____ 4. Were you late last week?   **d.** No, they weren't.

C | *Complete the conversation. Use the affirmative or negative form of **was** or **were**.*

A: How _____ your weekend?
                          1.

B: Great. I _____ at the park all day Saturday.
                          2.

A: _____ you with Ali?
              3.

B: Yes, I _____. We _____ together all day Saturday and
                    4.   5.

Sunday.

A: Ali _____ in class this morning. Where _____ he?
                    6.   7.

B: I don't know.

D | *Correct the paragraph. There are four mistakes.*

John is at a job interview yesterday. It were for a job at a bank. The questions no
were easy, but John's answers were good. He was happy. It a good day for John.

From Grammar to Writing

CAPITALIZATION

1 | *Look at A and B. What's wrong with A?*

A	B
mr. john smith	Mr. John Smith
342 dryden road	342 Dryden Road
ithaca, new york	Ithaca, New York 14850

2 | *Study the information about capitalization.*

1	Use a **capital letter** for the first word in every sentence.	• **We** are new students.
2	Use capital letters for **titles**.	• This is **Mr.** Winston. • She is **Dr.** Jones.
3	Use capital letters for the names of **people** and **places** (proper nouns).	• **Lila Roberts** is from **Vancouver**, **Canada**.
4	Use capital letters for the names of **streets**, **cities**, **states**, **countries**, and **continents**.	• 5 **Elm Street** • **West Redding, Connecticut** • **USA** • **Africa**
5	Use a capital letter for the word *I*.	• **I** am happy to be here.

3 | *Add capital letters.*

1. this is ms. herrera.

2. her address is 4 riverdale avenue.

3. i'm her good friend.

4. she was in bangkok and taiwan last year.

4 | *Correct the postcard from Ellen to Ruth. Add capital letters.*

Hi ruth,

john and i are in acapulco this week. it's beautiful here. the people are friendly, and the weather is great. it's sunny and warm.

   last week we were in mexico city for two days. i was there on business. my meetings were long and difficult, but our evenings were fun. hope all is well with you.

Regards,

ellen

To:

ms. ruth holland

10 oldwick st.

ringwood, new jersey 07456

usa

5 | *Write a postcard to a friend. Remember to use capital letters.*

To:

6 | *Exchange papers with a partner. Did your partner follow the directions? Correct any mistakes in grammar and spelling.*

7 | *Talk to your partner. Discuss the mistakes you made. Then rewrite your own paper and make any necessary changes.*

PART II

NOUNS, ADJECTIVES, PREPOSITIONS

UNIT 4

Count Nouns and Proper Nouns
PHOTOGRAPHS AND PHOTOGRAPHERS

STEP 1 GRAMMAR IN CONTEXT

Before You Read

PAIRS: Where do you keep your photos? Talk about a photo you have.

EXAMPLE: This is a photo of my sister. She's a nurse. She's 23 years old.

Read

Read the article about Henri Cartier-Bresson and one of his photographs.

A PHOTOGRAPHER AND A PHOTO

Henri Cartier-Bresson was **a photographer** and **an artist**. He was born in **France** in 1908. He died in 2004. At that time he was almost 96 **years** old. **Cartier-Bresson** traveled the **world**. He was in **West Africa**, the **United States**, **India**, **China**, **Egypt**, and **Russia**. His **photos** are from all over the **world**.

Cartier-Bresson is famous for "street" **photography**. Street **photographs** are about **people** in the **street** or other public **places** such as **parks** and **beaches**. They are sometimes about a special **moment** in **time**.

Look at this **photo** by **Cartier-Bresson**. Do you like it? It's **a photo** of **a woman** and **a man** on the **holiday** of **Easter**. They are both wearing fine **clothes**. The **woman** is wearing a big **hat** with many **flowers**. The man is wearing **a suit**. The **man** is looking at the **woman**. They are in **Harlem**, in **New York City**. It's 1947. **People** say **Cartier-Bresson's photos** are striking and beautiful. What do you think? Is it true for this **photo**?

After You Read

A | Practice *PAIRS: Now read the article aloud. Take turns reading each paragraph.*

B | Vocabulary *Circle the best meaning for the words in blue.*

1. Henri Cartier-Bresson **was born** in France.
   a. came into the world   b. lived

2. He was **almost** 96 years old.
   a. less than   b. more than

3. His photos are from **all over** the world.
   a. in some parts of   b. everywhere in

4. It's a **holiday**.
   a. a day when you do not work   b. a birthday or anniversary

5. His photos are **striking** and beautiful.
   a. very dangerous   b. unusual and attractive

6. A holiday is a **special** time. It is exciting and different.
   a. not ordinary   b. bad

C | Comprehension *Write T (**True**) or F (**False**) for each statement.*

_____ 1. The place of Henri Cartier-Bresson's birth was Russia.

_____ 2. Almost all of Cartier-Bresson's photos were of Europe.

_____ 3. Cartier-Bresson was in many countries during his life.

_____ 4. Cartier-Bresson is famous for "street" photography.

_____ 5. Street photography shows people in places like parks or beaches.

_____ 6. Harlem, New York, is not in the United States.

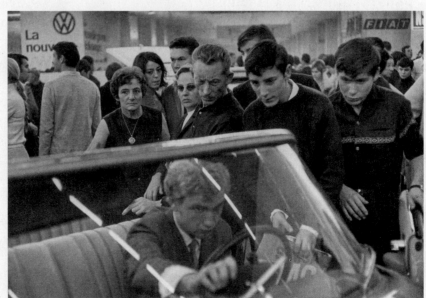

Cartier-Bresson,
Automobile Show, Paris. 1968

SINGULAR AND PLURAL COUNT NOUNS; PROPER NOUNS

Singular Nouns	Plural Nouns
He is **a photographer**.	They are **photographers**.
He is **an artist**.	They are **artists**.

Irregular Plural Nouns

Singular	Plural
man	men
woman	women
child	children
foot	feet
tooth	teeth
person	people

Proper Nouns

Harlem is in **New York City**.

The poet **Maya Angelou** has a home in **Harlem**.

GRAMMAR NOTES

1	**Nouns** are names of people, places, and things.	• a **student**, **Jung Eun** • a **country**, **Korea** • a **camera**, a **photograph**
2	**Count nouns** are easy to count. They have a singular and plural form.	• **one** photo, **two** photos, **three** photos
3	Use *a* before **singular count nouns** that begin with a **consonant sound** like / n / , / b / , / h /.	• She's **a n**urse. • He's **a b**aker. • It's **a h**ouse.
	BE CAREFUL! Use *a* before a *u* that sounds like "*yew*."	• This is **a u**nit about nouns.
	Use *an* before singular count nouns that begin with a **vowel sound**.	• She's **an a**rtist. • He's **an e**ngineer. • It's **an u**mbrella.
	BE CAREFUL! Use *an* before an *h* that is silent.	• It's **an h**our too early. (*Hour* sounds like *our*.)

4	To form the **plural** of most **count nouns**, add -*s* or -*es*.	• one **friend** three **friends** • one **class** three **classes**
	Some nouns have irregular plural endings.	• one **man** two **men** • one **tooth** two **teeth**
	Some nouns such as *clothes, glasses, jeans, scissors* are always plural.	• My **jeans are** blue.
	Do not put *a* or *an* before plural nouns.	• They are **photos** of **friends**. NOT: They are a photos of a friends.
5	Names of specific people and places are **proper nouns**. Write these with a capital letter.	• **Paris** is in **France**. • **Harlem** is in **New York City**.
	Do not put *a* or *an* before proper nouns.	NOT: A Paris is in a France.

REFERENCE NOTES

For a discussion of **non-count nouns and *the*** (the definite article), see Unit 27 page 311.

For the **spelling and pronunciation** rules for **plural nouns**, see Appendix 5 on pages A-5–A-6.

STEP 3 FOCUSED PRACTICE

EXERCISE 1: Discover the Grammar

A | *Read the conversation.*

MIKE: Is that you in the photo?

DOUG: Yes, it is. It's a photo of me with friends from college.

MIKE: Where are they now?

DOUG: Well, the woman on the left, Jasmine, is in Brazil.

MIKE: Really?

DOUG: Uh-huh. She's a teacher there. And the guy on the right, Bob, is here in New York. He's an accountant.

MIKE: Who's the woman in the center?

DOUG: That's Amy. She's a street photographer. Her camera is always with her. What a life! She travels all over the world. Last month she was in India. Before that she was in Central America. Now her photos are in a show at the library here.

MIKE: I'd love to see them.

DOUG: Them? Or her?

B | *Look back at the conversation in Part A. Find these nouns and write them:*

1. One noun that begins with a vowel: _____

2. Two singular nouns that begin with a consonant (not proper nouns):

_____, _____

3. Two proper nouns: _____, _____

4. Two plural nouns: _____, _____

EXERCISE 2: *A* or *An*

(Grammar Note 3)

A | *Write **a** or **an** before each word.*

1. __*a*__ man   **6.** ____ suit

2. ____ hand   **7.** ____ eye

3. ____ hat   **8.** ____ ear

4. ____ earring   **9.** ____ lip

5. ____ flower   **10.** ____ woman

B | *Look at the photo,* Harlem, 1947. *Label the parts of the photo with the words from Part A. Number them* **1–10**.

1

EXERCISE 3: *A* or *An*

(Grammar Notes 3–5)

Complete the sentences with **a** *or* **an**. *Write* Ø *if you don't need* **a** *or* **an**.

1. Henri Cartier-Bresson was __*a*__ photographer.

2. Cartier-Bresson and Ansel Adams were __Ø__ photographers.

3. Cartier-Bresson was _____ artist too.

4. All good photographers are _____ artists.

5. Adams was _____ pianist before he was _____ photographer.

6. Adams was born in _____ San Francisco, California.

7. For Adams, photography began with _____ trip to Yosemite National Park.

8. _____ Cartier-Bresson was born in _____ Normandy.

9. _____ Normandy is in _____ France.

10. Cartier-Bresson has _____ photos in the Louvre Museum.

EXERCISE 4: Regular and Irregular Plural Nouns

(Grammar Note 4)

Complete the sentences with the nouns from the box. Use the correct form. Look at the spelling rules for plural nouns in Appendix 5 on page A-5 for help.

artist	class	country	fish	life	person
~~city~~	clothes	earrings	flower	museum	watch

1. San Francisco and Los Angeles are _____*cities*_____ in California.

2. Brazil and France are _____.

3. The Louvre and the Prado are _____.

4. Seiko and Rolex are kinds of _____.

5. Your photos of _____ in the water are striking.

6. There are two _____, a man and a woman, in the photo *Harlem, 1947*.

7. The woman in *Harlem, 1947* has a hat with _____.

8. Her jewelry is beautiful, especially her _____.

9. The man and woman in the photo *Harlem, 1947* are wearing fine _____.

10. Many _____ and photographers live in New York City.

11. The _____ of famous artists are interesting to read.

12. I like photography. I'm taking two photography _____ at The New School in New York.

EXERCISE 5: Proper Nouns

(Grammar Note 5)

Change small letters to capital letters where necessary.

MIKE: Hi, are you ~~amy~~ lan? *Amy*

AMY: Yes, I am.

MIKE: I'm mike cho. I work with Doug.

AMY: Nice to meet you, mike.

MIKE: It's nice to meet you. Your photos are great.

AMY: Thanks. So, mike, are you from phoenix?

MIKE: No, I'm not. I'm from san francisco. I'm here for the Labor Day holiday.

AMY: Oh, san francisco is beautiful. I was there last year.

MIKE: Doug says you travel a lot.

AMY: Yes, I do. I was in india last year. And the year before that I was in almost every country in Central America.

MIKE: That's great.

AMY: Do you travel?

MIKE: When I can. I was in mexico last november during the thanksgiving vacation, and I was in canada with my family for a week last summer.

AMY: Any photos?

MIKE: No. My dad's brother sam is the photographer in our family.

EXERCISE 6: Editing

Correct the sentences. There are nine mistakes. The first mistake is already corrected. Find and correct eight more.

1. Henri Cartier-Bresson's photos are often of famous ~~person~~. *people*

2. This is photo of Henri Matisse.

3. Henri Matisse was great artist.

4. Before Matisse was artist, he was lawyer.

5. Matisse's paintings are in museum all over the world.

6. In this photo Matisse is in the south of france.

7. We see four bird outside their cages.

Matisse and His Doves, 1944

STEP 4 COMMUNICATION PRACTICE

EXERCISE 7: Pronunciation

A | *Read and listen to the Pronunciation Note.*

> **Pronunciation Note**
>
> When **nouns are plural**, the **ending** can have one of three sounds:
> / **s** /, / **z** /, or / **ɪz** /.
>
> **EXAMPLES:** students / **s** /
> teachers / **z** /
> buses / **ɪz** /

B | *Listen and complete each sentence with the correct word from the box. Then listen again and check the ending of the sound that you hear.*

artists	books	boxes	classes	glasses	~~photos~~	scissors

	/ s /	/ z /	/ ɪz /
1. The ___*photos*___ are ready.	☐	☑	☐
2. Her art _____ are from 10:00 to 1:00.	☐	☐	☐
3. Be careful. The _____ are sharp.	☐	☐	☐
4. The _____ are full of old photos.	☐	☐	☐
5. The paintings are by different _____.	☐	☐	☐
6. I need my _____ to see the names of the artists.	☐	☐	☐
7. I have some interesting _____ about Africa in that bookcase.	☐	☐	☐

C | *Listen again and repeat.*

EXERCISE 8: Listening

A | *Listen to a conversation between Doug and Lily. What is Lily telling Doug about? Circle the correct letter.*

a. a birthday party

b. a holiday

c. a family photo

| *Listen again. Then read the questions. Circle the correct letter.*

1. Who are the people in the photo?

    a. Lily's family and friends   **b.** Lily's family

2. What is the holiday?

    a. Easter   **b.** Thanksgiving

3. Who is the photographer?

    a. a cousin   **b.** an uncle

4. When is Lily's birthday?

    a. before Thanksgiving   **b.** after Thanksgiving

5. What is in the boxes?

    a. gifts   **b.** games

EXERCISE 9: Game: Describing Things

PAIRS: Look at these things. You have 15 minutes. Together list as many nouns as you can. The pair with the most correct nouns wins.

EXERCISE 10: Game: Comparing Choices

A | *PAIRS: Name the following people, places, and things.*

an artist or a photographer	
a music band	
three countries	
three things in your class	
three parts of the body	
two holidays	
three occupations	
two electronic items	

B | *Compare your choices with those of another pair. How many of the same choices do you have?*

EXERCISE 11: Writing

A | *Write a paragraph about a photo of a person you know. Tell about the person. Tell about the photo.*

EXAMPLE: This is a photo of my grandmother. She was born in China in 1945. She lives in Los Angeles now. She was a dancer. In this photo she's in her garden. It was her birthday. My grandmother is old, but she is still a striking woman.

B | *Check your work. Use the Editing Checklist.*

Editing Checklist

Did you . . . ?
☐ use singular and plural count nouns and proper nouns correctly
☐ check your spelling

UNIT 4 Review

Check your answers on page UR-1.
Do you need to review anything?

A | *Complete the sentences. Use **a, an,** or Ø.*

1. This is _____ photo of my best friend.

2. He is _____ actor.

3. He is _____ talented.

4. His friends are _____ actors too.

5. They all are _____ hardworking.

B | *Complete the sentences with the words from the box. Use the plural form.*

city	clothes	fish	person	watch

1. My favorite _____ are Venice and Rio de Janeiro.

2. The two _____ in the photograph show midnight.

3. The _____ in the photos are from the 1980s, so the photos are probably

   from that time.

4. We take photos of the _____ in the sea with our underwater camera.

5. We see three _____ in the photo: a man and two women.

C | *Add capital letters where necessary.*

ALI: Hi, are you the photographer?

AMY: Yes, I'm Amy lin.

ALI: Nice to meet you. I'm ali Mohammed.

AMY: Are you from london?

ALI: Yes, I am. I'm here for your thanksgiving Day holiday.

D | *Correct the paragraph. There are six mistakes.*

Melanie Einzig is artist and an photographer. She was born in Minnesota, but lives in New york. Einzig captures moments in time. Her photograph are striking. They are in museum in San francisco, Chicago, and Princeton.

50   Unit 4 Review: Count Nouns and Proper Nouns

Before You Read

Look at the photographs on this page. What words describe them?

beautiful   boring   exciting   ordinary   ugly   unusual

Read

Read the online article about an interesting place.

rock formations

underground caves

Cappadocia, a Place of Mystery

This place is like another world, but it is here on Earth. It's so **different**, it's **awesome**. What is this place? It's Cappadocia, in Turkey. Why is it so **different**? What's so **unusual** about it? **Beautiful** rock formations and **underground** cities make it a very **special** place.

Cappadocia has a **long** history. Many people lived in the **underground** cities to be **safe** from enemies.[1] These cities were **big**. One city, Derinkuyu, had room for more than 30,000 people.

Today only a few people live in these cave homes in **underground** cities. But many people from all over the world visit them. They are full of **interesting** things to see. From above, Cappadocia looks like another world, like a *Star Wars* movie.

The weather in Cappadocia is **comfortable** all year long. It has **warm**, **dry** summers and **cold**, **snowy** winters. There is a **big** difference between day and night temperatures. The **average** summer temperature is 73 degrees Fahrenheit, and the **average** winter temperature is 28 degrees Fahrenheit.

Awesome underground cities, **beautiful** rock formations, and an **interesting** history—these things make Cappadocia a place you won't forget.

---

[1] *enemies:* people who want to hurt you

After You Read

A | Practice *PAIRS: Now read the online article aloud. Take turns reading each paragraph.*

B | Vocabulary *Complete the sentences with the words from the box.*

average	awesome	comfortable	dry	safe	unusual

1. The _____ of the numbers 20, 25, and 30 is 25.

2. Be careful. It is not _____ to walk there.

3. That rock formation looks like a camel. It is _____.

4. Bring water. It is hot and _____ there.

5. We were happy with our hotel. It wasn't special, but it was

   _____.

6. I bought a(n) _____ rug in Turkey. It's very different

   from other rugs.

C | Comprehension *Read the questions. Circle the correct letter.*

1. Where is Cappadocia?
   a. not on this earth
   b. in Turkey

2. Why is Cappadocia so unusual?
   a. It has interesting rocks and cities under the ground.
   b. The people are awesome and the plants are beautiful.

3. How many people lived in Derinkuyu in the past?
   a. over 3,000
   b. over 30,000

4. Why does Cappadocia look like a scene from the movie *Star Wars*?
   a. The area looks like another world.
   b. It is a beautiful place with many rock formations.

5. How is the weather in Cappadocia?
   a. cool in summer and very cold in winter
   b. warm in summer and cold in winter

DESCRIPTIVE ADJECTIVES

Noun	*Be*	Adjective
The room	is	small.
The rooms	are	

	Adjective	Noun
It is a	small	room.
They are		rooms.

GRAMMAR NOTES

1	**Adjectives** describe nouns.	NOUN ADJECTIVE • **Cappadocia** is **beautiful**. ADJECTIVE NOUN • It's a **beautiful place**.
2	Adjectives can come • after the verb *be* • before a noun	• The room is **big**. • It's a **big** room. Nот: It's a ~~room big~~.
3	**BE CAREFUL!** Do not add *-s* to adjectives.	• a **hot** summer, a **cold** winter • **hot** summers, **cold** winters Nот: ~~colds winters~~
4	For **adjective** + **noun**: Use *a* before the adjective if the adjective begins with a **consonant sound**. Use *an* before the adjective if the adjective begins with a **vowel sound**.	• It's **a b**eautiful place. • It's **an u**nusual place.
5	Some adjectives end in *-ing*, *-ly*, or *-ed*.	• It's **interesting**. • They're **friendly**. • We're **tired**.

EXERCISE 1: Discover the Grammar

Maria is visiting Turkey. Read her travel blog about her hotel in Cappadocia. Underline eleven more adjectives.

○ ○ ○   maria.blogspot.com

I'm at a cave hotel in Cappadocia. Gamirasu Cave Hotel is in a <u>traditional</u> village. In the past it was a cave home. Now it's a hotel. The hotel is in a small village in the center of Cappadocia. My cave room is fun. It's old but has a modern bathroom and Internet service! The rooms are not expensive. The price of the room includes a delicious breakfast and

dinner. The food is good. The service is good too—the people are helpful and friendly. Also, it's easy to visit all of Cappadocia from the hotel. It was a great choice.

EXERCISE 2: Word Order   *(Grammar Notes 1–5)*

Complete the conversations with the words in parentheses. Remember to use a capital letter at the start of each sentence.

1. A: Where are we?

   B: *We are at an old market.* _____
   (market / at / we / are / old / an)

2. A: _____ Are they for sale?
   (awesome / carpets / the / are)

   B: Yes, they are.

3. A: How are the prices? Are they expensive?

   B: No, _____
   (the / prices / reasonable / are)

4. A: How's the weather?

   B: _____
   (warm / it / and / sunny / is)

5. A: How are you?

   B: _____
   (tired / happy / I'm / but)

EXERCISE 3: Sentences with Adjectives

(Grammar Notes 1–5)

Write sentences with the words in parentheses. Add the correct form of the verb **be.** *Add* **a** *if necessary.*

1. *Ali Baba Kitchen is a good restaurant.*_____

   (Ali Baba Kitchen / good restaurant)

2. _____

   (the food / delicious)

3. _____

   (the waiters / friendly and helpful)

4. _____

   (the Bilton / comfortable hotel)

5. _____

   (the rooms / not expensive)

6. _____

   (the outdoor market / safe)

7. _____

   (the carpets / expensive)

8. _____

   (that / beautiful carpet)

9. _____

   (the climate / mild)

10. _____

    (the weather / comfortable all year round)

EXERCISE 4: Editing

Correct the conversation. There are five mistakes. The first mistake is already corrected.
Find and correct four more.

A: Is that a ~~lamp new~~? *new lamp*

B: Yes, it is. It's from Turkey.

A: The colors are beautifuls.

B: Thanks. I got it at old market in Cappadocia.

A: Were there many things interesting to buy?

B: Yes. These plates are from the market too.

A: The colors unusual. I like them a lot.

B: Here. This one is for you.

EXERCISE 5: Listening

A | *Listen to the conversation. Sun Hi is talking to her friend Russ. What are they talking about? Circle the correct letter.*

a. Russ and Sun Hi's vacation

b. Sun Hi's visit to a national park

c. unusual places

B | *Listen again. Complete the sentences. Circle the correct letter.*

1. Sun Hi says Mesa Verde is _____.

    a. awesome   **b.** awful

2. The homes in the mountains are very _____.

    a. cold   **b.** old

3. The hotel is _____.

    a. clean   **b.** nice

4. The weather is _____.

    a. warm   **b.** cold

5. The park is _____.

    a. crowded   **b.** not crowded

EXERCISE 6: Pronunciation

A | *Read and listen to the Pronunciation Note.*

Pronunciation Note
Words have one or more **syllables**.
EXAMPLES: hat   happy
One syllable in a word is always **stressed**. Stressed syllables are long and loud.
EXAMPLE: happy

B | *Listen and repeat each adjective.*

One syllable	Two syllables	Three syllables	Four syllables
• cold	• boring	• usual • beautiful • expensive • important	• traditional

C | *Listen and mark the stressed syllable in each word.*

1. •
ugly

2. warm

3. unusual

4. friendly

5. modern

6. cheap

7. unimportant

D | *PAIRS: Take turns. Name an adjective from Parts B and C. Your partner names the opposite.*

EXAMPLE: **A:** Ugly.
            B: Beautiful!

EXERCISE 7: Guided Conversation

GROUPS: Each student writes the name of a city or place he or she knows well. The group asks questions about the place. Use the adjectives in Exercise 6 and the rest of the unit.

EXAMPLE: **A:** Woodside, Queens, in New York City.
            B: Are the homes in Woodside expensive?
            C: Are the people friendly?
            D: Is the weather mild?

EXERCISE 8: Writing

A | *Write a paragraph about an interesting place. Use* **be** *and adjectives.*

> EXAMPLE: JeJu Island is in South Korea. It is a popular vacation place. Many Koreans go to this island on their honeymoon. The people are friendly, and the climate is mild. It's a good place for hiking and horseback riding. It's safe and the beaches are awesome.

B | *Check your work. Use the Editing Checklist.*

Editing Checklist

Did you . . . ?

☐ use the correct form of descriptive adjectives
☐ use the correct word order with descriptive adjectives
☐ check your spelling

A | Complete the sentences. Add **a, an,** or **Ø**.

1. Mesa Verde has _____ long history.

2. We like to visit _____ big cities.

3. Miami has _____ hot, humid summers.

4. It is _____ interesting place.

5. The Grand Canyon has _____ beautiful rock formations.

B | Complete the sentences. Circle the correct letter.

1. We are at _____.

   a. a hotel small   **b.** small hotel   **c.** a small hotel

2. The hotel has _____.

   a. an interesting garden   **b.** an garden interesting   **c.** a garden interesting

3. Our room is _____.

   a. a big and a comfortable   **b.** big and comfortable   **c.** a big and comfortable

4. The people here are _____.

   a. kinds and helpful   **b.** kinds and helpfuls   **c.** kind and helpful

5. It was _____

   a. a choice great   **b.** a great choice   **c.** great choice

C | Write sentences with the words in parentheses.

1. (museum / I'm / the / at / new) _____

2. (full of / to see / things / interesting / It is) _____

3. (bowls / unusual / from / It has / long ago) _____

4. (has / It / carpets / beautiful / too) _____

5. (place / is / to visit / The museum / a great) _____

D | Correct the paragraph. There are five mistakes.

The Grand Canyon National Park in Arizona is a awesome place to visit. Almost five million people visit this park unusual each year. The weather is good in the late spring and summer, but it crowded is during those months. There are seven differents places to stay in the park. I like El Tovar. It is a old hotel with a great view.

UNIT 6 Prepositions of Place
LOCATIONS

STEP 1 GRAMMAR IN CONTEXT

Before You Read

PAIRS: Answer the questions. Look at the map to answer questions 1 and 2.

1. Where is the Chinese Garden? Where are the African Masks?

2. Where are the rest rooms?

3. Is there an art museum in your city? Where is it? What kind of art is there?

4. What kind of art do you like?

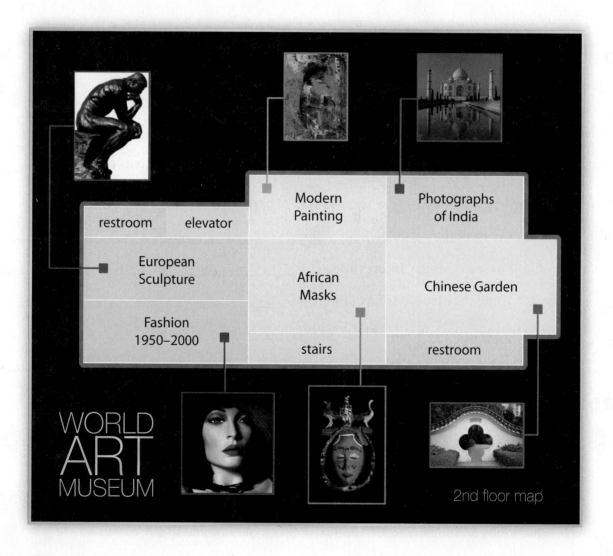

Read

Read Marina's posting and the conversation between Marina and a museum guard.

WALL
FRIENDS
PHOTOS

Marina Olitskaya Hey everyone. I want new glasses, and I need an eye exam. Any suggestions?[1] What's the best place to go?
September 3 at 10:16am · Comment · Like

George Rami Try *Your Color Eyes*. It's **at** 7 East 89th Street, **between** Madison and Fifth Avenue. The doctor there is really good. His name is Dr. Green. And the glasses are a great deal.[2]
September 3 at 12:31pm · Like

Marina Olitskaya So that's **near** the World Art Museum? Great! I'll go to the museum after I see the doctor. I want to see their African masks. Are you free then?
September 3 at 1:15pm · Like

AT THE MUSEUM

MARINA: Excuse me, where are the African masks?

GUARD: They're **on** the second floor. We're **on** the first floor.

MARINA: OK.

GUARD: So take the elevator or the stairs. The elevator is **on your left**, **behind** the gift shop. The stairs are **on your right**, **in back of** the information booth.[3] Then go up one flight.[4] The African Masks are just **up the stairs**. They're **between** the sculpture and the Chinese garden.

MARINA: Great. Oh, I'm sorry, one more thing. Where's . . .

GUARD: The restroom?

MARINA: No, the cafeteria. I'm starving.[5]

---

[1] **suggestions:** ideas
[2] **a great deal:** not very expensive
[3] **information booth:** a place where people ask questions
[4] **go up one flight:** go one floor upstairs.
[5] **I'm starving:** I'm very hungry.

A | Practice *PAIRS: Now read the posting and the conversation aloud. Take turns reading each part.*

B | Vocabulary *Complete the conversations with the words from the box. Use the correct form.*

appointment	be free	cafeteria	flight	restroom	sculpture

1. A: I'm hungry. Where's the _____?

   B: Downstairs.

2. A: What do you make in your _____ class?

   B: We make things from stone or metal.

3. A: Where is the garden with the unusual flowers?

   B: It's one _____ up, on the second floor.

4. A: Are you busy Thursday?

   B: No, I _____.

5. A: Where's Marina?

   B: At the eye doctor, I think. Her _____ is at 3:00.

6. A: Is the _____ in the back of the cafeteria?

   B: No, it's in the front, next to the elevator.

C | Comprehension *Write* **T** *(True),* **F** *(False), or* **?** *(it doesn't say) for each statement.*

_____ **1.** Dr. Green's office is on 98th Street.

_____ **2.** The glasses at *Your Color Eyes* are expensive.

_____ **3.** The African masks are on the second floor.

_____ **4.** The stairs are next to the elevator.

_____ **5.** At the museum, Marina is hungry.

_____ **6.** The cafeteria is closed.

PREPOSITIONS OF PLACE

 The glasses are **between** the book and the watch.

The glasses are **next to** the newspaper.

 The glasses are **behind** the box.

The glasses are **under** the table.

 The glasses are **in** his pocket.

 The glasses are **on** the table **near** the window.

 The man is **in back of** the woman.

 The man is **in front of** the woman.

GRAMMAR NOTES

1	**Prepositions of place** tell <u>where</u> something is. Some common prepositions of place are: *in* *on your left* *in front of* *behind* *in back of* *between* *on* *near* *on your right* *next to*	• My bag is **under** my seat. • Your umbrella is **near** the door.

(continued on next page)

2	For **prepositions in addresses**, use:	
	in before a country, a state, a province, a city, a room number	• He's **in** Canada. He's **in** British Columbia. • He's **in** Vancouver. He's **in** room 302.
	on before a street, an avenue, a road	• It's **on** Main Street. It's **on** 10th Avenue.
	at before a building number	• We're **at** 78 Main Street.
	on the before a floor	• We're **on the** second floor.
	on the corner of before a street or streets	• It's **on the corner of** Main Street.
	USAGE NOTE: In informal conversation, *street* or *avenue* is dropped.	• It's on the corner of **Main Street** and **Mott Avenue**. • It's on the corner of **Main** and **Mott**.

3	For **prepositions before places** use:	
	in school OR *at* school	• I'm **in** school from 9 to 11. • I'm **at** school now.
	at work	• She's **at** work right now.
	at home OR home	• No one is **at** home. OR No one is home.

REFERENCE NOTE

For lists of ordinal and cardinal numbers, see Appendix 3 on page A-3.

STEP 3 FOCUSED PRACTICE

EXERCISE 1: Discover the Grammar

Look at the eye chart. Then answer the questions to find the message. There are three words.

```
        E
      R T N
   I  L W O V
   E G S L I P H
```

1. The first word has one letter. This letter is next to an *L*. It isn't a *W* or an *S*. What's the word? _____/_____

2. The second word has four letters. The first letter is between the *S* and an *I*. The second letter is under the *N*. The third letter is a *V*. A *T* is under the last letter. What's the word? _____

3. The third word has seven letters. A *T* is under the first letter. The second letter is an *N*. The third letter is between an *E* and the *S*. The fourth letter is an *L*. The fifth letter

is an *I*. The sixth letter is between the *L* and the *G*. The last letter is an *H*. What's the

word? _____

4. What's the message? ____ ____ ____ ____ ____ ____ ____ ____ ____ ____!

EXERCISE 2: Prepositions of Place

(Grammar Notes 1–2)

Look at the map. Complete the sentences with the words from the box.

at	next to	on the	under
between	~~on~~	on the . . . of	

1. Fred's Flowers is _____*on*_____ Second Avenue.

2. Paul's Hair Salon is _____ Sam's Shoes.

3. Da Vinci's Bakery is _____ corner _____ Third Avenue and

   Fifth Street.

4. The café is _____ the drugstore and the toy store.

5. Paul's apartment is _____ 25 Second Avenue.

6. His apartment is _____ fourth floor.

7. The café and drug store are _____ a gym.

EXERCISE 3: Prepositions of Place

(Grammar Notes 1–3)

Complete the sentences. Choose from the words in the box. Use some words more than once.

at	between	in	of	on

1. My best friend lives in an apartment _____*in*_____ Lakeville.

2. He lives _____ 435 East Water Street.

3. He lives _____ the third floor.

4. His apartment is _____ a library and a bank.

5. The bank is _____ the corner of Lexington Avenue and 77th Street.

6. My friend is now _____ front _____ his building. He and a neighbor are talking.

7. His neighbor's little boy is _____ school for the first time. It is a big step for him.

EXERCISE 4: Prepositions of Place

(Grammar Notes 1–3)

Complete the sentences. Write true sentences.

1. I am _____*in*_____ school.

2. I am _____ room _____ .

3. My classroom is_____ .
   (floor)

4. My school is _____ .
   (school address)

5. I am not _____ home. I'm not _____ work.

6. I am in _____ , in _____
   (your city)   (your country)

EXERCISE 5: Editing

Correct the conversations. There are six mistakes. The first mistake is already corrected. Find and correct five more.

1. **A:** I'm in school until 2:00, but I'm free after that. Let's go to the Modern Art Museum.

   B: OK. Where is it?

   A: It's ~~in~~ *on* Fifth Avenue between Eight and Ninth Streets.

2. A: Excuse me. Are the masks the third floor?

   B: I don't know. Ask at the Information Booth.

   A: Where is that?

   B: It's in front the stairs, near to the gift shop.

   And the sculptures are on the second floor, in back the paintings.

STEP 4 COMMUNICATION PRACTICE

EXERCISE 6: Pronunciation

A | *Read and listen to the Pronunciation Note.*

Pronunciation Note
Stressed words are longer and louder. Sometimes we stress words to make our meaning clear. **EXAMPLE:** I'm not at school. I'm at the museum.

B | *Listen and mark a dot (•) over the stressed words.*

1. I'm on the first floor. I'm not on the fifth floor.

2. I'm on the first floor. He's on the fifth floor.

3. The museum is on Fifth Street. It's not on Fifth Avenue.

4. The museum is on Fifth Street. The library is on Fifth Avenue.

5. Your glasses are on the table. Your gloves are in the drawer.

C | *Listen and repeat each sentence.*

EXERCISE 7: Listening

A | *Look at the world map in Appendix 1 on pages A-0–A-1. Listen to the locations of countries. Find the countries on the map. Write the countries.*

1. __ __ __ __ __

2. __ __ __ __ __ __ __

3. __ __ __ __ __ __ __ __ __ __

4. __ __ __ __ __

B | *Listen again. Then compare your answers with a partner's.*

EXERCISE 8: Guessing Countries

A | *PAIRS: Write sentences about a country's location. Use the prepositions **between, near, next to,** and **in**.*

B | *Join another group. They guess the country. (See the map in Appendix 1, pages A-0—A-1.)*

> EXAMPLE: This country is in Central America. It is between Costa Rica and Colombia. What country is it?

EXERCISE 9: Game: Describing Locations

GROUPS: Name a place everyone knows. Each student describes its location in a different way. The group with the most correct sentences wins.

> EXAMPLE: **Central Park**
> **A:** It's between Fifth Avenue and Central Park West.
> **B:** It's in New York.
> **C:** It's near our school.
> **D:** It's between 59th Street and 110th Street.

EXERCISE 10: Writing

A | *Write an invitation to a party. Give the address and nearby places. Use prepositions with addresses and locations.*

> EXAMPLE:

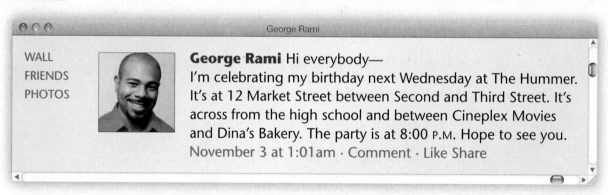

George Rami

George Rami Hi everybody—
I'm celebrating my birthday next Wednesday at The Hummer. It's at 12 Market Street between Second and Third Street. It's across from the high school and between Cineplex Movies and Dina's Bakery. The party is at 8:00 P.M. Hope to see you.
November 3 at 1:01am · Comment · Like Share

WALL
FRIENDS
PHOTOS

B | *Check your work. Use the Editing Checklist.*

Editing Checklist

Did you . . . ?
☐ use prepositions of place correctly
☐ check your spelling

A | Look at the picture. Complete the sentences with the words from the box.

behind	in front of	next to	on	under

1. The book is _____ the table.

2. The glasses are _____ the table.

3. The cup is _____ the book.

4. A watch is _____ the book.

5. A pencil is _____ the book.

B | Complete the sentences. Use prepositions.

1. I'm _____ work now, but I need to leave soon.

2. My appointment with Dr. McDonnell is _____ 4:30 P.M.

3. The doctor's office is _____ 235 West Second Street. He's

_____ second floor.

C | Follow the instructions. Draw in the space provided.

circle   square   triangle

1. Draw a circle on the left.
2. Draw a square on the right.
3. Draw a triangle between the circle and square.
4. Draw an X inside the circle.
5. Draw a Y inside the triangle.
6. Draw a Z under the square.

D | Correct the conversation. There are five mistakes.

A: Is Jon at the school?

B: No. He's in home.

A: Where does he live?

B: He lives at Oak Street, between First and Second Avenue at Lakeville.

A: Does he live in an apartment?

B: Yes. He lives in the third floor.

From Grammar to Writing

CONNECTING WITH *AND* AND *BUT*

We use the word *and* to add information. We use the word *but* to show a surprise or contrast. We usually use a comma before *and* and *but* when they connect two sentences.

> **EXAMPLES:** The book is good, **and** it is easy to understand.
> The book is good, **but** it is difficult to understand.

We can use *and* or *but* to connect two descriptive adjectives.

> **EXAMPLES:** I am hungry **and** tired.
> He is tired **but** happy.

1 | *Complete the sentences with* **and** *or* **but**.

1. She's friendly _____ popular.

2. She's friendly _____ unpopular.

3. Her last name is long, _____ it's hard to pronounce.

4. Her last name is long, _____ it's easy to pronounce.

2 | *Use* **and** *or* **but** *to complete the story about Henry. Then on a separate piece of paper, write a story about someone who made a big change in his or her life.*

Five years ago Henry was a banker. His home was big _____ expensive.
1.
His car was fast _____ fancy. His workday was long, _____
2. 3.
his work was stressful. He was rich, _____ he was stressed and unhappy.
4.
Today Henry works in a flower shop. His home is small _____
5.
inexpensive. His car is old _____ small. His workday is short,
6.
_____ his work is relaxing. He isn't rich, _____ he's relaxed
7. 8.
and happy.

3 | *On a separate piece of paper, write a story about a big change you made in your life.*

4 | *Exchange papers with a partner. Did your partner follow the directions? Correct any mistakes in grammar and spelling.*

5 | *Talk to your partner. Discuss the mistakes you made. Then rewrite your own paper and make any necessary changes.*

IMPERATIVES AND THE SIMPLE PRESENT

UNIT	GRAMMAR FOCUS	THEME
7	Imperatives; Suggestions with *Let's, Why don't we . . . ?*	Long Life
8	Simple Present: Affirmative and Negative Statements	Shopping
9	Simple Present: *Yes / No* Questions and Short Answers	Roommates
10	Simple Present: *Wh-* Questions	Dreams

Imperatives; Suggestions with *Let's, Why don't we . . . ?*

LONG LIFE

STEP 1 GRAMMAR IN CONTEXT

Before You Read

Some people live very long lives. Discuss the questions.

1. Who is the oldest person you know? How old is he or she?

2. What do you think is important for a long life?

Read

Read the online article. Then read the conversation between Joe and Mary on page 73.

Secrets to a Long Life

Yiannis Karimalis was 40 years old. He was a bridge painter in the United States. He was sick. His doctor said, "I'm sorry. You have stomach cancer.[1] It is very bad." Yiannis moved back to his hometown in Greece, to the island of Ikaria.

Yiannis is in his 80s and still alive today. His doctor is dead.

Many people in Ikaria live long lives. What are their secrets? Scientist Dan Buettner studies the lifestyle[2] of older people in different parts of the world. As a result of his studies in Ikaria, he offers this advice:

- **Eat** a lot of green vegetables, fresh fruit, olive oil, fish, and Greek honey.
- **Drink** herbal tea and goat milk.
- **Don't worry**.
- **Take naps**.
- **Walk**. **Don't use** a car, a bus, or a train.
- **Call friends** often.
- **Pray**.

Ikaria, Greece

---
[1] *cancer:* serious illness in which a growth spreads
[2] *lifestyle:* the way you live

JOE: Interesting article. But it's too healthy for me.

MARY: Come on, Joe, these suggestions are easy to follow. **Let's try** some of them.

JOE: I have a better idea. **Let's move** to Ikaria!

MARY: Um, **why don't we** just **take** a trip to Greece?

JOE: Stop right there. I'm on the phone with the airlines.

After You Read

A | Practice *PAIRS: Now read the online article and the conversation aloud. Take turns reading each paragraph of the article.*

B | Vocabulary *Complete the sentences with the words from the box.*

advice	dead	island	nap	pray	secret

1. You look very tired. Why don't you take a _____?

2. Don't tell him. It's a _____.

3. The flowers are _____ because nobody watered them.

4. The doctor's _____ to Mark was, "Walk more. Eat less."

5. We _____ for peace.

6. Ikaria is a Greek _____.

C | Comprehension *Circle the correct words to complete the sentences.*

1. At 40, Yiannis Karimalis was **sick / tired**.

2. Karimalis was a **house / bridge** painter.

3. Today Karimalis lives in **the United States / Greece**.

4. Dan Buettner is a **painter / scientist**.

5. Buettner tells people to **take it easy / work hard**.

6. **Mary / Joe** wants to follow Buettner's advice.

THE IMPERATIVE

Affirmative Statements			Negative Statements		
Base Form of Verb			*Don't*	**Base Form of Verb**	
Walk		to work.	**Don't**	**take**	a bus.

SUGGESTIONS

Affirmative Statements			Negative Statements			
Let's	**Base Form of Verb**		*Let's*	*Not*	**Base Form of Verb**	
Let's	**use**	olive oil.	**Let's**	**not**	**use**	butter.

Suggestions for You and Another Person			Suggestions for Another Person		
Why Don't We	**Base Form of Verb**		*Why Don't You*	**Base Form of Verb**	
Why don't we	**go**	on a bike tour?	**Why don't you**	**get**	the cameras?

RESPONSES TO SUGGESTIONS

Agree	Disagree
OK.	No, I don't feel like it.
That's a good idea. OR Good idea.	Why don't we . . . instead.
That sounds good to me. OR Sounds good to me.	Sorry, not today.
Sounds like a plan.	I can't. I . . .

GRAMMAR NOTES

1	The **imperative** uses the **base form of the verb**.	• **Walk** to work.
2	To make an imperative **negative**, use *don't* + **base form** of the verb.	• **Don't worry**. • **Don't be** late.
3	In an imperative statement, the subject is always *you*, but we don't say it or write it.	• (You) Be careful.
4	Use the **imperative** to a. give directions and instructions b. give orders c. give advice or suggestions d. give warnings e. make polite requests	• **Turn** right. • **Stand** there. • **Use** olive oil. **Don't use** butter. • **Be** careful! It's hot. • Please **call** before noon.

5	Use *please* to make orders, warnings, and requests more polite. *Please* can come at the beginning or the end of the sentence.	• **Please** be careful. • **Please** call before noon. • Call before noon, **please.**
6	Use *Let's* or *Let's not* + **base form** for suggestions that include you and another person.	• **Let's go**. • **Let's not eat** there.
7	Use *Why don't we* + **base form** for suggestions that include you and another person. Use *Why don't you* to make a suggestion or give advice to another person. Remember to put a question mark (?) at the end of sentences with *Why don't we* and *Why don't you.*	• **Why don't we go** to the pool? • **Why don't you look** on the Internet? • **Why don't we meet** at the gym? • **Why don't you call** home?

STEP 3 FOCUSED PRACTICE

EXERCISE 1: Discover the Grammar

*Read the conversations. Next to **line A**, write **I** for the imperative form and **S** for suggestions. Next to **line B**, write **A** when the person agrees. Write **D** when the person disagrees.*

__S__ **1. A:** Let's buy yogurt.

__D__   **B:** I don't like yogurt. Why don't we buy goat cheese?

_____ **2. A:** Please get more broccoli. It's on sale.

_____   **B:** OK. That's a good idea.

_____ **3. A:** Let's not drive to school. The weather is great.

_____   **B:** But it's late. Let's walk after school.

_____ **4. A:** Call Roberto and invite him to dinner.

_____   **B:** Good idea. What's his number?

_____ **5. A:** Why don't you take some time off? You look tired.

_____   **B:** Don't worry. I'm fine.

_____ **6. A:** Maria, don't get those flowers. Some are almost dead.

_____   **B:** OK. Thanks for telling me.

EXERCISE 2: Imperative and Suggestions: Affirmative and Negative (Grammar Notes 1–6)

Circle the correct words to complete the sentences.

1. The bread is still hot. **Eat / (Don't eat)** it now.

2. It's cold here. Please **close / don't close** the window.

3. It's a secret. Please **tell / don't tell** your brother about my plan.

4. For information about Dan Buettner, **check / don't check** the Internet.

5. **Let's walk / Let's not walk** to the store. It's not far.

6. **Let's buy / Let's not buy** those doughnuts. They're not very healthy.

7. Please **give / don't give** me directions to the gym. I want to go there today.

8. **Don't try / Try** this herbal tea. It's delicious.

9. **Take / Don't take** a nap now. Help me prepare dinner.

10. **Don't visit / Visit** that island in July. The weather is usually awful at that time.

EXERCISE 3: Imperative for Directions

(Grammar Notes 1, 3–4)

A | *Read the conversation. Joe gives Mary directions to Gold's gym. Then look at the map and put an **X** on the gym.*

MARY: Excuse me . . . Where's Gold's Gym?

JOE: Um, sure . . . The gym is on Second Avenue between 70th and 71st Street.

We're on Third Avenue at 73rd Street. Walk down Third Avenue to 71st Street. That's two blocks from here. Turn left at 71st Street. Walk one block to Second Avenue. Then turn right on Second Avenue. It's right there, on your right.

B | *Look at the map again. You are at the drug store. Continue the directions to the library.*

Walk down 71st Street to _____. _____

_____

EXERCISE 4: Editing

Correct the conversation. There are six mistakes. The first mistake is already corrected.
Find and correct five more.

JOE: Let's ~~to~~ go to the movies.

MARY: Why we don't go to the park first? It's a beautiful day.

JOE: OK. But first let have lunch. I'm hungry.

MARY: I'm hungry too. Why don't we have a fruit salad with nuts?

JOE: Good idea.

MARY: But you don't use those apples. They're bad. Throws them away.

JOE: OK.

MARY: And why you don't add honey to the yogurt? It's delicious that way.

JOE: You're right. This is really good.

STEP 4 COMMUNICATION PRACTICE

EXERCISE 5: Listening

🎧 **A** | *Listen. What kind of ad is this? Circle the correct letter.*

    a. an ad for a spa

    b. an ad for exercise classes

    c. an ad for healthy eating

🎧 **B** | *Listen again and check (✓) what the spa offers.*

    ___✓___ **1.** yoga classes

    _____ **2.** tai chi classes

    _____ **3.** fresh vegetables

    _____ **4.** healthy breakfast

    _____ **5.** healthy dinner

    _____ **6.** massage and shower

    _____ **7.** three weeks free

    _____ **8.** two weeks free

EXERCISE 6: Pronunciation

🎧 **A** | *Read and listen to the Pronunciation Note.*

Pronunciation Note
We often **link** *don't* + *you*. The two words sound like "doncha" / **doʊnʃə** /
EXAMPLE: Why don't you try that yogurt?

🎧 **B** | *Listen to the conversations. Notice the pronunciation of* **don't you.**

1. A: He's never sick.

  B: Maybe it's his healthy lifestyle. Why don't you try his exercise routine?

2. A: It's my mother's birthday tomorrow. I want to get her something.

  B: Why don't you get her Greek soap with olive oil? They say it's really good for

  the skin.

3. A: I don't want fried chicken. It's too fattening.

  B: Why don't you have the fish? It's broiled.

🎧 **C** | *Listen again. Repeat the suggestions with* **why don't you.**

EXERCISE 7: Making Suggestions for Another Person

PAIRS: Take turns. Read a problem. Your partner makes suggestions with **"Why don't you . . ."** *Agree if you like the suggestion. Disagree if you don't like the suggestion.*

1. I'm thirsty.   **2.** I'm bored.   **3.** I'm hungry.   **4.** I'm tired.

EXAMPLE: **A:** I'm thirsty.
  B: Why don't you have a soda?
  A: Soda? That's not healthy.
  B: Well, why don't you have some pineapple juice?
  A: OK. That's a good idea.

EXERCISE 8: Making Suggestions for You and Another Person

PAIRS: **Student A**, *make a suggestion for a healthy lifestyle.* **Student B**, *agree or make another suggestion and give a reason why. Continue until you both agree. Take turns. Use the topics from the list.*

- exercise with friends
- go to the gym
- sign up for a dance class
- go on a diet together
- hang out with friends
- your idea: _____

EXAMPLE: **A:** Let's go to the gym.
  B: Why don't we study first?
  A: OK. Let's study for an hour and then go to the gym.

EXERCISE 9: Giving Advice

PAIRS: What advice can you give for a healthy lifestyle? Make a list. Use the verbs **drink,** **eat, meet, nap, pray, walk,** *and* **worry.** *Then read your list to the class.*

EXAMPLE:
- Don't eat a lot of meat.
- Eat . . .

EXERCISE 10: Giving Directions

A | *PAIRS: Look again at the map on page 76. You are at the library. Ask your partner directions to the bank.*

B | *PAIRS: Now give directions to a place on the map from the bakery. Your partner names the place.*

EXERCISE 11: Writing

A | *Write an ad for a hotel on the island of Ikaria. Use imperatives.*

EXAMPLE: For a vacation you won't forget, come to Jean's "Hotel for Life" on the beautiful island of Ikaria. Enjoy a comfortable room with an awesome view of the beach. Eat three delicious and healthful meals in our dining room or on your terrace. Swim in our pool. Jog on the beach. Relax in our jacuzzi. Everything is there for you. Don't delay. Book a room today.

B | *Check your work. Use the Editing Checklist.*

Editing Checklist

Did you . . . ?
☐ use imperatives correctly
☐ check your spelling

Check your answers on page UR-2.

Do you need to review anything?

A | *Circle the correct words to complete the sentences.*

1. **Let's get / Let's not get** ice cream. It's on sale this week.

2. **Why don't we invite / Let's not invite** Bob? He's really nice.

3. **Please buy / Don't buy** peppers. I don't like them.

4. **Let's meet / Let's not meet** before 8. I have a lot of work.

5. **Touch / Don't touch** the wall. The paint is still wet.

B | *Complete the instructions with the verbs in parentheses. Use the imperative affirmative or negative form.*

1. _____ comfortable clothes to tai chi class. They're very important.
   (wear)

2. _____ tight clothes.
   (wear)

3. _____ a mat and water.
   (bring)

4. _____ coffee or soda inside the classroom. You can have those drinks in
   (bring)
   the nearby lounge.

5. Please _____ by check or cash. We don't accept credit cards.
   (pay)

C | *Write suggestions with the words in parentheses.*

1. _____
   (go to the gym / let's)

2. _____
   (watch a movie this afternoon / let's)

3. _____
   (take a trip together / why don't we)

4. _____
   (hang out with Pietro this weekend / why don't we)

D | *Correct the sentences. There are six mistakes. Check for punctuation.*

1. Why you don't ask Andrij for help?

2. You look really tired. You take a short nap.

3. Let's to walk to work. Let's not drive.

4. Don't ask Boris to fix the car. Asks Mickey.

5. I'm on a diet, so buy yogurt at the store. Don't to buy sour cream.

UNIT 8 Simple Present: Affirmative and Negative Statements

SHOPPING

STEP 1 GRAMMAR IN CONTEXT

Before You Read

A | Kawaii *is the Japanese word for "cute." In Japan, girls like* kawaii *things. In the United States, teens want "cool" things. What do young people say in your country?*

B | *Circle what's true about you.*

1. I **often / don't often** shop for clothes.

2. I look for **bargains / comfortable clothes / trendy clothes**.

Read

Read the online article about teenage shoppers in Japan.

SWEET LIFE magazine

SWEET LIFE *magazine*

This Japanese girl follows the fashion trend "anime." She is dressing as her favorite cartoon.

TEEN *TRENDS*

Yumi **is** 17 years old. She**'s** a senior in high school in Japan. Yumi **wears** *kawaii* boots and jeans. She **carries** a *kawaii* phone. Sometimes Yumi dresses as her favorite cartoon character. She wears makeup and *kawaii* costumes.

Yumi **uses** the word *kawaii* a lot. She **doesn't buy** non-*kawaii* things.

Businesses **look** at Yumi and her friends. They **study** their clothes. Companies **know** that Yumi **is** not alone. There **are** many other teens like Yumi. Yumi and her friends **buy** cool clothes. Their clothes **don't** always **cost** a lot. But the number of teenage shoppers is big. And that **means** a lot of money for businesses. In the 1990s, college girls were the trendsetters.[1] Now it**'s** high school girls. Maybe in the future middle school girls will set trends. And it**'s** not just girls. Nowadays guys **shop** and **want** a certain "look" too.

[1] *trendsetters:* people who start a new way of doing something

This Japanese girl follows the fashion trend "anime." She is dressing as her favorite cartoon.

Simple Present: Affirmative and Negative Statements **81**

A | **Practice** *PAIRS: Now read the article aloud. Take turns reading each paragraph.*

B | **Vocabulary** *Circle the letter of the best meaning for the words in blue.*

1. Yumi is a **senior**. She's in her _____ year of high school.

   a. first **b.** second **c.** last

2. She's a **teenager** (or teen). She is between _____ years old.

   a. 11 and 15 **b.** 13 and 19 **c.** 15 and 20

3. Her brother is in **middle school**. Middle school is between _____.

   a. high school and college
   b. primary school and high school
   c. kindergarten and first grade

4. Many **companies** study teens. These _____ believe that teenagers spend a lot of money.

   a. friends **b.** businesses **c.** families

5. You look **cute** in that photo. You look _____.

   a. pretty **b.** serious **c.** funny

6. Many teens **are like** Yumi. They _____ Yumi.

   a. are in love with **b.** are similar to **c.** are friends of

7. He lives **alone**. He lives _____.

   a. by himself **b.** with friends **c.** with relatives

C | **Comprehension** *Write **T** (**True**) or **F** (**False**) for each statement.*

_____ 1. Yumi wears boots.

_____ 2. Yumi works for a company.

_____ 3. Yumi has friends.

_____ 4. *Kawaii* means "cute."

_____ 5. Yumi doesn't like costumes.

_____ 6. Teenage boys don't like clothes.

_____ 7. Middle school girls set clothes trends today.

SIMPLE PRESENT: AFFIRMATIVE AND NEGATIVE STATEMENTS

Affirmative Statements			Negative Statements			
Subject	Verb		Subject	Do not / Does not	Base Form of Verb	
I You* We They	sell have	jeans.	I You* We They	do not don't	sell have	jeans.
He She It	sells has		He She It	does not doesn't		

*You is both singular and plural.

GRAMMAR NOTES

1	Use the **simple present** to tell about **things that happen again and again** (habits, regular occurrences, customs, and routines). **Now** Past —X—X—|—X—X→ Future *She shops every Saturday.*	• She **wears** boots. • He **shops** at the mall. • They **give** gifts on New Year's Day. • She **buys** her clothes at discount stores.
2	Use the simple present to tell **facts**.	• The word *kawaii* **means** "cute."
3	Use the simple present with **non-action verbs** such as: *be, have, know, like, need, want.*	• She **is** 17 years old. • She **likes** that store. • She **has** an expensive bag.
4	In **affirmative statements**, use the **base form** of the verb for all persons except the third person singular. Add **-s** or **-es** with *he, she,* or *it*.	• **I want** a new sweater. • **You need** a new suit. • **They have** a car. • **She wants** a new phone. • **He watches** TV every day.
5	In **negative statements**, use *does not* or *do not* before the base form of the verb. Use the contractions *doesn't* and *don't* in speaking or in informal writing. **BE CAREFUL!** When *or* connects verbs in a negative statement, do not repeat *don't* or *doesn't*.	• He **does not wear** ties. • We **do not shop** there. • He **doesn't wear** ties. • We **don't shop** there. • I **don't smoke** or **drink** coffee. Not: I don't smoke or ~~I don't~~ drink coffee.

(continued on next page)

6	The **third person singular affirmative** forms of *have*, *do*, and *go* are <u>irregular</u>.	• She **has** a new coat. • He **does** the laundry on Saturday. • He **goes** to the gym at 10:00.
	The **third person singular negative forms** of *have*, *do*, and *go* are <u>regular</u>.	• She **doesn't have** a new hat. • He **doesn't do** laundry on Sunday. • He **doesn't go** to the gym at 11:00.

7	**BE CAREFUL!** The verb *be* is irregular. It has three forms in the present: *is*, *am*, and *are*.	**BE** **REGULAR VERB** • I **am** tired. I **look** tired. • You **are** tall. You **look** tall. • He **is** bored. He **looks** bored.

REFERENCE NOTES

For a fuller discussion of **non-action verbs**, see Unit 17, page 188.
For **spelling and pronunciation rules for the third-person singular** in the **simple present**, see Appendix 6, pages A-6–A-7.
For a complete presentation of the **present tense of verb *be***, see Unit 1, page 5.

STEP 3 FOCUSED PRACTICE

EXERCISE 1: Discover the Grammar

Read the sentences. Underline all examples of the simple present.

1. Sometimes clothes <u>send</u> a message.

2. Sandy doesn't wear leather, and she doesn't eat meat.

3. Pierre and Katrina buy used clothes from thrift shops.

4. Marta makes her own clothes. She's very talented.

5. Ali wears gym clothes every day, and he exercises every day.

EXERCISE 2: Affirmative Sentences

(Grammar Notes 1–4)

Circle the correct word to complete the sentence.

1. My grandfather **work /** (**works**) for a big company, and he **wear / wears** a suit to work.

2. My brothers **like / likes** casual clothes. They almost never **wear / wears** suits.

3. His girlfriend **know / knows** about fashion.

4. They **shop / shops** online.

5. The word *cool* **mean / means** different things.

6. You **have / has** a cute hairstyle.

EXERCISE 3: Negative Statements

(Grammar Notes 5, 7)

Underline the verb in the first sentence. Complete the second sentence in the negative. Use the same verb.

1. He <u>shops</u> at flea markets. He _____ doesn't shop _____ at chain stores.

2. We buy name brands. They _____ name brands.

3. I like jeans. I _____ suits.

4. I need a new jacket. I _____ a new raincoat.

5. My mother wears high heels. She _____ sneakers.

6. That dress looks good. It _____ too tight.

7. We are 20 years old. We _____ teenagers.

8. He is in middle school. He _____ in high school.

EXERCISE 4: Affirmative and Negative Statements

(Grammar Notes 1–6)

Complete the sentences with the verbs in parentheses. Use the affirmative or negative form.

1. (cost) **a.** It's expensive. It _____ costs _____ a lot.

    b. It's cheap. It _____ doesn't cost _____ a lot.

2. (need) **a.** I'm hot. I _____ a sweater.

    b. I'm cold. I _____ a sweater.

3. (want) **a.** His jacket is old. He _____ a new one.

    b. His jacket is new. He _____ a new one.

4. (like) **a.** We _____ window shopping. We often look at store windows.

    b. They _____ window shopping. They never look at store windows.

5. (have) **a.** He's rich. He _____ a lot of money.

    b. She's poor. She _____ a lot of money.

6. (go) **a.** He doesn't like that new department store. He _____ there.

    b. She loves that new department store. She _____ there every week.

EXERCISE 5: Affirmative and Negative Statements

(Grammar Notes 1–7)

A | *Read this letter from a parent to an advice columnist. Complete the sentences with the verbs in parentheses. Use the correct form.*

Our son _____*is*_____ 14 years old. He _____ a good student at his
      1. (be)   **2. (be)**

middle school, and he _____ a lot of friends. But we _____ a
                    3. (have)   **4. (have)**

problem with him. He _____ clothes. He _____ trendy jeans
                  5. (love)   **6. (wear)**

with chains on them. And he _____ expensive hoodies and brand names.
                          7. (prefer)

We _____ poor, but I _____ it is wrong to spend a lot of
      8. (be / not)   **9. (think)**

money on clothes, especially for a growing boy. We _____ him spending
                                  10. (give)

money, but he _____ enough to buy all the clothes he wants. Now he
          11. (have / not)

_____ to get a part-time job. I _____ him to work, but my
    12. (want)   **13. (want / not)**

husband _____ it's OK. What do you think?
       14. (think)

Rosa Alvarado

B | *Complete the answer to the parent with the words from the box. Use the correct form.*

agree	sound	think	~~want~~	work

Your son is not alone. Most teens _____*want*_____ to look like other teens. It's very
                               1.

normal. And I _____ with your husband. When a person _____,
            2.   **3.**

that person _____ about the cost of things. A job for your son
             4.

_____ fine to me.
  5.

EXERCISE 6: Editing

Correct the paragraph. There are eight mistakes. The first mistake is already corrected.
Find and correct seven more.

> Miyuki Miyagi is a teenager. She ~~live~~ *lives* in Japan. She like clothes, and she shops in the Harajuku
>
> District in Tokyo. She say, "My friends and I love fashion. We goes to the stores, but we doesn't
>
> always buy much. Clothes are expensive. But we still look good. My friends and I know
>
> inexpensive ways to dress "kawaii." For example, sometimes we are make our own clothes. And
>
> we mix styles. Sometimes we put on gothic clothes with punk clothes or schoolgirl uniforms.
>
> Sometimes we wears lots of makeup. And sometimes we dresses like dolls, or like anime.

STEP 4 COMMUNICATION PRACTICE

EXERCISE 7: Pronunciation

A | *Read and listen to the Pronunciation Note.*

Pronunciation Note
In English, we pronounce the **third person singular ending / s / , / z / , or / ɪz / .**
EXAMPLES:
He lik**es** music. **/ s /**
She pla**ys** golf. **/ z /**
He watch**es** TV every day. **/ ɪz /**

B | *Underline the verb in each sentence. Then listen to each sentence and check (✓) the sound of the verb ending.*

	/ s /	/ z /	/ ɪz /
1. He <u>shops</u> a lot.	✓		
2. She uses that word a lot.			
3. She buys clothes at discount stores.			
4. He knows his business.			
5. It costs a hundred dollars.			
6. He misses her.			
7. She watches fashion shows on TV.			
8. He thinks about his clothes.			

EXERCISE 8: Listening

A | *Listen to the conversation between Elvia and Pedro. What does Elvia want?*

    a. something new

    b. something black

mannequin

B | *Listen to the conversation again. Complete the sentences.*

    1. Elvia wants something for _____*Bill's party*_____.

    2. There's a(n) _____ at the Wrap.

    3. She wants a(n) _____ in a(n)

    _____.

    4. It costs _____.

    5. Pedro thinks Elvia is a(n) _____.

EXERCISE 9: Conversation

A | *Check (✓) the sentences that are true for you.*

    1. ____ I wear colorful clothes.   ____ I don't wear colorful clothes.

    2. ____ I like leather jackets.   ____ I don't like leather jackets.

    3. ____ I buy designer clothes.   ____ I don't buy designer clothes.

    4. ____ I read fashion magazines.   ____ I don't read fashion magazines.

    5. ____ I like unusual clothes.   ____ I don't like unusual clothes.

    6. ____ I wear traditional clothes.   ____ I don't wear traditional clothes.

    7. ____ I have more than three pairs   ____ I don't have more than three pairs
        of jeans.   of jeans.

B | *PAIRS: Discuss the ways you and your partner are alike or different.*

    EXAMPLE: We don't wear colorful clothes. We like dark colors such as black and gray.

EXERCISE 10: Discussion

GROUPS: Talk about clothes customs in different parts of the world. For example, do people wear traditional clothes or Western clothes? Do people remove their shoes when they enter a home? Do people cover their heads?

EXAMPLE: **A:** In my country, Peru, some people wear colorful woven clothes.
B: What do they look like?
A: They have wide sleeves and full skirts.
B: In Argentina some men who work in the country wear "gaucho" clothing. They wear wide brimmed hats, ponchos, and loose pants in their boots.

EXERCISE 11: Writing

A | *Write about the way you and a relative dress. Use the simple present.*

EXAMPLE: I usually wear polo shirts and matching slacks to school. Sometimes I wear sneakers, and sometimes I wear boots. I have five polo shirts. They're blue, black, brown, beige, and green. Every day I wear a different shirt. My sister wears bright colors, and her clothes are very unusual. She's pretty, so everything looks great on her.

B | *Check your work. Use the Editing Checklist.*

Editing Checklist
Did you . . . ?
☐ use the simple present correctly
☐ remember to add **-s** or **-es** to the third person singular
☐ use correct spelling

8 Review

Check your answers on page UR-2.
Do you need to review anything?

A | *Circle the correct words to complete the sentences.*

1. John **shop / shops** at The Wrap.

2. He **like / likes** their clothes.

3. My sister and I **don't like / am not like** the clothes at The Wrap.

4. We **go / goes** to Blooms.

5. Blooms **has / have** interesting clothes.

B | *Complete the sentences with the verbs in parentheses. Use the affirmative or negative form.*

1. It's hot today. We _____ jackets.
   (need)

2. It's cold and windy today. They _____ jackets and sweaters.
   (need)

3. They _____ soccer. They enjoy the sport.
   (play)

4. He _____ sports. He prefers to watch movies or read books.
   (like)

C | *Complete the sentences with the words from the box. Use the correct form.*

be	be	not wear	wear	work

1. My brother _____ a fashion designer.

2. He _____ for a magazine.

3. He _____ a lot of trendy clothes. People always notice his clothes.

4. I _____ trendy clothes. I wear old jeans and a white T-shirt.

5. My brother and I _____ different in other ways too.

D | *Correct the sentences. There are six mistakes.*

1. My son doesn't has a suit.

2. He always wear jeans, T-shirts, and hoodies.

3. He need a suit for my brother's wedding.

4. Suits is expensive, and my son don't like to wear them.

5. We wants to rent or borrow a suit for him.

Simple Present: *Yes / No* Questions and Short Answers

ROOMMATES

STEP 1 GRAMMAR IN CONTEXT

Before You Read

GROUPS: Do you live alone? Do you have a roommate? Do you share a room with someone? Imagine you are looking for a roommate. What questions are important to ask?

Read

Colleges often use questionnaires to help students find the right roommate. Read the roommate questionnaire. Are Dan and Jon a good match? Why or why not?

Roommate Questionnaire[1]

	Dan		Jon	
	YES	NO	YES	NO
1. Do you **wake up** early?		✓		✓
2. Do you **stay up** late?	✓		✓	
3. Are you neat?	✓		✓	
4. **Does** a messy room **bother** you?	✓		✓	
5. Are you quiet?		✓	✓	
6. Are you talkative?	✓			✓
7. **Does** noise **bother** you?		✓		✓
8. Are you outgoing?	✓			✓
9. Are you a private person?		✓	✓	
10. Are you easygoing?	✓		✓	
11. Do you **listen** to loud music?	✓		✓	
12. Do you **watch** a lot of TV?	✓		✓	
13. Do you **study** and **listen** to music at the same time?	✓		✓	
14. Do you **study** with the TV on?	✓		✓	

[1]**questionnaire:** a list of questions

After You Read

A | Practice *PAIRS: Now read the questionnaire aloud. Take turns reading the questions.*

B | Vocabulary *Complete the statements with the words from the box. Use the correct form.*

bother	messy	outgoing	stay up
easygoing	neat	private	wake up

1. The room was _____, so we helped put things away. Now it is

   _____.

2. That smell _____ me. I feel a little sick.

3. We _____ late on Friday and Saturday nights.

4. She _____ at seven o'clock on weekdays.

5. He is pretty _____. He doesn't get upset about most things.

6. I don't know very much about my roommate. He's a very _____ person.

7. That little girl is very _____. She's not afraid to talk to anyone.

C | Comprehension *Write **T** (**True**) or **F** (**False**) for each statement.*

_____ 1. Dan and Jon wake up late.

_____ 2. Dan is neat, but Jon isn't.

_____ 3. Dan and Jon are quiet.

_____ 4. Dan is outgoing, but Jon isn't.

_____ 5. Jon is a private person.

_____ 6. Dan and Jon are both easygoing.

_____ 7. Dan and Jon listen to loud music.

_____ 8. Dan and Jon don't watch TV.

_____ 9. Dan and Jon study and listen to music at the same time.

STEP 2 GRAMMAR PRESENTATION

SIMPLE PRESENT: *YES / NO* QUESTIONS AND SHORT ANSWERS

Yes / No Questions			Short Answers					
Do / Does	Subject	Base Form of Verb	Affirmative			Negative		
Do	I you* we they	work?	Yes,	you I / we you they	do.	No,	you I / we you they	don't.
Does	he she it			he she it	does.		he she it	doesn't.

* *You* is both singular and plural.

92   UNIT 9

GRAMMAR NOTES

1	For **yes / no questions** in the **simple present**, use **do** or **does** before the subject. Use the base form of the verb after the subject.	SUBJECT • **Do** you **need** a roommate? • **Does** he **have** a roommate?

2	We usually use **short answers** in conversation. Sometimes we use **long answers**.	**A:** Do you need a roommate?
		B: Yes. OR **Yes, I do.** OR
		    Yes, I need a roommate.
		
		A: Does he have a roommate?
		B: Yes. OR **Yes, he does.** OR
		    Yes, he has a roommate.

3	**BE CAREFUL!** Do not use *do* or *does* for *yes / no* questions with **be**.	• **Are** you from Ecuador?
		• **Is** he from France?
		  NOT: ~~Do are you~~ from Ecuador?
		      ~~Does is he~~ from France?
		      ~~Does you~~ from Ecuador?

REFERENCE NOTE
For a discussion of **yes / no questions with be**, see Unit 2, page 17.

STEP 3 FOCUSED PRACTICE

EXERCISE 1: Discover the Grammar

Read about Dan and Jon. Then match the questions and answers on the next page.

   In many ways Dan and Jon are alike. Both Dan and Jon like music and sports, but Dan likes popular music, and Jon likes hip-hop. Both Dan and Jon like basketball, but Jon likes soccer and Dan doesn't. Dan and Jon are both neat. They don't like a messy room. They both like to go to bed late—after midnight. They watch about two hours of TV at night, and they study with the TV on. But in one way Dan and Jon are completely different. Dan is talkative, but Jon is quiet. Dan says, "We're lucky about that. It works out nicely. I talk, he listens." Jon says, "Uh-huh."

(continued on next page)

_b_ **1.** Do they both like music and sports?   **a.** It doesn't say.

____ **2.** Do they like to go to bed early?   **b.** Yes, they do.

____ **3.** Does Dan like popular music?   **c.** Yes, he does.

____ **4.** Dan is talkative. Jon is quiet. Does it matter?   **d.** No, they don't.

____ **5.** Do Dan and Jon like movies?   **e.** No, it doesn't.

EXERCISE 2: *Yes / No* Questions and Short Answers   *(Grammar Notes 1–2)*

Complete the questions with **Do** *or* **Does** *and the verbs in parentheses. Then complete the short answers.*

1. (listen)   **A:** _____ Do _____ you _____ listen _____ to music?

              B: Yes, _____ we do _____. OR Yes, _____ I do _____.

2. (have)   **A:** _____ your roommate _____ a TV?

              B: No, she _____.

3. (wake up)   **A:** _____ he _____ early?

              B: No, _____.

4. (stay up)   **A:** _____ they _____ late?

              B: Yes, _____.

5. (bother)   **A:** _____ the TV _____ you?

              B: No, _____.

6. (have)   **A:** _____ your room _____ a big window?

              B: Yes, _____.

7. (rain)   **A:** _____ it _____ a lot in your city?

              B: No, _____.

8. (have)   **A:** _____ I _____ Internet access?

              B: Yes, _____.

9. (go)   **A:** _____ she _____ to parties all the time?

              B: No, _____.

10. (need)   **A:** _____ we _____ another lamp?

              B: Yes, _____.

11. (sell)   **A:** _____ they _____ gum here?

              B: Yes, _____.

EXERCISE 3: *Yes / No* Questions and Short Answers   (Grammar Notes 1–3)

Complete the **yes / no** *questions with* **Do, Does, Am, Is,** *or* **Are***. Then complete the short answers.*

1. **A:** _____*Am*_____ I late?   **B:** No, ___*you aren't*___ .

2. **A:** _____ he come late?   **B:** Yes, _____ .

3. **A:** _____ you busy?   **B:** Yes, we _____ .

4. **A:** _____ they have a lot of work?   **B:** No, _____ .

5. **A:** _____ they roommates?   **B:** No, _____ .

6. **A:** _____ they live in a dormitory?   **B:** Yes, _____ .

7. **A:** _____ she your sister?   **B:** No, _____ .

8. **A:** _____ you live at home?   **B:** Yes, I _____ .

9. **A:** _____ your roommate play baseball?   **B:** No, he _____ .

10. **A:** _____ we in the right room?   **B:** Yes, you _____ .

11. **A:** _____ you friends?   **B:** Yes, _____ .

12. **A:** _____ you cook well?   **B:** No, I _____ .

EXERCISE 4: *Yes / No* Questions and Short Answers   (Grammar Notes 1–2)

Complete the conversation. Write questions with the words in parentheses. Then write short answers with **do, does, don't** *or* **doesn't***.*

A: So tell me about your new roommate, Edward. ____*Do you like*____ him?

                                                 1. (you / like)

B: ____*Yes, I do*____ . He's a really nice guy.

          2.

A: Where is he from? He sounds like a native speaker. _____ from England?

                                                     3. (he / come)

B: _____ . He comes from Australia.

          4.

A: Cool. What's he studying?

B: Music.

A: Oh, he's a music major. _____ an instrument?

                              5. (he / play)

B: Of course. He plays three instruments: violin, cello, and piano.

A: Wow. _____ with him?

                        6. (you / play)

B: _____ . I'm not a good musician. But sometimes his cousin plays with him.

          7.

(continued on next page)

A: _____ a lot of family close by?
     8. (he / have)

B: _____. His uncle, his aunt, three cousins, and his grandmother are
     9.

10 minutes away. I was at their home last night.

A: Really? _____ them often?
              10. (you / see)

B: _____. They invite us for a meal at least once a month. They all play music,
     11.

and they're interesting people. His uncle is a conductor, and she is an opera singer.

A: _____ them a small gift when you visit?
     12. (you / bring)

B: _____. I'm a poor student.
     13.

A: Hey, you're not that poor.

EXERCISE 5: Editing

*Correct the conversations. There are eight mistakes. The first mistake is already
corrected. Find and correct seven more.*

1. **A:** Does she ~~goes~~ go to school?

   B: Yes, she goes.

2. **A:** Does he needs help?

   B: Yes, he does.

3. **A:** Do they are like rock music?

   B: Yes, they do.

4. **A:** Do she live near the museum?

   B: Yes, she lives.

5. **A:** Does he has a roommate?

   B: Yes, he does.

6. **A:** Are you friends?

   B: Yes, we do.

STEP 4 COMMUNICATION PRACTICE

EXERCISE 6: Pronunciation

A | *Read and listen to the Pronunciation Note.*

> **Pronunciation Note**
>
> We **link the** words ***does it*** and ***does he***. The "s" in *does* makes a **/z/** sound.
>
> Join the **/z/** sound in *does* to the vowel sound **/ɪ/** in *it*.
>
> Join the **/z/** sound in *does* to the vowel sound **/i/** in *he*. Do not pronounce the "h" in *he*.
>
> **EXAMPLES:** Does it   Does he
>   ‿   ‿

B | *Listen to questions and repeat each question.*

1. Does it have Internet service?
2. Does it come with a desk?
3. Does it have two closets?
4. Does it have windows?

5. Does it have air conditioning?
6. Does he have a roommate?
7. Does he have a test?
8. Does he have a cold?

C | *PAIRS: Take turns. Look at Serge Lafitte's answers to a questionnaire. Ask your partner questions about Serge Lafitte. Remember to link **Does + he**.*

EXAMPLE: **A:** Does he like movies?
           B: Yes, he does.

NAME: *Serge*		
Do you _____?	**YES**	**NO**
1. like movies	✓	
2. stay up late	✓	
3. have a part-time job		✓
4. study and listen to music	✓	
5. like a clean, neat room		✓

EXERCISE 7: Listening

A | *Listen to the conversation. Why is Andrea talking to Valentina Gold?*

a. to find a roommate   **b.** to work out a problem with her roommate

B | *Listen again. Complete the chart with Andrea's answers.*

	Andrea	**Leyla**
parties		likes parties
music		likes rock
sports		plays basketball, soccer, swims
study habits		studies at night in her room

C | *Compare Andrea and Leyla. Are they a good match? Why or why not?*

_____

_____

EXERCISE 8: Discussion: Comparing Habits and Personality

PAIRS: Look at the roommate questionnaire again. Answer the questions for yourself. Then compare your answers with a partner's.

	YOU	
	YES	**NO**
1. **Do** you **wake up** early?	☐	☐
2. **Do** you **stay up** late?	☐	☐
3. **Are** you neat?	☐	☐
4. **Does** a messy room **bother** you?	☐	☐
5. **Are** you quiet?	☐	☐
6. **Are** you talkative?	☐	☐
7. **Does** noise **bother** you?	☐	☐
8. **Are** you outgoing?	☐	☐
9. **Are** you a private person?	☐	☐
10. **Are** you easygoing?	☐	☐
11. **Do** you **listen** to loud music?	☐	☐
12. **Do** you **watch** a lot of TV?	☐	☐
13. **Do** you **study** and **listen** to music at the same time?	☐	☐
14. **Do** you **study** with the TV on?	☐	☐

EXERCISE 9: Game: Find Someone Who . . .

Find out about your classmates. Ask these questions and add your own. Take notes. Tell the class something new about three classmates.

Do you . . . ?	Are you . . . ?
cook well	messy
text every day	outgoing
play a musical instrument	a private person
like sports	athletic
watch sports on TV	handy (good at fixing things)
have a lot of brothers and sisters	an only child
have a lot of electronics	interested in art
Your question:	*Your question:*

EXAMPLE: Ali is handy. He fixes things.
Sara plays the violin. She was in a concert last month.
Mi Young watches sports on TV. She loves the New York Yankees.

EXERCISE 10: Game: What's in Your Backpack?

Work in small groups. Ask questions. Check (✓) the items you have. The first group to check 10 items wins.

EXAMPLE: Do you have keys? OR Does anyone have keys?

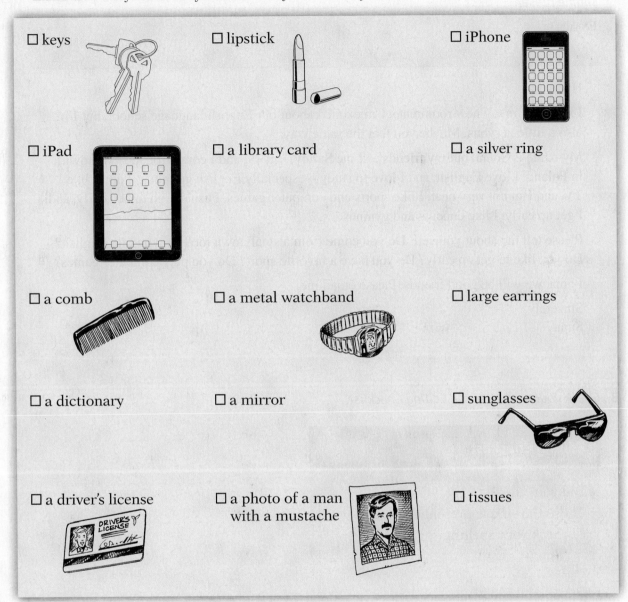

□ keys

□ lipstick

□ iPhone

□ iPad

□ a library card

□ a silver ring

□ a comb

□ a metal watchband

□ large earrings

□ a dictionary

□ a mirror

□ sunglasses

□ a driver's license

□ a photo of a man with a mustache

□ tissues

EXERCISE 11: Writing

A | *Imagine you plan to study English at a school for international students. The school has chosen a roommate for you. You do not know the roommate. Write your new roommate an email. Tell about yourself and ask your roommate questions. Use the simple present.*

EXAMPLE:

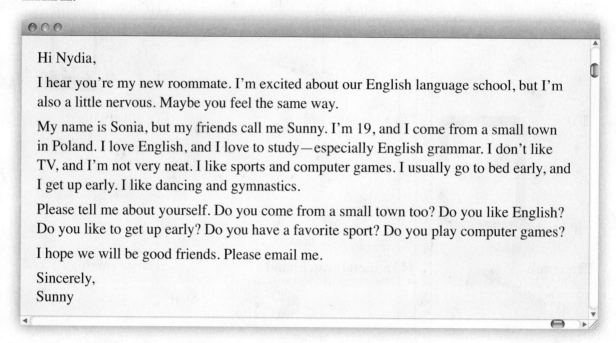

Hi Nydia,

I hear you're my new roommate. I'm excited about our English language school, but I'm also a little nervous. Maybe you feel the same way.

My name is Sonia, but my friends call me Sunny. I'm 19, and I come from a small town in Poland. I love English, and I love to study—especially English grammar. I don't like TV, and I'm not very neat. I like sports and computer games. I usually go to bed early, and I get up early. I like dancing and gymnastics.

Please tell me about yourself. Do you come from a small town too? Do you like English? Do you like to get up early? Do you have a favorite sport? Do you play computer games?

I hope we will be good friends. Please email me.

Sincerely,
Sunny

B | *Check your work. Use the Editing Checklist.*

Editing Checklist

Did you . . . ?
☐ use the simple present correctly
☐ check your spelling

UNIT

9 Review

Check your answers on page UR-2.
Do you need to review anything?

A | Complete the sentences with the words from the box.

Am	Are	Do	Does	Is

1. _____ you know his brother?

2. _____ his brother messy?

3. _____ he have a lot of friends?

4. _____ they easygoing?

5. _____ I your best friend?

B | Complete the questions with the verbs in parentheses. Use the correct form.

1. (have) _____ you _____ a roommate?

2. (speak) _____ his roommate _____ English fluently?

3. (watch) _____ your roommate _____ TV at night?

4. (be) _____ your roommate talkative?

5. (be) _____ your roommates' parents in the United States?

C | Write questions about an apartment. Use the words in parentheses.

1. _____ ?
   (be / the neighbors / noisy)

2. _____ ?
   (the apartment building / have / an elevator)

3. _____ ?
   (be / the apartment / near trains or buses)

4. _____ ?
   (the bedroom / have / two closets)

5. _____ ?
   (be / the bedroom / big)

D | Correct the conversations. There are five mistakes.

1. **A:** Does he have a big TV in his room?
   B: Yes, he has.

2. **A:** Does she needs help?
   B: No, she don't.

3. **A:** Do you are friends?
   B: Yes, we aren't.

UNIT 10 Simple Present: *Wh-* Questions
DREAMS

STEP 1 GRAMMAR IN CONTEXT

Before You Read

PAIRS: Do you dream? Do you remember your dreams? What do you dream about?

Read

Ask the Expert *is a radio talk show. Today Rob Stevens is talking to dream expert Helena Lee. Read the conversation.*

Dreams

RS: Good afternoon. I'm Rob Stevens. Welcome to *Ask the Expert*. This afternoon my guest is Helena Lee. She's the author of *Sleep and Dreams*. Thank you for coming.

LEE: Thanks, Rob. It's great to be here.

RS: Helena, we have a lot of questions about dreams. Our first question is from Carolina Gomes. She asks, "**Why do we dream?**"

LEE: That's a good question. Actually, nobody really knows why. But I think dreams help us understand our feelings.

RS: OK. . . . Our next question is from Jonathan Lam. He asks, "**Who dreams?** Does everyone dream?"

LEE: Yes, everyone dreams. People dream in every part of the world. And what's more, scientists believe animals dream too.

RS: Wow! That's really interesting. **How do we know?**

LEE: We have machines. They show when people or animals dream. But, of course, no one knows what animals dream about.

RS: Our next question is from Pablo Ortiz. He writes, "People don't remember *all* their dreams. **What dreams do they remember?**"

LEE: People remember their unusual dreams. And, unfortunately, people remember their bad dreams, or nightmares.

RS: Beata Green says, "I have the same dream again and again. **What does that mean?**"

LEE: That dream has special meaning for you. You need to think about it.

RS: Here's a question from Samuel Diaz. "**When do people dream?**"

LEE: They dream during deep sleep. It's called REM sleep. REM means *rapid eye movement.*

RS: I hear REM sleep is important. **Why do we need it?**

LEE: Without it, we can't remember or think clearly.

RS: Our last question for today is from Mike Morgan. He writes, "My roommate doesn't remember his dreams. **Why do I remember my dreams?**"

LEE: Well, a University of Iowa professor says, "Creative[1] people remember their dreams."

RS: Thank you so much, Helena. We look forward to reading your new book.

---
[1] *creative:* able to see things in a new way

After You Read

A | Practice *PAIRS: Now read the conversation aloud.*

B | Vocabulary *Complete the conversations with the words from the box.*

author	guest	nightmares	remember	unfortunately

1. **A:** Who's the _____ of that book?

   B: Helena Lee. She was a(n) _____ on *Ask the Expert.*

2. **A:** Do you _____ your dreams?

   B: No, I don't. _____, I remember my _____ because they

   wake me up.

C | Comprehension *Write* **T** (True), **F** (False), *or* **?** (it doesn't say) *for each statement.*

_____ 1. Only creative people dream.

_____ 2. Animals dream about food.

_____ 3. People dream during REM sleep.

_____ 4. REM stands for real eye movement.

_____ 5. A professor believes that smart people remember their dreams.

SIMPLE PRESENT: *WH-* QUESTIONS; SHORT AND LONG ANSWERS

Wh- Questions				Answers	
Wh- Word	Do / Does	Subject	Base Form of Verb	Short	Long
When	do	I	sleep?	From 10:00 P.M. to 5:00 A.M.	You sleep from 10:00 P.M. to 5:00 A.M.
Where	do	you	sleep?	On the futon.	I sleep on the futon.
Why	do	we	sleep?	Because we're tired.	We sleep because we're tired.
What	do	they	need?	Two pillows.	They need two pillows.
Who	does	she	know?	My brother.	She knows my brother.
How	does	it	feel?	Good.	The blanket feels good.

Wh- Questions about the Subject			Answers
Wh- Word	Verb		
Who	dreams?		Everyone does.
What	happens	during REM sleep?	People dream.

GRAMMAR NOTES

1 *Wh-* **questions** ask for <u>information</u>. Most questions use **wh- word + do** or **does** + **subject + base form of the verb**.

WH- WORD	DO / DOES	SUBJECT	BASE FORM	
• **When**	**do**	you	**go**	to bed?
• **What**	**does**	he	**dream**	about?

2 To ask a **question about the subject**, use *who* or *what* + **third-person singular form of the verb**.

SUBJECT
- **My brother** sleeps on the sofa.
- **Who sleeps** on the sofa?

SUBJECT
- **Milk** helps me fall asleep.
- **What helps** you fall asleep?

BE CAREFUL! Do not use *do* or *does* with questions about the subject. Do not use the base form of the verb.

Not: Who ~~does~~ sleeps on the sofa?
Not: Who ~~do~~ sleeps on the sofa?
Not: Who ~~sleep~~ on the sofa?

3

Who asks questions about a <u>subject</u>.
Who and whom ask questions about an <u>object</u>.

USAGE NOTE: *Whom* is very formal.

SUBJECT
• **Who helps** John? Mary does.

OBJECT
• **Who does** Mary **help**? John.

OBJECT
• **Whom does** Mary **help**? John.

REFERENCE NOTE
For more about **who**, **what**, **where**, **when**, and **why**, see Unit 2, page 17.

STEP 3 FOCUSED PRACTICE

EXERCISE 1: Discover the Grammar

Night owls like to stay up late at night. Early birds get up early. Read about a night owl and an early bird. Then match the questions and answers.

Felix is a night owl. He hates to get up in the morning. On weekends he goes to bed at 1:00 A.M. and gets up at noon. Unfortunately for Felix, during the week his first class starts at 8:15, and he needs to get up early.

At 7:00 A.M. Felix's alarm rings. He wakes up, but he doesn't get up. He stays in bed and daydreams. At 7:20 his mom comes in. She has a big smile. She says, "Felix, it's time to get up."

Felix's mother is an early bird. Even on vacations she is up at 6:00 A.M. When his mom wakes him, Felix says, "Leave me alone. I'm tired."

Finally, at about 7:30, Felix gets up. He jumps out of bed, showers, and gets dressed. At 7:50 he drinks a big glass of juice, takes a breakfast bar, and runs to the bus stop. The bus comes at 8:00.

___f___ 1. Who hates to get up in the morning?

_____ 2. How does Felix feel in the morning?

_____ 3. Why does Felix run to the bus stop?

_____ 4. What does Felix have for breakfast?

_____ 5. When does Felix sleep late?

_____ 6. What happens at 7:00?

a. On weekends.

b. Tired.

c. Felix's alarm rings.

d. A glass of juice and a breakfast bar.

e. Because he doesn't want to be late for school.

f. Felix does.

EXERCISE 2: Word Order of *Wh-* Questions

(Grammar Notes 1–3)

Complete the conversations. Read the answers. Then write questions with the words in parentheses.

1. (do / you / usually get up / When)

   A: _When do you usually get up?_

   B: At 7:00 on weekdays.

2. (Where / come from / your guest / does)

   A: _____

   B: She's from Sydney.

3. (at night / they / How / do / feel)

   A: _____

   B: They're never tired at night. They're night owls.

4. (does / Who / he / dream about)

   A: _____

   B: He dreams about me.

5. (What / she / dream about / does)

   A: _____

   B: Actually, she never remembers her dreams.

EXERCISE 3: *Wh-* Questions about the Subject

(Grammar Note 3)

Complete the conversations. Read the answers. Then write questions with the words in parentheses. Use the correct form.

1. (Who / daydream)

   A: _Who daydreams?_

   B: John does.

2. (Who / have / nightmares)

   A: _____

   B: Her brother Sam does. What's more, he sometimes screams during a nightmare.

3. (Who / get up / before 6:00 A.M.)

    A: _____

    B: Grandma Ilene does.

4. (Who / hate / early morning classes)

    A: _____

    B: Bob, Emiko, and Jill do.

5. (Who / need / more than eight hours of sleep)

    A: _____

    B: Feng does.

EXERCISE 4: *Wh-* Questions

(Grammar Notes 1–3)

Read the answers. Then ask questions about the underlined words.

1. <u>Sabrina</u> daydreams.

    Who *daydreams* _____?

2. Sabrina daydreams <u>during her math class</u>.

    When _____?

3. Sabrina daydreams about <u>her boyfriend</u>.

    Who _____?

4. Sabrina daydreams during math <u>because she doesn't like the class and doesn't</u>

    <u>understand the teacher</u>.

    Why _____?

5. Sabrina's boyfriend is <u>3,000 miles away in Alaska</u>.

    Where _____?

6. Sabrina feels <u>lonely</u>.

    How _____?

7. <u>Sabrina's boyfriend</u> has a good job.

    Who _____?

8. <u>He works for an oil company.</u>

    What _____?

EXERCISE 5: *Wh-* Questions: Subject and Object   *(Grammar Notes 2–3)*

*Label the subject (**S**) and object (**O**) in each sentence. Write one question about the subject and one question about the object. Then answer the questions. Use short answers.*

              S   O

1. My mother wakes me on weekdays.

    Q: *Who wakes you on weekdays?*   **Q:** *Who does your mother wake on weekdays?*

    A: *My mother.*   **A:** *She wakes me.*

2. In a dream Jake meets his boss at a party.

    Q: _____   **Q:** _____

    A: _____   **A:** _____

3. In a nightmare two giants hit Maya.

    Q: _____   **Q:** _____

    A: _____   **A:** _____

EXERCISE 6: Editing

Correct the questions. There are ten mistakes. The first mistake is already corrected. Find and correct nine more.

                      sleep

1. Where do they ~~sleeps~~?

2. Why they need two pillows?

3. Who sleep on the sofa?

4. When does she goes to bed?

5. Who wake you?

6. Who does you dream about?

7. How he feels about that?

8. What you dream about?

9. Where he sleep?

10. How long does she sleeps at night?

EXERCISE 7: Listening

A | *Mia often has the same dream. She tells a doctor about her dream.*
Listen to their conversation. What is Mia looking for?

_____

B | *Listen again to Mia's dream. Answer the questions.*

1. What important event does Mia have?   *She has an important test.*

2. What does the man in the dream say?   _____

3. What does Dr. Fox think Mia has?   _____

4. What do the two buildings symbolize?   _____

5. What does Mia's father want her to study?   _____

EXERCISE 8: Pronunciation

A | *Read and listen to the Pronunciation Note.*

> **Pronunciation Note**
>
> Some English words have an *r* or *l* after another consonant. For example, / **pr** / as in *price* or / **gl** / as in *glad*. If it is hard for you to pronounce these two consonants together, try saying the word with the second consonant and then add the first one.
>
> **EXAMPLES:** rice → **price**
> lock → **clock**

B | *Listen and repeat the words.*

black	bright	dream	free	price
blue	clock	dress	great	three

C | *PAIRS: Read a word from Part B. Your partner writes the word in his or her notebook. Take turns.*

D | *Listen and read about Olivia's dream. Underline the words with consonant groups that have an / r / or / l / .*

It was a great dream. Listen. I buy a black dress. The price is only thirty-three dollars. There's a problem with the dress. I bring it back. The salesperson says she's sorry.

She gives me a bright blue dress instead. I try it on. The dress is perfect. I wear the dress to a party. I have a great night out.

EXERCISE 9: Interview

Answer the questions. Then work with a partner. Ask your partner the questions.

	You	Your Partner
When do you go to bed?		
What days do you sleep in?		
Does anyone wake you? If so, who?		
Do you dream? If so, what do you dream about?		
Are you an early bird or a night owl?		

EXERCISE 10: Group Interview

A | *Ask five students these questions about sleep. Take notes on a separate piece of paper.*

EXAMPLE: YOU: Juan, do you snore?
          JUAN: No, I don't, but my sister Bianca snores.

1. Who snores?

2. Who gets up before 6:00 A.M.?

3. Who goes to bed after midnight?

4. Who needs more than eight hours of sleep?

5. Who needs less than five hours of sleep?

6. Who dreams in English?

7. Who daydreams?

8. Who has insomnia? (trouble sleeping)

9. Who falls asleep during the day?

B | *Tell the class interesting results.*

EXAMPLE: Juan's sister snores.
          Nobody gets up before 6:00 A.M., but sometimes Hasan goes to bed at 5:00 A.M.

EXERCISE 11: Information Gap: Understanding Dreams

PAIRS: **Student A,** *follow the instructions on this page.* **Student B,** *turn to page 112 and follow the instructions there.*

1. Student B often has the same dream. Find out about Student B's dream. Ask these questions.

   In your dream:

   - Where are you?
   - Who do you see?
   - Is the person big? little?

   - Are you big? little?
   - What does the person say?
   - What do you do?

2. You have the following dream again and again. Read about your dream. Then answer Student B's questions about it.

   > You are on an airplane. The pilot comes to you. He says, "I need your help." You go with the pilot. You fly the plane. You land the plane. Everyone claps. You feel good. You wake up.

3. Talk about your dreams. What do they mean?

EXERCISE 12: Writing

A | *Write about a dream or daydream you often have. Answer the questions:*
   - What do you dream or daydream about?
   - Where does it take place?
   - What happens?
   - How often do you have this dream?
   - What do you think? Why do you have this dream or daydream?

   EXAMPLE: I often daydream about my family. I daydream about my birthday. I am 14 years old. We are at my grandparents' home. My grandparents' friends are there. They have a granddaughter. She is beautiful. I want to talk to her, but I get nervous. I can't talk. I turn red. Everyone looks at me. Then I run home. I feel very embarrassed.

B | *Check your work. Use the Editing Checklist.*

Editing Checklist

Did you . . . ?
☐ use the simple present correctly
☐ check your spelling

1. You often have the following dream. Read about your dream. Then answer Student A's questions about it.

   > You are in the third grade. You see your third grade teacher. Your teacher is very big. You are small. Your teacher says, "Your schoolwork is great. You are my favorite student." You smile. Then you laugh. Then you wake up.

2. Student A often has the same dream. Find out about Student A's dream. Ask these questions.

   In your dream:

   - Where are you?
   - Who comes to you?
   - What does he say?

   - What do you do?
   - How do you feel?
   - What happens?

3. Talk about your dreams. What do they mean?

UNIT 10 Review

Check your answers on page UR-2.

Do you need to review anything?

A | Complete the **wh-** questions with the words from the box.

how	when	where	who	why

1. A: _____ does she snore?   **B:** I don't know why.

2. A: _____ do they get up?   **B:** At about 9:00 or 10:00.

3. A: _____ sleeps on the sofa?   **B:** Their uncle does.

4. A: _____ do you feel?   **B:** Sleepy.

5. A: _____ do you buy sheets?   **B:** At Bloom's department store.

B | Write questions with the words in parentheses. Use the correct form.

1. _____
   (Who / snore / in your family)

2. _____
   (What / you / dream about)

3. _____
   (What time / your mother / get up)

4. _____
   (What time / you / go to bed)

5. _____
   (Where / your brother / sleep)

C | Read the statement and answers. Then write the questions.

John meets his uncle at the diner on Saturdays.

1. A: _____   **B:** John does.

2. A: _____   **B:** His uncle.

3. A: _____   **B:** At the diner.

4. A: _____   **B:** On Saturdays.

D | Correct the questions. There are six mistakes.

1. Where you live and who you live with?

2. Why he daydreams in class?

3. When does she gets up?

4. How they feel about sleeping pills?

5. Who does you dream about?

From Grammar to Writing

TIME WORD CONNECTORS: *FIRST, NEXT, AFTER THAT, THEN, FINALLY*

1 | *Which paragraph sounds better, **A** or **B**? Why?*

Paragraph A

I like to watch my roommate prepare tea. She boils water and pours the boiling water in a cup with a teabag in it. She removes the teabag and adds sugar. She adds lemon. She adds ice. She sips the tea and says, "Mmm. This tea is just the way I like it."

Paragraph B

I like to watch my roommate prepare tea. First, she boils some water and pours the boiling water in a cup with a teabag in it. Next, she removes the teabag and adds some sugar. After that, she adds some lemon. Then she adds some ice. Finally, she sips the tea and says, "Mmm. This tea is just the way I like it."

You can make your writing clearer by using **time word connectors**. They show the order in which things happen. Some common ones are *first*, *next*, *after that*, *then*, and *finally*. We usually use a **comma** after these connectors.

> EXAMPLE: **First**, you add the water. **Next**, you add the sugar.

2 | *Add time word connectors to show the order of things in this paragraph.*

I take a shower. I have breakfast. I drive to the train station. I take a train and a bus. I get to work.

Now write a paragraph about a routine you follow. Use time word connectors. Here are some ideas:

> EXAMPLE: Every Saturday morning . . .
> Every New Year's Day . . .
> Every year on my birthday . . .

3 | *Exchange papers with a partner. Did your partner follow directions? Correct any mistakes in grammar and spelling.*

4 | *Talk to your partner. Discuss the mistakes you made. Then rewrite your own paper and make any necessary changes.*

PART V

There is / *There are*; Possessives; Modals: Ability and Permission

UNIT	GRAMMAR FOCUS	THEME
11	*There is* / *There are*	Shopping Malls
12	Possessives: Nouns, Adjectives, Pronouns; Object Pronouns; Questions with *Whose*	Possessions
13	Ability: *Can* or *Could*	Abilities of Animals
14	Permission: *Can* or *May*	Health and Diet

There is / There are

SHOPPING MALLS

Before You Read

PAIRS: Discuss the questions.

1. Do you like big malls? Why or why not?
2. Is there a mall near your school? Where is it? Do you go there? Why or why not?

Read

Read an advertisement for the West Edmonton Mall in Canada.

Come to Edmonton and see its top attraction,

West Edmonton Mall

West Ed Mall is a shopper's dream. **There are** more than 800 stores. They include everything from Old Navy® to Godiva® Chocolates to one-of-a-kind stores. Enjoy the mall's international flavor. **There's** Chinatown, where you can shop in a traditional Chinese marketplace. **There's** Europa Boulevard with its many European specialties. West Ed Mall also has over 110 eating places. And for the young and the young-at-heart **there are** seven world-class attractions including a water park, an amusement park, and an indoor skating rink. So make your travel plans now. **There isn't** a better time to get away.

After You Read

A | Practice *PAIRS: Now read the advertisement aloud. Take turns reading sentences.*

B | Vocabulary *Complete the conversations with the words from the box.*

amusement park	include	market
attraction	indoor	one of a kind
get away	international	

1. **A:** Why do you like that store?

   B: It's _____. It has unusual things for sale.

2. **A:** Does the bill _____ the tip at this restaurant?

   B: No. The tip is extra.

3. **A:** What kind of school is it?

   B: It's a(n) _____ school. Students come from all over the world.

4. **A:** There's a big _____ in the center of town. You can buy fresh fruit,

   vegetables, and handmade clothes.

   B: Let's go. It sounds great.

5. **A:** What's the main _____ at that mall?

   B: The prices. Everything is cheap.

6. **A:** What's your favorite ride at the _____?

   B: The Hurricane. It's fast and scary. I love it.

7. **A:** Does the school have a(n) _____ swimming pool?

   B: Yes, it does. The students can swim every day of the year.

8. **A:** He's tired and bored with his job.

   B: He needs to _____.

C | Comprehension *Read each question about the advertisement. Circle the correct letter.*

1. How many stores are there at the West Edmonton Mall?

    a. more than 80

    b. more than 100

    c. more than 800

2. What does the ad say about the mall?

    a. It has a chocolate flavor.

    b. It has a Canadian flavor.

    c. It has an international flavor.

(Top) Spinner and *(Bottom)* statue at West Edmonton Mall

3. What kind of traditional market is there?

    a. a Mexican market

    b. a Chinese market

    c. a Turkish market

4. How many eating places are there?

    a. more than 80

    b. more than 100

    c. more than 7

5. What does West Edmonton Mall include?

    a. a water park

    b. schools

    c. a golf course

THERE IS / THERE ARE

Affirmative Statements			
There	*Be*	Subject	Place / Time
There	is	a restaurant	on this level.
		a movie	at 6:30.
There	are	two restaurants	near the entrance.
		shows	at 7:00 and 9:00.

Negative Statements			
There	*Be + Not*	Subject	Place / Time
There	isn't	a restaurant	on the second level.
There	aren't	any movies	at 8:00.

Contractions	
there is	⟶ **there's**
there is not	⟶ **there isn't**
there are not	⟶ **there aren't**

Yes / No Questions			
Be	*There*	Subject	Place
Is	there	a pizza place	on Second Street?
Are	there	any banks	nearby?

Short Answers				
Affirmative		Negative		
Yes,	there is.	No,	there isn't.	
	there are.		there aren't.	

GRAMMAR NOTES

1	Use **there is** or **there's** to state facts about a **person** or **thing**.	• **There is a salesperson** near the door. • **There's a bookstore** next to the electronics store.
2	Use **there are** to talk about people or things. We often use *there is* or *there are* to tell the **location** of people or things or the **time** of events. **BE CAREFUL!** Don't confuse *there are* and *they are*.	• **There are five shoe stores** at the mall. • There's a woman's shoe store **on the second level**. (location) • There are concerts **on Friday and Saturday nights**. (time) • **There are two good restaurants. They are** on the third level.
3	In the negative, use the contractions **isn't** and **aren't**. The full forms, *is not* and *are not*, are rarely used with *there*. **BE CAREFUL!** Don't confuse *there aren't* with *they aren't*.	• **There isn't** a cloud in the sky. • **There aren't** any gyms near our school. • **There aren't any** gyms here. **There are** three restaurants nearby, but **they aren't** open this late.
4	We often use **any** with *yes / no* questions about plural nouns.	• Are there **any** malls nearby?
5	**BE CAREFUL!** **Here** and **there** are adverbs of place. *Here* is for something nearby, and *there* is for something far. Don't confuse the adverb of place *there* with *there is* or *there are* or with the possessive adjective *their*.	• Last summer we exchanged homes with friends near Banff. We went **there**, and they came **here**. • Banff National Park is good for hiking. **There are** high mountains **there**. • **Their** home is in the mountains.
6	We often use **There is** or **There are** the first time we talk about people or things. We use **he**, **she**, **it**, or **they** to tell more about the people or things.	• **There's a package** in the mail. **It's** heavy. • **There's a man** at the door. **He** wants to speak to you. • **There are three girls** in the dress store. **They** are choosing dresses for a party.

REFERENCE NOTE
For more about **any**, see Unit 27, page 311.

EXERCISE 1: Discover the Grammar

Look at the mall directory. Write **T (True)** *or* **F (False)** *for each statement.*

Mall Directory

Third Level	3a	3b	3c	3d	3e	
	Food Court	Thai food	Chinese food	Burgers	Sushi bar	Café
Second Level	2a	2b	2c	2d	2e	2f
	Women's clothes	Shoe store	Art supply store	Furniture store	Children's clothes	Cosmetics store
First Level	1a	1b	1c	1d	1e	1f
	Flower shop	Gift shop	Bookstore	Unisex hair salon	Electronics store	Women's clothes

___T___ **1.** There's a flower shop on the first level.

_____ **2.** There's a café on the second level.

_____ **3.** There aren't any toy stores.

_____ **4.** There are five places to eat.

_____ **5.** There isn't any Thai food at this mall.

_____ **6.** There's a bookstore on the first level.

_____ **7.** There aren't any office supply stores at the mall.

_____ **8.** There aren't any jewelry stores at the mall.

_____ **9.** There isn't an amusement park at this mall.

_____**10.** There's an art supply store at the mall.

EXERCISE 2: Affirmative and Negative Statements

(Grammar Notes 1–3)

Check (✓) each correct sentence. Change the sentences that don't make sense.

_____ **1.** There's a mall in the Chinese restaurant. _There's a Chinese restaurant in the mall._

_____ **2.** There's a second level on the shoe store. _____

_____ **3.** There are two women's clothing stores at the mall. _____

_____ **4.** There's an electronics store on the first level. _____

_____ **5.** There isn't a mall in the men's clothing store. _____

_____ **6.** There aren't any furniture stores in the desks. _____

EXERCISE 3: Affirmative and Negative Statements

(Grammar Notes 1–4, 6)

Complete the conversation. Use **there is, there isn't, there are, there aren't, they are,** *or* **they aren't.**

A: This pizza place is awful. _____ _There aren't_ _____ any tablecloths, and the
1.

placemats are dirty.

B: You're right. _____ any napkins either.
2.

A: Where is the busboy?

B: I don't know. _____ anyone here now except us.
3.

A: _____ a busboy here somewhere, but I don't see him now.
4.

Well, I need a fork and knife.

B: _____ some forks and knives on that table. Oh.
5.

_____clean.
6.

A: Oh my gosh. You won't believe this.

B: What is it? Boy, it's hot in here. _____ even a fan.
7.

A: _____ a mouse over there, near the wall!
8.

B: What? Ugh, _____ two mice! Let's leave!
9.

A: What about our food?

B: Let the mice have it. _____ hungry, too!
10.

EXERCISE 4: *There is / There are, There,* and *They are*   (Grammar Notes 1–2, 5)

Complete the conversation. Use **there's, there are, there,** *and* **they're.** *Remember to start sentences with a capital letter.*

A: How about some Chinese food?

B: Well, _____*there's*_____ only one Chinese food restaurant nearby, but

   1.

   it's not very good. _____ a lot of other restaurants though.

                        2.

A: Today is Sunday. Are they open?

B: _____ all open seven days a week.

      3.

A: Well, _____ a nice Mexican place over

              4.

_____.

   5.

B: Where?

A: Over _____ next to the diner.

            6.

B: That's right. I know the place. I was _____ a few months

                                            7.

ago. Let's go.

EXERCISE 5: **Agreement with** *There is / There are*   (Grammar Notes 1–2, 6)

Complete the sentences. Use **There's** *or* **There are** *in the first sentence. Use* **He's, She's, It's,** *or* **They're** *in the second sentence.*

1. _____*There's*_____ a good café over there. _____*It's*_____ next to the bookstore.

2. _____ a salesman behind the counter. _____ talking to that woman.

3. _____ a lot of wool sweaters. _____ in the back of the store.

4. _____ a scarf on the floor. _____ your new one, isn't it?

5. _____ some indoor parking spaces over there. _____ near the exit.

6. _____ a small mall on Route 4. _____ next to the amusement park.

7. _____ a lot of people in that line. _____ buying tickets for the movie.

EXERCISE 6: *Yes / No* Questions with *Is there / Are there*   (Grammar Notes 1–4, 6)

Look at the calendar. Complete the questions with **is there** or **are there**. *Then write answers. Remember to start sentences with a capital letter.*

---
www.findthingstodo.com/chicago

LOCATION
• Chicago
• Printers Row / South Loop
• Loop
• Lakeview
• Suburbs
DATE
This week

FIND THINGS TO DO

This week

Today
Carmen
Flamenco Dance
Dance Center
Columbia College
Tonight at 8:00

Friday
Buyers Flea Market
4545 West Division
8–5
Cheap clothing!

Saturday
The Misfits
Great Drama with
Marilyn Monroe!
Main Street Cinema
4:30, 6:30, 8:30

Sunday
**Chicago Symphony
Orchestra**
All Beethoven
Chicago Cultural Center
8:00 P.M.

---

1. A: _____Is there_____ a dance performance tonight? What is it?

   B: _____

2. A: _____ movies or concerts this weekend? When?

   B: _____

3. A: How many showings of the movie _____?

   B: _____

4. A: _____ a flea market? When and where is it?

   B: _____

EXERCISE 7: Editing

Correct the paragraph. There are six mistakes. The first mistake is already corrected.
Find and correct five more.

         are

There ~~be~~ pizza places at almost every mall. The pizzas come in all shapes and sizes. are

traditional pizzas with mushrooms, pepperoni, and broccoli. There is also pizzas with curry, red

herring, and coconut. In the United States they are over 61,000 pizza places. There represent

17 percent of all restaurants. There are popular with young and old.

EXERCISE 8: Pronunciation

A | *Read and listen to the Pronunciation Note.*

> **Pronunciation Note**
>
> The words **there**, **their**, and **they're** have the same sound.

B | *Listen to the sentences. Circle the correct letter of the word or words the speaker uses.*

1. **a.** there   **b.** their
2. **a.** There   **b.** There's
3. **a.** They are   **b.** There are
4. **a.** There   **b.** There's
5. **a.** There are   **b.** They are
6. **a.** There   **b.** They're

EXERCISE 9: Listening

A | *Listen to this conversation between two drivers. What is the speaker's first question?*

Excuse me, _____?

B | *Listen again. Mark the sentences **Y (Yes)**, **N (No)**, or **? (it doesn't say)**.*

___Y___ **1.** Is there a mall up ahead?

_____ **2.** Is the mall crowded?

_____ **3.** Is there a pizza place at the mall?

_____ **4.** Is the food court on the second level?

_____ **5.** Are there at least 10 places where you can eat?

EXERCISE 10: Comparing Pictures

PAIRS: Find 10 differences between Picture A and Picture B.

> **EXAMPLE:** In Picture A there's a shoe repair shop between the bakery and the pizza place. In Picture B there isn't a shoe repair shop between the bakery and the pizza place. The shoe repair shop is between the pizza place and the flower shop.

Picture A

Picture B

EXERCISE 11: Game: Tic Tac Toe

Use the phrases in the boxes to ask your classmates questions. Begin with **Is there** *or* **Are there any**. *If a student says "yes," write his or her name in the box. When you have three across, down, or diagonally, call out, "Tic Tac Toe!"*

a big mall near your home	an amusement park near your home	an international club in your school
twins in your family	an Italian restaurant near your home	a skating rink near your home
a pizza place on your street	credit cards in your purse or pocket	an indoor pool near your home

EXERCISE 12: Writing

A | *Write about a place where you like to shop. Use* **There is,** **There isn't,** **There are,** *or* **There aren't.**

EXAMPLE: There's a small store near my home. It's called "Village Gifts." It's on a street with two other small shops. The owners are a husband and wife. Their gifts include unusual crafts from all over the world. There are some great things to buy—colorful pottery from Mexico, beautiful jewelry from Thailand, traditional rugs from China, and baskets from Jamaica. The owners love the things they sell. There's a story behind every item. That's why I like to shop there. There aren't many shops like that.

B | *Check your work. Use the Editing Checklist.*

Editing Checklist

Did you . . . ?
- [ ] use *there is* and *there are* correctly
- [ ] check your spelling

UNIT 11 Review

Check your answers on page UR-2.
Do you need to review anything?

A | *Circle the correct words to complete the* **yes** / **no** *questions and short answers.*

1. **A:** **Are there / Are they** any soda machines in the building?

   B: Yes, **there are / they are.**

2. **A:** **Are there / Are they** any amusement parks near your school?

   B: No, **there aren't / they're not.**

3. **A:** **Is it / Is she** the teacher?

   B: Yes, **she's / she is.**

4. **A:** **Are there / Are they** new students?

   B: No, **they aren't / she isn't.**

5. **A:** **Are there / Is there** a men's room on this floor?

   B: No, **they aren't / there isn't.**

B | *Complete the sentences with* **There's, There are, She's, It's,** *or* **They're.**

1. _____ a new pizza place on Elm Street. _____ next to the post office.

2. _____ a lot of people outside the pizza place. _____ in a long line.

3. _____ a great pizza chef there. _____ funny, and her pizzas are delicious.

C | *Correct the paragraph. There are four mistakes.*

> Visit the new Shopper's Mall on Route 290. There's over 100 stores. There a movie theater, and they are ten great places to eat. Come early. Every morning at 10:30 there are a free show for children. The mall is three miles from the Tappan Bridge on Route 290.

UNIT 12

Possessives: Nouns, Adjectives, Pronouns; Object Pronouns; Questions with *Whose*

POSSESSIONS

STEP 1 GRAMMAR IN CONTEXT

Before You Read

A | *Is your handwriting neat? Is it difficult to read?*

B | *Look at Michelle and Rick's handwriting. Whose handwriting is neat? Whose is messy?*

My name is Michelle Young.

Read

A teacher is returning student compositions. Read the conversation.

TEACHER: **Whose** composition is this?

BORIS: Is it a good paper?

TEACHER: It's excellent.

BORIS: It's **my** composition.

YOLANDA: No, that's not **your** handwriting. It's **Kim's** composition. **Her** name is right there. She's absent today.

TEACHER: Thanks, Yolanda. **Whose** paper is *this*?

BORIS: Is it a good paper?

TEACHER: It's OK.

BORIS: Then it's **mine**.

JUAN: It's not **yours**. It's **mine**. See, **my** name is on the back.

TEACHER: You're right, Juan. I recognize your handwriting. Here, Boris. *This* is **your** composition.

BORIS: Is it a good paper?

TEACHER: It needs some work.

BORIS: I don't think it's **mine**.

TEACHER: Uh . . . I think it is. I have a grade for everyone else.

After You Read

A | Practice *GROUPS OF 4: Now read the conversation aloud.*

B | Vocabulary *Complete the sentences with the words from the box.*

back	composition	grade	handwriting	recognize

1. It's his letter. I can _____ the _____.

2. We had to write a _____ about a favorite childhood possession. Mine was about my blue blanket.

3. Are the answers in the _____ of the book?

4. What was your _____ in English? Mine was an A+.

C | Comprehension *Whose compositions are these? Write **Kim**, **Juan**, and **Boris** below the correct composition.*

1. _____   2. _____   3. _____

STEP 2 GRAMMAR PRESENTATION

POSSESSIVES, OBJECT PRONOUNS; QUESTIONS WITH *WHOSE*

Possessive Nouns	
Singular Nouns	**Plural Nouns**
John's last name is Tamez. **Russ's** last name is Stram.	The **girls'** gym is on this floor.
My **mother's** name is Rita. The **woman's** name is Carmen.	My **parents'** car is in the garage. The **women's** restroom is on the first floor.

Subject Pronoun	Possessive Adjective	Possessive Pronoun	
I	**my**	**mine**	That is **my** book. That book is **mine**.
You*	**your**	**yours**	Do you have **your** key? Do you have **yours**?
He	**his**	**his**	This is **his** car. This car is **his**.
She	**her**	**hers**	That's **her** house. That house is **hers**.
It	**its**		Look at that bird. **Its** feathers are red and gold.
We	**our**	**ours**	We lost **our** notes. We lost **ours**.
They	**their**	**theirs**	They can't find **their** tickets. They can't find **theirs**.

You can be singular or plural.

	Object Pronoun (Singular)		Object Pronoun (Plural)
Raul likes	**me**. **you**. **him**. **her**.	Sarah knows	**us**. **you**. **them**.

Questions with *Whose*	
Questions	**Answers**
Whose hair is long?	Carmen**'s**. Carmen**'s** is. Carmen**'s** hair is long.
Whose eyes are green?	Igor**'s**. Igor**'s** are. Igor**'s** eyes are green.
Whose compositions are finished?	Yoko**'s** and Kaori**'s**. Yoko**'s** and Kaori**'s** are. Yoko**'s** and Kaori**'s** compositions.

GRAMMAR NOTES

1	**Possessive nouns** and **possessive adjectives** show belonging or a relationship.	• **Kim's car** (the car belongs to Kim) • **her aunt** (relationship)
2	To show possession, add: **apostrophe (')** + *s* to a **singular noun**. **apostrophe (')** to a **plural noun** ending in *-s*. **apostrophe (')** + *s* to an **irregular plural noun**.	• That's **Juan's** composition. • My **parents'** home is near my home. • The **women's** restroom is on the first floor.
3	**Possessive adjectives** replace **possessive nouns**. Possessive adjectives agree with the possessive noun they replace.	**His** • ~~My father's~~ sisters are in Busan and Daegu. **Her** • ~~My mother's~~ brother is in Seoul.
4	A **noun** always follows a possessive noun or a possessive adjective.	• Bekir's **book** is new. • His **book** is new.
5	A **possessive pronoun** can replace a **possessive adjective** and noun. **BE CAREFUL!** A noun never follows a possessive pronoun. **BE CAREFUL!** The verb after a possessive pronoun agrees with the noun it replaces.	• This isn't **my umbrella**. **Mine** is blue. *(My umbrella is blue.)* • This is my hat. This is **mine**. NOT: This is mine ~~hat~~. • Her **notebook** is blue. = **Hers is** blue. • Her **notebooks** are red. = **Hers are** red.
6	Use *whose* for questions about possessions. **BE CAREFUL!** *Who's* is short for *who is*.	• **Whose** notebook is this? • **Who's** absent?
7	**BE CAREFUL!** Don't confuse possessive pronouns with **object pronouns**. Object pronouns come after a verb.	• Do you need to see **me**? • The baby loves baths. We give **him** a bath every day.
8	**BE CAREFUL!** A noun + apostrophe (') + *s* may be short for *is* in conversation and very informal writing. Do not confuse *its* and *it's*. *its* = possessive adjective; *it's* = *it is*	• "**Anna's** late." (Anna **is** late.) • This is my turtle. **Its** name is Tubby. • **It's** a hot day.

REFERENCE NOTES

For more rules about possessive nouns, see Appendix 7 on page A-7.
For more about irregular plural nouns, see Appendix 5 on pages A-5–A-6.

EXERCISE 1: Discover the Grammar

Read the conversations. Then complete the sentences. Circle the correct letter.

Conversation 1:

FENG: Whose book is on the table next to the printer?

LI: It's mine.

1. *Whose* refers to _____.
   a. book   b. table

2. *Mine* means _____.
   a. my book   b. my printer

Conversation 2:

JOSE: Maria, is that your translator?

MARIA: No, it's Marco's. Mine is in my backpack. His is over there.

3. *Marco's* means _____.
   a. Here is Marco.   b. Marco's translator

4. *Mine* means _____.
   a. my translator   b. my backpack

5. *His* means _____.
   a. Marco's backpack   b. Marco's translator

Conversation 3:

SUN HI: How is Mi Young related to you?

JUN: She's my father's brother's wife.

6. My *father's brother's wife* is _____.
   a. my uncle   b. my aunt

Conversation 4:

EROL: Where are the workbooks?

AYLA: I put on them on the bookshelves near the door.

7. *Them* refers to _____.
   a. the bookshelves   b. the workbooks

EXERCISE 2: Possessive Nouns

(Grammar Notes 1–2)

A | *Read about the Zhang family. Underline the possessive nouns in the reading.*

This is the Zhang family. The older man is Lao Zhang. Lao's wife is Feng. They have two daughters, Hua and Mei. Hua's husband is Gang. They have a son, Bao. Mei's husband is Jinsong. They have a daughter, Ting.

B | *Complete the sentences. Underline the correct noun or possessive noun form.*

1. Ting's **mothers / mother's** mother is Ting's **grandmother / grandmother's**.

2. Hua's **sister / sister's daughter / daughters** is Hua's niece.

3. Gang's **wife / wife's sister / sister's** is his sister-in-law.

4. Bao's **uncle / uncle's** apartment is in Shanghai.

5. Bao and Ting are **cousins / cousin's**. Their **mothers / mother's** are **sisters / sister's**.

6. Lao Zhang is the **families / family's** oldest member.

EXERCISE 3: Possessive Adjectives

(Grammar Notes 1, 3)

Complete the sentences. Use a possessive adjective.

1. My sister studies in Toronto. _____*Her*_____ school is on Victoria Street.

2. She goes to Edgewood University. She likes _____ classes.

3. Carlos's parents work at the United Nations. _____ jobs are interesting.

His mother is a translator, and his father is an interpreter.

4. Right now my brother is in Peru, _____ wife is in Belize, and

_____ children are in the United States.

5. The children have a rabbit. _____ fur is soft.

6. Does your brother like _____ job?

7. Do you use _____ calculator every day in math class?

8. Does your grandmother like _____ new apartment? Is she happy there?

EXERCISE 4: Possessive Pronouns

(Grammar Note 5)

Replace the underlined words with a possessive pronoun.

1. **A:** Is that your notebook?

   B: No, it's not ~~my notebook~~. It's <u>his</u> notebook. <u>My notebook</u> is in my book bag.
           mine
          a.   **b.**   **c.**

2. **A:** Is this their house?

   B: No. <u>Their house</u> is in back of the library.
           a.

   A: Whose house is this?

   B: It's <u>our house</u>.
         b.

3. **A:** Are those your sunglasses?

   B: No, they're <u>her sunglasses</u>. <u>My sunglasses</u> are in my bag.
          a.   **b.**

EXERCISE 5: Possessive Adjectives and Possessive Pronouns

(Grammar Notes 1–2, 5, 7)

Complete the conversations with the words in parentheses. Write the correct form.

1. **A:** I think you have my umbrella.

   B: No. This is _____*my*_____ umbrella. _____ is over there. It's next
              a. (my / mine)   **b. (You / Yours)**

   to _____ translator.
       c. (her / hers)

2. **A:** Whose gloves are these? Yours or Julie's?

   B: _____ are black leather. _____ are wool.
      a. (Her / Hers)   **b. (My / Mine)**

3. **A:** Where is _____ car?
           a. (their / theirs)

   B: _____ car is in the garage.
      b. (Their / Theirs)

   A: Is _____ there too?
        c. (your / yours)

   B: No. _____ is on the street.
        d. (Our / Ours)

EXERCISE 6: Subject and Object Pronouns, Possessives
(Grammar Notes 1, 3–5, 7)

Complete the sentences with the words in parentheses. Write the correct form.

1. It's _____*mine*_____. Please give it to _____.
   a. (I / my / me / mine)   b. (I / my / me / mine)

   _____ need it.
   c. (I / My / Me / I)

2. I don't think _____ is on the train. I don't see _____.
   a. (he / him / his)   b. (he / him / his)

3. Our family is from Edmonton. _____ family is from Vancouver,
   a. (They / Their / Theirs / Them)

   but _____ live in Edmonton now. We live next door to
   b. (they / their / theirs / them)

   _____.
   c. (they / their / theirs / them)

EXERCISE 7: Possessives: Questions and Verb Agreement
(Grammar Notes 3, 5–6)

Complete the conversations with the words in parentheses. Write the correct form.

1. **A:** _____*Whose*_____ shoes are these?
   (Who's / Whose)

   B: They're my shoes. His _____ over there.
   (is / are)

2. **A:** _____ key is this? _____ it yours?
   (Who's / Whose)   (Is / Are)

   B: No it isn't.

3. **A:** _____ in room 401?
   (Who's / Whose)

   B: Florian and David.

   A: _____ that their usual classroom?
   (Is / Are)

4. **A:** _____ books are those? _____ they hers?
   (Who's / Whose)   (Is / Are)

   B: No, _____ his.
   (they're / it's)

5. **A:** _____ notes are those?
   (Who's / Whose)

   B: Bob's. His notes are messy. Mine _____ neat.
   (is / are)

6. **A:** _____ that woman?
   (Who's / Whose)

   B: Her name is Wu-Shen. She's an English teacher.

7. **A:** My parents live in Italy. Hers _____ in Argentina.
   (live / lives)

EXERCISE 8: Pronouns and Possessive Adjectives

(Grammar Notes 1–4, 7)

Read and complete the article with the words in parentheses. Write the correct form.

International Language Institute Newsletter
Vol. 22

Get to Know New Students at the ILI

New Student of the Month

Sandra Gomes

My name is Sandra Gomes. ___*I'm*___ from São Paulo,
                                              1. (I / I'm)
Brazil. _____ happy to be a student at the International
        2. (I / I'm)
Language Institute. _____ great to learn English and meet
                    3. (Its / It's)
people from all over the world. _____ parents and brother
                                4. (Me / My)
are in Brazil, but _____ sister is here with _____.
                   5. (my / mine)   **6. (I / me)**
_____ share an apartment. _____ nice, but
7. (We / Our)   **8. (It / It's)**
_____ far from school. _____ each have a bedroom.
9. (it's / its)   **10. (We / Us)**
_____ is small, but it has a big closet. _____ is large,
11. (My / Mine)   **12. (Her / Hers)**
but it doesn't have a closet. _____ spend a lot of time
                             13. (We / Us)
together in _____ apartment. That's because _____
            14. (us / our)   **15. (we / our)**
have a TV, a computer, and a lot of friends who visit _____.
                                                     16. (we / us)

EXERCISE 9: Editing

Correct the conversations. There are seven mistakes. The first mistake is already corrected. Find and correct six more.

1. **A:** Is that ~~you~~ *your* dictionary?

   B: No. It's his dictionary.

   A: Who's?

   B: Dans.

2. **A:** Is Maria sister here?

   B: No, she's not.

   A: Is Maria here?

   B: No, but his brother is.

   A: Where is Maria?

   B: I think she's with his sister. Their at the movies.

EXERCISE 10: Pronunciation

🎧 **A |** *Read and listen to the Pronunciation Note.*

Pronunciation Note

When you use a possessive, add the sound of / **z** /, / **s** / or / **ɪz** /.

EXAMPLES:

Lisa	Lisa's	/ **z** /
Jack	Jack's	/ **s** /
Ross	Ross's	/ **ɪz** /

🎧 **B |** *Listen to the sentences. Circle the word you hear.*

1. Maria   (Maria's)   Marias   4. partner   partner's   partners

2. Maria   Maria's   Marias   5. partner   partner's   partners

3. Maria   Maria's   Marias   6. partner   partner's   partners

EXERCISE 11: Listening

🎧 **A |** *Listen to the conversation. What are Boris and Jasmine talking about? Circle the correct letter.*

     a. bikes   **b.** baskets   **c.** sales

🎧 **B |** *Listen again. Write the name of the owner above each bicycle. Use the names from the box.*

Amy	Jasmine	Johnny	Roger and Ted

1. _____   2. _____   3. _____   4. _____

EXERCISE 12: Talking about Family Photos

Bring in photos of family members. Write on the back of the photo how the person is related to you (for example, my sister, my mother, my aunt). Your teacher collects the photos and gives you a different photo. You and your classmates ask questions about the photos.

EXAMPLE: ANYA: Whose sister is this?
          PABLO: I think it's Juan's.
          JUAN: You're right. She's my sister.

EXERCISE 13: Game: Find Someone Whose / Who's . . .

A | *Complete the questions. Use* **whose** *or* **who's**.

1. _____Whose_____ birthday is in December? _____

2. _____Who's_____ good in art? _____

3. _____ name means something? _____

4. _____ a good athlete? _____

5. _____ eyes aren't dark brown? _____

6. _____ a good cook? _____

7. _____ first name has more than eight letters? _____

8. _____ birthday is in the summer? _____

9. _____ a good dancer? _____

10. _____ handwriting is beautiful? _____

B | *Look back at Part A. Ask your classmates the questions. Write their names. Report to the class.*

EXAMPLE: MARIA: Juan, is your birthday in December?
          JUAN: No, it's not. Is yours?
          MARIA: Yes, it is. (Juan writes Maria's name on the line.)

EXERCISE 14: Writing

A | *Look at Exercise 8 on page 138. Write about yourself and your family for a school newsletter. Use pronouns and possessive adjectives.*

EXAMPLE: I'm from Recife in Brazil. I live with my parents and my younger brother. My older brother, Jose, is married. He is a pilot, and his wife is a pilot too. My mother worries about them, but she is proud of them. My dream is to become a pilot one day too, but it's my secret for now.

B | *Check your work. Use the Editing Checklist.*

Editing Checklist

Did you . . . ?

☐ use possessive adjectives, possessive pronouns, and object pronouns correctly

☐ check your spelling

UNIT 12 Review

Check your answers on page UR-3.
Do you need to review anything?

A | Cross out the underlined words. Replace them with **His, Her, Its,** or **Their.**

1. The Browns' car is big.

2. My brother's best friend is a history teacher.

3. That bird is injured. That bird's wing is broken.

4. The students' tests are on the teacher's desk.

5. Our aunt's store is on Main Street.

B | Underline the correct words to complete the conversations.

1. **A:** You need an umbrella. Take **me / mine**.

   B: I don't want to use **your / yours**.

   A: It's OK. I have **you / your** rain hat.

2. **A:** **Who / Whose** dictionary is on the floor?

   B: It's **Ali / Ali's**.

3. **A:** Who's talking?

   B: **My / Mine** children have a parrot. **Its / It's** name is Polly. Polly's talking.

4. **A:** **Her / Hers** composition is here, but where is **your / yours**?

   B: **My / Mine** is at home. Sorry.

C | Correct the conversation. There are five mistakes.

A: Who's bag is that on the floor?

B: I think it's Maria.

A: No. Her bag is on her arm.

B: Well, it's not mine bag. Maybe it's Rita.

A: Rita, is that bag your?

13 Ability: *Can* or *Could*

ABILITIES OF ANIMALS

STEP 1 GRAMMAR IN CONTEXT

Before You Read

GROUPS: Do you have a pet or know someone who has one? What kind? Does it have any unusual talents?

Read

Read the online article about an amazing parrot.

WILD NATURE   Home | **Animal Facts** | Photos | Quizzes | Wild TV

A Genius Parrot

Everyone knows parrots **can talk**. By "talk" we mean they **can repeat** words. Most parrots **can't** really **express** ideas.

N'kisi is different. N'kisi is an African gray parrot. He **can say** almost 1,000 words. He **can use** basic grammar. He **can talk** about the present, past, and future. When he doesn't know a form, he **can invent** one. For example, he used the word "flied," not "flew," for the past of the verb "fly."

N'kisi lives in New York City with his owner, Aimee Morgana. He **couldn't talk** much at first. At first he **could** only **say** a few words. But Aimee was a great teacher, and N'kisi was a good student. Now N'kisi talks to anyone near him.

Donald Broom, a professor of Veterinary Medicine at the University of Cambridge, is not surprised. He says that parrots **can think** at high levels. In that way, they are like apes and chimpanzees.

Les Rance of the Parrot Society says, "Most African grays are intelligent. They **can learn** to do easy puzzles. They **can say** 'good night' when you turn the lights off at night. They **can say** 'good-bye' when you put a coat on. But N'kisi **can do** many more things. N'kisi is an amazing[1] bird. He's not just smart. He's a genius."

---

[1] *amazing:* surprising in a good way

A | Practice *PAIRS: Read the article again aloud. Take turns reading each paragraph.*

B | Vocabulary *Complete the sentences with the words from the box. Use the correct form.*

be surprised	genius	intelligent	invent	professor

1. Monkeys and dolphins are very _____

   animals. They can learn many things.

2. Many people _____ by the abilities of

   African gray parrots.

3. Mozart was a _____.

   He wrote great music at the age of six.

4. Try and take his course. He's a very good

   _____.

5. We need to _____ a way to learn languages while we sleep.

C | Comprehension *Write* **T** *(True),* **F** *(False), or* **?** *(it doesn't say) for each statement.*

_____ 1. N'kisi can say more than 1,100 words.

_____ 2. N'kisi can't use basic grammar.

_____ 3. N'kisi can talk about the past and the future.

_____ 4. N'kisi can understand Italian.

_____ 5. Parrots can't think at high levels.

_____ 6. N'kisi could only say a few words at first.

CAN / CAN'T FOR ABILITY AND POSSIBILITY; COULD FOR PAST ABILITY

Affirmative Statements		
Subject	Can / Could	Base Form of Verb
I You* He We	can could	talk.

*You is both singular and plural.

Negative Statements		
Subject	Can't / Couldn't	Base Form of Verb
She It They	can't couldn't	talk.

Yes / No Questions		
Can / Could	Subject	Base Form of Verb
Can	you	understand?
Could		

Short Answers	
Affirmative	Negative
Yes, I can.	No, I can't.
Yes, we could.	No, we couldn't.

GRAMMAR NOTES

1	*Can* expresses **present ability** or **possibility**. It comes before the verb. The verb is always in the **base form**.	• He **can say** 950 words. • We **can teach** your bird to talk.
2	The **negative** of *can* is *can't*. *Cannot* is a form of the negative. It is not common.	• I **can't** understand you. • I **cannot** understand you.
3	Reverse the subject and *can* for *yes / no* questions.	• **He can** speak about the past. • **Can he** speak about the past?
4	*Could* expresses **past ability**. *Could not* is the full negative form. The more common form is the contraction, *couldn't*.	• I **could** run fast in high school. • I **could not** drive five years ago. • I **couldn't** drive five years ago.
5	Reverse the subject and *could* for *yes / no* questions.	• **You could** speak English last year. • **Could you** speak English last year?
6	We usually give short answers to questions with *can, can't, could,* or *couldn't*.	• Can he understand me? **Yes, he can.**

EXERCISE 1: Discover the Grammar

A | *Read the sentences in column A. Underline* **can, can't,** *or* **couldn't** *and the base form verbs. Circle the negative statements.*

A	B
__e__ **1.** N'kisi can invent new words.	**a.** He's very strong.
____ **2.** We can't understand our professor.	**b.** She speaks too fast.
____ **3.** I'm sorry. I can't help you now.	**c.** He was too short.
____ **4.** I can't hear you.	**d.** They never talk about their feelings.
____ **5.** He can lift 110 pounds (50 kilos).	**e.** He's a smart bird.
____ **6.** They can't express their love.	**f.** I'm busy.
____ **7.** The boy couldn't reach the button.	**g.** It's very noisy here.

B | *Look back at Part A. Match the sentences in column A with the possible reasons in column B.*

EXERCISE 2: *Can and Can't*   *(Grammar Notes 1–2)*

Complete the sentences with **can** *or* **can't** *and the verbs in parentheses.*

1. Many parrots _____*can learn*_____ to speak. My parrot _____, "You're a
                            (learn)   **(say)**
    genius."

2. My dog _____, but he _____ me my shoes. I'm trying to
                       (sit)   **(bring)**
    teach him to bring things to me.

3. My cat _____ mice. He's very good at
                 (catch)
    that. Her cat _____ mice. He just sits and
                        (catch)
    watches them.

4. Her dog _____ two languages, Spanish
                 (understand)
    and English. She speaks to her dog in English, and her
    husband speaks to the dog in Spanish.

5. Dolphins _____ people in trouble. They are
                 (help)
    smart and show feelings.

EXERCISE 3: *Can / Can't*: *Yes / No* Questions and Answers

(Grammar Note 3)

Read the real conversation between Aimee Morgana and N'kisi, her parrot. Then write
yes / no *questions with the words in parentheses. Answer the questions.*

> **N'KISI:** Wanna (I want to) go in a car right now.
>
> **AIMEE:** I'm sorry. We can't right now—
>
> maybe we can go later.
>
> **N'KISI:** Why can't I go in a car now?
>
> **AIMEE:** Because we don't have one.
>
> **N'KISI:** Let's get a car.
>
> **AIMEE:** No, N'kisi, we can't get a car now.
>
> **N'KISI:** I want a car.

1. **A:** _____ Can N'kisi talk? _____
    (N'kisi / talk)
   B: _____ Yes, he can. _____

2. **A:** _____
    (he / ask questions)
   B: _____

3. **A:** _____
    (he / make suggestions)
   B: _____

4. **A:** _____
    (Aimee / buy a car now)
   B: _____

5. **A:** _____
    (N'kisi / ask for things)
   B: _____

6. **A:** _____
    (Aimee and N'kisi / go in a car now)
   B: _____

EXERCISE 4: Past Abilities: *Could / Couldn't*

(Grammar Notes 4–5)

Complete the sentences with **could** *or* **couldn't** *and the verbs in parentheses.*

1. My cat was smart. She ___could close___
   (close)

   the door with her paws. _____

   your cat _____ the door?
   (open)

2. Michael was a smart gorilla. He

   _____ sign language. He
   (use)

   _____ 600 different gestures.
   (make)

3. My dog Charlie was a good watchdog, but

   he _____ any tricks.
   (do)

4. My dog Spot was not a good watchdog, but he _____ me my slippers.
   (bring)

5. My bird _____, but he could sit on my finger.
   (talk)

6. _____ your bird _____ anything? My bird
   (say)

   _____, "I love you." That's why everyone smiled at him.
   (say)

EXERCISE 5: Editing

*Correct the conversation. There are seven mistakes. The first mistake is already
corrected. Find and correct six more. Add* **can** *to fix one mistake.*

A: Can you ~~coming~~ to my party? It's next Saturday night. You can to meet my new dog.
come

B: Yes, I'd love to. How I get to your home?

A: You can to take the train or a taxi.

B: Can you meet me at the train station?

A: I'm sorry. I can't. I no can drive. Maybe Bob can meets you. He has a car, and he can
   to drive.

EXERCISE 6: Pronunciation

A | *Read and listen to the Pronunciation Note.*

Pronunciation Note

When **can** is followed by a base form verb, we usually pronounce it **/ kən /** and stress the base form verb:

EXAMPLE: *We can **dance**.*

When **can't** is followed by a base form verb, we usually pronounce it **/ kaent /** and stress both *can't* and the base form verb:

EXAMPLE: *We **can't dance**.*

B | *Listen and complete the sentences with* **can** *or* **can't** *and the verb.*

1. A zebra _____*can see*_____ the color blue, but it _____ the color orange.

2. You _____ a cow upstairs, but you _____ a cow downstairs.

3. Dolphins _____ with their eyes open, but dolphins _____ on dry land.

4. A pet cat _____ a black bear, but a cat _____ a jaguar.

5. Dogs _____ feelings, but they _____ them.

6. Elephants _____ their trunks to spray water, but they _____.

C | *Listen again and repeat the sentences.*

EXERCISE 7: Listening

A | *Listen to a conversation about dolphins. Circle three things the dolphins in Florida could do.*

catch a ball   paint pictures   play basketball   talk

B | *Listen again to the conversation. Read the questions. Check (✓) the correct answers.*

1. What can all the dolphins at a marine institute in Mississippi do?

   _____ **a.** hold onto a paper and play with it

   _____ **b.** exchange paper for fish

2. Which four things can Kelly do?

   _____ **a.** hide paper under a rock

   _____ **b.** use paper to catch fish

   _____ **c.** tear paper

   _____ **d.** eat paper

   _____ **e.** catch a bird

   _____ **f.** exchange pieces of paper for fish

EXERCISE 8: Game: Find Someone Who...

A | *Walk around the classroom. Ask your classmates questions with **can** or **could**. Ask about now and about five years ago. If they answer **yes**, write their names in the chart.*

EXAMPLE: VICTOR: Can you play an instrument?

CAROLINA: Yes, I can. I can play the guitar.

VICTOR: Could you play the guitar five years ago?

CAROLINA: No, I couldn't.

	Now	Five Years Ago
play an instrument	Carolina	
teach a bird to talk		
design a Web page		
ride a motorcycle		
train a dog		

B | *Report your answers to your class.*

EXAMPLE: Erna can play the piano and design a Web page. Five years ago she could play the piano, but she couldn't design a Web page.

EXERCISE 9: Game: What Can Your Group Do?

Work in small groups. Read the questions. When your group can do one of the tasks, raise your hand. The first group to do a task wins.

1. Can you think of 12 different animals that start with 12 different letters of the alphabet?

    EXAMPLE: a = ape   b = bear

2. Can you say "I love you" in more than four languages?

3. Can you name the colors of the flags of six countries?

4. Can you name the capitals of eight countries?

EXERCISE 10: Writing

A | *Write about an interesting pet or other animal. Use* **can** *or* **can't**. *Answer these questions in your paragraph:*

- What kind of animal is it? What does it look like?
- Where does it live?
- Is it your pet? Does it have a name?
- What can this animal do? What can't it do?

EXAMPLE: I have a beautiful parakeet. His feathers are bright green. His name is Chichi. He is two years old. He lives in a cage in the living room. Sometimes he flies around the room. Chichi can sing very beautifully. Chichi couldn't do anything when he was younger. But now he can sit on my finger and eat from my hand. He can't speak, but I'm happy about that. I tell him all my secrets, and he doesn't tell anyone. That's a wonderful quality. I love my Chichi.

B | *Check your work. Use the Editing Checklist.*

Editing Checklist

Did you . . . ?
☐ use **can** and **can't** correctly
☐ check your spelling

A | Complete the sentences with **can, could, can't,** or **couldn't** and the verbs in parentheses.

1. Last year I _____ much English. Now I _____ a lot more.
   (understand)   (understand)

2. Jill doesn't have time to exercise these days, so she _____ fast. In high
   (run)
   school she was on a team, and she _____ a mile in seven minutes
   (run)

3. I _____ five years ago. Now I have a driver's license, and I
   (drive)
   _____ well.
   (drive)

B | Complete the questions and answers. Use **can, could, can't** or **couldn't.**

1. **A:** _____ you understand your dreams?

   B: Yes, I _____. They're easy to understand.

2. **A:** _____ you write reports last year?

   B: No, I _____, but now I _____.

3. **A:** _____ he fix cars?

   B: Yes, he _____. He's a good mechanic.

C | Correct the conversation. There are seven mistakes.

A: Can you to get online?

B: No, I can't not. I couldn't got online last night either.

A: My brother is good with computers. Maybe he can helps.

B: Great. I can no figure out what's wrong.

A: I no can reach him now, but I can to call him after 6 P.M.

Permission: *Can* or *May*
HEALTH AND DIET

STEP 1 GRAMMAR IN CONTEXT

Before You Read

Foods are mainly made of protein, carbohydrates, and fat. Which category do these foods belong in? Write them below. Then check your answers on page 154.

| ~~beef~~ | ~~bread~~ | ~~butter~~ | cake | chicken | fish | oil | pasta | rice |

Protein: *beef,*

Carbohydrate(s): *bread,*

Fat: *butter,*

Read

Read the online article about diets. What do you think about them?

www.healthandnutritionmagazine.com/therightdiet

Health & Nutrition

fashion | beauty | health & fitness | shopping

The Right Diet

Marita is a college junior. She was 5 pounds overweight. She gained those 5 pounds in her freshman year. She tried many diets, but they didn't work. Then three months ago she joined Weight Watchers®. Most nutritionists say that exercise and calorie reduction is the best way to lose weight. The Weight Watchers® diet follows both principles. It also uses a point system. You **can eat** any food, but you **may not eat** more than a certain number of points each day. Different foods have different numbers of points. For example, an orange has 1 point. A piece of chocolate cake has 7 points. Dieters **can follow** a weekly class or follow the program online. Marita is happy. She lost the extra weight and feels terrific.

(continued on next page)

Bill Morgan is a businessman. He eats many meals out. He was 25 pounds overweight. Bill doesn't want to count points, so he's following the Atkins™ diet. In this diet you **may eat** foods high in protein and fat, such as red meat and cheese, but you **can't eat** carbohydrates such as bread, cereal, pasta, and rice. The first two weeks are especially strict. You **can't have** fruit, grains, cereals, bread, or most vegetables. You also **can't drink** any milk or juice. But after three weeks Bill weighs 10 pound less. He's thrilled.

Many people, like Marita and Bill, lose weight on diets, but they don't keep it off. So they have to start all over again. Dieters don't always agree on the best diet, but almost every dieter would like to take a pill one day, become slim the next, and never regain the weight.

Comments (115)   Post a comment   Share

After You Read

A | Practice *PAIRS: Now read the article aloud. Take turns reading each paragraph.*

B | Vocabulary *Complete the sentences with the words from the box. Use the correct form.*

especially	gain	lose	overweight	pound

1. These days many people eat more than they need, and they become

   _____. They need to _____ weight.

2. That diet is _____ hard to keep.

3. People often lose weight, but after a while they _____ it back.

4. How many _____ does he want to lose?

C | Comprehension *Write* **T** *(True),* **F** *(False), or* **?** *(it doesn't say) for each statement.*

_____ 1. You can eat small portions of everything on the Weight Watchers® diet.

_____ 2. You can't eat meat on the Atkins™ diet.

_____ 3. You may follow the Weight Watchers® diet online.

_____ 4. You can't eat cereal in the first two weeks of the Atkins™ diet.

_____ 5. An overweight person can take a pill and become slim the next day.

_____ 6. You may not drink coffee on the Atkins™ diet.

Answers to Before You Read, page 153: Protein: beef, chicken, fish; **Carbohydrates:** bread, cake, pasta, rice; **Fat:** butter, oil

CAN OR MAY FOR PERMISSION

Statements			
Subject	**Can / Can't May / May Not**	**Base Form of Verb**	
You	can can't	start	today.
He	may may not	eat	nuts.

Yes / No Questions				Answers
Can / May	**Subject**	**Base Form of Verb**		**Yes, you can.**
Can May	I	have	the day off?	**Yes, you may.** **Sure.** **Of course.** **I'm sorry. We're too busy.**

Wh- Questions				
Wh- Word	**Can**	**Subject**	**Base Form of Verb**	
When	can	I	**borrow**	the car?
Where		we	**park**?	

GRAMMAR NOTES

1	Use **can** or **may** to **give permission**. (It's OK to . . .) *Can* and *may* are followed by the base form of the verb. Use **can't** or **may not** to **deny permission**. (Something is not OK.) There is no contraction for *may not*.	• You **can see** the doctor now. • You **may eat** fish. • You **can't drive** a truck on this road. • You **may not use** my car. NOT: You ~~mayn't~~ drive a car without a license.
2	Use *can* or *may* to **ask for permission**. *May* is more formal than *can*. We respond with a short affirmative response (*Yes, you may*) or a short apology and a reason. (*Sorry, I . . .*)	**A:** **May** I see the doctor this afternoon? **B:** **Yes, you may.** OR No, I'm sorry. The doctor is out.
3	We use **Can I help you?** or **May I help you?** to offer help to someone. We thank the speaker or say no thank you and give a reason.	**A:** Can I help you? OR May I help you? **B:** **Thanks.** I'm looking for a winter jacket. OR **No thanks. I'm just looking.**

EXERCISE 1: Discover the Grammar

A | *Read the conversation. Underline* **can, can't, may,** *or* **may not.** *Then complete Part B.*

_A_ **A:** <u>Can</u> I eat meat?

_____ **B:** Yes, you can, but you can only have boiled, grilled, or baked meat.

_____ **A:** What about fried chicken? Can I have it? I love fried chicken.

_____ **B:** Sorry. You may not have any fried food on this diet.

_____ **A:** Can I eat nuts?

_____ **B:** Yes, you may, but don't eat too many. And remember, there are many things on this diet that you can eat. You may eat as many green vegetables as you want, and you can drink as much green tea as you want.

A: Well, that sounds good.

_____ **B:** If you have any more questions, you can call me weekdays between 11:00 and 1:00.

B | *Look back at Part A. Write* **A** *for sentences that ask for permission,* **G** *for sentences that give permission, and* **D** *for sentences that deny permission.*

EXERCISE 2: *Can / May*: **Affirmative, Negative,** *Yes / No* **Questions**   (*Grammar Notes 1–3*)

Complete the conversations with **can** *or* **may** *and the verbs from the box.*

drive	help	~~return~~
eat	keep	see
have	look	take

1. (Can)

A: You're doing great.

B: I feel good too, Dr. Lam. When __*can*__ I __*return*__ to work?

A: Next week.

B: And when _____ I _____?

A: Wait another week. Take the train next week.

B: OK.

A: But remember. Watch your diet. Don't eat heavy food and stay away from dessert.

B: _____ I _____ out?

A: Sure. Just watch what you order.

2. (May)

A: _____ I _____ you?

B: Thanks. I'd like to make an appointment with Ms. Stein.

A: She's free next Tuesday at 10:00. Here are some booklets about nutrition. You _____ _____ them home and read them.

B: Thanks. Do you want them back?

A: No. You _____ _____ them.

3. (Can)

A: Your fish comes with a salad.

B: OK. _____ I _____ the dressing on the side?

A: Of course.

B: And _____ we _____ the dessert menu?

C: Bob, you're on a diet! You can't have dessert.

B: But I _____ _____ at the desserts and dream about them.

EXERCISE 3: Permission: *May / Can*

Complete the conversation. Write questions with **can** or **may** and the information in parentheses.

RECEPTIONIST: (May) _May I help you?_____

                          1. (Do you need my help?)

NURAY: Yes, thanks. I'm Nuray Attaturk. I have an appointment with Dr. Lee for 2:00.

RECEPTIONIST: Thanks Ms. Attaturk. (May) _____

                          2. (I want to see your health insurance card.)

DR. LEE: OK, Nuray. Here's your diet. Any questions?

NURAY: (Can) _____

                          3. (Is it OK to eat snacks?)

DR. LEE: Yes, but you can only have light snacks.

NURAY: (Can) _____

                          4. (Is it OK to eat ice cream?)

DR. LEE: No, you can't, but you can have low-fat yogurt instead.

NURAY: (May) _____

                          5. (Is it OK to call you with questions?)

DR. LEE: Certainly. But don't worry. Everything is on these papers. Just read the diet

      and follow the directions. You'll feel better in no time.

NURAY: Thanks, Dr. Lee.

EXERCISE 4: Editing

Correct the conversations. There are six mistakes. The first mistake is already corrected. Find and correct five more.

1. **A:** Can we ~~paid~~ *pay* in two installments?

   B: Yes, you can pays half now and half next month.

2. **A:** May I speaks to the doctor?

   B: I'm sorry. He's with a patient now. Give me your number and he'll call you back.

3. **A:** Can I to use salt?

   B: Yes, but not a lot.

4. **A:** Can I drink coffee or tea?

   B: You may drink tea, but you mayn't drink coffee.

5. **A:** May I helping you?

   B: Thanks. I'd like to make an appointment for next week.

EXERCISE 5: Listening

A | *Listen to a telephone conversation. A patient calls a doctor. What is the woman's problem?*

    a. her ankle

    b. her elbow

    c. her knee

B | *Listen again and answer the questions.*

    1. What can she do for the swelling and pain? _____

    2. What activities can she do? _____

    3. What activities can't she do? _____

EXERCISE 6: Pronunciation

A | *Read and listen to the Pronunciation Note.*

> **Pronunciation Note**
>
> The vowel **/ eɪ /** as in **lay**, is tense. The vowel **/ ɛ /**, as in **egg**, is lax. The tongue is higher and the lips are more spread for **/ eɪ /** than for **/ ɛ /** .

B | *Listen and repeat the words with the / eɪ / sound.*

    break   **day**   **explain**   **late**   **name**   **plate**   **play**   **say**   **scale**

C | *Listen and repeat the words with the / ɛ / sound.*

    egg   **get**   **guess**   **leg**   **less**   **let**   **mess**   **met**   **stress**   **west**

D | *Listen to the sentences. Check (✓) the sound of the underlined word.*

	/ eɪ /	/ ɛ /
1. He drinks <u>eight</u> bottles of water a day.	✓	
2. The doctor can't see you until <u>May.</u>		
3. Can I eat <u>eggs</u> on this diet?		
4. You can have <u>steak</u> on the Atkins™ diet.		
5. They met at a <u>Weight</u> Watchers® session.		
6. <u>May</u> I help you?		
7. The nutritionist's office is on <u>West</u> Street.		

EXERCISE 7: Information Gap

*Work in pairs (**A** and **B**). **Student A,** follow the instructions on this page. **Student B,** look at the Information Gap questions on page 161. Ask Student A the questions.*

1. Read the information for patients of Dr. Green.

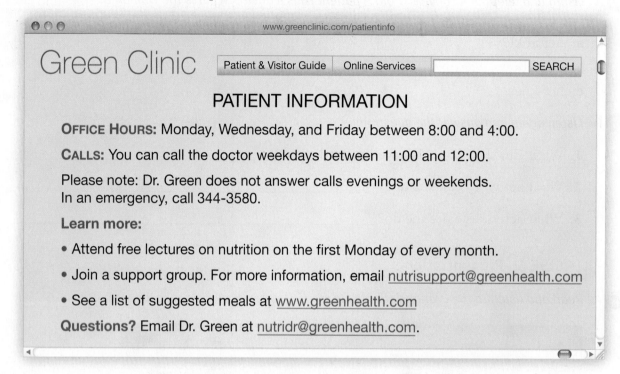

www.greenclinic.com/patientinfo

Green Clinic

Patient & Visitor Guide   Online Services   [ ]   SEARCH

PATIENT INFORMATION

OFFICE HOURS: Monday, Wednesday, and Friday between 8:00 and 4:00.

CALLS: You can call the doctor weekdays between 11:00 and 12:00.

Please note: Dr. Green does not answer calls evenings or weekends.
In an emergency, call 344-3580.

Learn more:

• Attend free lectures on nutrition on the first Monday of every month.

• Join a support group. For more information, email nutrisupport@greenhealth.com

• See a list of suggested meals at www.greenhealth.com

Questions? Email Dr. Green at nutridr@greenhealth.com.

2. Answer Student B's questions. Use ***can***, ***may***, ***can't***, or ***may not***.

EXERCISE 8: Writing

A | *You and your friend want to lose weight. You found three diets online: The Skinny, 8-Minutes, and The Biggest Loser. Write an email to your friend. Tell your friend the requirements of each diet. Use **can** or **may**.*

Can I . . . ?	The Skinny	8-Minutes	The Biggest Loser
Eat out	Yes, often. The Skinny gives advice for foods in restaurants.	Occasionally.	It's difficult.
Drink coffee	Three times a day.	Not too much.	Yes.
Follow a vegetarian diet	Yes. There are many vegetarian possibilities.	Yes.	No. Many suggestions include meat.

EXAMPLE: On the Skinny diet, we can eat out often.

B | *Check your work. Use the Editing Checklist.*

> ## Editing Checklist
>
> Did you . . . ?
> □ use *may* and *can* for permission
> □ check your spelling

INFORMATION GAP FOR STUDENT B

Ask Student A the questions about the Green Clinic.

1. When can I see the doctor?

2. When can I call her?

3. Can I contact her by email?

4. What can I do in an emergency?

5. Are there any free lectures on nutrition?

6. Can I join a support group?

7. How can I get good meal suggestions?

Check your answers on page UR-3.

Do you need to review anything?

A | *Complete the paragraph with the words in parentheses. Use the correct form of the affirmative or negative.*

It's a great diet. You _____ whatever you like. You just
                        1. (may / eat)

_____ a lot. For example, for breakfast you _____ a slice of
  2. (can / eat)   **3. (can / have)**

toast, an egg, and an orange. You can put jelly on the toast, but you _____
                                                  4. (may / use)

butter. You _____ coffee, tea, or milk.
       5. (may / drink)

B | *Write John's questions for his doctor. Use* **can** *and the words in parentheses.*

1. _____
                         (When / I / return to work)

2. _____
                         (When / I / take a shower)

3. _____
                         (I / go / to the gym)

4. _____
                         (I / ride / my bike)

C | *You are taking a language test. Read the rules. Then write sentences with* **may** *or* **may not**.

NO	OK
food	a bottle of water
pencil	a black or blue pen
phone calls	dictionary

1. _____   4. _____

2. _____   5. _____

3. _____   6. _____

D | *Correct the conversation. There are five mistakes.*

A: May I sees a menu?

B: Sure, you might. Here you go.

A: And can we to have some water?

B: I'll be right back with the water. . . . Ready?

A: Yes. I want the chicken with mushroom sauce. But may I has the sauce on the side?

B: You may not. We cook the chicken in the sauce.

A: Oh? Well, then I'll have grilled chicken with rice.

From Grammar to Writing

PUNCTUATION I: THE APOSTROPHE, THE COMMA, THE PERIOD, THE QUESTION MARK

1 | *Read this email. Circle all the punctuation marks.*

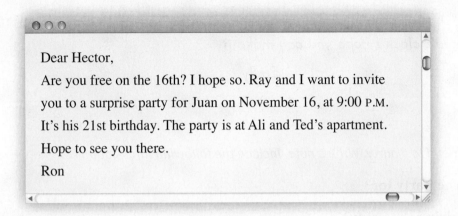

Dear Hector,

Are you free on the 16th? I hope so. Ray and I want to invite you to a surprise party for Juan on November 16, at 9:00 P.M. It's his 21st birthday. The party is at Ali and Ted's apartment. Hope to see you there.

Ron

2 | *Study these rules of punctuation.*

1	**The apostrophe (')** Use an apostrophe to show possession and to write contractions.	• **Carol's** book is here. • We **aren't** late.
2	**The comma (,)** Rules for commas vary. Here are some places where commas are almost always used: **a.** in a list of more than two things **b.** after the name of a person you are writing to **c.** after *yes* or *no* in a sentence **d.** when you use *and* to connect two sentences.	• He is wearing **a shirt, a sweater,** and a **jacket**. • Dear **John,** • **Yes,** I am. OR **No,** I'm not. • His house is huge, **and** his car is expensive.
3	**The period (.)** **a.** Use a period at the end of a statement. **b.** Use a period after abbreviations.	• We are English language **students**. • The party is on **Nov.** 16.
4	**The question mark (?)** Use a question mark at the end of a question.	• Are you planning a **party?** • Where are you **going?**

3 | *Add punctuation marks to this note.*

> Dear Uncle John
>
> Bob and I want to invite you to a party for my parents 25th wedding anniversary Its on Sunday Dec 11
>
> The party is at our home at 23 Main St Its at three o'clock I hope you can make it
>
>   Emily

4 | *Invite a friend to a party. Write a note. Include the following information.*

Who is the party for?

Who is giving the party?

What is the occasion?

When is the party?

Where is the party?

5 | *Exchange papers with a partner. Did your partner follow the directions? Correct any mistakes in grammar and spelling.*

6 | *Talk to your partner. Discuss the mistakes you made. Then rewrite your own paper and make any necessary changes.*

PRESENT PROGRESSIVE

15 Present Progressive: Affirmative and Negative Statements

HIGH SCHOOL

STEP 1 GRAMMAR IN CONTEXT

Before You Read

PAIRS: Answer the questions.

1. How many hours a day do high school students spend in school?
2. Were you very busy during your high school years?
3. Is a very busy schedule good for high school students? Why or why not?

Read

🎧 *Read the online article about two cousins.*

---

www.nineteen.com/lifestyle

Nineteen

| quizzes & games | fashion | lifestyle | celebrities | guys |

Mi Young and Julie are cousins. Mi Young lives in Seoul, and Julie lives in New York City. Both teens are *juniors*[1] in high school. It's the second week of the semester.

It's 10:00 at night. Mi Young is still in school. She**'s working** on some tough math problems. She's tired, but she**'s not giving up**. Mi Young goes to public school from 8:00 to 3:00. Then she goes to a private study school from 3:30 to 10:00. Her friends are in the study school with her. Like Mi Young, they**'re hoping to** go to a top college. There is a lot of competition and pressure to get into top schools. These private schools—or "cram" schools—are popular with middle class[2] and wealthy families all over East Asia.

12 hours later

It's 10 P.M. in New York City. Julie is in her family's apartment. She**'s texting** her friend. They**'re making plans** to study together. Julie goes to school from 9:00 to 3:00. She swims on the school swimming team. Then she does her homework. Julie and her friends **are** all **working** hard this year. They**'re going** to school. They**'re preparing** for the SATs.[3] They**'re playing** on teams, and they**'re doing** a lot of other extra-curricular activities. They**'re not getting** enough sleep. They**'re feeling** a lot of pressure.[4] Julie only takes a break[5] once in a while.

Just like Mi Young and her friends, they**'re doing** all this work because they want to attend a top-rated college.

But is a "top" school really so important? What are they learning and what are they missing?

---
[1] *juniors:* students in their third year of high school
[2] *middle class:* the group of people in a society who are not rich and not poor
[3] *SAT:* a test students take to get into many colleges
[4] *pressure:* things in your life that make you worry
[5] *take a break:* rest

After You Read

A | Practice *PAIRS: Now read the online article aloud. Take turns reading each paragraph.*

B | Vocabulary *Match the words from the article with their meaning.*

____ 1. tough	**a.** in addition to school work
____ 2. give up	**b.** people trying to be better than others
____ 3. extracurricular	**c.** stop doing something
____ 4. top	**d.** rich
____ 5. competition	**e.** best
____ 6. wealthy	**f.** difficult

C | Comprehension *Look back at the online article. Complete the chart. Check (✓) what is true about Mi Young and Julie or both. It's 10 P.M.*

	Mi Young	Julie
1. in school		
2. at home		
3. working hard		
4. hoping to get into a top college		
5. texting a friend		
6. feeling a lot of pressure		
7. doesn't have a lot of free time		

STEP 2 GRAMMAR PRESENTATION

PRESENT PROGRESSIVE

Affirmative Statements				Negative Statements			
Subject	**Be**	**Base Form of Verb + -ing**		**Subject**	**Be**	**Not**	**Base Form of Verb + -ing**
I	am			I	am		
He				He			
She	is			She	is		
It		relaxing.		It		not	sleeping.
We				We			
You*	are			You	are		
They				They			

*You can be both singular and plural subjects.

GRAMMAR NOTES

1	Use the **present progressive*** to talk about an **action** that is or is not **happening now**.	• I **am** driving • We **are not** walking.
	Now Past ———X———→ Future	
	We can use the time expressions *now*, *right now*, and *at the moment* with the present progressive.	• The machine **isn't working now.** • **Right now** she**'s resting.** • **At the moment** he**'s talking** on the phone.
	BE CAREFUL! We don't usually use non-action verbs in the present progressive.	• The textbook costs $80. Not: ~~The textbook is costing $80.~~
2	Use **contractions** in speaking and informal writing.	• **I'm** not studying. **I'm** resting. • Luis **isn't** playing a game. **He's** reading. • We **aren't** playing a game. **We're** practicing.
3	Do not repeat the verb *be* when the subject is doing two things.	• They**'re singing** and **dancing.** Not: ~~They're singing and are dancing.~~
4	If a verb ends in a silent -*e*, drop the final -*e* and add -*ing*.	• She's **driving** home. (drive) • I'm **taking** a test. (take)
5	We sometimes use the present progressive for an action that is taking place at this time, but may not be happening at this moment.	• **These days** Julie **is working** hard.

*The present progressive is also called present continuous.

REFERENCE NOTES

See Unit 17, page 188 for a discussion of non-action verbs.
See Appendix 8, page A-8 for more spelling rules for the present progressive.

STEP 3 FOCUSED PRACTICE

EXERCISE 1: Discover the Grammar

A | *Read about Mi Young and Julie. Underline the present progressive.*

1. 6:00 A.M.   Mi Young is getting ready for school. She's putting on her school

   uniform. Julie is still sleeping.

2. 7:00 A.M.   Mi Young and her classmates are taking the bus to school. Julie is

   washing her face and combing her hair.

3. 3:30 P.M.   Mi Young is studying English. Julie is swimming at her high school pool.

4. 7:00 P.M.   Mi Young is having dinner with her classmates. Julie is eating at home.

5. 11:00 P.M.   Mi Young is riding home on the bus. Julie is studying physics.

B | *Write the base form of the words you underlined in Part A.*

1. _____*get*_____   4. _____   7. _____   10. _____

2. _____   5. _____   8. _____   11. _____

3. _____   6. _____   9. _____   12. _____

EXERCISE 2: Present Progressive Statements   *(Grammar Notes 1–4)*

Write about Julie's day with the words in parentheses. Use the present progressive.

1. It's 9:00 A.M. on Saturday morning.

(Julie / get / up) _____*Julie is getting up*_____. She's late.

(She / not / eat breakfast) _____

2. 9:40 A.M.

(Julie / take the bus) _____ to her SAT prep class.

3. 1:00 P.M. Julie is at her school for a swimming competition.

(Julie / compete) _____ against 20 swimmers.

Three swimmers are ahead of Julie.

(Julie / not / give up) _____

4. 4:00 P.M. Julie is home.

(She / study / physics) _____

5. 8:00 P.M.

(Julie / hang out) _____ with

some friends.

(They / not / study) _____

(They / not / compete) _____

(They / relax and have fun) _____

EXERCISE 3: Present Progressive Statements

(Grammar Notes 1–2, 4)

It's 10:00 P.M. at Julie's home. Complete the sentences with the words from the box. Use the present progressive form.

chat	go / not	sleep / not	study / not	~~turn~~
do / not	hang out	study	take	worry

1. Julie's brother Jay _____*is turning*_____ off his

   computer. He's tired. He _____ any more

   homework.

2. Julie's sister Grace _____ her notes for

   biology class. She has a test tomorrow. She's tired,

   but she _____ to bed.

3. Julie _____ a short break from studying math. Julie and her friend

   _____ online.

4. Julie's mom _____ about her children. Julie and Grace

   _____ enough. They're always tired. Jay _____ enough. He

   doesn't care about school. Most of the time he _____ with his friends,

   instead.

EXERCISE 4: Present Progressive Statements

(Grammar Notes 1–5)

Complete the paragraph with the verbs in parentheses. Use the present progressive.

Hye Won is the manager of an international company. This week she _____*is traveling*_____
                                                                1. (travel)
on business. She _____ with clients in Spain. It's 8:00 in the evening. Hye Won
                    2. (meet)
_____ dinner with a manager and a client. They _____ at a top
        3. (have)   4. (eat)
restaurant in Madrid. Hye Won _____ about Spanish customs from the client.
                                    5. (learn)
On this business trip, Hye Won and the other manager _____ two days in
                                                    6. (spend)
Madrid and two days in London.

Hye Won loves her job and her lifestyle. She says, "I'm glad I'm not married. School

was hard. Now I _____ my freedom, and I _____ a lot of money.
                7. (enjoy)   8. (earn)
I _____ for the future. I _____ for a husband right now, maybe
       9. (save)   10. (look / not)
later." Hye Won's parents _____ to worry, but Hye Won is very happy.
                    11. (begin)

EXERCISE 5: Editing

Correct the journal entry by a high school student. There are eight mistakes. The first mistake is already corrected. Find and correct seven more.

> *sitting*
> I'm ~~sit~~ in the park. It's a beautiful day. The leaves changing color. Today there
>
> are a lot of children in the park. They laughing and are playing. They no are studying.
>
> They're lucky. It's hard to study on a beautiful day.
>
> I trying to memorize vocabulary words for the SATs. I'm wait for my friend
>
> Grace. She's in my Saturday SAT prep class. We planning to study together all
>
> afternoon and evening.

STEP 4 COMMUNICATION PRACTICE

EXERCISE 6: Listening

A | *Listen to a telephone conversation. Where is the mother calling from?*

She's _____.

B | *Listen again and answer the questions.*

1. What's the father doing?

   <u>He's cooking.</u>

2. What's Jay doing?

   _____

3. What's Julie doing?

   _____

4. Where's Grace?

   _____

5. What time will the mother arrive?

   _____

EXERCISE 7: Pronunciation

🎧 **A** | *Read and listen to the Pronunciation Note.*

🎧 **B** | *Read and listen to the sentences. Then listen and repeat.*

1. She's taking a test.
2. He's not giving up.
3. We're trying out for the play.
4. We're studying together.
5. He's driving home.
6. They're watching the news.

EXERCISE 8: Game: Describing a Photo

A | *GROUPS: You have 10 minutes. Look at the photo. Write as many affirmative and negative statements as you can. Use the present progressive.*

B | *Now compare the class in the photo to your own class.*

EXERCISE 9: Writing

A | *Look at people in a school cafeteria, a park, a mall, or on a train or a bus. Write about two people. Answer these questions. Use the present progressive.*

- Where are you? What time is it?
- What are the people doing? What are they wearing?

EXAMPLE: I'm in our school cafeteria. It's 12:30 P.M. Two girls are paying for their food. One girl is very tall. The other is not. The tall girl is wearing black pants and a black T-shirt. The shorter girl is wearing jeans and a red sweater. They're carrying a lot of books. The tall girl isn't smiling. She's carrying a tray with a cup of yogurt and a salad. The shorter girl is carrying a tray with a sandwich, a salad, an apple, and cookies. She's talking a lot. The tall girl is listening. She isn't saying a word. I think they're in the same class. I don't think they're close friends.

B | *Check your work. Use the Editing Checklist.*

A | *Circle the correct words to complete the sentences.*

1. I'm **not getting / no am getting** enough sleep.

2. We **are prepare / 're preparing** for the SATs now.

3. She **isn't playing / no is playing** tennis now.

4. They **doing / 're doing** a lot of extracurricular activities.

5. He **is feel / 's feeling** a lot of pressure.

B | *Complete the sentences with the words from the box. Use the present progressive form.*

carry	drive	listen to	run	stand and talk

1. A man _____ music on his iPod.

2. Two women _____ on a street corner.

3. Some children _____ to catch their school bus.

4. A young man _____ a red sports car.

5. An older man _____ a briefcase.

C | *Complete the sentences with the verbs in parentheses. Use the affirmative or negative form of the present progressive.*

1. John _____ his friend. He _____ him. John says texting is
   (text)   (call)
   faster.

2. Mary and Lulu _____ on some tough physics problems. The problems
                        (work)
   are difficult, but they _____.
                              (give up)

3. Julie _____ fast. She _____ to win a race.
          (swim)   (try)

D | *Correct the paragraph. There are four mistakes.*

   My classmates and I am sitting in a computer lab. One student writing a
composition. Two students are check their email. A teacher is helps a student. The
other students are surfing the Internet.

UNIT 16 Present Progressive: *Yes / No* and *Wh-* Questions

MOVIES

STEP 1 GRAMMAR IN CONTEXT

Before You Read

A | *Where do you like to watch movies? Check (✓) your favorite place:*

☐ on a flat-screen TV

☐ at the theater

☐ on your computer

☐ on your phone

Movie theater in India

B | *Look at the stamps that show famous movies. Do you like these kinds of movies? Check (✓) the types that you like.*

☐ Fantasy/Adventure   ☐ Romance   ☐ Action

C | *Look at the list of other kinds of movies. Check (✓) each kind of movie you like.*

☐ animation   ☐ crime / horror   ☐ mystery

☐ comedy   ☐ drama   ☐ science fiction

Read

Abby has a cold. Her co-worker Greg is calling to see how she is. Read their conversation.

ABBY: Hello.

GREG: Hi, Abby. **How are you feeling?** Any better?

ABBY: Uh-huh. I'm coughing less, and the fever is going down.

GREG: Good. **Are you resting?**

ABBY: Yes, and I'm watching a DVD.

GREG: Oh? **What are you watching?**

ABBY: *The Wizard of Oz.*[1]

GREG: *The Wizard of Oz?*

ABBY: I know its a kid's movie, but I really like it.

GREG: So **what part are you watching? What's happening?**

ABBY: I'm watching the scene where Dorothy meets the Tin Man.

GREG: **Is Dorothy giving the Tin Man oil?**

ABBY: Yes, she's putting oil in his mouth.

GREG: **Is he talking?**

ABBY: No, not yet. Dorothy and the Scarecrow are talking to him, but he can't talk.

GREG: I remember the scene. It's amazing. The film is still popular after so many years.

ABBY: Well, it's a classic. **So what's going on at work?**

GREG: Same old same old.[2] We're working on ten things at once.

ABBY: **Is Mr. Brooks going crazy?**[3]

GREG: Uh-huh. And tomorrow he'll be worse.

ABBY: Why?

GREG: I'll be out. I think I'm catching your cold.

---

[1] *The Wizard of Oz:* 1939 film about a Kansas farm girl. Her house goes up in the air during a storm and she lands in a magical place called Oz.

[2] *same old same old:* nothing new

[3] *going crazy:* feeling very upset because many things are happening all at once

After You Read

A | Practice *PAIRS: Now read the conversation aloud.*

B | Vocabulary *Complete the sentences with the words from the box.*

catching a cold	classic	coughing	favorite	fever	scene

1. In this _____ Dorothy meets the Tin Man.

2. I don't feel well. I think I'm

   _____.

3. Do you feel hot? Do you have a

   _____.

4. Take this medicine. But if you're

   _____ a lot, maybe you

   should see a doctor.

5. The movie *Casablanca* is a

   _____. It's still popular after more than 60 years.

6. Eddie Murphy is my _____ actor. I watch every comedy he is in.

Eddie Murphy

C | Comprehension *Correct the false statements to make them true.*

1. Abby is staying home from work because her daughter has a cold and fever.

2. Greg is taking care of Abby.

3. Greg and Abby are watching *The Wizard of Oz*.

4. Dorothy is giving the Tin Man water.

5. The Tin Man is talking.

6. Greg's boss, Mr. Brooks, isn't going crazy.

STEP 2 GRAMMAR PRESENTATION

PRESENT PROGRESSIVE: *YES / NO* QUESTIONS AND *WH-* QUESTIONS

Yes / No Questions

Be	Subject	Base Form of Verb + *-ing*
Am	I	
Are	you	
Is	he she it	resting?
Are	we you they	

Short Answers

	Affirmative			Negative	
Yes,	you	are.	No,	you're	not.
	I	am.		I'm	
	he she it	is.		he's she's it's	
	you we they	are.		you're we're they're	

Wh- Questions

Wh- Word	Be	Subject	Base Form of Verb + *-ing*	
Why	are	you	staying	home?
What	are	you	watching?	
Where	are	they	going?	
Who	is	she	meeting?	

Answers

I'm sick.
The Wizard of Oz.
To the movies. They're going to the movies.
Her teacher. She's meeting her teacher.

Wh- Questions about the Subject

Wh- Word	Be	Base Form of Verb + *-ing*
Who	is	reading?
What	is	happening?

Answers

My friend (is).
They're singing.

GRAMMAR NOTES

1	Use the **present progressive** to ask about **something that is happening now**. Reverse the subject and *be* when asking a **yes / no** question.	**I'm singing** in the rain. • He is singing. • Is he singing?
2	Most **wh- questions** in the present progressive use the same word order as *yes / no* questions. Use *whom* only for formal English.	• **Where is** he **working**? • **What are** they **doing**? • **Who are** you **meeting**? • **Whom** is the president meeting?
3	**Who** and **What** questions about the subject use statement word order.	STATEMENT • Dorothy is singing. WH- QUESTION • Who is singing? What is happening?

STEP 3 FOCUSED PRACTICE

EXERCISE 1: Discover the Grammar

A | *Read the conversation again on page 175. Write the three other* **yes** / **no** *questions.*

1. *Are you resting?*   3. _____

2. _____ 4. _____

B | *Look at the conversation again. Write the four other* **wh-** *questions in the charts.*

Wh- word + *be*	Subject	Base Form of Verb + *-ing*
1. How are	you	feeling?
2.		
3.		

Wh- word + *be*	Base Form of Verb + *-ing*
4.	
5.	

EXERCISE 2: Present Progressive: *Yes / No* and *Wh-* Questions (*Grammar Note 1*)

Write questions with the words in
parentheses. Use the present progressive.
Then match the questions with the
answers below.

__b__ **1.** (you / watch / a movie) _Are you watching a movie?_____

_____ **2.** (what / Johnny Depp / do / now?) _____

_____ **3.** (you / watch / it / on your DVD) _____

_____ **4.** (you / tape / it / for me) _____

    a. No, sorry, but it will be on again.

    b. Yes. I'm watching *Pirate of the Caribbean: Curse of the Black Pearl*
       with Johnny Depp.

    c. No. It's on TV.

    d. He's standing on the deck of his ship.

EXERCISE 3: Present Progressive: *Yes / No* and *Wh-* Questions (*Grammar Notes 1–3*)

Abby and Greg are talking on the telephone. Complete their conversation with the words
in parentheses. Use the present progressive.

ABBY: Hi, Greg. _____ _How are you feeling_ _____? _____?
                     1. (How / you / feel)   **2. (you / feel / any better)**

GREG: No, I'm not.

ABBY: _____?
         3. (you / take / the medicine)

GREG: Yes, I am. _____?
             4. (Where / you / call from)

ABBY: I'm at an Italian restaurant. Greg. Listen to this. Meryl Streep is eating here.

GREG: No kidding! _____?
                5. (Who / she / eat / with)

ABBY: I think she's with her daughter. I'm not sure.

GREG: _____?
      6. (people / ask for her autograph)

ABBY: No. Nobody's bothering her, but everyone knows she's there.

GREG: Well, when you pass her table, say, "Bon appétit!" That was my favorite line in *Julie
     and Julia*.

EXERCISE 4: Common Two-Word Verbs

(Grammar Notes 1–2)

Complete the questions with the words from the box. Use the present progressive.

listen to	look at	look for	~~wait for~~

1. **A:** Is that *Shrek 3*?

   B: No. I __*'m waiting for*__ *Shrek 3* to start. I'm watching a preview of some other film.

2. **A:** _____ you _____ a good

   movie to watch?

   B: Yes, I am. Why? Do you have an idea?

3. **A:** What _____ she _____?

   B: She's looking at some online movie reviews.

4. **A:** What _____ they _____?

   B: The music from *The Wizard of Oz*.

EXERCISE 5: Editing

Correct the conversations. There are six mistakes. The first mistake is already corrected. Find and correct five more.

1. **A:** Excuse me, who's collecting tickets?

   B: He isn't here now. Wait a minute. He'll be right back.

2. **A:** What you doing?

   B: I'm turning off my cell phone.

3. **A:** Is Dad buy popcorn?

   B: Yes, he is.

4. **A:** What taking him so long?

   B: He's waiting in a long line.

5. **A:** Excuse me, is someone sits here?

   B: No, no one sitting here. Please sit down.

EXERCISE 6: Listening

A | *Listen to the conversation. What is Dan shopping for? Circle the correct letter.*

    a. an HDTV   **b.** a DVD player   **c.** a DVR player

B | *Listen again and answer the questions.*

   1. Who is Dan getting a gift for?   *for his dad*

   2. What's the occasion?   _____

   3. When can he use the gift?   _____

   4. What does Dan's friend tell him to buy?   _____

   5. What's happening at Goodbuys this week?   _____

EXERCISE 7: Pronunciation

A | *Read and listen to the Pronunciation Note.*

Pronunciation Note
When letters are used in abbreviations, we usually stress the last syllable.
EXAMPLES:
MTV   PC

B | *Listen and repeat the abbreviations.*

   CD   **DVD**   **DVR**   **TV**   **ISBN**   **BA**

C | *Change the underlined words to abbreviations. Then take turns reading the sentences. Stress the last letter of each abbreviation.*

                           DVD

   1. We're buying a new <u>digital video disc</u> player.

   2. That 50-inch flat screen <u>television</u> is on sale.

   3. Do you have an extra <u>compact disc</u>?

   4. Give me the <u>international standard book number</u>.

   5. We want to get a <u>digital video recorder</u> so we can record shows.

   6. He has a <u>bachelor of arts</u> in film.

D | *Listen to the sentences in Part C. Then repeat the sentences.*

EXERCISE 8: Role Play

PAIRS: Write a telephone conversation with your partner. Student A is watching a movie when Student B calls. Student B, ask Student A questions about his or her movie. Use the present progressive. Continue the conversation.

B: Hi, _____? This is _____. Are you busy?

A: Oh, hi, _____. I _____ a movie.
                                        (watch)

B: What _____?
              (watch)

A: _____.

B: What's happening?

A: _____.

EXERCISE 9: Describing Pictures

A | *PAIRS: On a separate piece of paper, write questions about the picture. Use the present progressive. Ask another pair your questions.*

B | *Draw a picture. Include four people or more and a basket. Use four of these actions:* **sing, dance, wear, look at, look for, carry.** *Do not show your partner your picture.*

C | *PAIRS: Ask your partner questions about his or her picture. Then try to draw the picture your partner describes. Answer your partner's questions about your picture. Compare pictures.*

> EXAMPLE: **A:** Who is singing?
>   **B:** Two girls are singing.
>   **A:** What are they wearing?

EXERCISE 10: Writing

A | *PAIRS: Interview each other about your favorite movies. Ask some questions with the present progressive:*

- What's the name of the movie? Who's the director? Who's the star? What language is it in?
- What do you like best about the movie?
- What's your favorite in the scene?
- Where is it taking place? When?
- What are the people doing?

B | *Now write about the movie you talked about. Use the present progressive when possible.*

EXAMPLE: The movie is *Avatar*. The director is James Cameron. It's a science fiction fantasy. It takes place in a world called Pandora. The digital art is the best part of the movie. In this scene the hero Jake is an avatar. He's flying on Pandora with his girlfriend. He is helping her people and trying to save Pandora from greedy people from Earth.

C | *Check your work. Use the Editing Checklist.*

Editing Checklist

Did you . . . ?
- ☐ use the present progressive correctly
- ☐ check your spelling

A | Complete the conversations with the verbs in parentheses. Use the present progressive.

1. **A:** The kids are screaming. _____ they _____ a horror
   (watch)
   show?

   B: Yes, _____.

2. **A:** What _____ you _____?
                               (do)
   B: I _____ to my favorite CD.
          (listen)

3. **A:** What _____ outside?
              (happen)
   B: Uncle John _____ up a new fence.
                      (put)

B | Write **yes** / **no** questions with the words in parentheses. Use the present progressive.

1. _____
                     (you / work)
2. _____
                 (he / buy tickets online)
3. _____
                (they / watch a mystery)
4. _____
                (she / enjoy the movie)

C | Write **wh-** questions in the present progressive with the words in parentheses.

1. _____
                   (Where / they / go)
2. _____
              (What music group / perform)
3. _____
                   (Where / they / play)
4. _____
                 (Why / Bob stay home)

D | Correct the conversations. There are four mistakes.

1. **A:** Is it's raining outside?

   B: Yes. I hope it stops.

2. **A:** Are they playing soccer?

   B: No, they not. They're playing rugby.

3. **A:** You watching a good movie?

   B: It's OK.

4. **A:** What they doing?

   B: They're fixing the cabinets.

Simple Present and Present Progressive; Non-Action Verbs

SMARTPHONES

STEP 1 GRAMMAR IN CONTEXT

Before You Read

Do you have a cell phone? How many ways do you use it?

Read

🎧 *Read the online article about today's phones.*

ARTS	SCIENCE	POLITICS	TECHNOLOGY	SEARCH:

Cell Phone Mania | Technology Today

More than 4½ billion people **have** them. People under 30[1] **don't know** a world without them. They **come** in all colors and shapes. Some **are** waterproof and shockproof.[2] What **are** they? Cell phones.

Today's cell phones **have** many different features. Take Xavier. He**'s** at a picnic in a park. He **needs** a ride to a party that evening. He**'s texting** a friend. The couple in the car were in a minor accident. The man **is taking** a photo with his phone. And John **is checking** email from his phone.

It**'s** easy to understand the popularity of these phones. People **want** to connect with others, and at the same time, they **want** to be *mobile*.[3] Cell phones **make** it possible to do both. Cell phones **are** big business, and the technology **is** constantly **improving**. What about the future? What will it bring? Nobody **knows**, but here **are** the wishes of two people.

Emily, age 15, **says**, "I often **forget** to charge my phone. I **want** a phone with endless power."

Robert, a college freshman **says**, "I **want** a phone that can teach me a foreign language while I **sleep**."

Well, Emily may get her wish a lot sooner than Robert. But of course, with the speed at which things **are changing**, you never **know** what the future will bring.

---

[1]*under 30:* less than 30 years old
[2]*shockproof:* doesn't break when it falls
[3]*mobile:* able to move around

After You Read

A | Practice *PAIRS: Now read the article aloud. Take turns reading each paragraph.*

B | Vocabulary *Circle the best meaning for the words in blue.*

1. We **connect** through Facebook®.

   a. join   **b.** make contact

2. That watch is **waterproof**. You can swim with it on.

   a. not hurt by water   **b.** dry

3. That new computer comes with a lot of **features**.

   a. parts that make it better   **b.** memory

4. He calls her **constantly**. Is he in love?

   a. all the time   **b.** from time to time

5. Your work is **improving**.

   a. getting better   **b.** changing.

6. There's a **minor** problem with my computer.

   a. serious   **b.** small

C | Comprehension *Complete the sentences. Circle the correct letter.*

1. More than _____ people have cell phones today.
   a. 450,000   **b.** 4,500,000   **c.** 4,500,000,000

2. The man in the car accident is using the phone as a _____.
   a. radio   **b.** camera   **c.** computer

3. Telephone technology is _____.
   a. making phones harder to use   **b.** using video   **c.** improving all the time

4. Emily wants her phone to _____.
   a. have power all the time   **b.** have a beeper   **c.** teach her a language

SIMPLE PRESENT AND PRESENT PROGRESSIVE

The Simple Present	The Present Progressive
I **eat** at eight o'clock.	I**'m eating** now.
He **eats** at 8:00 too.	He**'s eating** now.
She **doesn't eat** with me.	She **isn't eating** with him.
They **don't eat** with us.	They **aren't eating** with us.
Does he **eat** meat?	**Is** he **eating** chicken?
Do you **eat** in the cafeteria?	**Are** you **eating** chicken?

NON-ACTION (STATIVE) VERBS

State of Being	Emotion	Sense / Appearance	Need / Preference	Mental Action	Possession	Measurement
be	love hate like dislike	hear see feel taste smell sound look	want need prefer	agree disagree guess understand know remember believe think mean worry	have own belong	cost weigh owe

GRAMMAR NOTES

1	Use the **simple present** to tell or ask about **habits**, **customs**, **routines**, or **facts**. Now Past —X—X—|—X—X—→ Future *She shops every Saturday.*	• I **check** Facebook® every morning. • **Do** you **check** Facebook® in the morning?
2	Use the **present progressive** to tell or ask about an action happening **right now** or **these days**. Past ———————X————————→ Future Now	• He**'s checking** email now. • **Is** Enrique **checking** email? • Jon **is teaching** computer science this year.
3	Some verbs do not describe actions. These verbs are called **non-action** or **stative verbs**.	• I **have** a great idea. • This **belongs** to me. • They **love** that phone.
4	**Non-action verbs** do the following: **a.** express emotion **b.** describe sense or appearance **c.** express a need or preference **d.** describe a thought **e.** show possession **f.** give a measurement **g.** *Be* expresses a state of being.	• We **like** that computer. • The music **sounds** relaxing. • I **prefer** email. • Jennifer **knows** you. • It **belongs** to me. • It **costs** a lot of money. • I **am** tired now.
5	We usually do not use non-action verbs in the present progressive (*-ing*) form.	• I **own** a smartphone • It **costs** a lot. Not: ~~I'm owning~~ a smartphone. It~~'s costing~~ a lot.

EXERCISE 1: Discover the Grammar

Underline the simple present. Circle the present progressive. Underline twice all non-action verbs.

Raisa <u><u>has</u></u> a new phone with a lot of great features. She likes her phone a lot. Her phone keeps her in touch with her friends wherever she is. Right now Raisa is texting friends. They are making plans for the evening. She and her friends often text. They don't talk much on the phone. They also connect through Facebook®. Raisa often adds new friends to her site. Sometimes she doesn't know them very well. Raisa's mother, Olga, worries about that. Olga doesn't use social networks. She prefers to talk on the phone or connect through email.

EXERCISE 2: Simple Present; Non-Action Verbs; Present Progressive *(Grammar Notes 1–5)*

Complete the conversation with the words in parentheses. Use the simple present or present progressive. Use contractions when possible.

A: What ____*are*____ you ____*doing*____?
　　　　　　1.　　　　　　　2. (do)

B: I _____ my messages. Look. That's my friend from high school.
　　　3. (check)

　　She _____ three kids now. They _____ happy birthday to
　　　4. (have)　　　　　　　　　　　　5. (sing)

　　their father.

A: Oh. That's nice.

B: _____ you _____ social networking sites?
　　6.　　　　　　　　7. (use)

A: No, I _____. I _____ to email my friends. I _____
　　　8.　　　　　　　9. (prefer)　　　　　　　　　　　10. (think)

　　it's more personal. Also, I _____ there are privacy features in social
　　　　　　　　　　11. (know)

　　networking sites, but I _____ about my privacy.
　　　　　　　　　12. (worry)

EXERCISE 3: Simple Present; Non-Action Verbs; Present Progressive (Grammar Notes 1–5)

Complete the conversation with the words in parentheses. Use the simple present or
present progressive. Use contractions when possible.

A: I'm worried about Tim. This term he _____*is*_____ always online or

_____ friends. He _____ well in school. I _____
     2. (text)   **3. (do / not)**   **4. (think)**

he _____ Spanish.
     5. (fail)

B: Oh. What _____ he _____?
                      6.   **7. (say)**

A: Nothing. Right now he _____ some new game. He _____
                              8. (play)   **9. (love)**

computer games. I _____ he _____ a computer addict.
                      10. (think)   **11. (become)**

EXERCISE 4: Simple Present; Non-Action Verbs; Present Progressive (Grammar Notes 1–5)

Complete the paragraph with the verbs from the box. Use the correct form. Use contractions.

answer	ask	be	talk	think	want	~~work~~

Phuong is a fisherman. He _____*works*_____ on a boat. His old phone is broken. Phuong
                                1.

_____ a new phone. He _____ about getting a waterproof smart
     2.   **3.**

phone with a lot of features. Right now he _____ to a saleswoman in a wireless
                                              4.

phone store. He _____ a lot of questions. The saleswoman _____
                   5.   **6.**

his questions. She _____ very helpful.
                      7.

EXERCISE 5: Editing

Correct the paragraph. There are six mistakes. The first one has been corrected for you.
Find and correct five more.

>   *hate*
> I ~~hates~~ cell phones. My boss is thinking he can call me anytime, even on weekends.
>
> I'm dislike email for the same reason. People in my company work all the time.
>
> There's no "off" time. Look at John over there. It's his lunchtime, but he answering
>
> calls and is checking email. This wasn't possible in my parents' day. I don't think
>
> it's right. Technology great in some ways, but it's awful in other ways.

EXERCISE 6: Listening

A | *Listen to the phone messages. Which calls are from co-workers? Which calls are from family? Check (✓) co-worker or family next to the call.*

Phone Message	Co-worker	Family	Message
1.			Please send me a copy of the Smith report.
2.			She's _____.
3.			She needs to _____.
4.			She's looking for _____.

B | *Look back at Part A. Listen again. Complete the messages.*

EXERCISE 7: Pronunciation

A | *Read and listen to the Pronunciation Note.*

Pronunciation Note

We can use intonation to express emotions such as surprise or anger.

EXAMPLES: I'm surprised at you! (surprised)   I'm surprised at you! (angry)

B | *Listen to this conversation. How does the woman sound? Circle the correct letter.*

  a. surprised   **b.** angry

C | *Listen to this conversation. How does the woman sound? Circle the correct letter.*

  a. surprised   **b.** angry

D | *PAIRS: Practice the conversation. Take turns reading each part. Practice showing surprise. Then practice showing anger.*

  A: I have a call coming in. It's my boss.

  B: But it's 2:00 A.M.! Why is he calling now?

EXERCISE 8: Conversation

PAIRS: Read about these people. Guess why they're doing something different today.

1. Paul and Ana usually shop at Electronics Plus for their electronics. Today they're shopping at Goodbuys.
   EXAMPLE: Paul and Ana are shopping at Goodbuys today because there is a big sale.

2. Maria usually texts friends. Today she's calling and speaking to them.

3. Joaquin usually wears jeans and a T-shirt in class. Today he's wearing a suit.

4. Ali usually brings his lunch to work. Today he's eating out.

EXERCISE 9: Survey

A | GROUPS: Match the pictures and sentences. Write the correct letter.

1. <u> d </u>   2. _____   3. _____

a. She's checking her messages.

b. He's texting a friend

c. They're reading e-books.

d. He's using a landline.

e. He's using a desktop computer.

4. _____   5. _____

B | Complete the survey for yourself. Write your preference and a reason why.

Which do you prefer?	I prefer_____.
using email or Facebook®	Facebook®. I think it's more fun. It's easy to connect with everyone at once.
texting or talking on the phone	
ebooks or printed books	
cell phones or landlines	
laptops or desktop computers	

C | *GROUPS: One student asks the others for their preferences and takes notes. Another student reports the results to the class.*

EXAMPLE: **Juan:** Marta, do you prefer social network sites or email?

MARTA: I prefer email.

JUAN: Emiko, what about you? Do you prefer . . .

PAUL: In our group four people prefer social networking sites, and two prefer email.

EXERCISE 10: Writing

A | *Look at the pictures. Write about the people. They are doing many things at once. What are they doing? Use the present progressive.*

EXAMPLE: The man is drinking a cup of tea . . .

B | *Now write about times when you do many things at once. Use the simple present.*

EXAMPLE: I'm always busy in the morning. I usually walk to school. Sometimes I look at the other people and I wonder about their lives.

C | *Check your work. Use the Editing Checklist.*

Editing Checklist

Did you . . . ?
☐ use simple present, present progressive and non-action verbs correctly
☐ check your spelling

Check your answers on page UR-4.

Do you need to review anything?

A | Complete the sentences with the words in parentheses. Use the affirmative or negative form of the simple present.

1. They _____ a car.
   (own / not)

2. He _____ to drive.
   (like / not)

3. She _____ a new bike.
   (have)

4. She _____ a lock for it.
   (need)

5. They _____ to buy bikes too.
   (want)

B | Complete the paragraph with the verbs in parentheses. Use the simple present or present progressive.

John _____ his new computer now. He _____ the
  1. (use)   2. (surf)
Internet. He _____ information about events in his area. His computer
              3. (get)
_____ a lot of great features. John _____ to learn how to use
      4. (have)   5. (want)
all of them.

C | Complete the conversation with the words in parentheses. Use the simple present or present progressive.

A: What _____ Tom _____?
                                    1. (do)

B: He _____ to fix his printer again.
          2. (try)

A: What _____ the problem now?
              3. (be)

B: I _____.
        4. (know / not)

A: _____ he _____ a new printer? This one is pretty old!
                                    5. (need)

D | Correct the conversations. There are five mistakes.

1. **A:** Where you calling from?

   B: Downtown. I walk along Second Street.

2. **A:** Is she play tennis at West Park?

   B: No, she's not. She no like those courts.

3. **A:** Does he understands Greek?

   B: Yes, he does. He was in Greece for a year.

From Grammar to Writing

SUBJECTS AND VERBS

1 | *What's wrong with these sentences?*

1. He a handsome man.
2. She a red skirt.
3. I from Argentina.

4. Am wearing blue pants.
5. Are tired?
6. Is a cool day.

Sentences 1–3 are missing a verb. Sentences 4–6 are missing a subject.

2 | *Study the information about subjects and verbs.*

Every sentence needs a subject and verb.	SUBJECT VERB My **mother works**.
The **subject** is a noun or pronoun. It tells who or what the sentence is about.	• **John** is running. • **They** are watching TV.
The **verb** tells the action or links the subject with the rest of the sentence.	• It **is raining**. • He **is** a doctor.

3 | *Correct this paragraph. Then underline the subject and circle the verb in each sentence.*

I in Central Park. It a sunny day in September. Is crowded. Some children soccer.

They're laughing and shouting. Some people are running. Three older women on a bench.

Are watching the runners and soccer players. A young man and woman are holding

hands. Are smiling. Are in love. Central Park a wonderful place to be on a beautiful day.

4 | *Imagine you are in one of these places. Write a paragraph about the people you see.*

an airport   a busy street   a park   a train station

5 | *Exchange papers with a partner. Did your partner follow the directions? Correct any mistakes in grammar and spelling.*

6 | *Talk to your partner. Discuss the mistakes you made. Then rewrite your own paper and make any necessary changes.*

SIMPLE PAST

Simple Past: Affirmative and Negative Statements with Regular Verbs

TRAVEL

STEP 1 GRAMMAR IN CONTEXT

Before You Read

Discuss the question.

• In which countries are these tourist attractions? (See answers on page 202.)

Read

Read a message from Karen to Dahlia and Dahlia's answer. What city did Karen visit? (See answer on page 202.)

WALL
FRIENDS
PHOTOS

Karen van der Broek
Hi Dahlia,
You were so right! This city is awesome.
Yesterday morning Julian and I **watched** foot-volley on Ipanema Beach. The players were great. Then in the afternoon we **visited** Sugarloaf. What a view! In the evening we **enjoyed** a delicious meal at a churrascuria (a barbecued meat restaurant).
Our flight here was the only bad part of the trip. It was bumpy, and we **didn't land** until 11:30 at night. But someone from the hotel **picked** us **up**, and we **arrived** at the hotel before 1:00 A.M. Everyone here is helpful, and our room is beautiful. The weather is great. I **didn't need** to pack my umbrella or my jacket.
Say hi to everyone at the office.
Love, Karen

Dahlia Gold

Hey Karen,

   I'm glad *you're* having such a great time. It's freezing here. Yesterday it **snowed** all day, and last week it **rained**.

   I **stayed** late Monday and Tuesday preparing for the spring conference. I **dined** on sandwiches from the vending machines downstairs. Then guess what happened? Mr. Grimes **canceled** the conference.

   So enjoy every minute of your vacation.
   —Miss you.

Love, Dahlia

WALL
FRIENDS
PHOTOS

After You Read

A | Practice *PAIRS: Now read the messages aloud. Take turns.*

B | Vocabulary *Complete the sentences with the words from the box.*

bumpy	canceled	freezing	landed	picked / up

1. Our flight was very _____. I felt sick during the flight.

2. Our airplane _____ on time. I was glad the flight was over.

3. Someone from the hotel _____ us _____.

4. It's _____ in this room. I need a sweater.

5. I ordered french fries and a shake but then I _____ my order because I need to diet.

C | Comprehension *Make the false statements true.*

                           watched
1. Karen and Julian ~~played~~ foot-volley on Ipanema Beach.

2. Karen and Julian enjoyed dessert at a café.

3. Karen and Julian's plane arrived in the afternoon.

4. The people at the hotel were unhelpful.

5. Mr. Grimes attended the spring conference.

THE SIMPLE PAST: STATEMENTS WITH REGULAR VERBS

Affirmative Statements		Negative Statements		
Subject	**Base Form of Verb + -ed**	**Subject**	*Did Not*	**Base Form of Verb**
I He She It We You* They	land**ed**. arrive**d**. cr**ied**.	I He She It We You* They	did not didn't	land. arrive. cry.

*You can be both singular and plural subjects.

Past Time Markers		
Yesterday	*Ago*	*Last*
yesterday **yesterday** morning **yesterday** afternoon **yesterday** evening	two days **ago** a week **ago** a month **ago** a year **ago** a couple of days **ago**	**last** night **last** Monday **last** week **last** summer **last** year

GRAMMAR NOTES

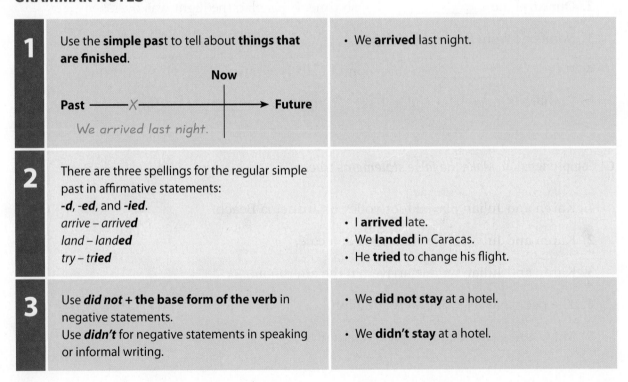

1   Use the **simple past** to tell about **things that are finished**.

Now

Past ——X———|———→ Future

We arrived last night.

- We **arrived** last night.

2   There are three spellings for the regular simple past in affirmative statements:
-d, *-ed*, and *-ied*.
arrive – arrived
land – landed
try – tried

- I **arrived** late.
- We **landed** in Caracas.
- He **tried** to change his flight.

3   Use *did not* + **the base form of the verb** in negative statements.
Use *didn't* for negative statements in speaking or informal writing.

- We **did not stay** at a hotel.

- We **didn't stay** at a hotel.

4	The **verb form** is the **same for all subject pronouns**.	• **I visited** Seoul. • **She visited** Mexico City. • **They visited** Madrid.
5	**Time markers** usually come at the beginning or end of a sentence.	• **Yesterday** I studied. • I studied **yesterday**.
	You can use *yesterday* alone. You can also use it before *morning*, *afternoon*, or *evening*.	• I visited my friends **yesterday**. • I visited my friends **yesterday evening**.
	Use *ago* after a length of time.	• I started this class a month **ago**.
	Use *last* before words like *night*, *week*, or *year*.	• I arrived here **last** month.

REFERENCE NOTE
For complete simple past spelling and pronunciation rules, see Appendix 10 on page A-10.

STEP 3 FOCUSED PRACTICE

EXERCISE 1: Discover the Grammar

A | *Underline the simple past affirmative verbs. Circle the simple past negative verb. Then write the base form of the verb next to each sentence.*

Base Form

1. We arrived in Washington, D.C., last Friday.   *arrive*

2. Yesterday afternoon we walked around the National Zoo.   _____

3. Some friends invited us for dinner last night.   _____

4. Ana baked a cheesecake yesterday morning.   _____

5. The cheesecake didn't look good, but it tasted delicious.   _____, _____

6. Miguel cooked enchiladas.   _____

7. The enchiladas looked delicious, but they didn't taste good.   _____, _____

8. We visited Dupont Circle with Ana and Miguel.   _____

9. An hour ago I called and thanked them for a wonderful evening.   _____, _____

B | *Write the five time markers in Part A.*

_____, _____, _____,

_____, _____

EXERCISE 2: Affirmative Statements

(Grammar Notes 1, 2, 4)

Complete the sentences with the verbs from the box. Use the simple past form.

~~borrow~~	cook	land	walk
cancel	hug	visit	watch

1. We _____borrowed_____ a guidebook from our friends.

2. His plane _____ on time.

3. Yesterday she _____ the art museum.

4. He _____ a meal for us. It was terrific.

5. I'm tired. I _____ up a lot of hills in San Francisco this morning.

6. The airlines _____ many flights because of bad weather.

7. Two nights ago they _____ a movie.

8. Everyone _____ and kissed us when we left.

EXERCISE 3: Negative Statements

(Grammar Notes 3–4)

Underline the verb in the first sentence. Then complete the second sentence with the negative simple past form of the verb.

1. He <u>stayed</u> with friends. He _____ *didn't stay* _____ at a hotel.

2. I wanted coffee. I _____ tea.

3. It rained in the morning. It _____ in the afternoon.

4. She only invited you. She _____ your whole family.

5. He helped you. He _____ me.

6. I watched a movie. I _____ the news.

7. He picked her up from the airport. He _____ her

   _____ from the train station.

EXERCISE 4: Affirmative and Negative Statements

(Grammar Notes 2–3)

Complete Camila's travel notes with the verbs in parentheses. Use the simple past.

Carlos and I _____*arrived*_____ in San

1. (arrive)

Francisco last Wednesday night at 9:00. The

next day it _____, but the weather

2. (rain)

_____ us from sightseeing.

3. (stop / not)

We _____ our umbrellas and

4. (carry)

_____ at Fisherman's Wharf. Then the

5. (shop)

rain _____, so we _____

6. (stop)   **7. (climb)**

Telegraph Hill. We _____ around there a bit, and then we _____ a

8. (walk)   **9. (board)**

bus to Baker Beach. We _____ the sun set next to the Golden Gate Bridge, and

10. (watch)

we _____ to the ocean waves. I was so tired. I _____ to stay out. I

11. (listen)   **12. (want / not)**

_____ to go back to our hotel. On the way home we _____ to eat,

13. (want)   **14. (need)**

though. Chinatown was the perfect spot. We _____ a "bird's nest" and red bean

15. (order)

soup. It was delicious. Everything in San Francisco was amazing.

EXERCISE 5: Past Time Markers

(Grammar Note 5)

*Complete the conversations. Use **last** or **ago**, or **yesterday**.*

1. **BEN:** Were you away?

   SAM: Yes, I was in Mexico City _____*last*_____ week.

                                             a.

   BEN: Oh. I was there a couple of months _____. By the way, Ian called

                                                        b.

   me _____ night. He wants us to meet for lunch.

          c.

2. **STEVE:** Where is Demetrios? I never see him anymore!

   ALLY: I know. He's always traveling. He was in Montreal _____

                                                               a.

   weekend. He was in Prague _____ month. And two months

                                b.

   _____ he visited his family in Greece.

          c.

   STEVE: Where is he now?

   ALLY: I'm not sure. I called him _____ but he didn't answer.

                                       d.

EXERCISE 6: Simple Past and Simple Present Statements

Complete the conversations with the words in parentheses. Use the simple past or simple present.

1. A: When do you usually travel?

   B: We usually _____*travel*_____ in the summer, but last year we _____
                          (travel)   **(travel)**

     in the fall.

2. A: Does John like guided tours?

   B: No. He _____ most guided tours, but he _____ the one
                (like / not)   **(like)**

     yesterday in Chicago.

3. A: When does that restaurant open?

   B: It usually _____ at 7:00 A.M., but it _____ until 7:30
                       (open)   **(open / not)**

     today.

4. A: Do you travel on business a lot?

   B: No, I don't. I usually _____ on business, but last month I
                            (travel / not)

     _____ twice on business.
        (travel)

5. A: When do you start work?

   B: I usually _____ at 9:00, but I _____ at 8:00 this morning
                 (start)   **(start)**

     because I was very busy.

6. A: Does Jade always take the bus?

   B: She usually _____ a bus or train, but this week she
                   (take)

     _____ public transportation. She _____ a car.
     (use / not)   **(rent)**

7. A: Where do you have lunch?

   B: I usually _____ something from home, but last Friday was a
                 (bring)

     co-worker's birthday, so five of us _____ in a Thai restaurant.
                                      (eat)

EXERCISE 7: Editing

Correct the postcard. There are six mistakes. The first mistake is already corrected. Find and correct five more.

Dear Ilene,

Paris is unbelievable at night! It's 10 P.M., and I'm writing to you from a café. We arrived here ~~ago two days~~ *two days ago*. Paul's friend Pierre picks us up. We toured the city during the day, and at night we did walked along the Seine River. Today we dining in Montmartre, and we visited the Louvre Museum. I not like the food in Montmartre, but I did loved the area.

We hope all is well with you. Don't work too hard.

Love,

Michelle and Paul

To:
Ilene Carson
85 Maple Street
Plymouth, DE 19905
USA

STEP 4 COMMUNICATION PRACTICE

EXERCISE 8: Listening

A | *Listen to the conversation. Write* **T** (**True**) *or* **F** (**False**) *for each statement. Then correct the false statements.*

_F_ **1.** Marta visited ~~Mexico~~. *Japan*

____ **2.** Marta stayed with friends.

____ **3.** Marta stayed at a traditional Japanese inn.

____ **4.** Marta rented a car.

____ **5.** Marta didn't enjoy her trip.

ryokan

B | *Listen again. Write the amount of time.*

1. Marta was in Japan: _____

2. Marta stayed in a ryokan: _____

3. Marta visited Kyoto: _____

4. Marta and her friend talked about Marta's trip: _____

EXERCISE 9: Pronunciation

A | *Read and listen to the Pronunciation Note.*

Pronunciation Note
Regular simple past verbs end in three sounds: / **d** /, / **t** /, or / **ɪd** /.
EXAMPLES: He arriv<u>ed</u> late. / **d** /   They work<u>ed</u> at a hotel. / **t** /   We wait<u>ed</u> a long time. / **ɪd** /

B | *Listen to the sentences. Check (✓) the final sound of each verb.*

Last weekend, . . .	/ t /	/ d /	/ ɪd /
1. I watched TV.	✓		
2. I rented a movie.			
3. I listened to music.			
4. I played a sport.			
5. I visited friends.			
6. I worked.			

C | *PAIRS: Ask your partner what he or she did last weekend. Then tell your partner what you did. Use the verbs in Part B or other regular simple past verbs.*

> **EXAMPLE:** **A:** What did you do last weekend, Zofiya?
> **B:** I listened to music at a concert in the park.

EXERCISE 10: Game: Truths and Lies

A | *On a separate piece of paper, write five things you did on your last trip. Four of them are true, and one is a lie. Use five verbs from the unit. Use the past tense.*

> **EXAMPLE:** On my last trip, . . .
> 1. I toured Seattle.
> 2. I rented a car.
> 3. I stayed with friends.
> 4. I visited the Space Needle.
> 5. It rained every day.

B | *GROUPS: Take turns reading your sentences. Guess which one is not true.*

> **EXAMPLE:** **A:** On my last trip, I toured Seattle. I rented a car. I stayed with friends. I visited the Space Needle. It rained every day.
> **B:** I think "I rented a car" is not true. You don't drive!

EXERCISE 11: Writing

A | *Write about a city you would like to visit. Imagine you traveled to that city last summer. Write a postcard to a classmate about the trip. Use the words from the box, the simple past, and at least two time markers.*

arrive	like	shop	travel	walk
enjoy	rent	stay	visit	watch

EXAMPLE:

Hola Jack,

Guadalajara is amazing. I landed here four days ago. I stayed at a hotel the first night. Then Hugo invited me to stay with his family.

Yesterday morning we visited the palace and rented a horse-drawn carriage. In the afternoon I shopped for ceramics. Now I can't buy anything else unless I buy another suitcase.

See you soon.

Emily

To:
Jack Spence
10 Arbor Lane
Alexandria, VA
22315

Guadalajara

B | *Check your work. Use the Editing Checklist.*

Editing Checklist

Did you . . . ?
☐ use the simple past with regular verbs correctly
☐ check your spelling

A | *Circle the correct words to complete the sentences.*

1. I **watch / watched** TV last night.

2. We **did visit / visited** Chile last summer.

3. He picked her up from work **an hour ago / last hour**.

4. **Last night / A night ago** I stayed home.

5. Our plane **didn't land / no landed** on time.

B | *Complete the sentences with the verbs in parentheses. Use the simple past.*

1. I'm helping them now. I _____ them last week too.
   (help)

2. She's staying with me. Last year I _____ with her.
   (stay)

3. It snowed during the night, but it _____ in the morning.
   (snow / not)

4. She only asked you. She _____ him.
   (ask / not)

5. We wanted to fly first class. We _____ to fly coach.
   (want / not)

C | *Complete the sentences with the verbs from the box. Use the simple past affirmative or negative.*

cancel	enjoy	play	rain	stay

1. My boss _____ the conference. He's trying to save money.

2. She _____ late at work. She needed to get home to her children.

3. I didn't need my umbrella. It _____.

4. We _____ soccer for three hours. It was a lot of fun.

5. He _____ the movie. It was very boring.

D | *Read the paragraph. Find the five mistakes.*

Hello from London. Our friends did invited us here for a week. We're having a great time. Yesterday we visit Big Ben, and we tour the Royal Palace. This morning we watch the Changing of the Guard. We wanted to shop this afternoon, but we didn't. The prices were high, but we are enjoyed looking at the store windows.

Simple Past: Affirmative and Negative Statements with Irregular Verbs

YOU NEVER KNOW

STEP 1 GRAMMAR IN CONTEXT

Before You Read

Some people say, "In life, you never know what will happen." What does that mean?

a. Life never changes.　　　　**b.** Life has surprises.

Read

Read this Chinese folktale.

YOU NEVER KNOW WHAT WILL HAPPEN

A long time ago there lived a poor Chinese peasant.[1] One day a beautiful horse appeared on his farm. When the peasant's friends **saw** the horse they **said**, "How lucky you are!"

The peasant answered, "You never know what will happen."

Two days later the horse **ran** away. The peasant's friends **came** and **said**, "What a terrible thing. How unlucky you are! The fine horse **ran** away." The peasant **didn't get** excited. He simply **said**, "You never know what will happen."

Exactly one week later the horse returned. And it **brought** three other horses. When the peasant's friends **saw** the horses they **said**, "Oh. You are so lucky. Now you have four horses to help you." The peasant looked at them and once again **said**, "You never know what will happen."

The next morning the peasant's oldest son **was** in the field.[2] Suddenly one of the horses **ran** into him, and the boy **fell** to the ground. He **was** badly hurt. He **lost** the use of his leg. Indeed, this **was** terrible, and many people **came** to the peasant and expressed their sadness for his son's misfortune. But again the peasant simply **said**, "You never know what will happen."

[1] *peasant:* person who works on a farm
[2] *field:* large grassy area

A month after the accident, soldiers **rode** into the village. They shouted, "There is a problem along the border! We are taking every healthy young man to fight." The soldiers **took** all the other young men, but they **didn't take** the peasant's son. All the other young men **fought** in the border war, and they all died. But the peasant's son lived a long and happy life. As his father **said**, you never know what will happen.

After You Read

A | **Practice** *PAIRS: Read the folktale again aloud. Take turns reading paragraphs.*

B | **Vocabulary** *Complete the sentences with the words from the box.*

appeared	border	lucky	shouted	suddenly	terrible

1. I didn't like the story because it had a(n) _____ ending.

2. He showed his passport to cross the _____ into Mexico.

3. We didn't expect the rain. The weather changed _____.

4. It's a folktale about a(n) _____ man. Good things always happen to him.

5. He _____, but nobody heard him.

6. A beautiful red bird _____ on my window sill.

C | **Comprehension** *Number the events in the order they occurred (1 to 6).*

_____ A week later the horse came back with three other horses.

_1_ A horse appeared on a peasant's land. Two days later it ran away.

_____ The next morning one of the horses ran into the peasant's son; he was hurt.

_____ A month later soldiers rode into the village.

_____ The other young men died. The peasant's son lived a long, happy life.

_____ The soldiers took all the healthy young men to fight, but they didn't take the peasant's son.

SIMPLE PAST: IRREGULAR VERBS—AFFIRMATIVE AND NEGATIVE STATEMENTS

Affirmative Statements		
Subject	Verb	
I You He We	bought rode saw	the horses.

Negative Statements			
Subject	*Did Not / Didn't*	Base Form of Verb	
I You He We	did not didn't	buy ride see	the horses.

Be: Affirmative Statements		
Subject	*Was / Were*	
She	was	lucky.
They	were	unlucky.

Be: Negative Statements		
Subject	*Was / Were not*	
I	was not	home.
We	were not	nearby.

Contractions
was not → **wasn't**
were not → **weren't**

GRAMMAR NOTES

1	Many common verbs are irregular. **Irregular past verbs** do not add *-ed*. They often look different from the base form.	• We **saw** a beautiful horse. (**see**) • They **went** to work. (**go**) • She **came** late. (**come**) • He **brought** a friend to school. (**bring**) • He **ate** a big lunch. (**eat**)
2	For **negative statements** in the past, use *did not* + **base form of the verb** (except for *be*). Use the short form *didn't* for speaking and informal writing. **BE CAREFUL!** Do not use the simple past form after *didn't*.	• They **did not see** him. • She **did not eat** lunch. • They **didn't** see him. NOT: They didn't ~~saw~~ him. They didn't ~~ate~~ lunch.
3	The **past tense of *be*** is *was* or *were*. The **negative** is *was not* or *were not*. Use *wasn't* and *weren't* for speaking and informal writing.	• I **was** at the library last night. • They **were not** home this morning. • It **wasn't** late. • They **weren't** in Mexico City.
4	We use *was* or *were* + *born* to tell when or where people were born.	• I **was born** in Nicaragua. • She **was born** in 1989.

REFERENCE NOTES
See Appendix 11, page A-11 for a list of irregular past forms.
See Unit 3, page 28 for a discussion of the past of *be*.
See Unit 18, pages 200–201, and Unit 20, pages 222–223 for more about the simple past.

EXERCISE 1: Discover the Grammar

Circle the verbs in the past. Then write the verbs and the base form of each verb in the chart.

I have two brothers. My older brother (was) a great student. He (brought) home prizes and won awards. My younger brother felt bored by school. He never did well. My parents worried about him. Then in his second year of high school, he had a great chemistry teacher. He became interested in chemistry. He began to study hard. He's now a chemistry professor at a university. So, you never know what will happen.

Past	Base Form
was	be
brought	bring

EXERCISE 2: Simple Past: Irregular Verbs

(Grammar Notes 1–3)

Complete the paragraph with the words in parentheses. Use the simple past.

Abe _____was_____ nine when his mother died in 1818. His family
    1. (be)

_____ very little money and lived in a log cabin with one room. Still,
    2. (have)

Abe _____ to school. He _____ strong and very tall. He
    3. (go)   **4. (grow)**

_____ wood for money, then he _____ himself the law and
    5. (split)   **6. (teach)**

_____ a law firm. For a short time, he _____ a soldier, but he
    7. (begin)   **8. (be)**

_____ any action. He _____ home, _____ speeches,
    9. (see / not)   **10. (come)**   **11. (give)**

and _____ for political office. People _____ of him because he
    12. (run)   **13. (make fun)**

was so tall, but he _____ it bother him. He _____ president of
    14. (let / not)   **15. (become)**

the United States and _____ the country during a difficult civil war. His army
    16. (lead)

_____ the war. He _____ one of the most admired American
    17. (win)   **18. (become)**

presidents in history. His name, as you guessed, _____ Abraham Lincoln.
    19. (be)

EXERCISE 3: Simple Past: Irregular Verbs

(Grammar Notes 1–4)

Complete the paragraphs with the words in parentheses. Use the simple past.

James Earl Jones _____was born_____ in Mississippi in 1931. At five his family moved

                           1. (be born)

to Michigan. Soon after that, he _____ to stutter. For many years he

                                        2. (begin)

_____ more than a few words. In high school a teacher tried to help him. After

3. (say / not)

Jones _____ a poem, this teacher _____ him read it aloud. Jones

            4. (write)   **5. (make)**

_____ the poem by heart, and he _____ it without stuttering. It

       6. (know)   **7. (say)**

_____ his first success at public speaking. Later, Jones _____ a

    8. (be)   **9. (get)**

scholarship to the University of Michigan. At first, he

studied medicine, but then he changed to theater.

After college, he _____ to New York. He

                           10. (go)

_____ money, and he _____

11. (have / not)   **12. (do)**

all sorts of jobs to pay his bills. After a few years, people

_____ his talent. He _____ a

    13. (see)   **14. (become)**

famous and admired

actor. Maybe you

know his deep,

powerful voice. It

is the voice of Darth Vader in the *Star Wars* movies and

Mufasa in *The Lion King*.

In 2009 Jones _____ a Lifetime

                        15. (win)

Achievement Award of the Screen Actors Guild. Jones's

life is amazing when you think that as a child, speaking

_____ his biggest challenge. So in life you

    16. (be)

never know what will happen.

EXERCISE 4: Simple Past: Irregular Verbs

(Grammar Notes 1–4)

Complete each paragraph with the words from the box. Use the simple past.

~~be born~~	become	begin	be / not	read

Joanne Kathleen _____was born_____ in 1965 in England. She _____ writing
                    1.   **2.**
at the age of five, and she always _____ a lot. She majored in French at the
                                       3.
university and _____ a bilingual secretary. But she _____ very
                  4.   **5.**
good at it.

begin	go	have	teach

At 26, she _____ to Portugal. She _____ English there. At this
              6.   **7.**
time she first _____ working on a story about a boy with special powers named
                  8.
Harry. She met a journalist in Portugal. They married and _____ a daughter in
                                                              9.
1993. Unfortunately, the marriage ended in divorce.

be	give	have / not	sell	want / not	write

She moved to Scotland to be near a sister and finish

her book. In Scotland life _____ hard
                              10.

because she _____ much money. She tried
                11.

to sell her book, but the publishers _____
                                         12.

it. She finally _____ her book for about
                  13.

$4,000. Several months later, an American company

_____ her money to write full time. Soon
   14.

her book became a bestseller. She _____
                                      15.

several more Harry Potter books. Today, J. K. Rowling is

rich and famous. So you never know what will happen.

Actor Daniel Radcliffe, star of *Harry Potter*

EXERCISE 5: Editing

Correct the sentences. There are nine mistakes. The first mistake is already corrected.
Find and correct eight more.

>   *was*
> My grandfather⸝born in Peru. He had an older brother and sister. Their dad
>
> (my great-grandfather) were a dreamer. The family have not much money.
>
> When my grandfather was 13, his mother did died and his dad remarried.
>
> My grandfather no like his stepmother so he move in with his sister and her
>
> husband. All three leave for America. They did begin a small business. They
>
> worked hard, and the business grow. Today my sister and I direct the
>
> company.

STEP 4 COMMUNICATION PRACTICE

EXERCISE 6: Listening

A | *Listen to Paul's story. Answer the question. Circle the correct letter.*

The story is about _____.

    a. a father and son   **b.** a man and his grandfather

B | *Listen again and complete the sentences.*

1. Paul's grandfather gave him a(n) _____*blanket*_____.

2. After a couple of years it _____ _____ good.

3. Paul's mother made it into a(n) _____ _____.

4. Then the _____ _____ tore.

5. His mother made it into a(n) _____ _____.

6. Paul _____ the _____.

7. He felt _____.

8. His friends said, "_____ _____ _____."

9. Paul didn't _____ about it. He _____ about it instead.

10. Many years later Paul's _____ found the story.

EXERCISE 7: Pronunciation

A | *Read and listen to the Pronunciation Note.*

> **Pronunciation Note**
>
> The / æ / sound, as in *have*, is slightly more open than the / ɛ / sound, as in *bed*.
>
> To pronounce the / ɛ / sound, keep your mouth open and your lips spread. Keep your tongue low in your mouth. Touch the lower front teeth lightly with the tip of your tongue.

B | *Listen to the / æ / sound in the underlined words. Then repeat the sentences.*

1. The story <u>happened</u> in China.
2. A Chinese peasant's horse <u>ran</u> away.
3. It came <u>back</u> with three more horses.
4. The son lived a <u>happy</u> life.
5. The peasant <u>laughed</u> and said, "You never know what will <u>happen</u>."

C | *Listen. Check (✓) if the underlined word has the / æ / sound or the / ɛ / sound.*

	/ æ /	/ ɛ /
1. They <u>had</u> a hard life.	☑	☐
2. The boy's <u>head</u> hurt from his fall.	☐	☐
3. He told us the <u>end</u> of the story.	☐	☐
4. We liked the story <u>and</u> the movie.	☐	☐
5. The <u>man</u> was lucky.	☐	☐
6. The <u>men</u> fought on the border.	☐	☐

EXERCISE 8: A Memory Game

GROUPS: Sit in a circle. Take notes. The first student tells one thing he or she did last weekend. The next student tells what the first one did and then what he or she did. Continue until every student speaks.

> EXAMPLE: ANN: I went to the movies.
>
> JOE: Ann went to the movies, and I read a book.

EXERCISE 9: Discussion

SMALL GROUPS: Tell about a wonderful day and a terrible day. Use **First, Then,** *and* **After that.**

EXAMPLE: I had a wonderful day. First, I saw my grandmother. Then, I went to the park. After that, I rented a video.
Yesterday I had a terrible day. First, I got up late. Then, I broke my glasses. After that, I lost my keys.

EXERCISE 10: Writing

A | *Write your autobiography. The year is now 2066. Think about these questions as you write.*

- Where and when were you born?
- Where did you go to school?
- What did you do in your free time?
- What did you become? (businessperson, etc.) Why?
- Where did you live?
- Did you marry? Did you have children?
- Did you travel?
- Did you become rich or famous?
- Did you make a difference in the world?
- Were you happy?

EXAMPLE: Right now I'm celebrating my eightieth birthday with my four children, their children, and their children's children. I am a lucky man. I was born in 1980 in Korea. My family didn't have much money, but we were hardworking. I was the fourth of five children. My parents were . . .

B | *Check your work. Use the Editing Checklist.*

Editing Checklist

Did you . . . ?
☐ use the simple past of irregular and regular verbs correctly
☐ check your spelling

A | Complete the sentences with the verbs in parentheses. Use the simple past.

1. One day a fox _____ some delicious grapes.
   (see)

2. He _____ hungry, and he _____ the grapes.
   (be)   (want)

3. He _____ to reach the grapes, but they were too high.
   (try)

4. He _____ angry and said, "I really _____ them anyway."
   (get)   (want / not)

B | Complete the paragraph with the verbs from the box. Use the simple past.

become	find	keep	steal	use / not

A lucky man _____ a pot of gold. He _____ the pot of gold in

a hole in the ground of his garden. A jealous worker _____ the gold from

the man. The man _____ upset. But a neighbor laughed because the man

_____ the gold. He just enjoyed counting it.

C | Complete the sentences with the verbs in parentheses. Use the affirmative or negative form.

1. The concert was terrible. I _____ until the end.
   (stay)

2. He _____ his keys. He needs to get a new set of keys.
   (lose)

3. We _____ 5 miles yesterday. We're practicing for a big race.
   (run)

4. We _____ him in school. Was he sick?
   (see)

5. It _____ him a long time to get to school. I wonder why?
   (take)

D | Correct the sentences. There are four mistakes.

1. William Sidney Porter born in North Carolina in 1862.

2. He was a famous American short story writer. He wrote under different names, but
   he did became best known as O. Henry.

3. His stories were had surprise endings.

4. O. Henry had many talents, but he did get into trouble and spent time in prison.

20 Simple Past: *Yes/No* and *Wh-* Questions

INTERVIEWS

STEP 1 GRAMMAR IN CONTEXT

Before You Read

PAIRS: Read these lines by the greatest writer in the English language. Who wrote these famous lines? In what play did he write them?

- "Romeo, Romeo! Wherefore art thou Romeo?"
- "Parting is such sweet sorrow."

William Shakespeare wrote these words in the play *Romeo and Juliet*. Altogether Shakespeare wrote between 37 and 38 plays and many poems.

Leonardo DiCaprio starred in the 1996 movie version of *Romeo and Juliet*

Read

Read a radio talk show interview between English professor Robert Gibbons and Carla Jonas.

CARLA: Thank you for coming today Professor Gibbons. I see your new book ***Who Wrote the Greatest Plays of All?*** is out. It's about Shakespeare, right?

PROFESSOR GIBBONS: Yes, it is. It's about Shakespeare and the time period he lived in.

CARLA: So, **why did you write the book?**

PROF: I wanted to explore some questions we have about Shakespeare and his life. Shakespeare probably wrote all the plays and poems that we say he did, but we don't know for sure. You see, Shakespeare's life is a mystery. There are many things we don't know about him. And the questions are interesting.

(continued on next page)

CARLA: Well, what can you tell us about him? **When was Shakespeare born?**

PROF: He was born in 1564 in Stratford-on-Avon, but we don't know the exact date.

CARLA: What about his family?

Juliet's castle, Castle Vecchio

PROF: His father was a landowner and a town leader. His mother was the daughter of a wealthy landowner. But his father was illiterate.[1]

CARLA: **Did Shakespeare go to school?**

PROF: Yes, but we don't know too much about Shakespeare's education because there is no paper trail.[2] We think he went to grammar school.[3] But he did not attend a university. He probably studied Latin and Greek. But . . . **was his education good enough? How did Shakespeare learn to write so well? Did he really write the plays himself**, or **did someone else write them for him?**

CARLA: What do you mean?

PROF: At that time, many people wrote under a different name, a pen name. Some people think that Shakespeare's friend, Ben Jonson, wrote the plays.

CARLA: That's interesting. I have a question about Shakespeare. He wrote many plays about English kings and queens. **How did he know so much about the life of royalty?**[4] He wasn't in that class.[5]

PROF: That's a good question. We think he read about them. We're pretty sure the story of *Macbeth* and parts of *King Lear* came from a book by Raphael Holinshed. That book tells all about English, Scottish, and Irish kings. Still . . . we don't know, **was Shakespeare the writer?** And could one person write so many great works? Most scholars[6] believe Shakespeare was the author. We think he was a man of great genius and imagination . . . but perhaps it was someone else. We may never know for certain.

CARLA: Such interesting points! I'm looking forward to reading your book, Professor. For those of you who like a good mystery, buy Professor Mark Gibbons's new book, *Who Wrote the Greatest Plays of All?* And Professor, thank you for coming here today.

PROF: And thank you, Carla, for inviting me.

---

[1] *illiterate:* not able to read or write

[2] *paper trail:* a written record

[3] *grammar school:* basic English schooling for boys in the 1500s

[4] *royalty:* a king, queen, and their family

[5] *class:* a group of people classified by income and education

[6] *scholar:* someone who studies a subject deeply

After You Read

A | Practice *PAIRS: Now read the interview aloud.*

B | Vocabulary *Complete the sentences with the words from the box.*

author	be out	mystery	play	poem

1. Shakespeare wrote the _____ *Romeo and Juliet* between the years 1591 and 1595.

2. Shakespeare is the _____ of between 37 and 38 plays.

3. Nobody knows Shakespeare's exact birthday. It's a(n) _____.

4. The words in that _____ are beautiful, but they don't rhyme.

5. When will that new book about *Romeo and Juliet* _____?
   I'd like to read it.

C | Comprehension *Read the questions. Circle the correct letter.*

1. Where was Shakespeare born?
   a. London   **b.** Stratford-on-Avon

2. When was he born?
   a. 1654   **b.** 1564

3. Did his parents come from poor families?
   a. Yes, they did.   **b.** No, they didn't.

4. Did Shakespeare attend a university?
   a. Yes, he did.   **b.** No, he didn't.

5. What was *Macbeth* the name of?
   a. a play by Shakespeare   **b.** a town in England

6. Do most scholars believe that Shakespeare wrote all of his plays?
   a. Yes, they do.   **b.** No, they don't.

Stratford-on-Avon

THE SIMPLE PAST: *YES / NO* AND *WH-* QUESTIONS AND ANSWERS

Yes / No Questions		
Did	Subject	Base Form of Verb
Did	I you he she it we they	help?

Short Answers					
Affirmative			Negative		
Yes,	you I he she it you they	did.	No,	you I he she it you they	didn't.

Wh- Questions				Answers
Wh- Word	*Did*	Subject	Base Form of Verb	
What		I	ask?	You asked about his name.
Where		you	go?	I went to the library. (To the library.)
When	did	he	write?	He wrote at night, after work. (At night, after work.)
Why		we	leave?	We went someplace else.
Who		you	call?	We called the doctor. (The doctor.)
How long		they	stay?	They stayed for an hour. (For an hour.) (An hour.)

Wh- Questions about the Subject			Answers
Wh- Word	Past Form of Verb		
Who	wrote	*Romeo and Juliet?*	William Shakespeare did.
What	happened	in the play?	Romeo and Juliet fell in love.

GRAMMAR NOTES

1	*Yes / No* questions in the simple past have the same form (*Did* + subject + base form) for regular and irregular verbs. The verb *be* is the one exception.	REGULAR VERB • **Did** you **call** your classmate? IRREGULAR VERB • **Did** you **write** your report? • **Was** Shakespeare an actor?
2	Most *wh-* questions in the past begin with the question word followed by *did* + the subject + the base form of the verb.	• **What did** he **write**? • **Why did** he **write**? • **Where did** he **write**? • **Who did** he **work** for?

3	Wh- questions in the past **do not use *did*** when the **question is about the subject**.	**SUBJECT** • Shakespeare wrote *Romeo and Juliet*. **Q: Who wrote *Romeo and Juliet*?** **A:** William Shakespeare. NOT: **Q:** Who ~~did write~~ *Romeo and Juliet*?
4	We usually give **short answers** to *yes / no* and *wh-* questions, but we can also give **long answers**. **NOTE:** *Yes / No* questions use **rising** intonation. *Wh-* questions use **falling** intonation.	**Q:** Did you work yesterday? **A:** Yes. OR Yes, I did. OR Yes, I worked yesterday. • Did you hear the story? • What did you think about it?

REFERENCE NOTE
See Unit 3, page 28 for more about the past of *be*.

STEP 3 FOCUSED PRACTICE

EXERCISE 1: Discover the Grammar

A | *Underline all the base form verbs.*

1. Did you watch a Shakespeare play last summer?

2. What did you see?

3. Did anyone go with you?

4. Did you understand it?

5. Did you enjoy it?

6. Did you read the whole play?

B | *Match the questions with the responses from the box. Write the responses.*

> **a.** I read *Hamlet*.
>
> **b.** William Shakespeare.
>
> **c.** Yes, I saw it three times.
>
> **d.** No, I didn't. I got it at the library.

1. A: What did you read for English class?

B: _____

2. A: Who wrote it?

B: _____

3. A: Did you buy the book?

B: _____

4. A: Did you see the movie?

B: _____

EXERCISE 2: Simple Past: *Yes / No* Questions

(Grammar Note 1)

Write **yes / no** questions in the simple past. Use the verb from the first sentence.

1. I read all his plays. _____Did_____ you _____read_____ them too?

2. We enjoyed the movie. _____ you _____ it too?

3. The movie had good acting. _____ it _____ a good story?

4. I didn't understand everything. _____ she _____ everything?

5. We didn't like the ending. _____ he _____ the ending?

6. I expected a happy ending. _____ you _____ a happy ending?

7. We saw a review online. _____ they _____ the review online?

EXERCISE 3: Simple Past: Short Answers

(Grammar Note 4)

Complete the conversations with the simple past. Write affirmative or negative short answers.

1. **A:** Did you finish your homework?

   B: _____Yes, I did._____ I finished it before dinner.

2. **A:** Did they go to the movies?

   B: _____. They stayed home and watched TV.

3. **A:** Did I call too late?

   B: _____. I'm usually up at this hour.

4. **A:** Did we get any mail?

   B: _____. We got our tickets for *King Lear*.

5. **A:** Did the package arrive?

   B: _____. It just came.

6. **A:** Did you buy the DVD?

   B: _____. I plan to buy it next weekend.

7. **A:** Did she lose her phone?

   B: _____. She thinks she left it on the bus.

EXERCISE 4: Simple Past Questions

(Grammar Notes 1–3)

Sherryl Woods is a best-selling romance and mystery writer. She has written more than 100 books that are available in over 20 countries. Read the interview. Complete the questions with the words in parentheses. Use the simple past.

I = INTERVIEWER

SW = SHERRYL WOODS

I: _____When did you write_____ your first
        1. (When / you / write)
book?

SW: In 1980. It came out in 1982.

I: _____ to be a
        2. (you / always / want)
writer?

SW: No, I didn't. For many years I wanted to be a

graphic artist.

I: _____ always good
        3. (be / you)
at writing?

SW: Well, my first-grade teacher wrote, "Sherryl is good at everything except making up
stories."

I: _____ your first-grade teacher?
        4. (you / like)
SW: I can't remember.

I: _____ to write?
        5. (When / you / start)
SW: After I graduated from college, I became a journalist.

I: _____ as a journalist?
        6. (How long / you / work)
SW: I worked for newspapers for 14 years.

I: _____ writing romance novels?
        7. (Why / you / start)
SW: Romances were new when I started. I read one and said, "I can do this too."

I: _____ the most?
        8. (Who / help / you)
SW: My agent did. She was there for me from the beginning.

I: _____ when your books became popular?
        9. (How / you / feel)
SW: I felt terrific. I remember the first time I saw someone with my book. I said, "That's
my book." The woman looked at me and said, "No, it's not. It's mine." I said, "No, no,
no. It's my book. I wrote it."

EXERCISE 5: Editing

John Steinbeck was a great American writer. Correct the questions and answers about him. There are ten mistakes. The first mistake is already corrected. Find and correct nine more.

Q: When John Steinbeck ~~was~~ born?   *(was inserted after "When")*

A: He born in 1902.

Q: Where he was born?

A: He was born in Salinas, California.

Q: Where did he studied writing?

A: He studied writing at Stanford University.

Q: He graduate from Stanford?

A: No, he didn't.

Q: Does he marry?

A: Yes, he did. He married in 1930.

Q: When he published *Tortilla Flat*?

A: In 1936.

Q: What year did *The Grapes of Wrath* come out?

A: In 1938. It was his best book.

Q: What were it about?

A: It was about a family who lost their farm and became fruit pickers in California.

Q: Did he won many prizes?

A: Yes, he did. He won a Pulitzer Prize and a Nobel Prize in Literature.

Q: When did he died?

A: He died in New York in 1968.

EXERCISE 6: Pronunciation

A | *Read and listen to the Pronunciation Note.*

> **Pronunciation Note**
>
> When you pronounce / ʤ / as in *jump*, place the tip of your tongue high and pulled back from the teeth.
>
> When you pronounce / y / as in *young*, the center of your tongue slides up toward the front of your mouth.
>
> **EXAMPLES:** / ʤ / jet
> / y / yet

B | *Listen and repeat the sentences.*

1. I like yellow.
2. I like Jell-O.™
3. He's going to Yale.
4. He's going to jail.
5. There's no juice.
6. There's no use.

C | *PAIRS: Your partner says a sentence from Part A. Read a sentence from the list below that follows your partner's sentence.*

1. Why? Did he rob a bank?
2. I do too. It's delicious.
3. Do I need to buy some?
4. You mean we can't change anything?
5. That's a great university.
6. It's my favorite color, too.

D | *Listen to the sentences. Underline the / ʤ / sounds and circle the / y / sounds that you hear.*

1. His initials are J. S.

2. He's good at storytelling, and some say he's a genius.

3. Does the J stand for Jack or John?

4. What year was he born?

5. We saw the movie *The Grapes of Wrath* yesterday.

6. At what age did he write his first book?

7. The language is not so difficult to understand.

8. Steinbeck wrote, "A journey is like marriage."

EXERCISE 7: Listening

A | *Listen to the conversation between Jon and Elena. Then read the questions. Circle the correct letter.*

1. What movie did Jon see last night?
   a. *I Love Shakespeare*   b. *Shakespeare in Love*

2. Where did it take place?
   a. in London   b. in Rome

3. When did it take place?
   a. in the 1500s   b. in the 1600s

B | *Listen again. Complete the sentences about the play* Romeo and Juliet.

Romeo and Juliet fell _____. They couldn't _____

because _____. In the last scene, they _____.

EXERCISE 8: Describing a Performance or Event

PAIRS: Name a play, a movie, a concert, a TV show or an athletic event you attended. Your partner asks **wh-** *questions and* **yes / no** *questions about the event.*

EXAMPLE: **A:** I saw the play *West Side Story*.
            B: What was it about?
            A: It was a play about two people who fell in love.
            B: When did it take place?
            A: In the 1950s.

EXERCISE 9: Writing

A | *Work in small groups. Complete the chart with names of famous people from the past.*

Artists	Writers	Musicians	Scientists / Inventors	Actors	Athletes

B | *Write 10 questions about one of the people from Part A. Use the words in parentheses.*

1. _Where was Leonardo diCaprio born?_
    (Where / he or she / born?)

2. _____
    (When / he or she / born?)

3. _____
    (Where / he or she / grow up?)

4. _____
    (What / he or she / do in his or her free time?)

5. _____
    (he or she / have / a happy childhood?)

6. _____
    (he or she / travel?)

7. _____
    (he or she / work hard?)

8. _____
    (he or she / make a lot of money?)

9. _____
    (YOUR QUESTION)

10. _____
    (YOUR QUESTION)

C | *Check your work. Use the Editing Checklist.*

Editing Checklist
Did you . . . ? ☐ use **yes/no** and **wh-** questions with the simple past correctly ☐ check your spelling

Check your answers on page UR-4.
Do you need to review anything?

A | Write **yes** / **no** questions with the verbs in parentheses. Use the simple past.

1. _____
   (they / go to the theater)

2. _____
   (she / get there by bus)

3. _____
   (you / have good seats)

4. _____
   (he / understand everything)

5. _____
   (we / miss the beginning)

6. _____
   (it / have a happy ending)

B | Complete the questions with the words in parentheses. Use the simple past.

1. _____?
   (what play / see / you)

2. _____?
   (where / you / see / it)

3. _____?
   (how long / be / the show)

4. _____?
   (you / enjoy / the performance)

5. _____?
   (who / be / the stars)

6. _____?
   (you / go out / after the show)

7. _____?
   (Where / you / go)

8. _____?
   (What / you / order)

C | Correct the sentences. There are six mistakes.

1. Where he did go last night?

2. What saw he?

3. Did he enjoyed it?

4. Who he met?

5. When they go?

6. Who did pay for it?

From Grammar to Writing

PUNCTUATION II: THE EXCLAMATION POINT (!), THE HYPHEN (-), QUOTATION MARKS (". . .")

1 | *What's wrong with the sentences? Discuss them with a partner.*

1. You're kidding

2. She's 21 years old

3. He said I love you

4. He worked for many years before he became rich. Then he invest

   ed his money and became even richer.

2 | *Study this information about punctuation.*

The exclamation point (!) Use the exclamation point after **strong, emotional statements**. (Don't use it too often.)	• What a surprise! • You're kidding! • How wonderful!
The hyphen (-) **a.** Use a hyphen in **compound numbers** from twenty-one to ninety-nine. **b.** Use a hyphen **at the end of a line** when dividing a word. Words must be divided by syllables. (Check your dictionary if you are unsure.)	• There were **twenty-two** students in the class. • We visited them at the **begin-ning** of the year.
Quotation marks (". . . ") Use quotation marks **before** and **after the exact words** of a speaker. Use a comma before the quote.	• She said, "I just love your new sweater."

3 | *Add the correct punctuation to the sentences in Exercise 1.*

4 | *Read the story. Circle the exclamation marks. Add quotation marks where necessary.*

Whose Baby Is It?

Solomon was a king. He lived about 3,000 years ago. Everyone came to Solomon because he was very wise.

One day two women approached King Solomon. One carried a baby. The woman said, We live nearby and had our babies three days apart. Her baby died in the night, and she changed it for mine. This baby is really mine.

The other woman said, No! That woman is lying. That's my baby.

The two women started arguing. They continued until King Solomon shouted, Stop!

He then turned to his guard and said, Take your sword and chop the baby in two. Give one part to this woman and the other to that one. The guard pulled out his sword. As he was about to harm the baby, the first woman screamed, No! Don't do it. Give her the baby. Just don't kill the baby.

King Solomon then said, Now I know the real mother. Give the baby to the woman who has just spoken.

5 | *Work in small groups. Follow the steps.*

1. Think about these questions. Take notes.
   • What was your favorite story as a child?
   • When did you first hear it? Who told it to you? Why did you like it?

2. Tell your story to your group.

3. Write your story. When you are finished, read your story twice. First pay attention to the story. Next pay attention to the grammar and punctuation.

6 | *Exchange papers with a partner. Did your partner follow the directions? Correct any mistakes in grammar and spelling.*

7 | *Talk to your partner. Discuss the mistakes you made. Then rewrite your own paper and make any necessary changes.*

8 | *Hang your story on the wall. Go around and read the stories of your classmates.*

PART VII

VERB REVIEW AND CONTRAST AND EXPANSION

UNIT	GRAMMAR FOCUS	THEME
21	Simple Past Review	Biographies
22	Gerunds and Infinitives	Careers and Abilities
23	Simple Present, Present Progressive, and Simple Past	Creativity

Simple Past Review

BIOGRAPHIES

STEP 1 GRAMMAR IN CONTEXT

Before You Read

PAIRS: Look at the words in the box. Tell your partner about people or pets with these qualities. Tell why.

generous	innovative	loyal	powerful
hardworking	loving	passionate	understanding

EXAMPLE: My cousin is very passionate about his work. He's an architect and spends hours working on projects.

Read

Read the article about a very unusual dog.

A Loyal Friend

Many people say dogs are loving and loyal. For one dog named Hachiko that description is especially true. He **won** the hearts of people all over the world because of his love and faithfulness to his master.

Hachiko **was** an Akita Inu dog. Akita Inus are large dogs from Japan. Hachiko **was born** in 1923. His owner, Ueno, **was** a professor at Tokyo University. Every morning Ueno and Hachiko **walked** to the Shibuya train station together. Every evening Hachiko **met** Ueno at the station. This routine **continued** for a couple of years. One evening, however, Hachiko **went** to the station, but Ueno **didn't get** off the train. That day, Ueno **was** at work when he suddenly **had** a cerebral hemorrhage[1] and died.

Hachiko **didn't know** what to do. He **looked** everywhere for Ueno. He **was** very sad, and he **missed** his master a lot. Every day for nine years he **went** to the train station and **waited** for his master's return. After a while people at the station **noticed** the dog and **began** to bring him food. They **admired** his loyalty. In 1934 they **hired** a well-known sculptor to build a statue of Hachiko. Hachiko **was** there when the statue was unveiled. A year later, in 1935, Hachiko **died**.

After Hachiko's death, Ueno's students **wrote** articles about the amazing dog. People **wrote** books about him. In 2004 Leslie Newman **wrote** and Machiyo Kodaira **illustrated** *Hachiko Waits*. This book **received** many awards. In 2009 Richard Gere **starred** in a movie based on Hachiko's life.

These days when people are near the Shibuya train station in Tokyo, they often say, "Let's meet at the statue of Hachiko!"

One thing is certain. Hachiko's life will not be forgotten.

---

[1]**cerebral hemorrhage:** bleeding in the brain

After You Read

A | Practice *PAIRS: Now read the article aloud. Take turns reading each paragraph.*

B | Vocabulary *Circle the letter of the best meaning for the words in blue.*

1. I **noticed** that he had a good memory.
   a. forgot
   b. saw

2. When I'm away from home, I **miss** my brothers.
   a. wish to be with
   b. don't think about

3. He **illustrated** a children's book.
   a. wrote
   b. drew pictures for

4. The movie **is based on** the book.
   a. comes from ideas in
   b. is different from

5. I **admire** his ability in art. He is a very good sculptor.
   a. think highly of
   b. admit

6. There is a stone **statue** of our first president in front of the park.
   a. figure that looks like a person
   b. painting that looks like a person

C | Comprehension *Read the questions. Circle the correct letter.*

1. What kind of dog is Hachiko?
   a. a Collie
   b. an Akita Inu

2. What did Hachiko's master do?
   a. He was a professor.
   b. He was a train conductor.

3. When was Hachiko born?
   a. in 1934
   b. in 1923

4. Where did Hachiko wait for his master every evening?
   a. at the university
   b. at the train station

5. What did Hachiko do after Ueno died?
   a. He waited for Ueno at the train station.
   b. He looked for Ueno at the university.

6. Why did people admire Hachiko?
   a. He was loyal and patient.
   b. He was strong and powerful.

7. What is *Hachiko Waits*?
   a. a story based on Hachiko's life
   b. a TV show based on Hachiko's life

THE SIMPLE PAST

Affirmative Statements (All Verbs Except *Be*)

Subject	Verb	
I	stayed	home.
We	went	

Affirmative Statements with *Be*

Subject	Verb	
I	was	at home.
We	were	

Negative Statements (All Verbs Except *Be*)

Subject	*Did Not (Didn't)*	Base Form of Verb	
I	did not	stay	with them.
We	didn't	go	

Negative Statements with *Be*

Subject	Verb	
I	was not wasn't	at work.
We	were not weren't	

Yes / No Questions (All Verbs Except *Be*)

Did	Subject	Base Form of Verb
Did	she	leave?
	they	

Yes / No Questions with *Be*

Was / Were	Subject	
Was	he	home last night?
Were	they	

Wh- Questions (All Verbs Except *Be*)

Wh- Word	*Did*	Subject	Base Form of Verb
When		you	arrive?
Where		he	work?
How	did	it	begin?
Why		he	leave?
Who(m)		they	help?

Wh- Questions with *Be*

Wh- Word	Past Form	Subject	
When		she	there?
Where	was	he	from?
How		his	tests?
Why	were	you	late?
Who(m)		they	with?

Wh- Questions About the Subject (All Verbs Except *Be*)

Wh- Word	Past Form	
Who	walked	to the station?
What	happened	to him?
How many people	waited	there?

Wh- Questions About the Subject with *Be*

Wh- Word	Past Form	
Who		his friend?
What	was	his last name?
How many people	were	there?

GRAMMAR NOTES

1	Use the **simple past** to tell about **something that happened in the past**. For all verbs except *be*, the simple past form is the same for all persons.	• **He liked** that book. • **We liked** that book. • **I liked** that book.
2	**Regular verbs** end in *-d*, *-ed*, or *-ied*. Many common verbs are **irregular** in the past.	• They **noticed** the dog. • He **missed** his master. • He **worried** about him. • She **wrote** a book. • He **had** a special dog.
3	For **negative statements** use *did not (didn't)* + **the base form of the verb**.	• He **did not know** him. • He **didn't know** him.

4	For *yes / no* questions use *Did* + subject + the base form of the verb.

	DID	SUBJECT	BASE FORM	
•	**Did**	you	**see**	the dog?
•	**Did**	they	**go**	to work?

5	Most *wh-* **questions** use a *wh-* question word and *yes / no* question order.

	WH- WORD	DID	SUBJECT	BASE FORM	
•	**What**	did	he	do?	
•	**Where**	did	she	go?	
•	**Who**	did	he	marry?	
•	**How**	did	he	do	it?

6	**Questions about the subject** use statement word order. They do not use *did*.

	SUBJECT	VERB		SUBJECT	
•	**Who helped** him? His **friend** did.
	Not: Who ~~did~~ helped him?
	Not: Who ~~did help~~ him?

7	The verb *be* has **different forms** from all other verbs.	**STATEMENTS** • He **was** happy. • They **weren't** happy. **QUESTIONS** • **Was** he in a movie? • **Were** you in the audience? • Where **were** they? Who **was** on TV? Not: ~~Did they were~~ famous? Not: He was ~~be~~ a loyal dog.
	BE CAREFUL! Do not use *did* or the base form of the verb for questions or negative statements with *be*.	

REFERENCE NOTES

For a more complete discussion of the past, see Unit 3, page 28, Unit 18, page 201, Unit 19, page 211, and Unit 20, page 222.

For more about the past of *be*, see Unit 2, page 17.

For a list of irregular verbs see Appendix 11, page A-11.

For pronunciation and spelling rules for the simple past of regular verbs, see Appendix 10, pages A-10–A-11.

EXERCISE 1: Discover the Grammar

Read the conversation. Then write the sentences (both statements and questions) that use the past on the lines below.

BORIS: Who's the man in the picture?

TEACHER: George Washington. He was the first president of the United States.

BORIS: When was that?

TEACHER: He became the president in 1789.

RODRICA: How long was he president?

TEACHER: For eight years.

RODRICA: Was he a good leader?

TEACHER: Yes, he was. And before he became president, he led the army during the American Revolution.

BEKIR: He sounds a lot like Ataturk. Kemal Ataturk was the father of modern Turkey. He was also a great soldier and leader. He gave Turkey many things including a modern alphabet. Now spelling is easy in Turkish.

TEACHER: Well, George Washington didn't do anything about the English alphabet. Spelling is still hard in English.

EUN YOUNG: King Sejong gave Korea an alphabet. He was one of Korea's greatest leaders.

JOSÉ: In South America, Simón Bolívar led many countries to independence. He didn't change our alphabet, but spelling is not so hard in Spanish.

Sentences with *Be* in the Past

1. George Washington was the first president of the United States.

2. _____

3. _____

4. _____

5. _____

6. _____

7. _____

Sentences with Other Verbs in the Past

1. He became the president in 1789.

2. _____

3. _____

4. _____

5. _____

6. _____

7. _____

EXERCISE 2: Affirmative and Negative Statements

(Grammar Notes 1–2, 7)

Complete the paragraph with the words in parentheses. Use the correct form of the simple past.

Pierre Omidyar _____was born_____ in Paris, France. His parents
                    1. (be / born)

_____were_____ from Iran. His mother _____was_____
        2. (be)   3. (be)

a professor, and his father _____practiced_____ medicine. His
                                4. (practice)

family _____moved_____ to the United States when Omidyar
            5. (move)

_____turned_____ six years old. He _____went_____ into the
        6. (turn)   7. (go)

field of computer science. At age 28, Omidyar _____wrote_____
                                                    8. (write)

the computer code for eBay. eBay _____became_____ extremely
                                      9. (become)

successful. In July 2008, eBay _____had_____ shares that were
                                    10. (have)

worth $4.45 billion. In 2004 Omidyar _____started_____ the Omidyar Foundation. In
                                          11. (start)

2005, Omidyar and his wife _____gave_____ $100 million to the foundation. The money
                                12. (give)

will help poor people in developing countries. In 2010, Omidyar _____joined_____
                                                                      13. (join)

40 billionaires. They all _____promised_____ to give away at least half of their money
                              14. (promise)

before they die.

EXERCISE 3: Affirmative and Negative Statements

(Grammar Notes 1–3, 7)

Read the article. Complete the sentences with the words in parentheses. Use the correct form of the simple past.

Recluse Leaves Millions

Anne Schreiber _____was_____ a recluse. Recluses live apart from other people.
                    1. (be)

Anne Schreiber never _____married_____. She also never _____had_____ close friends.
                          2. (marry)   3. (have)

She _____lived_____ alone in a tiny studio apartment and _____wore_____ the same
        4. (live)   5. (wear)

outfit every day—a black coat and a black hat. For many years she _____worked_____
                                                                        6. (work)

for the tax department of the U.S. government. She _____was_____ an auditor. She
                                                        7. (be)

_____made_____ sure people paid their taxes. However, she _____didn't like_____ to pay
    8. (make)   9. (like / not)

taxes. She _____didn't like_____ to pay for anything.
                10. (like / not)

(continued on next page)

As a young woman, Anne ____followed____ the suggestions of a brother and
11. (follow)

____invested____ all her money in his company. His company ____went____
12. (invest)   13. (go)

bankrupt, and she ____lost____ her life savings. She ___didn't forgive___ her
14. (lose)   15. (forgive / not)

brother. Anne ____started____ investing again in 1944 when she ____was____
16. (start)   17. (be)

49 years old. This time she ____used____ her own ideas. By investing well, she
18. (use)

____turned____ $5,000 into $22,000,000. She ____did____ better than the biggest
19. (turn)   20. (do)

businessmen. But she ___did not go___ her relatives to know she had so much money
21. (want / not)

because she ___didn't go___ to give them any of it. And she didn't. Anne Schreiber
22. (want / not)

____died____ in 1995 at the age of 101. She ____left____ her money to
23. (die)   24. (leave)

universities to help poor, bright women get an education.

EXERCISE 4: Simple Past: Questions and Answers   (Grammar Notes 1–7)

A | *Read the article. On the next page, write **wh-** questions that the underlined words answer.*

When you think of basketball, do you think of Michael

Jordan, LeBron James, Shaquille O'Neal . . . or Dr. James

Naismith? Dr. Naismith? Who was he? What did he do for

basketball?

James Naismith was born <u>in Ontario, Canada</u>, <u>in 1861</u>.
                                    1.   2.

He was a good athlete and a good student. He always

loved <u>school</u>.
       3.

Dr. Naismith earned <u>four</u> degrees, including one in medicine. But his biggest
                        4.

contribution to the world did not come from his work as a

medical doctor. <u>In the winter of 1891</u> he worked as a gym
                              5.

instructor in Massachusetts. where

His students were <u>active and hard to control</u>. He wanted them
                         6.

to play an indoor sport <u>because it was too cold to play outdoors</u>.
                                        7.

He invented the game of <u>basketball</u>. It became an instant success
                              8.

Basketball team around 1900

in the United States. Soon it spread to other countries.

1. <u>*Where was James Naismith born?*</u>
2. <u>when was James Naismith born?</u>
3. <u>what did he always love?</u>
4. <u>How many did he earhe?</u>
5. <u>When did he work as a gym instructor?</u> in Massachusetts
6. <u>How were has students</u>
7. <u>why did he want?</u>
8. What game <u>did he invettet?</u> ?

B | *Write* **yes** / **no** *questions about James Naismith with the given words. Use the correct form. Then write short answers.*

1. be / he good at sports?

   Q: <u>*Was he good at sports?*</u>

   A: <u>*Yes, he was.*</u>

2. be / he a good student?

   Q: <u>Was he a good student?</u>

   A: <u>Yes, he was.</u>

3. he / finish college?

   Q: <u>Did he finish college?</u>

   A: <u>Yes, he did.</u>

4. he / become a lawyer?

   Q: <u>Did he become a lawyer?</u>

   A: <u>No, he didn't</u>

5. he / invent the game of volleyball?

   Q: <u>Did he invent the game of volleyball?</u>

   A: <u>No, he Didn't</u>

EXERCISE 5: Editing

Correct the conversation. There are eleven mistakes. The first mistake is already corrected. Find and correct ten more.

1. **Q:** Who ^was^ Elizabeth Blackwell?

   A: She was the first woman physician in the United States.

2. **Q:** Where she was born?

   A: She was born in England.

3. **Q:** When was she born?

   A: She ^was^ born in 1821.

4. **Q:** When she did come to the United States?

   A: She did ^came^ come to the United States in 1833.

5. **Q:** Was it hard for her to become a doctor?

   A: Yes, it ~~were~~ ^was^. Most medical schools didn't want women.

6. **Q:** How ~~was~~ ^were^ her grades in medical school?

   A: She was an outstanding student. Her grades were excellent.

7. **Q:** When ^did^ she graduate?

   A: In 1849.

8. **Q:** What did Dr. Blackwell fight for?

   A: She did ^fought~~fight~~ for the admission of women to medical schools.

9. **Q:** Where did she ^go~~goes~~ in 1869?

   A: She returned to London. She worked and wrote there for many years.

10. **Q:** When ^did^ she die?

    A: She died in 1910.

STEP 4 COMMUNICATION PRACTICE

EXERCISE 6: Pronunciation

A | *Read and listen to the Pronunciation Note.*

> **Pronunciation Note**
>
> The words **work** and **walk** are sometimes hard to pronounce correctly. Listen to the difference between the vowel sound / ɜ / in *work* and / ɔ / in *walk*. Also remember the / kt / ending in words like **work**ed and **walk**ed is one sound.

B | *Listen and repeat the words.*

work   works   worked   walk   walks   walked

C | *Listen to the sentences and repeat.*

1. I walked fast.   **3.** Do you walk after school?   **5.** Who works with you?

2. I worked fast.   **4.** Do you work after school?   **6.** Who walks with you?

EXERCISE 7: Listening

A | *Two people are watching TV. Listen to their conversation. Then circle the letter of the correct answer to the question.*

What kind of a TV show are they watching?
    a. a quiz show   **b.** a talk show

B | *Listen again. Complete the questions. Write the answers.*

1. Q: Who _____*painted*_____ *The Night Watch*?   **A:** Rembrandt.

2. Q: In what century _____?   **A:** The _____ century.

3. Q: Where _____?   **A:** In _____.

4. Q: What is _____?   **A:** Rembrandt van Rijn.

5. Q: Who _____ Yoko Ono?   **A:** _____

6. Q: What _____ of John
Lennon's _____?   **A:** _____

7. Q: Where _____?   **A:** _____

8. Q: When _____ their last
appearance together?   **A:** _____

EXERCISE 8: A Quiz Show

SMALL GROUPS: Prepare a quiz show. On a separate piece of paper, write questions in the past. Choose a host or hostess from your group. Choose classmates in other groups to be contestants.

EXAMPLES: Who starred in the *Twilight* movies?
What was the *Titanic*?
Who wrote *One Hundred Years of Solitude*?

EXERCISE 9: What Were You Like As a Child?

PAIRS: Ask your partner what he or she was like as a child. Use boxes A and B for ideas.

EXAMPLE: **A:** When you were a child, were you talkative?
B: Yes. Once my teacher wrote a note to my mother, "Bernie never stops talking. He's smart, but he needs to give other children a turn." What about you? What were you like? Did you study hard?
A: No, I didn't. I began to study hard in high school.

A: Were you _____ ?	B: Did you _____ ?
athletic / uninterested in sports	study hard
naughty / well behaved	listen to your parents
stubborn / easygoing	watch a lot of TV
talkative / quiet / shy	play a lot of computer games
cheerful / moody	like music / art / dance

EXERCISE 10: Information Gap: Guess the Musician

Work in pairs (A and B). Student A, follow the instructions on this page. Student B, turn to page 246 and follow the instructions there.

1. Read about the life of the musician Ray Charles. Do not tell your partner his name. Your partner will ask you questions about the person and guess. Answer your partner's questions.

> He was born in Albany, Georgia, in 1930. His family was very poor. He became blind at the age of seven. He learned to read Braille and play music at the St. Augustine School for the Deaf and the Blind in Florida. His mother died when he was a teenager. He left school at 15 and began his career as a musician. He moved to Seattle and started his rise to fame. He started out as a jazz and blues pianist and singer, but over more than 50 years he built a career that combined many types of music. In 2004, he died in Beverly Hills, California. He was 73 years old.

2. Now you will ask your partner questions about a different musician. First, write questions with the words given and the simple past.

1. When / he / born <u>*When was he born?*</u>

2. Where / he / born _____

3. What / he / teach himself to play _____

4. Where / he / begin his career _____

5. Who / discover him _____

6. Where / be / he from 1958 to 1960 _____

7. What / he / appear in after that _____

8. When / die _____

3. Ask your partner the questions from Part 2 and then guess who the musician is.

EXERCISE 11: Writing

A | *Write a short biography of a musician. Use the simple past. Read your biography to a partner.*

B | *Check your work. Use the Editing Checklist.*

Editing Checklist

Did you . . . ?
☐ use the simple past correctly
☐ check your spelling

1. You will ask your partner questions about a musician. First, write questions about the person. Use the words given and the simple past.

   1. Where / be / born _Where was he born?_____

   2. When / he born _____

   3. What / happened to him at the age of seven _____

   4. Where / he / go to school _____

   5. What / he / learn at school _____

   6. Where / he / move _____

   7. How many years / he / be / in the music business _____

   8. When / he / die _____

2. Ask your partner the questions from Part 1 and then guess who the musician is.

3. Now read about the life of the musician Elvis Presley. Do not tell your partner his name. Your partner will ask you questions about the person and guess. Answer your partner's questions.

> He was a popular singer. He was born in Tupelo, Mississippi, in 1935. He began singing in a local church, and he taught himself to play the guitar. Sam Phillips, the president of Sun Records, discovered him in 1953. By 1956 he was the most popular performer in the United States. Soon after that he became popular all over the world. His music combined country and western music with rhythm and blues. He spent two years, from 1958 to 1960, in the army. He appeared in several movies, but none were very successful. He died in 1977. He is known as the King of Rock and Roll.

A | Complete the sentences with the verbs in parentheses. Use the correct form and the simple past.

1. Craig Newmark ___was born___ on December 6, 1952.
   (be born)
2. He ___grew up___ in New Jersey.
   (grow up)
3. He ___attended___ Morristown High School.
   (attend)
4. He ___went___ to college in Ohio.
   (go)
5. In 1995 he ___started___ an email list.
   (start)
6. It ___became___ a Web-based service in 1996.
   (become)
7. It ___expanded___, and today almost everyone knows about Craigslist®.
   (expand)

B | Write questions with the words in parentheses. Use the simple past.

1. ___When did go to college?___
   (when / she / go to college)
2. ___who did they meet?___
   (who / they / meet)
3. ___where did he study?___
   (where / he study)
4. ___How long did they live in canada?___
   (how long / they live in Canada)

C | Complete the questions with **be** or **do**. Use the correct form and the simple past.

1. ___were___ you late yesterday?
2. ___Did___ they work last night?
3. ___was___ he at the park with his son?
4. ___Did___ she marry him?
5. ___Did___ he move?

D | Correct the paragraph. There are four mistakes.

   Steve Paul Jobs did start college in 1970, but he no did finish it. In 1976 Jobs and his friend begin to make their own computers. They worked in the Jobs' garage. That was the beginning of Apple® Computers. Their company become a big success. Apple® changed the field of computers, and by the age of 30, Jobs was a multimillionaire.

Gerunds and Infinitives

CAREERS AND ABILITIES

Before You Read

Look at the photos. Why do people choose a particular career? For example, why do people become fashion designers, makeup artists, or models? Would you like these jobs? Or others?

Read

To get the right job and be successful, you need to know yourself. Read these people's comments and the jobs that match their needs.

1. **I like to learn new things. I hope to continue** learning throughout my career.

doctor	software developer
scientist	teacher

2. **I enjoy working** with my hands.

auto mechanic	chef
carpenter	farmer

3. I don't like routine work. I **expect to do** something different every day. I don't like things to be predictable.

actress   musician
fire fighter   police officer

4. I'm very competitive. I **hate losing**. People say I have a type A personality.

attorney   politician
investment banker   professional athlete

5. I love the outdoors. I **can't stand wearing** a suit. I **avoid wearing** formal clothes.

anthropologist   gardener
farmer   park ranger

6. I **enjoy interacting** with people. I **love helping** them with their problems.

hotel manager   psychologist
physical therapist social worker

A | Practice *PAIRS: Now read the comments aloud. Take turns reading the comments.*

B | Vocabulary *Circle the letter of the best meaning for the words in blue.*

1. He's not good at math. He **avoids** working with numbers.
   a. tries not to   b. is afraid of

2. He **can't stand** speaking with angry customers.
   a. is good at   b. hates

3. He always does the same thing. He's **predictable**.
   a. not surprising; expected   b. suprising

4. Everyone likes her. She has a pleasant **personality**.
   a. way of behaving   b. way of smiling

5. She needs **formal** clothes for her brother's graduation and her sister's wedding.
   a. dresses   b. dress clothes

6. He hates losing. He's **competitive**.
   a. wants to play sports   b. wants to win

C | Comprehension *Read the descriptions. Circle the letter of the career that **doesn't** belong.*

1. You expect to make a lot of money. You always want to win.
   a. lawyer   b. investment banker   c. social worker

2. You often need to wear a suit.
   a. banker   b. farmer   c. lawyer

3. You're a "people person." You enjoy interacting with others.
   a. teacher   b. physical therapist   c. computer programmer

4. Your work routine changes every day.
   a. chef   b. artist   c. actress

5. You don't wear formal clothes at work.
   a. teacher   b. carpenter   c. politician

GERUNDS AND INFINITIVES

Subject	Verb	Gerund (Verb + -ing)
I	**enjoy**	**dancing**.

Subject	Verb	Infinitive
She	**wants**	**to sing**.

Subject	Verb	Infinitive or Gerund
They	**like**	**driving**.
		to drive.

Verb + Gerund	Verb + Infinitive		Verb + Infinitive or Gerund
avoid	agree	refuse	hate
enjoy	decide	want	like
finish	expect		continue
keep	hope		love
keep on	intend		prefer
regret	need		try
think about	plan		

GRAMMAR NOTES

1	A **gerund** is a noun that is formed by the **base form of a verb** + **-ing**. Some verbs, such as *enjoy*, *finish*, and *keep*, can be followed by a gerund.	• I **enjoy singing**. • We **finished studying** at 8:00. • She **keeps asking** about the job.
2	An **infinitive** is **to** + **the base form of the verb**. Some verbs, such as *want* and *need*, can be followed by an infinitive.	• I **want to work**. • She **needs to write** a résumé. • He **wants** to change jobs.
3	Some verbs, such as *like* and *hate*, can be followed by a gerund (*-ing* form) or an infinitive (*to* + base form).	• I **like writing**. • I **like to write**.

EXERCISE 1: Discover the Grammar

Write **I** *(verb + infinitive)* or **G** *(verb + gerund) for each statement.*

G **1.** I enjoy working with people.   *G* **5.** I avoid wearing a suit.

I **2.** He needs to get a job.   *I* **6.** He refused to work late.

I **3.** She prefers to work at night.   *I* **7.** They hope to move in July.

G **4.** I prefer working in the daytime.   *G* **8.** They finished eating at 10:00.

EXERCISE 2: Infinitives   *(Grammar Note 2)*

Complete the sentences with the words from the box. Use infinitives.

| complete | ~~find~~ | leave | ~~move~~ | ~~send~~ | ~~work~~ |

1. John's looking for a job. He hopes _____ *to find* _____ a job in this city.

2. He likes this city. He doesn't want *to more* _____ away.

3. He sees his friends every weekend. He refuses *to work* _____ on weekends.

4. He plans *to send* _____ out some letters of application this afternoon.

5. In two years he intends *to leave* _____ his job and go to business school.

6. He hopes *to complete* _____ his M.B.A. in four years.

EXERCISE 3: Gerunds   *(Grammar Note 1)*

Complete the sentences with the words from the box. Use gerunds.

| ~~apply~~ | ~~do~~ | go | ~~leave~~ | ~~take~~ | ~~work~~ |

1. He finished _____ *taking* _____ final exams last week.

2. He is thinking about _____ *applying* _____ for a part-time job for the summer.

3. He enjoys _____ *doing* _____ sales work.

4. He doesn't like _____ *working* _____ with his hands.

5. He regretted _____ *leaving* _____ his part-time job, but he needed time to study.

6. He avoided _____ *going* _____ out with friends for a month before his final exams.

EXERCISE 4: Gerunds and Infinitives

(Grammar Notes 1–3)

Complete the conversation. Use gerunds or infinitives with the verbs in parentheses.
One verb can be used with both a gerund or an infinitive.

ELENA: Do you enjoy _____*acting*_____?
　　　　　　　　　　　　1. (act)

JULIAN: Yes. I love ___*acting*___. *to act.*
　　　　　　　　　　　2. (act)

ELENA: Is it hard to find work as an actor?

JULIAN: Very hard. Many people want ___*to become*___ actors. You need
　　　　　　　　　　　　　　　　　　　3. (become)

　　　___*to have*___ talent, patience, and luck.
　　　　　4. (have)

ELENA: Do you ever want ___*to change*___ careers? Do you ever regret
　　　　　　　　　　　　　　5. (change)

　　　___*spending*___ so much time
　　　　6. (spend)

looking for work?

JULIAN: No. I refuse ___*to give up*___.
　　　　　　　　　　　7. (give up)

my dream. I keep

___*I trying out*___ for new parts.
　　　8. (try out)

I think I'm a great actor, and

I plan ___*to show*___ the
　　　　9. (show)

world!

Actors trying out for a role

EXERCISE 5: Gerunds and Infinitives

(Grammar Notes 1–2)

Complete the sentences with the words from the box. Use infinitives and gerunds.

~~get~~	~~look~~	meet	study	~~tell~~	~~work~~

1. Do you enjoy ___*working*___ with children?

2. Do you plan ___*to get*___ an advanced degree?

3. He hoped ___*to meet*___ with the president of the company. Instead he met with

   the vice president.

4. I regret ___*telling*___ him about my problem with my previous employer.

5. He keeps ___*looking*___ at his watch. I hope he isn't bored.

6. Many people decide ___*to study*___ law after watching courtroom dramas.

EXERCISE 6: Editing

Correct the letter. There are seven mistakes. The first mistake is already corrected.
Find and correct six more.

35 Main Street, Apt. 6
New Hope, New Jersey 07675

May 27, 2012

Head Librarian
Kennedy Library
7 West Street
New Hope, New Jersey 07675

To Whom It May Concern:

I want *to* apply for a part-time job at Kennedy Library. I am in my senior year of high school.

I expect *to* attend State College next year, and I plan to majoring in library science. I enjoy *to*

read and *to* work with the public. I'm good at computers, and I like *to* keep things in order.

I've enclosed a résumé. I hope *to* hearing from you soon.

Sincerely,

Joe Reed

STEP 4 COMMUNICATION PRACTICE

EXERCISE 7: Pronunciation

A | *Read and listen to the Pronunciation Note.*

> **Pronunciation Note**
>
> ***Of*** is usually pronounced with the unstressed sound / əv / . When *of* comes
> after a consonant sound, we link the consonant with *of*.
>
> **EXAMPLE:**　out of ice cream

B | *Listen and repeat.*

1. out of town
2. out of everything
3. out of juice
4. out of eggs
5. out of order

C | *PAIRS: Answer the questions. Use the phrases in Part B.*

1. **A:** Do we have any orange or grape juice?

   B: No, we're _____.

2. **A:** Does the copy machine work?

   B: No, it's _____.

3. **A:** Is he in town?

   B: No he's _____.

4. **A:** Do we have any eggs?

   B: No, we're _____.

5. **A:** Where are you going?

   B: Shopping for food. We're _____.

EXERCISE 8: Listening

A | *Listen to a conversation between two friends. When do the friends meet?*

    a. every week   **b.** for the first time in years

B | *Listen again. Write **T** (**True**) or **F** (**False**) for each statement. Change the false statements to make them true.*

_____ **1.** Ken plans to go back to school for more training.

_____ **2.** Cindy got tired of working for a big company.

_____ **3.** Cindy plans to write a book.

_____ **4.** Cindy enjoys planning conventions.

_____ **5.** Cindy likes to work with animals.

_____ **6.** Ken wants to have lunch with Cindy on Saturday.

EXERCISE 9: Discussion: Likes

PAIRS: For each category, write something that you enjoy doing. Then tell your partner. Use infinitives and gerunds. Your partner then agrees or tells about something he or she prefers.

    EXAMPLE: **A:** I like playing golf.
                     B: I do too. OR I prefer to play tennis.

1. sports: _____*golf*_____   **3.** books: _____   **5.** desserts: _____

2. movies: _____   **4.** music: _____   **6.** cars: _____

EXERCISE 10: Game: What Do I Do?

SMALL GROUPS: Each group thinks of an occupation and gives the other groups hints. Use only the verbs in the chart on page 251.

> EXAMPLE: MOHAMMED: You want to help people.
> TATIANA: You need to study for many years.
> HECTOR: (Student from another group): Are you thinking about a doctor?
> MOHAMMED: Yes, we are.

EXERCISE 11: Problem Solving: Finding the Right Job

PAIRS: Ask your partner the questions. Talk about possible jobs.

- Do you enjoy working with people?
- Do you want to make a difference in the world?
- Do you want to be rich?
- Do you dislike traveling?
- Do you want to be famous?
- Do you want a safe job (one that you can keep when times are bad)?
- Do you want to help others?
- Do you like to "do your own thing"?

EXERCISE 12: Writing

A | *Write about your future career goals. Use gerunds and infinitives.*

> EXAMPLE: I enjoy window shopping and studying all the latest fashions. I also love to draw. I hope to combine my two passions and become a fashion designer. I plan to study art and fashion in college this year. I hope to get an internship with a design company in the summer. I expect to graduate in four years. In 10 years I hope to have my own fashion design business.

B | *Check your work. Use the Editing Checklist.*

Editing Checklist

Did you . . . ?
- ☐ use infinitives and gerunds correctly
- ☐ check your spelling

22 Review

Check your answers on page UR-5.
Do you need to review anything?

A | Underline the correct words to complete the sentences.

1. Do you regret **to start** / **starting** a business?

2. I hope **to sell** / **selling** my business next year.

3. She decided **to return** / **returning** to school.

4. She hopes **to become** / **becoming** a pilot.

5. She enjoys **to fly** / **flying** and **to see** / **seeing** the world.

6. Her parents plan **to help** / **helping** her reach her goal.

B | Complete the sentences with the words in parentheses. Use the correct form.

1. She doesn't want _to work_ evenings.
   (work)

2. Her boss refuses _to change_ her hours.
   (change)

3. She's thinking about _quitting_ her job and _going_ back to
   (quit)   **(go)**
   school.

4. She wants _to study_ computer science.
   (study)

5. She enjoys _doing_ Web design.
   (do)

C | Correct the paragraph. There are eight mistakes.

Carol volunteers at a hospital. She enjoys to take care of patients. Some patients

refuse to do exercise, but Carol keeps to push them. Carol intends to study physical therapy

in college. She needs taking a lot of science courses. She expects to went to college

next fall. She hopes get a degree in physical therapy in five years. She prefers to

working with teenagers, but she will work with adults too.

Simple Present, Present Progressive, and Simple Past

CREATIVITY

STEP 1 GRAMMAR IN CONTEXT

Before You Read

A | *GROUPS: What can you do with the items below? Write as many ideas as you can. Be as creative as possible.*

aluminum foil   **hairdryer**   **straws**   **Ziploc® bag**

EXAMPLE: You can wrap your hair with aluminum foil to make it curly.

B | *Share your ideas with the class. Now vote. Which ideas were the most interesting?*

Read

Read the online article about creativity.

| ARTS | SCIENCE | POLITICS | TECHNOLOGY | SEARCH: |

What does it **mean** to be creative? To be creative **means** to see things in a new way. New inventions often **come** from old ideas. **Do** you **know** a new invention that **came** from an older one?

Glue **is** a very old invention, from 250,000 B.C., but Krazy Glue® **is** a new kind of glue. It **is** extremely strong. In fact, it **can glue** your fingers together. Dr. Harry Coover **invented** this kind of glue in 1942. He **wanted** to use it for airplanes, but it **didn't work**. Later, in 1962, scientists **realized** they could use the glue in surgery.[1] They **used** it to save lives in wars. Nowadays doctors **are** still **using** a kind of Krazy Glue® during surgery.

How **do** new inventions **come** about? Sometimes, a new invention **is** the result of two old ideas combined. The motorcycle, for example, **is** a combination of a car and bicycle. New inventions can also **happen** over time, in steps. One creative idea **comes** after another, and the invention **changes**— adjustments **take** place—and the invention **improves**. We **see** this in today's computers and phones, which **are changing** all of the time.

Picturephone, 1965

New ideas **do not** always **meet** with public approval at first. Often it **takes** time for people to accept new ways of thinking. In France, in the late 1800s, painters **came up with** a style of painting called Impressionism. At first people **disliked** this art and **rejected** the style, but later they **accepted** and **admired** it. And in this century, the public first **rejected**, and then **began** to accept ebooks.

---
[1] *surgery:* medical treatment in which a doctor cuts open the body to fix or remove something inside

These days we **are learning** more about creativity through a recent invention. The MRI[2] **takes** pictures of the body which **are** more powerful and accurate than X-rays. Scientists **are** now **using** MRIs to study the human brain. MRIs **show** them what happens in the brain when a person **is thinking** creative thoughts. So in the future, we may have a deeper understanding of the creative process. One day scientists may even invent a pill for creativity. Would you try such a pill?

_____
[2] **MRI:** magnetic resonance imaging

After You Read

A | Practice *PAIRS: Now read the article aloud. Take turns reading each paragraph.*

B | Vocabulary *Complete the sentences with the words from the box.*

accepted	came up with	comes after	invented	rejected

1. Who ___came up with___ with the idea for Krazy Glue®?

2. What number ___comes after___ 9,999?

3. At first, they ___rejected___ his suggestion, but later they agreed to it.

4. We ___accepted___ his invitation to the party.

5. Thomas Edison ___invented___ the lightbulb.

C | Comprehension *Read the statements. Write **T** (**True**) or **F** (**False**).*

_____ 1. To be creative means that you are an artist.

_____ 2. Glue is not a new invention.

_____ 3. Krazy Glue® is not used by doctors any more.

_____ 4. Sometimes a new invention is a combination of two older ones.

_____ 5. The art movement Impressionism ended around 1800.

_____ 6. It took people time to like Impressionism.

_____ 7. Scientists are using MRIs to understand the human brain and creativity.

SIMPLE PRESENT

Affirmative Statements			Negative Statements		
Subject	Verb	Time Marker	Subject	Verb	Time Marker
I	**paint**		I	**don't paint**	
He	**paints**	sometimes.	He	**doesn't paint**	often.
They	**paint**		They	**don't paint**	

PRESENT PROGRESSIVE

Affirmative Statements			Negative Statements		
Subject	Verb	Time Marker	Subject	Verb	Time Marker
I	**'m painting**		I	**'m not painting**	
He	**'s painting**	now.	He	**'s not painting** **isn't painting**	now.
They	**'re painting**		They	**'re not painting** **aren't painting**	

SIMPLE PAST

Affirmative Statements			Negative Statements		
Subject	Verb	Time Marker	Subject	Verb	Time Marker
I			I		
He	**painted**	last week.	He	**didn't paint**	last week.
They			They		

GRAMMAR NOTES

1	REMEMBER: Use the **simple present** to tell about **things that happen again and again** or to **tell facts**. Use the simple present with **non-action verbs** even when something is happening now.	• He **goes** to work every day. • Some doctors **use** glue during surgery. • I **like** your idea.
2	REMEMBER: Use the **present progressive** to talk about **an action that is happening now or nowadays**.	• He **is looking** at your MRI now. • Scientists **are studying** the brain these days.
3	REMEMBER: Use the **simple past** to tell about **things that are finished**.	• He **had** a good idea. • At first people **rejected** his work.

STEP 3 FOCUSED PRACTICE

EXERCISE 1: Discover the Grammar

Read the conversation. Underline the present progressive verbs once. Underline the simple present verbs twice. Circle the simple past verbs.

A: What <u>are</u> you <u>doing</u>?

B: I'm <u>looking</u> at a plan of my apartment. It's really tiny. Now with a baby we need more space. I'm trying to redo it.

A: Check out Gary Chang of Hong Kong. He's an architect. He lives in a 333-square-foot apartment, but he divided his small apartment into 24 rooms.

B: Are you kidding?

A: I'm not kidding. I read about it online. And I even saw it on YouTube.™

EXERCISE 2: Simple Present and Simple Past

(Grammar Notes 1, 3)

Complete the conversation with the verbs in parentheses. Use the correct form.

A: When _____*did*_____ you _____*get*_____ a cat?
1. 2. (get)

B: I _____*got*_____ Yume a month ago.
3. (get)

A: She _____*is*_____ cute! But you _____*travel*_____
4. (be) 5. (travel)

a lot for your job. What _____*do*_____ you
6.

_____ when you're away? Who
7. (do)

_____*takes*_____ care of her and _____*feeds*_____ her?
8. (take) 9. (feed)

B: Nobody.

A: What _____*do*_____ you _____*mean*_____?
10. 11. (mean)

B: Take a better look. She's a robotic cat. She

_____*movs*_____ and _____*makts*_____ sounds like a cat, but she's a robot.
12. (move) 13. (make)

A: That's amazing. Where _____*are did*_____ you _____*get*_____ her?
14. 15. (get)

B: She's from Japan. I _____*bugther*_____ her online.
16. (buy)

EXERCISE 3: Simple Present, Present Progressive, and Simple Past (Grammar Notes 1–3)

Complete the paragraph with the verbs in parentheses. Use the correct form.

Where _____*do*_____ new ideas _____*come*_____ from? Sometimes they
1. 2. (come)

_____*comes*_____ from the world of science fiction.
3. (come)

Mary and Bill _____*are*_____ on a train now. They _____*are using*_____ their laptop
4. (be) 5. (use)

computers on their way to work. Mary and Bill _____*arewit*_____ unusual. Millions of
6. (be / not)

people _____*have*_____ laptops and _____*uses*_____ them on their way to work.
7. (have) 8. (use)

The laptop computer _____*didn't exist*_____ in the 1970s. However, in 1977 James Hogan
9. (exist / not)

_____*write*_____ about one in *Inherit the Stars*. In this science fiction book, Hogan
10. (write)

_____*descriibs*_____ a small computer that fit into a briefcase.
11. (describe)

Now Mary and Bill _____*are entering*_____ their office building. The office doors
12. (enter)

_____*open*_____ automatically. In 1899 doors _____*didn't open*_____ automatically. But
13. (open) 14. (not / open)

H. G. Wells _____*write*_____ about such doors in his novel *When the Sleeper Wakes*.
15. (write)

These are just two examples in which science fiction showed us the future.

EXERCISE 4: Editing

Correct the paragraph. There are seven mistakes. The first mistake is already corrected.
Find and correct six more.

Jay Leno is a comedian. He also ~~love~~ *loves* to collect cars. One of his cars needs *does* not gas. It's a Baker electric car. Baker invent an electric car in 1909. In the early 1900s, electric cars was popular in the United States. Then Henry Ford did produce inexpensive cars that used gas. People stopped buying electric cars. But nowadays people is trying to keep the air clean. So electric cars are become popular once again.

STEP 4 COMMUNICATION PRACTICE

EXERCISE 5: Listening

A | *Listen to a talk about X-rays. Then circle the correct letter.*

Doctors, dentists, and _____ use X-rays.

    a. airline companies   **b.** baggage companies   **c.** airplane manufacturers

B | *Listen again. Read the questions. Circle the correct letter.*

1. Where was Wilhelm Roentgen from?

    a. Germany   **b.** Austria

2. When did he discover X-rays?

    a. 1859   **b.** 1895

3. Whose hand did he first X-ray?

    a. his hand   **b.** his wife's hand

4. How did people learn about X-rays?

    a. from Roentgen   **b.** from newspapers

5. What did Roentgen win?

    a. the Nobel Prize   **b.** the Pulitzer Prize

6. What did Roentgen's friends tell him to call X-rays?

    a. X-rays   **b.** Roentgen rays

EXERCISE 6: Pronunciation

A | *Read and listen to the Pronunciation Note.*

B | *Listen and repeat these compound nouns.*

1. bike trip
2. office building
3. houseboat
4. motorbike
5. library book
6. wedding ring

C | *PAIRS: Student A, choose a sentence. Student B, say the compound noun Student A is thinking of. Remember to stress the first noun. Take turns.*

EXAMPLE: **A:** I'm thinking of a trip by bicycle.
             B: A bike trip.

1. I'm thinking of a building with offices.
2. I'm thinking of a bicycle with a motor.
3. I'm thinking of book you can borrow from the library.
4. I'm thinking of a ring you wear when you are married.

EXERCISE 7: Information Gap

Work in pairs (A and B). **Student A,** *follow the instructions on this page.* **Student B,** *turn to page 266. Follow the instructions on that page.*

turn to page 266

1. Ask your partner questions to complete your chart.

EXAMPLE: **Student A:** Who invented the ATM?
             Student B: Don Wetzel invented the ATM.
             Student A: When did he invent it?
             Student B: In 1968.
             Student A: Where is he from?
             Student B: He's from the United States.

Invention	Inventor	Year	Country
ATM	Don Wetzel	1968	United States
credit card			
dishwasher			
eyeglasses			
fork			
paper money			
subway			
YouTube™			

2. Now your partner will ask you questions. Answer the questions with information from the chart.

Answers to Student B's Questions

Invention	Inventor	Year	Country
bicycle	Baron Karl von Drais de Sauerbrun	1818	Germany
disposable diapers	Marion Donovan	1950	U.S.
mirror (glass)	the Venetians	c. 1200	Italy
paper	Ts'ai Lun	c. 105	China
pencil	Conrad Gessner	1565	Switzerland
satellite	Soviet Space program	1957	Russia
thermometer	Galileo	1592	Italy
World Wide Web	Tim Berners-Lee	1989	U.K.

3. GROUPS: Talk about the inventions. Are they still good? Are there newer and better inventions?

EXERCISE 8: Writing

A | *Imagine you are living in the future. Choose the year. Write about life in that year. Write about something you're doing now and something you did. Include the simple present, present progressive, and simple past.*

EXAMPLES: It's 3010. As usual the weather is sunny and 65 degrees. It never rains or snows. Sometimes people complain. They say, "We want some bad weather."

I live in France, but I go to school in Spain. Right now I'm flying to school in my new aeromobile. It's a lot of fun. I'm flying across the border and looking at the beautiful mountains below.

Last month two exciting things happened. On the first of the month, scientists announced a cure for the cold. Finally. On the 15th of last month, my great granddad celebrated his 150th birthday. The whole family met, and we had a party for him in his new home on the bottom of the ocean.

B | *Check your work. Use the Editing Checklist.*

Editing Checklist

Did you . . . ?

☐ use correct forms of the simple present, present progressive, and simple past

☐ check your spelling

---

1. Your partner will ask you questions. Answer the questions with information from the chart.

Answers to Student A's Questions

Invention	Inventor	Year	Country
ATM	Don Wetzel	1968	U.S.
credit card	Frank McNamara, Ralph Schneider	1950	U.S.
dishwasher	Josephine Cochrane	1886	U.S.
eyeglasses	Salvino degli Armati or Alessandro di Spina	1280s	Italy
fork	—	2000 B.C.E.	China
paper money	—	late 900s	China
subway	Sir John Fowler	1863	U.K.
YouTube	Steven Chen, Chad Hurley, and Jawed Karim	2005	U.S.

2. Now ask your partner questions to complete your chart.

EXAMPLE: **Student B:** Who invented the bicycle?
Student A: Baron Karl von Drais de Sauerbrun.
Student B: When did he invent it?
Student A: In 1818.
Student B: Where was he from?
Student A: Germany.

Invention	Inventor	Year	Country
bicycle	Baron Karl von Drais de Sauerbrun	1818	Germany
disposable diapers			
mirror (glass)			
paper			
pencil			
satellite			
thermometer			
World Wide Web			

3. GROUPS: Talk about the inventions. Are they still good? Are there newer and better inventions?

A | Complete the sentences with the verbs in parentheses. Use the simple present, present progressive, or simple past.

1. My brother _is taking_ a sculpture class now.
(take)
2. Each week the students _made_ sculptures out of recycled materials.
(make)
3. Last month he _made_ a sculpture out of soda cans.
(make)
4. He really _likes_ the class.
(like)

B | Complete the paragraph with the verbs in parentheses. Use the simple present, present progressive, or simple past.

Whitcomb Judson _invented_ a zipper in 1893. His zipper
1. (invent)
didne work, and nobody _____ it. Later the B. F. Goodrich
2. (work / not)   3. (want)
company _became_ interested in a zipper for rain shoes, and Judson's zippers
4. (become)
started to sell. Today we still _use_ zippers. Right now factory
5. (start)   6. (use)
workers _are sewing_ zippers in clothes, bags, shoes, and many other things.
7. (sew)

C | Complete the questions with the words in parentheses. Use the correct form.

1. _____
(Where / you / go / last weekend)
2. _____did_____
(How / you / get there)
3. _____did_____
(What / you / see / at the museum)
4. _____was_____
(How / be / the museum)
5. Do, _____
(you / often/ go there)

D | Correct the sentences. There are four mistakes.

1. Last night I did watch~ed~ a movie about fish.

2. The fish were beautiful, and I enjoy~ed~ the movie.

3. My brother is watching the movie now, but he don't _does_ like it.

4. He is only lik~e~ing action films.

From Grammar to Writing

ORGANIZATION: TIME SEQUENCE MARKERS

1 | *Look at these sentences. Which words show the time?*

1. He studies at home in the evening.
2. At present I live on Bleeker Street.

2 | *Study the information about time sequence markers.*

> You can organize your writing by using **time sequence markers**. Some common markers for the time of day are *in the morning*, *in the afternoon*, *in the evening*, and *at night*.
> **EXAMPLE:**
> Monique works **in the morning**.
>
> Some common markers for the past, present, and future are *in the past*, *at present*, and *in the future*.
> **EXAMPLE:**
> **At present**, I'm a student.

3 | *Read this story about a country doctor. Underline the time sequence markers. Then write about a day in the life of someone you know well.*

> Michelle Hirch-Phothong is a country doctor. Her day begins at 6:30 in the morning. At seven o'clock she is at the hospital. She visits her patients and discusses their problems with the nurses and other doctors. Michelle enjoys talking to her patients. She listens carefully and never rushes.
>
> In the afternoon Michelle works at a clinic. The clinic is busy, and patients are often worried about their health. Michelle and the other doctors try to help them.
>
> At six o'clock in the evening Michelle leaves the clinic. She goes home and relaxes. Every evening at seven o'clock Michelle goes to Bangkok in the Boondocks. That's my restaurant, and Michelle is my wife. Michelle and I usually enjoy a delicious Thai dinner alone.
>
> Sometimes, however, people come to the restaurant and tell Michelle their medical problems. I say, "Tell them to go to the clinic." But Michelle never sends them home without listening to their problems and offering advice. Michelle is a wonderful doctor.

4 | *Exchange papers with a partner. Did your partner follow the directions? Correct any mistakes in grammar and spelling.*

5 | *Talk to your partner. Discuss the mistakes you made. Then rewrite your own paper and make any necessary changes.*

THE FUTURE

UNIT	GRAMMAR FOCUS	THEME
24	*Be going to* for the Future	City and Campus Planning
25	*Will* for the Future; Future Time Markers	The Future
26	*May* or *Might* for Possibility	Weather

Be going to for the Future
CITY AND CAMPUS PLANNING

STEP 1 GRAMMAR IN CONTEXT

Before You Read

PAIRS: Do you ever read or write letters to the editor of a newspaper? Tell your partner about a letter you remember.

> EXAMPLE: This city is going to increase the cost of transportation. Last week there was a letter against the increase. I agree with the writer.

Read

Read the letters from students to the editor of their school newspaper.

---

www.dailycolumbus.com/letters_to_the_editor

DAILY COLUMBUS
The website of Columbus College

| Home | Campus | City | Sports | Classifieds |

LETTERS TO THE EDITOR

To the Editor:

Last week President Clark talked about plans for a new fitness center[1] for our college. The center sounds great. It**'s going to have** a beautiful gym, a track for running, an Olympic size pool, saunas, steam rooms, a basketball court, exercise machines, and weight-lifting equipment.[2] But this fitness center **is going to cost** a lot of money.

Where is the money **going to come** from? You guessed it. Most of the money **is going to come** from us. Our tuition **is going to increase**. That's why I'm against the plan. With a tuition increase, more students **are going to need** to work while they go to school. We**'re not going to have** time to enjoy the fitness center. We**'re not going to have** time to study.

Why is President Clark doing this? He only wants a fitness center because other schools have them. He thinks more students **are going to come** to our school if we have a fancy fitness center. But we're here for a good education, not to enjoy a state-of-the-art fitness center.

—*Joe Molina*

To the Editor:

A week ago President Clark announced plans for a new fitness center for our college. I love the idea. It**'s going to give** us a chance to relax and unwind[3] before and after classes. College is not just a time to sit in a library and study. It's a time for us to make our bodies *and* our minds stronger.

When the gym is built, **I'm going to go** there every day. Yes. We**'re going to pay** for it. There **is going to be** a tuition hike.[4] But in my opinion, it's worth it. It**'s going to improve** our lives.

Last month a study showed that most students gain 10 pounds in their freshman year. I'll bet that**'s not going to happen** once we have our new fitness center.

—*Alison Meadows*

---

[1] *fitness center:* a place to exercise
[2] *equipment:* machines
[3] *unwind:* to relax and feel no stress
[4] *hike:* an increase

A | Practice *PAIRS: Read the Letters to the Editor again aloud. Take turns reading each paragraph.*

B | Vocabulary *Circle the letter of the best meaning for the words in **blue**.*

1. Is the **tuition** at your school the same as it was last year?

   a. work   **b.** money for school

2. Our teacher **announced** that there will be a school party next Thursday.

   a. said   **b.** answered

3. They **increased** the number of students from 22 to 25 per class.

   a. raised   **b.** changed

4. The train is two dollars more than the bus. **Is it worth it?**

   a. How much is the train?   **b.** Is there value in paying extra for the train?

5. I am **against** the idea of raising taxes.

   a. not for   **b.** worried about

6. **In my opinion** students need a fitness center.

   a. I know   **b.** I think

C | Comprehension *Read the sentences. Is the statement for or against the fitness center? Write the letter in the correct box.*

   a. "It's going to cost a lot of money."
   b. "It's going to be a place to relax and unwind."
   c. "It's going to keep students in good shape."
   d. "More students are going to need to work during the school year."
   e. "Tuition is going to increase."
   f. "It's going to attract more students."

For the Fitness Center	Against the Fitness Center
	a

BE GOING TO FOR THE FUTURE

Affirmative Statements			
Subject + *Be*	***Going to***	**Base Form of Verb**	
I'm He's We're You're* They're	going to	study	tonight.
It's		rain	

Negative Statements			
Subject + *Be*	**Not**	***Going to***	**Base Form of Verb**
I'm He's We're You're They're	not	going to	sleep.
It's			rain.

You're can be both singular and plural subjects.

Yes / No Questions						Short Answers	
Be	**Subject**	***Going to***	**Base Form of Verb**			**Affirmative**	**Negative**
Am	I	going to	drive	tomorrow?		Yes, you are.	No, you're not.
Are	you					Yes, I am.	No, I'm not.
Is	he					Yes, he is.	No, he's not.

Wh- Questions						Short Answers
Wh- Word	***Be***	**Subject**	***Going to***	**Base Form of Verb**		
What	is	she	going to	do?		Meet her friend.
Where	are	they		go?	there?	To the library.
How	am	I		get		By bus.

GRAMMAR NOTES

1	There are different ways to express **the future**. **USAGE NOTE:** In speaking, *be going to* is more common than *will*.	• We **are going to buy** a car. • We **are buying** a car next month. • We **will buy** a car.
2	One way to express the future is with a form of ***be* + *going to* + the base form of the verb**. Use **contractions** of ***be*** in speaking and informal writing. Remember to use a form of *be* before *going to*. Remember to use the base form of the verb after *going to*.	• He **is going to start** at 9:00. • They **are going to start** at 9:00. • He's **going to start** at 9:00. • They're **going to start** at 9:00. NOT: He ~~going to~~ start at 9:00. NOT: He's going to ~~starts~~ at 9:00.

3	Use *be going to* + base form • **to state facts about the future** • **to make predictions** • **to talk about plans**	• The politicians **are going to meet** in Rome. • There **is going to be** a change in the climate. • I can't go to the restaurant. I**'m going to take** my friend to the airport.
4	Use *probably* with *be going to* to say that **you think something will happen, but you are not sure.**	• We're **probably** going to start at 9:00. • It's **probably** going to rain.
5	**Future time markers** usually come at the beginning or the end of a sentence. Some common future time markers are: *tomorrow*, *next week*, *next month*, *this weekend*, and *in 2100*.	• They are going to start construction **next week**. • **Next week** they are going to start construction.
6	Sometimes we use **the present progressive + a future time marker** to talk about the future. This is especially true with the verb *go* and verbs such as *drive* or *fly*. We do not use the present progressive with non-action verbs to talk about the future.	• We**'re going** there **next week**. • He**'s driving** to the country **this weekend**. • He**'s going to need** a new car next year. Not: He's needing a new car next year.

STEP 3 FOCUSED PRACTICE

EXERCISE 1: Discover the Grammar

A | *Read the sentences. Underline all examples of* **be going to** *and the base form of the verb that follows.*

1. Last week Mayor Jonas talked about building a sports stadium. It's going to seat 300,000 people.

2. They're going to build a garage for the stadium. It's going to have spaces for 5,000 cars.

3. The mayor is giving a speech on Wednesday here at our school. She's going to talk about raising money for the stadium.

4. They're going to build stores around the stadium. The stores are going to provide jobs for a lot of people.

5. Some people don't want the city to build a new stadium. They're against it because the city is going to destroy some historic buildings when they build the stadium.

B | *Look at Part A. Circle the sentence that uses present progressive for the future.*

EXERCISE 2: *Be going to* for the Future

(Grammar Notes 2–4)

*Complete the sentences with **be going to** and the verbs in parentheses.*

A: The city needs money.

B: What _____ _is_ _____ the mayor _____ _going to do_ _____ about it?
1.   2. (do)

A: He ___ is going to increase ___ taxes.
3. (increase)

B: _____ Is _____ he ___ going to lay off ___ city workers?
4.   5. (lay off)

A: No. Two thousand city workers ___ are going to retire ___. The city
6. (retire)

___ is not going to hire ___ new police or teachers.
7. (hire / not)

B: That's not good. Crime ___ is probally going to ___.
8. (probably / increase)

A: I agree.

B: And children ___ are not going to Probably ___ good education.
9. (probably get / not)

A: I ___ am going to write ___ a letter to the mayor.
10. (write)

B: What _____ are _____ you ___ going to say ___?
11.   12. (say)

A: I ___ am not going to tell ___ him to bring more business to the city.
13. (tell)

B: How _____ is _____ he ___ going to do ___ that?
14.   15. (do)

A: Tourism. That's the answer.

EXERCISE 3: *Be going to* for the Future: *Wh-* Questions

(Grammar Notes 2–5)

*Read the news announcement. Write questions with **be going to** and the words in parentheses on the next page. Then answer the questions. Use short answers.*

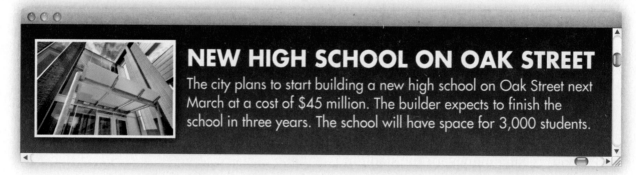

NEW HIGH SCHOOL ON OAK STREET

The city plans to start building a new high school on Oak Street next March at a cost of $45 million. The builder expects to finish the school in three years. The school will have space for 3,000 students.

1. (What / city / build)

   A: _What's the city going to build?_

   B: _A new high school._

2. (Where / it / be)

   A: _Where is it going to be?_

   B: _On street_

3. (When / the builders / start)

   A: _When are the builders going to start_

   B: _next March_

4. (How much / it / cost)

   A: _How much's it going to cost?_

   B: _$45 mi_

5. (How long / it / take)

   A: _How long's it going to take?_

   B: _in three years_

EXERCISE 4: *Be going to* for the Future

(Grammar Notes 1–3)

The West Street Association is against the construction of a new building on West Street.
Complete their letter to the editor with the affirmative or negative form of **be going to**.

To the Editor:

Mr. Romp wants to build a 20-story building on West Street. The West Street Association is

against the plan. It_'s going to change_ the area. All the buildings on West
            1. (change)

Street are only four or five stories high. A very tall building _is not going to look_
                                            2. (look)

good. The new building _'s going to have_ garage spaces
                  3. (have)

for 50 cars, but there _are going to be_ 200 apartments.
                  4. (be)

There _are probably not going to be_ enough parking spaces. There
      5. (probably / be)

is going to be a lot more traffic in the area and
  6. (be)

is going to look terrible. Let's stop construction of the Romp Tower!
  7. (look)

EXERCISE 5: Simple Past, Simple Present, *Be going to*   (Grammar Notes 1–4)

Complete the conversations with the verbs in parentheses. Use the simple past, the simple present, or **be going to** *for the future.*

CONVERSATION A

INEZ: _____*Did*_____ you _____*listen*_____ to the weather report?
1. 2. (listen)

ROBERTO: Yes. It _is going to be_ sunny and warm today and tomorrow.
3. (be)

INEZ: Good. There _____*is*_____ a town meeting outdoors in East Park
4. (be)

tomorrow.

CONVERSATION B

DANIEL: The mayor _____*wanted*_____ to close Maple Street to cars next month. He
1. (want)

is going to make it a place for people to walk. No cars will be allowed.
2. (make)

ALISA: How _____*Do*_____ you _going to know_ about it?
3. 4. (know)

DANIEL: The mayor _____*announced*_____ it last night on his weekly radio show.
5. (announce)

ALISA: I _____*thinked*_____ it's a great idea.
6. (think)

DANIEL: Well, storeowners aren't happy. They say they _are going to lose_ business.
7. (lose)

ALISA: What else _____*Did*_____ the mayor _____*say*_____ last night?
8. 9. (say)

DANIEL: In the next five years he _is going to turn_ this city into a center for the arts.
10. (turn)

ALISA: How _____*is*_____ he _going to do_ that?
11. 12. (do)

DANIEL: He _is going to offer_ cheap housing for artists. He _is going to build_ a
13. (offer) 14. (build)

concert hall, and he _is going to put_ artwork in the park.
15. (put)

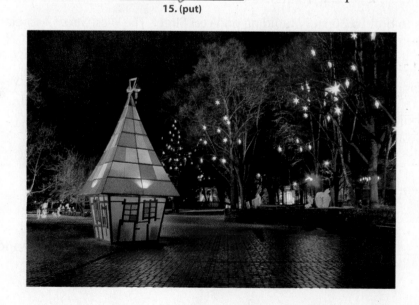

EXERCISE 6: Present Progressive for the Future

(Grammar Note 6)

*Look at the mayor's schedule for next Monday and Tuesday. Write questions with the given words. Use the **present progressive for the future.** Then write short answers.*

1. Who / he / have lunch with on Monday?   *hase*

   Q: _Who is he having lunch with on Monday?_

   A: _He's having lunch with community leaders._

2. What / he / do / Monday afternoon?   *meet*

   Q: _What is he doing to do Monday afternoon?_

   A: _He is going to do Lunch with community leaders._

3. Who / he / meet / at 7:00 P.M. on Monday?   *meet*

   Q: _who is he meeting at 7.00. PM on Monday_

   A: _He is meeting_

4. What time / he / fly home from Los Angeles?

   Q: _what time is he flying_

   A: _He is flying_

(continued on next page)

5. Where / he / speak/ in Washington, D.C.?

Q: _where's he speaking?_

A: _he's speaking_

6. When / he speak to the senior citizens?

Q: _when is he speaking_

A: _____

7. Where he / go / to a dinner for the police chief?

Q: _where's he going to a di_

A: _____

EXERCISE 7: Editing

Correct the newsletter article. There are five mistakes. The first mistake is already corrected. Find and correct four more.

VILLAGE GREEN APARTMENTS

Dear Residents:

Last week the mayor talked about building a sports stadium in our neighborhood. I think it's a terrible idea. It's going ~~to~~ cost taxpayers millions of dollars. It's going to mean traffic jams. Parking is ~~being~~ going to difficult, and it's going to ~~bringing~~ noise to the area.

Next Monday at 7:00 P.M. the mayor is ~~goes~~ going to answer questions at the public library. Please come out and speak out against the new stadium.

Sincerely,

Dale Ortiz

President, Residents' Association

EXERCISE 8: Pronunciation

A | *Read and listen to the Pronunciation Note.*

Pronunciation Note
In informal speaking, ***going to*** is often pronounced **"gonna"** when it comes before a verb.
EXAMPLE: We're "gonna" win this race. (***going to*** + **verb**)
Do not pronounce *going to* as "gonna" when *going* comes before the preposition ***to*** + **a place**.
EXAMPLE: We're going to the movies. (***going to*** + **place**)

B | *Listen to the sentences. Check (✓) when you hear **going to** and when you hear* **"gonna."**

going to	"gonna"
1.	
2.	
3.	
4.	
5.	
6.	
7.	

C | *Listen and repeat the sentences.*

1. He's going to a concert.
2. They're going to be late.
3. It's going to rain.
4. We're going to the library.
5. I'm going to think about it.

EXERCISE 9: Listening

🎧 A | *Listen to a conversation about a new building. Circle the correct letter.*

Why does the man want to buy the newspaper?

a. He wrote a letter and wants to see if his letter is in the paper.

b. He wants to see if the paper is for the new building.

🎧 B | *Listen again. Answer the questions.*

1. What are two reasons for building the new apartment building?

a. _____

b. _____

2. What are two reasons against building it?

a. _____

b. _____

3. Is the man for or against the new building? _____

EXERCISE 10: Conversation: Changes in Your Life

PAIRS: Tell about an upcoming change in your life or the life of someone you know well. For example, a move or a new job. Your partner asks questions about the change. Then talk about a good and a bad thing about the change. Take turns.

EXAMPLE: **A:** My sister is moving away from the city.
B: Why is she moving?
A: She needs a larger home. She has two children. She's going to have more space, but she and her husband are going to have a long commute to work.

EXERCISE 11: Writing

A | *GROUPS: Read the changes in the chart for Columbus College and the city of Columbus. Choose one school change and one city change. Discuss reasons why you are for or against the change.*

School Changes	City Changes
50% of courses will be online.	No cars on Main Street on weekends
No tests, just written reports	Higher taxes on clothes and entertainment to pay for better schools
No smoking on college campus	Restaurants need to show calorie and fat content of all food on menus.

EXAMPLE: Fifty percent of classes will be online courses.
A: I think that's a terrible idea. Online courses will be boring.
B: I disagree. In my opinion, we're going to have great online discussions.

B | *Write an email letter to the editor. Explain why you are for or against one of these changes. Explain what the change is going to mean. Use* be going to *for the future.*

EXAMPLE:

Dear Editor:

　　Last week the college president spoke about a law to ban cars on Main Street on weekends. I think that's a great idea. The street is going to be safer for students. The air is going to be cleaner. It's going to be quieter. The change is going to make the campus area a better place to walk, shop, and dine.

Sincerely,

Daniel Rivera

C | *Check your work. Use the Editing Checklist.*

Editing Checklist

Did you . . . ?
☐ use correct forms of ***be going to*** for the future
☐ check your spelling

Check your answers on page UR-5.

Do you need to review anything?

A | Complete the sentences with **be going to** and the words in parentheses. Use the future. Use contractions when possible.

The city ___is going build___ a waterfront park. It ___'s going to cost___ millions of dollars.
1. (build)   2. (cost)

It _____ an amusement park. There _____ a few restaurants.
3. (have)   4. (be)

Construction ___is going be___ until next summer.
5. (begin / not)

B | Complete the sentences with **be going to** and the words in parentheses. Use the future and the affirmative or negative form. Use contractions when possible.

1. Everyone is happy. Taxes ___ar's not going to increase___. No one likes to pay taxes.
(increase)

2. It's raining hard. We ___are go___ soccer in the park.
(play)

3. John is in the hospital. We ___are___ him. Do you want to come?
(visit)

4. It's Mary's last year. She ___is going to retire___ in December and move away.
(retire)

5. I'm tired and it's late. I ___am___ any more work.
(do)

C | Look at Eun Young's schedule. Write questions with the words in parentheses. Use the present progressive for the future. Write short answers.

| MONDAY: dentist 5:30 | TUESDAY: meet Yu Chen Pappa Pizza 6:30 |

1. (When / she / go to the dentist)

Q: ___when's she going t___ A: ___on Monday at 5:30___

2. (Where / she / meet / Yu Chen)

Q: ___Where's she meet Y___ A: ___meet Yu Chen Pappa Pizza___

3. (she / meet / Yu Chen / on Monday)

Q: ___Is she meet___ A: _____

D | Correct the paragraph. There are four mistakes.

   This city 's going to change under our new mayor. People are 's going to ride bikes, and they're gonna going to use public transportation. They're no going to drive big cars. There are probably going to be higher tolls on bridges and more bike paths on the roads.

Before You Read

What do you think will be different by the year 2025? 2050? By 2100?

EXAMPLE: I think people will travel to the past and the future.

Read

Future Science Magazine *asked scientists to make predictions for the year 2050. How will we look? How will we travel? How long will we live? Read their predictions.*

www.futuresciencemag.com

FUTURE SCIENCE

What's in Store¹ for Us in 2050?

1. More people **will be** vegetarians. They **won't eat** any meat or fish.
2. People **will look** bigger than people today.
3. People **will read** each other's thoughts.
4. They **will take** memory pills.
5. Cars **will run on** solar² energy.
6. Private planes **will be** common.
7. Travel to the moon **will be** common.
8. Robots **will cook** our meals. We **won't spend** a lot of time in the kitchen.
9. On average, people **will weigh** 11 pounds (5 kilograms) more, and they **will be** about 5 inches (12.5 centimeters) taller.
10. People **will live** to be 100 years old on average, and the majority of people **will be** over 60.
11. People **won't need** so many tissues. There **will be** a cure for the common cold.
12. Paper money and coins³ **will disappear**. People **will use** credit cards for all their purchases.

---

¹*be in store:* to be about to happen to someone
²*solar:* from the sun
³*coins:* metal money such as quarters or dimes

A | Practice *PAIRS: Read the predictions again aloud. Take turns reading each prediction.*

B | Vocabulary *Complete the sentences with the words from the box.*

common	disappear	meal	spend time	vegetarian

1. He never eats meat. He's a ___meal___.

2. In the future, travel to the moon will be ___vegetarian___

3. Did the moon ___will come___ behind a cloud?

4. What's your favorite ___disappear___ of the day?

5. We like to ___spend time___ in the laboratory.

C | Comprehension *Read the questions. Circle the letter of the correct answers based on the article in* Future Science Magazine. *There may be more than one correct answer.*

1. How will people look?

   a. taller   **b.** shorter   **c.** smaller

2. Where will people travel?

   a. to the moon   **b.** to Mars   **c.** to the past

3. What will increase?

   a. the number of vegetarians   **b.** the average life span   **c.** the number of colds

4. What will be common in 2050?

   a. coins   **b.** private planes   **c.** travel to the moon

WILL FOR THE FUTURE

Affirmative Statements			
Subject	Will / 'll	Base Form of Verb	Time Marker
I You* He She It We They	will 'll	leave	tomorrow.

Negative Statements			
Subject	Will Not / Won't	Base Form of Verb	Time Marker
I You* He She It We They	will not won't	leave	tonight.

*You is both singular and plural.

Yes / No Questions			
Will	Subject	Base Form of Verb	Time Marker
Will	I you he she it we they	arrive	tonight?

Short Answers					
Affirmative			Negative		
Yes,	you I he she it we they	will.	No,	you I he she it we they	won't.

Future Time Markers	
today tonight tomorrow	
this	morning afternoon evening
tomorrow	morning afternoon evening night
Saturday	night

Future Time Markers with Next and In	
next	week month year Monday weekend
in	2020 the 22nd century 20 years two weeks a few days

GRAMMAR NOTES

1 Use *will* + **the base form of the verb** to talk about things that will take place in the future.

BE CAREFUL! Use the base form of the verb after *will* or *won't*. Remember, the base form does not change.

- The class **will begin** on November 2.
- We **will meet** tomorrow at 10:00 A.M.
- The plane **will arrive** at 6:00 P.M.

Nот: The plane will ~~to arrive~~ at 6:00 P.M.
Nот: The plane will ~~arrives~~ at 6:00 P.M.

2 Use **contractions** of *will* **with pronouns** in speaking and informal writing.

BE CAREFUL! Do not use contractions in affirmative short answers.

- **We'll** be there before 3:00.

A: Will they be there?
B: Yes, they will.
   Nот: Yes, ~~they'll.~~

3 Use *will* to make **predictions**.

USAGE NOTE: In writing, we often use *will* in one sentence and *be going to* in the next sentence.

- In 2050 there **will be** more megacities. Those cities **are going to be** very crowded.

4 Use *will* to make a **promise** or **give assurance**.

- I**'ll be** back in five minutes.
- I **won't do** that again.

5 Use *will* to **ask for** or **offer** something.

A: **Will** you **help** me?
B: Don't worry. I**'ll help**.

6 *Won't* is the contraction of *will* + *not*. It has two meanings.
Use *won't* to mean the **negative future**.
Use *won't* to mean "**refuse(s) to.**"

- He **won't be** in school tomorrow.
- The child **won't eat** carrots.

7 To say that something is not definite, use *probably* with *will* for the future.

- People will **probably** take more vacations.

8 Some **time markers** are used only for the future. Other time markers can be used for the past or the future.

FUTURE
- She won't be home **tomorrow**.

FUTURE
- She'll be home **this afternoon**.

PAST
- She was at the library **this afternoon**.

EXERCISE 1: Discover the Grammar

*Read the sentences. How is **will** used? Match the sentences with the descriptions.*

___b___ **1.** I won't do it. I think it's wrong.

___d___ **2.** Will you show me how to use that computer?

___c___ **3.** I'll be back by 9:00.

___e___ **4.** There won't be any meeting on February 8.

___a___ **5.** By 2020 people will fly to the moon for fun.

a. predicts something

b. refuses to do something

c. promises to do something

d. asks for something

e. tells about something that is not going to happen

EXERCISE 2: *Will* for the Future

(Grammar Notes 1–7)

*Complete the conversations with **will** or **won't** and the verbs in parentheses.*

1. A: Mom, when ____will____ dinner ____be____ ready?
(be)

B: Robot Bob says it ____will be____ ready in 22 minutes.
(be)

2. A: Do you really think scientists ____will find____ a cure for the cold?
(find)

B: I hope so. It ____will save____ a lot of money. People ____will miss____ work
(save) (miss)

so often.

3. A: Dr. Smith, my great grandmother ____will not take____ her memory pills. She says
(take)

they taste bad. ____will____ you ____give____ her some that taste
(give)

good?

B: Don't worry. I ____will give____ her some that taste like candy.
(give)

4. A: When do you think we ____will send____ astronauts to the planet Mars?
(send)

B: No one knows. Right now we're spending less money on space exploration. So it

____will probably take____ longer than we thought.
(probably / take)

5. A: Where ____will____ the wedding ____take place____?
(take place)

B: The wedding ____will be____ on the moon.
(be)

A: And where ____will____ you ____go____ for your honeymoon?
(go)

B: We ____will probably go____ to Mars.
(probably / go)

EXERCISE 3: *Will* for the Future

(Grammar Notes 1–7)

Complete the conversation with **will** *and the verbs in parentheses.*

A: So, Laura, when _____*will*_____ you _____*finish*_____ the article about the future?
        1.   2. (finish)

B: It _will not be_ ready until 4:00 P.M., but I think you _will like_ it.
        3. (not / be)   4. (like)

A: You interviewed Dr. Reicher, right?

B: Yes, I did. He says computers _will help_ us stay healthy.
                                          5. (help)

A: Oh, yeah? How's that?

B: In the future, we _will have_ computers inside our bodies. They
                          6. (have)

_____*will*_____ constantly _____*check*_____ things such as our blood sugar and
        7.   8. (check)

blood pressure.

A: _____*Will*_____ diabetes and heart disease _disappear_?
        9.   10. (disappear)

B: No, but people _will not probably die_ from those diseases so often, and people
                        11. (probably / die / not)

_____*will live*_____ longer.
        12. (live)

A: And when _____*will*_____ this _happen_?
                  13.   14. (happen)

B: By 2030.

A: That's really not so far away.

EXERCISE 4: *Will* for the Future

(Grammar Notes 2–3, 8)

Look at the chart of predictions. Write questions about Fogville with the words in parentheses. Use **will** *for the future. Answer the questions.*

Predictions for Fogville in 2050				Key	
The cost of housing	↓	Crime	→	Increase	= ↑
The cost of health care	↓	The percent of people under 25	↑	Stay the same	= →
Taxes	↓	The percent of people over 65	→	Decrease	= ↓

1. A: _Will the cost of housing increase?_
                 (the cost of housing / increase)

   B: _No, it won't. The cost of housing will decrease._

2. A: _will t_
                 (the cost of health care / stay the same)

   B: _No, it will not_   _It will decarse_

288   UNIT 25

3. A: _will taxes stay the sam?_

(taxes / stay the same)

B: _They will d_

4. A: _____

(the percent of people under 25 / decrease)

B: _____

5. A: _____

(the percent of people over 65 / decrease)

B: _____

EXERCISE 5: Review of Present, Past, Future

(Grammar Notes 3–4, 6–8)

Complete the conversation. Use the verbs in parentheses. Use the simple present, the simple past, or the future with **will**. *Use contractions where possible.*

A: _____ *Did* _____ you _____ *hear* _____ the lecture last week?

         1.   2. (hear)

B: No, what _____ *was* _____ it about?

          3. (be)

A: The future. According to Professor Johns, by the year 2100 there _____ *will be* _____

                                             4. (be)

cities in the ocean, we _____ *will take* _____ trips to the moon, and we _____ *will learn* _____

                5. (take)   6. (learn)

everything from computers.

B: By 2100? We _____ *will* _____ all _____ *be* _____ gone by then. _____ *Did* _____

            7.   8. (be)   9. (like)

the people _____ *like* _____ his lecture?

           10.

A: Yes, they did. They always do. He _____ *know* _____ how to make any subject

                              11. (know)

fascinating.

EXERCISE 6: Editing

Correct the conversation. There are six mistakes. The first mistake is already corrected. Find and correct five more.

A: What did he say?

B: He said there ^*will* be an increase in the population. Many young people will move~~s~~ to the area. Taxes will increase~~s~~. The value of homes will also ~~to~~ increase.

A: How about crime? Will it increase~~s~~?

B: No, it *will not* ~~doesn't~~.

A: Well, it sounds like a great place to live.

EXERCISE 7: Pronunciation

A | *Read and listen to the Pronunciation Note.*

> **Pronunciation Note**
>
> In conversation we often **link** the **subject pronoun** (*I, you, he, she, it, we,* OR *they*) and *will*. The final vowel sound of *will* often sounds like / əl /.
>
> **EXAMPLES:** I'll   she'll   it'll   we'll

B | *Listen and repeat the contractions.*

I'll   you'll   he'll   she'll   it'll   we'll   they'll

C | *Now listen and repeat the sentences.*

1. You'll fly to the moon.
2. He'll visit you on the moon.
3. They'll be there too.
4. She'll help you fly the spaceship.
5. I'll be with you shortly.
6. It'll cost a lot of money.
7. We'll see them the following year.

EXERCISE 8: Listening

A | *Listen to a conversation between a TV news reporter and two people. Read the question. Circle the correct letter.*

Why is the man talking to the two people?

    a. They made a lot of money.   **b.** They won a lot of money.

B | *Listen again. Answer the questions.*

1. What will the woman do with her money?

    a. _____

    b. _____

2. What will the man do with his money?

    _____

3. What does the man mean when he says, "They'll get over it."

    _____

EXERCISE 9: Class Survey

SMALL GROUPS: Look at the predictions in the Future Science *article on page 283. Do you agree? What are your predictions? Discuss your answers. Report to the class.*

> **EXAMPLE:** We all think paper money will disappear. People will use credit cards or check cards to pay for everything. Coins are heavy, and bills are not clean. These cards are the way of the future.

EXERCISE 10: Survey: In the Future

A | *Complete the information.*

1. Write the name of something that is very popular today.

_____

2. Write the name of a country and a time in the future.

_____

B | *Complete the questions below with your answers from Part A. Then survey five classmates. Ask them the questions.*

1. Will _____ still be popular in _____?

2. Will _____ be a popular tourist destination in _____?

C | *Report your results to the class.*

> **EXAMPLE:** I asked five people this question: "Will DVDs still be popular in 10 years?" Four out of six students said, "No."

EXERCISE 11: Making Predictions

A | *Make predictions about these fields for the year 2050. Tape them on the wall.*

environment   health   jobs   medicine   sports   technology

> **EXAMPLE:** Nobody will be hungry.

B | *Number all the predictions. Go around and read each prediction. Choose four predictions. Tell if you agree or disagree with them.*

EXERCISE 12: Writing

A | *GROUPS: Talk about how life will be in the future. Use these topics:*

education   fashion   food   homes   tourism   travel

> **EXAMPLE:** **A:** I think people will wear paper clothes.
> **B:** I disagree. People will worry about the environment. They won't wear throwaway clothes.
> **C:** I think people will wear special clothes in the summer. They will be light, but they will protect them from the sun.
> **D:** And in the winter they will wear clothes that are light in weight, but very warm.

B | *Choose a year. Choose a topic from Part A. Write about how things will be different.*
Use **will** *for the future and* **be going to** *for the future.*

EXAMPLE: TRAVEL IN 2050

In 2050 people will have new ways to travel. First of all, people will have their own wings. They're going to use them to fly distances of 50 miles or less. The wings won't take up much space, so people won't have to "park" their wings. People will also travel with flying cars. These cars will go up to 200 miles an hour. People are going to use their flying cars to travel 200 to 400 miles. There will be regular planes and jets, and there will be spaceships for trips to other planets.

C | *Check your work. Use the Editing Checklist.*

Editing Checklist

Did you . . . ?
- ☐ use **will** for the future correctly
- ☐ use **be going to** for the future correctly
- ☐ check your spelling

25 Review

Check your answers on page UR-5.
Do you need to review anything?

A | *Write questions with **will** and the words in parentheses.*

1. _Where will_ _____
   (Where / people / travel / in 20 years)

2. _will_ _____
   (people / fly / to the moon)

3. _____ _will_ _____
   (How / they / get around)

4. _____ _will_ _____
   (the climate / change)

5. _____ _will_ _____
   (people / look / different)

B | *Circle the correct word to complete the sentences.*

1. He doesn't like hats. He **will /** ~~**won't**~~ wear them.

2. I'm busy tomorrow morning. I **will /** ~~**won't**~~ be at work until noon.

3. He's good at computers. He probably ~~**will**~~ **/ won't** be able to fix your computer.

4. The sale ends today, but there **will /** ~~**won't**~~ be a sale next month.

5. I need more time. I **will /** ~~**won't**~~ be ready for at least a half an hour.

C | *Write questions with **will**. Use the same ideas in all sentences.*

1. Yesterday was hot. Today is hot. ____will____ it ___not be___ tomorrow too?

2. Last week he had a test. This week he has a test. ____will____ he ___has a test___ next week too?

3. Last September there was a storm. This September there was a storm.
   ____will____ there _be a storm_ next September too?

4. Yesterday it rained. Today it rained. ____will____ it ___rain___ tomorrow too?

5. He worked late yesterday. He worked late today. ____will____ he ___work___
   tomorrow too?

D | *Correct the paragraph. There are five mistakes.*

I usually bring my lunch to work, but tomorrow I ~~no will~~ bring it because it's my birthday. My co-workers will ~~takes~~ me out to a restaurant. We'll ~~to~~ order a few different dishes, and we'll share them. They'll ~~singing~~ "Happy Birthday," and they'll give me a small gift. I'm sure it will ~~is~~ be a lot of fun.

UNIT 26 *May* or *Might* for Possibility

WEATHER

STEP 1 GRAMMAR IN CONTEXT

Before You Read

Answer the questions.

1. How do you know what the weather will be? (*I watch TV, check my phone or computer, listen to the radio, read the newspaper*)
2. How often do you think the weather report is wrong? (*rarely, sometimes, often, almost always*)

Read

Read the conversation and TV weather report.

MOTHER: Shh. The weather report is **coming on.**[1]

ANNOUNCER: It's Sunday, May 15. The time is 9:00 A.M. And now here's the weather forecast with Luis Malina.

METEOROLOGIST: Good morning, everyone. If you plan to be outdoors today or Monday, wear a warm jacket and bring an umbrella. The weather will continue to be unseasonable.[2] Today will be cold and windy. And heavy rain will begin

[1] **coming on:** starting
[2] **unseasonable:** unusual for the time of year

294   UNIT 26

tonight or tomorrow. For your morning commute, there **may be** flooding on the highways.

So, if you can, take public transportation. And don't put away those umbrellas too soon because we'll have more rain on Tuesday and Wednesday. By Thursday the weather **may become** milder with only a 20 percent chance of showers.[3] We **might** even **see** some sun. But until then, my friends, my best advice is stay indoors with a good book or movie.

ALEX: I guess that means no soccer tomorrow.

MOTHER: Don't be too sure. You **may** still **have** a game. The meteorologist[4] is often wrong. Remember last Friday. He predicted a beautiful day, but it was awful. And last week he said we **might have** a major[5] storm. It turned out to be sunny and dry.

ALEX: Maybe.

MOTHER: I just hope you don't play in the rain.

ALEX: We **might**. The last time it rained we played the entire game. Playing in the mud was great! And we won!

---

[3] **chance of showers:** a short period of heavy rain
[4] **meteorologist:** weather reporter
[5] **major:** big

After You Read

A | Practice *GROUPS OF THREE: Now read the conversation aloud.*

B | Vocabulary *Complete the sentences with the words from the box.*

commute	entire	flooding	highways	mild	predicted	storm

1. They canceled the game because they expected rain the _____ day.

2. He lives outside the city. His _____ to work is an hour and a half each way.

3. There is always _____ on that street when it rains. The city needs to fix the problem.

4. The meteorologist _____ beautiful weather for the next three days.

5. There is bad traffic on all the major _____. I think we should wait to go home.

6. The _____ is getting worse. They may close the airport.

7. I want to live someplace where the weather is sunny and _____.

C | Comprehension *Circle the correct weather for each day, according to the forecast.*

Sunday	
sunny and warm	cold and windy

Monday	
light rain	heavy rain

Tuesday	
rainy	sunny

Wednesday	
sunny	rainy

Thursday	
sunny—no chance of rain	sunny—20% chance of rain

STEP 2 GRAMMAR PRESENTATION

MAY OR *MIGHT* FOR POSSIBILITY

Affirmative Statements			
Subject	***May / Might***	**Base Form of Verb**	
I You* He She We They	**may might**	**play**	soccer.
It	**may might**	**rain**	tonight.

Negative Statements				
Subject	***May / Might***	***Not***	**Base Form of Verb**	
I You* He She We They	**may might**	**not**	**play**	soccer.
It	**may might**	**not**	**rain**	tonight.

*You is both singular and plural.

GRAMMAR NOTES

1	Use *may* or *might* to express **possibility** about the present or the future.	**A:** Where's John? **B:** I don't know. He **may be** on vacation. **A:** What are you going to do this weekend? **B:** We **might go** to a movie.
	May and *might* have almost the same meaning, but *may* means something is a little more possible than *might*.	• It **might** rain. *(It's possible.)* • It **may** rain. *(It's more possible.)* • It**'ll probably** rain. *(It's likely.)* • It **will** rain. *(It's definite.)*
2	*May* and *might* are **followed** by the **base form of the verb**.	• He **might go** to the movies. NOT: He might ~~goes~~ to the movies. NOT: He might ~~to go~~ to the movies.
	There are no contractions for *may* or *might*.	He might not go to the movies. NOT: He ~~mightn't~~ go to the movies.
3	**USAGE NOTE:** We usually use *will* or *be going to*, not *may* or *might*, to **ask yes / no questions about the future**.	**A: Will** you **go** to the party? **B:** I might. OR I may. **A: Are** you **going to see** that movie tonight? **B:** We might. OR We may. NOT: ~~May~~ you go to the party?
4	We use *I think I might* for possibility. We use *I'm sure* + **subject** + *will* for certainty.	• **I think I might** have the flu. • **I'm sure I will** be there. NOT: I'm sure I ~~might~~ buy that book.
	We use *I think I will* for something that is likely.	• **I think I'll call** the doctor.
5	*May* and *might* are modals. ***Maybe*** is an adverb. It means "there's a possibility."	**Maybe I'll go** to the party. = **I might go** to the party. OR **I may go** to the party.
	Maybe I will has a similar meaning to *I might* or *I may*.	**A:** Are you going to the game? **B: Maybe.** = **I may**. OR **I might**.
6	We use ***it might*** or ***it may*** to talk about the weather.	• **It might** rain tonight. • **It may** snow tomorrow.

EXERCISE 1: Discover the Grammar

Match the sentences. Write the correct letter.

___d___ **1.** It's definitely going to rain.

_____ **2.** There's an 80 percent chance of rain.

_____ **3.** There's about a 50 percent chance of rain.

_____ **4.** There's a 10 percent chance of rain.

_____ **5.** It's definitely not going to rain.

a. It probably won't rain.

b. It'll probably rain.

c. It won't rain.

d. It will rain.

e. It may rain.

EXERCISE 2: Affirmative of *May* or *Might*   *(Grammar Notes 1–2, 4)*

*Complete the conversations with **may** or **might** and the verbs from the box. Use the affirmative or negative form.*

be	cancel	have	leave	~~rain~~	take

1. A: Take your umbrella. I think it _____ *might rain* _____ this afternoon.

   B: Really? The forecast was for sun.

2. A: Start dinner without me. It _____ me a long time to get

   home. The rain is causing flooding on the highway.

   B: That's OK. We'll wait.

3. A: Sandy looks upset.

   B: She is. She _____ her trip. Her sister is in the hospital.

4. A: Why are you so worried?

   B: The kids are camping tonight, and the forecast is for unusually cold weather. They

   _____ enough clothes.

5. A: Where's John? The meeting will start in a few minutes.

   B: He _____ late. All flights are delayed because of the wind.

6. A: How are you feeling now?

   B: Terrible. I _____ the office early.

EXERCISE 3: *May/ Might / Will / Will probably*

(Grammar Notes 1–3)

Read today's weather forecast. Complete the sentences with the correct words in parentheses.

Today

Cloudy with periods of rain
High of 50°

Winds SSE
at 30 to 40 mph

60 percent
chance of rain

1. It _____ *will be* _____ a very windy day.
   (will be / won't be)

2. It _____, but it _____ all
   (will probably rain / probably won't rain)   (may not rain / won't rain)
   day.

3. The temperature _____ 60 degrees.
   (may reach / probably won't reach)

4. _____ they _____ the ball
   (Will cancel / Might cancel)
   game for this afternoon?

5. They _____ the game if the rain is heavy.
   (might cancel / won't cancel)

EXERCISE 4: *Maybe* and *May / Might*

(Grammar Note 5)

Replace **maybe** with **may** or **might**. In some cases you may need to add a subject or a subject and a verb.

1. **A:** Do you have an extra umbrella?

   B: I'm not sure. ~~Maybe I have one~~ *I may have one* in that closet.

2. **A:** Where are the baby's shoes?

   B: Maybe they are in the top drawer.

3. **A:** Are they going to cancel the barbecue?

   B: Maybe. The forecast is for heavy rain.

4. **A:** Where will you meet if it rains?

   B: Maybe we'll meet at the mall.

5. **A:** Will she bring her daughter in the rain?

   B: Maybe.

EXERCISE 5: Editing

Correct the conversations. There are six mistakes. The first mistake is already corrected.
Find and correct five more.

1. **A:** Where's Bill?

   B: ~~I'm sure~~ *I think* he might be on vacation in Florida.

   A: He may needs his winter jacket. It's 40 degrees there today.

2. **A:** We maybe go to the park. Do you want to join us?

   B: No thanks. It's very windy. Why don't you do something indoors?

3. **A:** May you take the highway?

   B: Yes, I may. It's usually faster than the city streets.

4. **A:** Are you going to finish your paper on climate change today?

   B: I want to, but I mightn't have enough time.

5. **A:** What's the weather report?

   B: It's sunny now, but it may to rain this afternoon.

STEP 4 COMMUNICATION PRACTICE

EXERCISE 6: Pronunciation

A | *Read and listen to the Pronunciation Note.*

> **Pronunciation Note**
>
> For numbers that end in **-ty** such as *thirty, forty, fifty*, etc., we stress the **first syllable** of the word. For numbers that end in **-teen**, we usually stress the **second syllable**.

B | *Listen and circle the word you hear.*

1. 16   60

2. 13   30

3. 19   90

4. 15   50

5. 18   80

| *Now listen and complete the conversations. Write the words you hear. Then practice the conversation with a partner.*

1. **A:** This tornado has winds of _____

   miles an hour.

   B: Did you say 115 or 150?

   A: _____.

2. **A:** It's _____ degrees.

   B: Was that 60 or 16?

   A: _____.

3. **A:** There are _____ inches of snow.

   B: Was that 14 or 40?

   A: _____.

4. **A:** It's _____ degrees below zero.

   B: Did you say 13 or 30?

   A: _____.

Tornadoes have wind speed from 40 to 300 miles an hour.

EXERCISE 7: Listening

🎧 **A** | *A couple is taking a trip to Oregon. Listen to their conversation. What is the conversation about? Circle the correct letter.*

   a. The things the man is taking with him on the trip

   b. The things the man is going to do on the trip

🎧 **B** | *Listen again. What reason does the man give for packing these things in his suitcase?*

1. boots _They may go mountain climbing._

2. a raincoat _____

3. two hats _____

4. two books _____

5. a sports jacket _____

EXERCISE 8: Discussion

PAIRS: Take turns asking about your partner's plans for tonight. Use **may, might,** *and* **will probably** *in your answers. Use the ideas in the list or your own. Explain your answer.*

- stay indoors
- listen to the weather report
- go running
- watch a movie
- study English
- eat out
- cook dinner

EXAMPLE: **A:** Are you going to stay indoors?
B: I think so. I'll probably stay home and watch a movie tonight. How about you?
A: I might eat out. I may try that new Korean restaurant. My friend says it's very good.

EXERCISE 9: Writing

A | *You are a reporter for UpToDateWeather.com. Write a weather report for the next three days for your region. Look at pages 294–295 for ideas. Use* **may** *and* **might** *where possible.*

EXAMPLE: Good evening. This is Hye Won Paik with the three-day forecast. Tomorrow you will want to take out your running shoes. We're going to have perfect weather. It's going to be sunny and warm. On Wednesday, it will still be warm, but we may see some clouds. Then on Thursday, temperatures will drop, and we might have a shower in the evening.

B | *Check your work. Use the Editing Checklist.*

Editing Checklist

Did you . . . ?
☐ use *may* and *might* correctly
☐ check your spelling

26 Review

Check your answers on page UR-5.
Do you need to review anything?

A | Circle the correct words to complete the sentences.

1. She may **to go / go** to the library.

2. He may **buy / buys** a new car.

3. It **mightn't / might not** rain tonight.

4. They **maybe / may** return the TV.

5. **Will / Might** you go to the party?

B | Complete the sentences with **may** or **might** and the verbs from the box. Use the affirmative or negative form.

get	need	see	snow	stay

1. Take your boots. It _____ this afternoon.

2. Start dinner without me. I _____ home from work until 10:00 P.M.

3. Karina is upset. The doctor says she _____ surgery.

4. Here's a gift. I _____ you before your birthday.

5. Traffic is heavy now. I _____ here for a while.

C | Rewrite the sentences. Replace **Maybe** with **may** or **might** and the correct word order.

1. Maybe there's a restroom in the library. _____

2. Maybe he's the director. ____he may be the i____

3. Maybe the plane is late. ____The plane may late____

4. Maybe they are cousins. ____they may be c____

5. Maybe it's his coat. _____

D | Correct the sentences. There are five mistakes.

1. He might goes on vacation next week.

2. He may works late tomorrow.

3. They might to visit him tomorrow. Are you free?

4. I might not help him. I might to help her instead.

5. She maybe take a yoga class.

From Grammar to Writing

TIME CLAUSES WITH *WHEN*

1 | *Study this information about time clauses.*

1. I was six years old. I loved to play with dolls.

   _____

2. I graduate next year. I will work for a bank.

   _____

2 | *Combine the sentences using* **when**. *Look at the chart below for help.*

1	We can combine two sentences that tell about time by using a **time clause** and a **main clause**. *When I was six* is a **time clause**. It is not a sentence and can never stand alone. It needs a main clause.	• I was six. I started school. TIME CLAUSE MAIN CLAUSE • **When** I was six, I started school.
2	When we use **present time clauses**, the verbs in both the time clause and the main clause are written in the **present**.	PRESENT TIME CLAUSE MAIN CLAUSE • When I **get** home, I **have** dinner.
3	When we use **past time clauses**, the verbs in both the time clause and the main clause are written in the **past**.	PAST TIME CLAUSE MAIN CLAUSE • When I **got** home, I **had** dinner.
4	When we use a **future time clause**, the future time clause uses the **simple present**. The main clause uses the **future**.	FUTURE TIME CLAUSE MAIN CLAUSE • When I **get** home, I **will have** dinner. (First I'll get home. Then I'll have dinner.)
5	You can begin a sentence with the time clause or the main clause. When the time clause begins the sentence, put a **comma** before the main clause. There is no comma when the main clause begins the sentence.	PRESENT TIME CLAUSE MAIN CLAUSE • When I get home**,** I will have dinner. MAIN CLAUSE PRESENT TIME CLAUSE • I will have dinner when I get home.

3 | *Rewrite this paragraph using three time clauses.*

> ## My Dream
>
> I was a child. I loved to play "make-believe" games. Sometimes I was a cowboy, and sometimes I was a prince. I became a teenager. I got a job at a video store. I saw many movies. I also made a couple of videos, and I acted in all the school plays. Now I'm studying film and acting at school. I will finish college next year. I will move to Hollywood. I hope to become a movie star.

4 | *Write a paragraph about yourself at different times of your life. Include a part about your future.*

5 | *Exchange papers with a partner. Did your partner follow the directions? Correct any mistakes in grammar and spelling.*

6 | *Talk to your partner. Discuss the mistakes you made. Then rewrite your own paper and make any necessary changes.*

My Dream

COUNT / NON-COUNT NOUNS;
MUCH / *MANY*; QUANTIFIERS

Count and Non-Count Nouns, Quantifiers, Articles

RESTAURANTS AND FOOD

STEP 1 GRAMMAR IN CONTEXT

Before You Read

*What do you usually look for in a restaurant? Check (✓) three things that are important to you. Put an **X** next to three things that are not important.*

____ unusual food	____ a quiet place
____ polite service	____ a lively place
____ fast service	____ low prices
____ a beautiful atmosphere	____ food I like
____ an unusual atmosphere	____ big portions

Read

Read the online restaurant reviews.

www.kassandrasfoodreview.com

Kassandra's Food Reviews

Al Hambra ★ ★ ★ ★

Rich **spices** are the **draw**[1] at **Al Hambra**. The **flavor** of **ginger**, **garlic**, **cumin**, and **lemon** make the **chicken** in a **tagine** (ceramic pot) our favorite **choice**. Another great **choice** for the main **course** is the **lamb** with **ginger**. Note: There isn't **much beef** on the **menu**, and there isn't **any pork**. However, there are **many choices** of fresh **fish**, **chicken**, and **lamb**. All the **appetizers** are great. We especially like an **appetizer** called *zaalouk*. This is a **salad** made of **eggplant and tomato**. For **dessert** we recommend **the** almond **cookies**. There aren't **many tables** at Al Hambra, so be sure to make a **reservation** well in advance.

[1]*draw:* attraction

Topkapi ★★★

Topkapi serves Turkish **food** in a colorful **atmosphere**. The **mirrors**, **lights**, and yellow and red **colors** give this **restaurant a** warm, inviting **look**. The **food** is delicious. Try the vegetable **combo**[2] to begin. The pita **bread** with **hummus**, **yogurt**, and **tahini** is excellent. For the main **course** I suggest the lamb **kebab** with rice and salad. The best **dessert** is the **baklava**. This is **a** sweet **pastry** made with pistachios or walnuts. Enjoy your **baklava** with Turkish **coffee**. But beware, Turkish **coffee** is very strong.

Note: You may need to wait **a few minutes** even with a **reservation**, but the **atmosphere**, **food**, and **service** are worth the **wait**.

[2]**combo:** combination

After You Read

A | Practice *PAIRS: Now read the restaurant reviews aloud.*

B | Vocabulary *Complete the sentences with the words from the box.*

atmosphere	delicious	main course	menu	reservation	service

1. The food was _____. We will definitely go back to that restaurant.

2. Everything on the _____ is fresh and tasty. Order whatever you like.

3. I ordered steak for my _____. My friend ordered a pasta dish.

4. All the servers are polite and helpful. The _____ was excellent.

5. The restaurant has soft lights, slow music, and beautiful flowers everywhere. The _____ is romantic.

6. Be sure to make a _____ in advance. That restaurant is always crowded.

C | Comprehension *Read the descriptions of the restaurants. Write **AH** (**Al Hambra**) or **T** (**Topkapi**) for each statement.*

_____ **1.** People come here for the spices.

_____ **2.** There is no pork on the menu.

_____ **3.** They serve chicken cooked in a ceramic pot.

_____ **4.** The reviewer recommends the lamb kebab.

_____ **5.** The best dessert is the baklava.

COUNT AND NON-COUNT NOUNS; QUANTIFIERS, ARTICLES

Affirmative Statements

Singular Count Nouns		
	Article or *One*	Singular Noun
She wants	a	banana.
	an	apple.
	one	banana. apple.

Plural Count Nouns		
	Number or Quantifier	Plural Noun
He owns	seven	restaurants.
	a few	
	some	
	a lot of	
	many	

Non-count Nouns		
	Quantifier	Non-count Noun
Carol needs	a little	help.
	some	coffee.
	a lot of	

Negative Statements

Singular Count Nouns		
	Article or *One*	Singular Noun
I didn't buy	a	pear.
	an	apple.
	one	pear. apple.

Plural Count Nouns		
	Number or Quantifier	Plural Noun
I didn't buy	two	pears.
	any	
	many	
	a lot of	

Non-count Nouns		
	Quantifier	Non-count Noun
I didn't buy	any	milk.
	much	
	a lot of	

The Definite Article *The*		
Count Noun	Plural Count Noun	Non-count Noun
I need **the menu**.	She has **the napkins**.	He has **the butter**.

GRAMMAR NOTES

1	*A*, *an*, and *the* are **articles**. An article comes before a noun. It can also come before an adjective + noun.	• **The** pears are delicious. • **a** pear / **a** juicy pear • **an** avocado
2	There are two kinds of nouns: **count nouns** and **non-count nouns**. **Count nouns** are ones that we can count. We cannot count **non-count nouns**.	• **Count:** a pear, an apple • **Non-count:** milk, water, salt

3	Use *a*, *an*, or *one* before a singular count noun. Use *a* before a **consonant sound**. Use *an* before a **vowel sound**.	• **a salad**, **an onion**, **one olive** • **a c**upcake • **an a**vocado
	BE CAREFUL! Do not put *a*, *an*, or a number before a non-count noun. Do not add *-s* or *-es* to a non-count noun.	• There's **salt** on the table. Not: There's a salt on the table. Not: There's salts on the table.
4	*A* and *an* are **indefinite** articles. *The* is a **definite** article.	• (You're hungry. You are looking for a restaurant. You see one and say, "There's **a restaurant**.")
	We use *a* or *an* to talk about a person or thing for the first time, or when it is not clear which person or thing you mean.	I want to go to a **Thai restaurant**, but I don't know a good one.
	We use *the* when it is clear which person or thing you mean.	• We ate chicken and rice. **The chicken** was good, but **the rice** was bad.
5	You can use the **definite article** *the* before singular count nouns, plural nouns, and non-count nouns.	• **The restaurant** is open. • **The menus** are there. • **The soup** is delicious.
6	Use *some* before plural count nouns and non-count nouns in affirmative statements.	• He wrote **some invitations.** • He drank **some juice**.
	Use *any* before plural count nouns and non-count nouns in negative statements.	• He didn't mail **any invitations**. • He didn't drink **any soda**.
	We usually use *any* in *yes/no* questions.	YES / NO QUESTIONS • Did you buy **any** milk? • Did you buy **any** bananas?
	We can also use *some* in *yes/no* questions when we offer something or ask for something.	AN OFFER • Would you like **some** juice? A REQUEST • Can I have **some** more coffee?
7	Use *a few* for small amounts and *many* for large amounts with count nouns. Use *a little* for small amounts and *much* for large amounts with non-count nouns.	• I ate **a few peanuts**. • I ate **many grapes**. • I used **a little salt**. • I didn't use **much pepper**.
	BE CAREFUL! *Much* is not usually used in affirmative statements. We usually use *a lot of* instead.	• I drank **a lot of water**. Not: I drank much water.

(continued on next page)

8 Some nouns can be <u>both</u> **count** and **non-count** nouns.

COUNT NOUN
• He bought three **cakes** for the party.

NON-COUNT NOUN
• He ate some **cake**.

USAGE NOTE: In informal speaking, some non-count nouns are used as count nouns.

• I'd like **two coffees** and **two sodas**.
(I'd like two cups of coffee and two cans of soda.)

REFERENCE NOTES
See Unit 4, page 43 for count nouns and the indefinite article *a/an*.
See Appendix 5 on page A–5 for spelling and pronunciation rules for plural nouns.
See Appendix 12 on page A–12 for a list of common non-count nouns.

STEP 3 FOCUSED PRACTICE

EXERCISE 1: Discover the Grammar

A | *Read the sentences. Circle the noun in each sentence. Then check (✓) whether the noun is used as a singular count noun, a plural count noun, or a non-count noun.*

	Singular Count Noun	Plural Count Noun	Non-count Noun
1. We ate a little (chicken).	☐	☐	☑
2. I need some information.	☐	☐	☐
3. There's a menu over there.	☐	☐	☐
4. There aren't many customers.	☐	☐	☐
5. We ate some bread.	☐	☐	☐
6. We need one more napkin.	☐	☐	☐
7. There was one server there.	☐	☐	☐
8. It's about 6 miles (10 kilometers) from here.	☐	☐	☐
9. The coffee is expensive.	☐	☐	☐
10. There aren't any rolls.	☐	☐	☐
11. There isn't any food left.	☐	☐	☐
12. The people here are very kind.	☐	☐	☐

B | *Read the situations. Circle the correct letter.*

1. You're in a restaurant. You need a napkin. Your friend sees one and says,

   _____.

   a. "Here's a napkin."   **b.** "Here's the napkin."

2. You ask about a person's job. Someone says, _____.

   a. "He's the lawyer."   **b.** "He's a lawyer."

3. It's your child's 10th birthday. You ask her what she wants for her party. She says,

   _____.

   a. "Please bake a cake."   **b.** "Please bake some cake."

4. You're at a restaurant. You say, _____.

   a. "Please pass some salts."   **b.** "Please pass the salt."

EXERCISE 2: *A, An, The*

(Grammar Notes 3–4)

Complete the conversation with **a, an,** *or* **the.**

A: Where's _____the_____ party?
                    1.

B: At Rectangles Restaurant.

A: Are _____ Garcias coming?
              2.

B: Yes, they are.

A: He's _____ chef, right?
              3.

B: Yes, he is. His wife is _____ chef
                              4.

too.

A: I hope they like _____ food at Rectangles.
                        5.

B: I'm sure they'll like _____ atmosphere and _____ service.
                            6.   **7.**

A: Where do they work?

B: She works at _____ Spanish restaurant, and he works at _____
                    8.   **9.**

Peruvian one.

A: Where are their restaurants?

B: _____ Spanish restaurant is in downtown Manhattan. _____ Peruvian
      10.   **11.**

restaurant is on Queens Boulevard in Rego Park in New York.

EXERCISE 3: *A, An, The*

(Grammar Notes 3–5)

Correct this paragraph. Add **a, an,** *or* **the**. *There are 10 more missing articles.*

> Kel Warner is ^a college student. He's English major. He has great part-time job. He writes
>
> for school paper. He's food critic. Kel goes to all restaurants in his town and writes about
>
> them. He can take friend to restaurants, and school newspaper pays bill. Kel really has
>
> wonderful job.

EXERCISE 4: *Some, Any*

(Grammar Note 6)

Complete the conversation with **some** *or* **any**.

MAN: Could you bring _____*some*_____ more bread, please?
1.

SERVER: Certainly. . . . Here you go. Anything else?

MAN: _____ water, please. With ice.
2.

SERVER: Would you like _____ water too, ma'am?
3.

WOMAN: No thanks, I don't feel like having _____ water. Hmm, maybe . . . how
4.

about a glass of ginger ale?

SERVER: Sure.

WOMAN: Also, could we have _____ more butter?
5.

SERVER: Of course.

MAN: Do you have _____ fish dishes? I don't eat meat, and I don't see
6.

_____ fish on the menu.
7.

SERVER: I'm sorry—we don't have fish, but we have _____ delicious vegetarian
8.

dishes.

EXERCISE 5: *Many, Much*

(Grammar Note 7)

Complete the sentences with **many** *or* **much**.

1. Boston's South End has _____*many*_____ good restaurants.

2. You can find _____ delicious dishes from different parts of the world

including Brazil, France, Italy, Ethiopia, the Middle East, and Korea.

3. There isn't _____ parking on Saturday night, so it's better to use public

transportation.

4. If you don't have _____ time, try Falafel King. The service is fast, and the

food is tasty.

5. If you don't have _____ money, try the Bakery Café. There are

_____ delicious choices at reasonable prices.

6. _____ of the best restaurants are on Tremont Street. _____

people call that street "restaurant row."

EXERCISE 6: *Many, Much* *(Grammar Note 7)*

Complete the conversations. Use **much** *or* **many** *and the words from the box.*

choices	people	time
information	restaurants	~~traffic~~

1. A: How long did it take you to get to the South End?

   B: There wasn't _____*much traffic*_____, but it still took us an hour to get

there.

2. A: It was a holiday. Were _____ open?

   B: Yes, we had a lot of choices.

3. A: Was your boyfriend with you?

   B: Yes, but he didn't have _____. He had to leave at 9:00,

and we only got to Tremont Street at 8:15.

4. A: How _____ were you with?

   B: There were six of us. We chose a small Italian restaurant.

5. A: How was the food?

   B: Delicious, but there weren't _____.

6. A: Did you find out about the area from your hotel concierge?

   B: No, he didn't have _____. I got everything from the

Internet.

EXERCISE 7: *A few, A little, Much,* or *Many*

Complete the sentences with **a few, a little, much,** *or* **many.**

1. We need to get some more apples. We only have _____*a few*_____ left.

2. There's _____ pea soup in the refrigerator. I didn't finish it all.

3. There's just _____ milk. We need to stop for more.

4. I want to buy _____ onions for an onion soup.

5. We don't have _____ cheese. Let's add that to the list.

6. We don't have _____ rolls. I'll stop at the bakery and buy some more.

7. Hurry. There isn't _____ time. The supermarket will close in half an
   hour.

EXERCISE 8: Editing

*Correct the paragraph. There are nine mistakes. The first one is already corrected. Find
and correct eight more.*

My friend Mario is ^the^ chef at a small French restaurant. He does most of the

cooking. He doesn't have the easy job. He works nights and weekends in an

hot kitchen. He manages lot of people. Any days the restaurant is very busy

from 6:00 p.m. to 8:00 p.m. Few times a year the restaurant has a special

deal. Mario has much friends.

They often eat at the

restaurant. Mario's dishes are

always delicious. He uses

many wine in his sauces.

Mario would like to go to a

French cooking school, but

he doesn't have some time.

EXERCISE 9: Pronunciation

🎧 **A** | *Read and listen to the Pronunciation Note.*

Pronunciation Note
The indefinite article *a* is usually unstressed and sounds like / ə / . **EXAMPLE:** a little sugar

🎧 **B** | *Listen and repeat the phrases.*

a delicious dish	**a little butter**	**a little salt**
a few eggs	**a little cheese**	
a few minutes	**a little pepper**	

🎧 **C** | *Now listen and complete the recipe. Then listen again and repeat each sentence.*

1. Put _____ in a frying pan.

2. Heat the pan and add _____ and _____.

3. Scramble the eggs for _____.

4. Add _____ and _____.

5. Enjoy _____ of scrambled eggs.

EXERCISE 10: Listening

🎧 **A** | *Listen to a conversation. Miguel helps Theresa prepare for a party. Circle the food Miguel buys.*

cheese	ice	nuts	soda
chips	ice cream	salsa	tuna

🎧 **B** | *Listen again. Answer the questions.*

1. What's the problem?

   _____

2. Why is Miguel upset?

   _____

EXERCISE 11: Presentation

A| *Imagine that you are a TV chef. Think of an appetizer, a main course, and a dessert. Write notes on the steps for your presentation. Remember to include articles and quantifiers.*

B| *Now tell about the meal you will prepare. The class asks questions about the meal.*

> **EXAMPLE:** Good afternoon and welcome to Pietro's Cooking Class. Today I will prepare a meal fit for a king. I'll begin with the salad. It's easy to make. The salad will have a lot of lettuce, a few pieces of carrot, a few walnuts, and some mango. I'll add a little creamy Italian dressing. Next I'll show how to make some carrot soup. Then for the main course I'll prepare lamb shish kebab with rice and some mixed vegetables.

> **EXAMPLE:** **STUDENT A:** What will you make for dessert?
> **STUDENT B:** For dessert, I will prepare an orange almond cake.

EXERCISE 12: A Restaurant

A| *Think of a restaurant you know. Complete the sentences with true statements about the restaurant. Use the suggestions from the box or your own ideas.*

big selection	fast service	lower prices	organic ingredients
cool design	free parking	music	tables outside
desserts	garden	new drinks	vegetarian choices

Name of restaurant: _____

There's a(n) _____

There aren't any _____

There aren't many _____

There isn't any _____

There isn't much _____

It doesn't have any _____

B| *SMALL GROUPS: Tell your group about the restaurant.*

> **EXAMPLE:** The name of my restaurant is Tiramisu Restaurant.
> There's a beautiful garden in the back of Tiramisu Restaurant.
> There aren't any rooms for private parties.

EXERCISE 13: Writing

A | *Write a review of the restaurant you described in Exercise 12 or any other restaurant, coffee shop, or cafeteria. Rate the restaurant and give the address and phone number. Tell about the food, the atmosphere, and the prices.*

EXAMPLE:

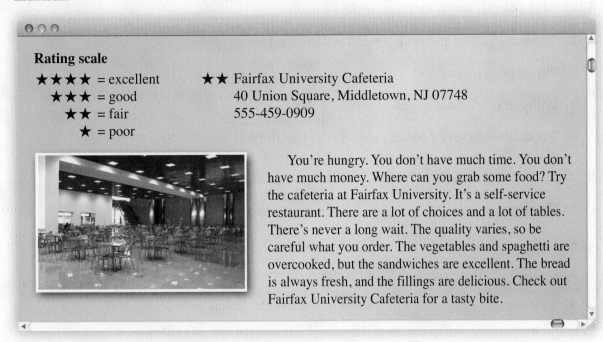

Rating scale

★★★★ = excellent   ★★ Fairfax University Cafeteria
  ★★★ = good   40 Union Square, Middletown, NJ 07748
    ★★ = fair   555-459-0909
     ★ = poor

You're hungry. You don't have much time. You don't have much money. Where can you grab some food? Try the cafeteria at Fairfax University. It's a self-service restaurant. There are a lot of choices and a lot of tables. There's never a long wait. The quality varies, so be careful what you order. The vegetables and spaghetti are overcooked, but the sandwiches are excellent. The bread is always fresh, and the fillings are delicious. Check out Fairfax University Cafeteria for a tasty bite.

B | *Check your work. Use the Editing Checklist.*

Editing Checklist

Did you . . . ?
☐ use count and non-count nouns correctly
☐ use indefinite and definite articles correctly
☐ use quantifiers correctly
☐ check your spelling

UNIT **27 Review**

Check your answers on page UR-6.
Do you need to review anything?

A | *Circle the correct words to complete the sentences.*

1. The baby spilled his milk. I need **a little / a few** napkins.

2. Please pass **a / the** salt.

3. Will you buy **a / an** avocado for the salad?

4. We didn't find **any / some** avocados at the store.

B | *Complete the sentences with* **a few, a little, many** *or* **much.**

1. There weren't _____ people at the party, only 10 or 12.

2. These days I don't have _____ free time. I work and study.

3. I only had _____ money with me. I couldn't pay for everyone.

4. We spent _____ days at the beach. It was great.

C | *Complete the sentences with* **a, an,** *or* **the.**

We bought grandpa _____ watch and _____ tie. I hope he
                 1.   **2.**

liked _____ watch. He didn't like _____ tie. Next year we'll take
   3.   **4.**

him to _____ restaurant. He always likes _____ good meal.
   5.   **6.**

D | *Correct the conversations. There are six mistakes.*

1. **A:** What are you looking for?

   B: I need a little stamps. I wrote any postcards, and I want to mail them.

2. **A:** There isn't some yogurt in the refrigerator. There's only half a container.

   B: There isn't much eggs either. We need to go shopping, but we don't have many

   time.

UNIT 28 How much / How many, Quantifiers, Enough, Adverbs of Frequency

DESSERTS, COOKING, AND BAKING

STEP 1 GRAMMAR IN CONTEXT

Before You Read

PAIRS: Ask your partner these questions.

- Do you have a favorite dessert? What is it?
- Where is it from?
- Do you know the recipe?
- How often do you eat it?

Read

Read the conversation. Each month Robert Fertita's English class has a party. A student brings a typical dessert from his or her country and tells the class about it.

WASANA: Carlos, try some of my dessert. It's very popular in Thailand. It's a mango and rice dessert.

CARLOS: No thanks, Wasana. I'm not that hungry.

WASANA: Just try **a little.** I think you'll like it.

CARLOS: OK, but just **a little**. That's **enough**. . . . Hmm. It's not bad.

WASANA: What do you mean, not bad. It's delicious.

CARLOS: Actually, it is pretty good. It's just that color . . . I don't **usually** eat purple rice. **How often** do you have it?

WASANA: My mom **often** makes it when mangoes are in season.

CARLOS: What's in it?

WASANA: Well, there's white rice and black rice, coconut milk, sugar, salt, and mangoes. It's not so hard to prepare.

CARLOS: Maybe I'll try to make it. **How much rice** do you use?

WASANA: A cup of white rice and a cup of black rice. The black rice gives it that dark color.

CARLOS: **How much coconut milk**?

WASANA: Two cups.

CARLOS: And **how many mangoes**?

(continued on next page)

How much / How many, Quantifiers, Enough, Adverbs of Frequency **321**

WASANA: Three.

CARLOS: I have an idea, Wasana. How about if I buy the ingredients, and I watch you prepare the dessert? Then I'll really know how to make it.

WASANA: OK. But then you have to show me how to make those delicious cookies from your country.

CARLOS: You mean the ones with the *dulce de leche* filling?

WASANA: Yes. They were wonderful.

CARLOS: Um. I er . . . I just went to the grocery store and bought them. They sell them all over my neighborhood.

After You Read

A | Practice *PAIRS: Now read the conversation aloud.*

B | Vocabulary *Complete the sentences with the words from the box.*

ingredients	in season	neighborhood	prepare	pretty good	taste

1. This lemon chicken has an amazing _____.

2. Peaches are not _____ right now, so I bought apples.

3. It takes a long time to _____ that dish.

4. There are two good fruit and vegetable stores in my _____.

5. This cake is _____, but I prefer the ice cream.

6. Do you know the _____ of this cake? I want to make it.

C | Comprehension *Make the false statements true based on the conversation.*

1. Wasana doesn't want Carlos to try her dessert.

2. Wasana's dessert is popular in Turkey.

3. Carlos likes the look of Wasana's dessert.

4. Wasana's dessert has two kinds of fruit.

5. Carlos brought fruit from his country.

HOW MUCH / HOW MANY, QUANTIFIERS, ENOUGH

Questions with *How Much*			Answers
How Much	**Non-count Noun**		**Quantifier**
How much	milk	do you need? did she buy?	**A lot.** (A lot of milk.) **Two quarts.** (Two quarts of milk.) **A carton.** (A carton of milk.) **A glass.** (A glass of milk.) **A cup.** (A cup of milk.) **A little.** (A little milk.)

Questions with *How Many*			Answers
How Many	**Plural Count Noun**		**Quantifier**
How many	apples	do we need? did he buy?	**A lot.** (A lot of apples.) **One bag.** (One bag of apples.) **Two pounds.** (Two pounds of apples.) **One or two.** (One or two apples.) **A few.** (A few apples.)

Statements with *Enough*			
		Enough	**Noun (Plural Count or Non-count)**
We	have don't have	enough	vegetables. meat.

Questions with *Enough*			
		Enough	**Noun (Plural Count or Non-count)**
Do you Does he	have	enough	vegetables? milk?

QUESTIONS ABOUT FREQUENCY

Questions with *How Often*				Answers
How often	**do**	I you we they	**bake?** **cook?**	Three times a day. Every (Sunday). Once a week. Rarely. Once in a while. Never.
	does	he she it	**break?**	

ADVERBS AND EXPRESSIONS OF FREQUENCY

Adverbs of Frequency			
Subject	**Adverb**	**Verb**	
I		**cook**	
He She It	usually almost never	**cooks**	on Tuesdays.
We You* They		**cook**	

Adverbs of Frequency with *Be*			
Subject	***Be***	**Adverb**	
I	am		
He She It	is	usually almost never	busy.
We You* They	are		

You is both singular and plural.

Adverbs of Frequency	
always	100%
almost always	
frequently	
usually / often	
sometimes	50%
rarely / seldom	
almost never	
never	0%

Expressions of Frequency	
Emiko cooks	every day. twice (a day). three times (a month). several times (a year). once in a while.

GRAMMAR NOTES

1	Use *how much* or *how many* to ask about quantity. Use *how much* with non-count nouns. Use *how many* with count nouns. Use *a little* with non-count nouns. Use *a few* with count nouns.	**A: How much** juice do you have? **B: A little**. OR I have **a little juice**. **A: How many** lemons do you need? **B: A few**. OR We need **a few** lemons.
2	It is not necessary to repeat the noun after *how much* or *how many* if the noun was named before or if the noun is understood.	**A: How much** does it cost? (*How much money is it?*) **B:** Ten dollars. **A:** I bought some cupcakes. **B: How many did you buy**? (*How many cupcakes did you buy?*)
3	You can **count non-count nouns** by using **measure words** or **containers**. Measure words include *a quart, a liter, an ounce, a kilogram, a teaspoon,* and *a tablespoon*. Containers include *a cup, a glass, a can, a jar,* and *a box*.	• Please get me **one quart of milk**. • He drank **two glasses of water**.

4	**Enough** means the amount you need. Use *enough* before plural count nouns and non-count nouns. **Not enough** means less than the amount you need. Use *not enough* before plural count nouns and non-count nouns.	• We have **enough eggs**. *(We need six eggs, and we have six eggs.)* • We have **enough juice**. • There **aren't enough apples**. • There **isn't enough milk**.
5	**How often** asks questions about **frequency**. *How often* is usually used with the simple present or simple past. It is rarely used with the present progressive.	• **How often** do you bake? NOT: How often ~~are you baking?~~
6	**Adverbs** and **expressions of frequency** tell **how often** we do something. Adverbs and expressions of frequency are often used with the simple present. They rarely occur with the present progressive.	• Tim **always** shops at the Farmer's Market. • Marta goes to class **every day**. • They **usually** open the market at 9:00. NOT: They ~~are usually opening~~ the market at 9:00.
7	Adverbs of frequency usually come **after the verb be**. They usually come **before other verbs** in the simple present. **Sometimes**, **usually**, and **often** can also come at the beginning of a sentence. **BE CAREFUL!** Don't begin a sentence with **never** or **always**. **BE CAREFUL!** Don't use negative adverbs of frequency (*rarely*, *seldom*, *almost never*) in negative sentences.	• Yoko **is usually** on time. She **isn't usually** late. • She **rarely eats** dessert. • She **doesn't often eat** dessert. • He **sometimes goes** to the bakery. • **Sometimes** he **goes** to the bakery. • I **never** cook. NOT: ~~Never~~ I cook. NOT: I ~~rarely don't~~ cook.
8	**Expressions of frequency** are time markers. They usually come at the beginning or at the end of a sentence.	• He eats an orange **every day**. • **Every week** she goes to the bakery.

REFERENCE NOTES

See Unit 35 page 411 for a discussion of *enough* after an adjective.
See Appendix 12, page A-12 for a list of quantity expressions.

EXERCISE 1: Discover the Grammar

A | *Underline the noun in each phrase. Then check (✓) the category.*

	Singular Count Noun	Plural Count Noun	Non-count Noun
how much <u>milk</u>			✓
how many eggs			
a lot of raisins			
enough sugar			
a little juice			
a lemon			

B | *Underline the adverbs of frequency. Circle the expressions of frequency.*

1. He almost <u>always</u> cooks.

2. She usually bakes.

3. Once in a while he bakes.

4. Every weekend they go to a café.

5. They often meet friends there.

6. It is frequently crowded.

EXERCISE 2: *How much / How many / How often* (Grammar Notes 1–2, 4)

Complete the conversations with **How much, How many,** *or* **How often.** *Complete the answers with* **much, many,** *or* **often.**

1. **A:** _____How many_____ meals do you prepare in a week?

   B: Not _____. I eat breakfast and lunch at school.

2. **A:** _____ does he eat out?

   B: Not _____. He likes to eat at home.

3. **A:** On average _____ time does it take you to prepare dinner?

   B: Not _____. Only about 15 or 20 minutes.

4. **A:** _____ times a week do you shop for food?

   B: Not _____. We usually shop once or twice a week.

5. **A:** _____ do they spend on food each week?

   B: Not _____. They shop when there are sales.

6. **A:** _____ do you bake?

   B: Not _____. There's a great bakery in our neighborhood.

EXERCISE 3: Word Order: Adverbs and Expressions of Frequency   *(Grammar Notes 5–7)*

Write sentences with the words in parentheses.

   1. (chocolate / Hugo / and / Every afternoon / has coffee / a piece of)

   Every afternoon Hugo has coffee and a piece of chocolate.

   2. (hot / is / always / The coffee)

   _____

   3. (almost always / dark / is / The chocolate)

   _____

   4. (never / It / white chocolate / is)

   _____

   5. (Hugo / never drinks / in the evening / coffee)

   _____

   6. (hot chocolate / drinks / usually / He)

   _____

   7. (drinks / Sometimes / he / ginger tea)

   _____

EXERCISE 4: *Enough*   *(Grammar Note 4)*

*Complete the sentences with **enough** and the words from the box.*

chairs	cupcakes	drinks	ice	plates	room	~~time~~

   1. We can't bake a cake. There isn't _____ *enough time* _____. People will be here soon.

   2. People get thirsty. Are there _____?

   3. Is there _____ for the drinks? The drinks aren't cold.

   4. You can't put those cupcakes on that table. There isn't _____.

   5. There aren't _____ for everyone. Why don't you cut them in half?

   6. People won't want to stand. Are there _____?

   7. People will want to put their dessert on something. Are there _____?

EXERCISE 5: Containers

(Grammar Note 3)

Complete the conversation with the words in parentheses. Write the correct words.

blender   pint   container   jar   can   tablespoon

A: Can you show me the ingredients for your berry dessert drink?

B: Sure. _____*A can*_____ of chick peas, a _____ of orange juice, a
         1. (can / box)   2. (container / jar)
_____ of fresh strawberries, and a _____ of honey.
      3. (bag / pint)   4. (box / jar)

A: And how do you make this drink?

B: I put the _____ of chick peas, 1½ _____ of orange juice,
                   5. (can / box)   6. (cups / bags)
2 _____ of strawberries, and 2 or 3 _____ of honey in a
      7. (cups / cans)   8. (tablespoons / cans)
blender. When it's smooth, I add six ice cubes. Then I blend it again. Delicious!

EXERCISE 6: Editing

Correct the conversations. There are seven mistakes. The first mistake is already corrected. Find and correct six more.

1. **A:** How ~~much~~ *many* cookies are there in the box?

   B: Only one. Mary ate the rest.

2. **A:** How often do you bake?

   B: Always I bake on the weekend.

3. **A:** Do we have cake enough for everyone?

   B: Yes, we do.

4. **A:** How many flour do you need?

   B: Two cups.

5. **A:** How many egg are there in the cake? And how much sugars?

   B: Four eggs and three cup of sugar.

EXERCISE 7: Pronunciation

A | *Read and listen to the Pronunciation Note.*

> **Pronunciation Note**
>
> Sometimes when people get hurt they say, "Ow." That's the **/ aʊ /** sound in words such as **how** or **flour**.

B | *Listen and underline the / aʊ / sound in the sentences.*

1. Now, add the eggs.

2. How much brown sugar do you need?

3. You need about two cups of sugar.

4. How many pounds of flour did you buy?

5. Take the cupcakes out of the oven.

6. How many ounces of milk does this need?

C | *Listen again and repeat the sentences.*

EXERCISE 8: Listening

A | *Listen to a conversation. Write T (True) or F (False) for each statement.*

_____ 1. Robert is giving Laura a recipe.

_____ 2. Laura thinks Robert's red velvet cupcakes are good.

_____ 3. Robert doesn't want to give Laura the recipe.

_____ 4. Laura writes down the recipe.

B | *Listen again and check (✓) the ingredients in the recipe.*

✓ flour	_____ butter	_____ red food color
_____ cocoa powder	_____ eggs	_____ vanilla extract
_____ baking soda	_____ sour cream	_____ cream
_____ salt	_____ milk	_____ sugar

EXERCISE 9: Survey

Survey five students. Report the results to the class. Ask "How often do you
_____*?" with the activities in the list.*

bake   cook   do dishes   eat dessert   eat out   go to a bakery

EXAMPLE: Mi Young frequently eats dessert. But she rarely bakes or cooks. So she often eats out.
Sometimes she eats at a bakery.

EXERCISE 10: Information Gap

Work in pairs. **Student A,** *follow the instructions on this page.* **Student B,** *turn to page 332 and follow the instructions there.*

1. Look at the list of ingredients. Ask your partner questions to find out how much you need of each ingredient to make chocolate chip cookies. Write the amounts.

Chocolate Chip Cookies
7 ounces chocolate chips
_____ flour
_____ teaspoons baking powder
1 cup chopped walnuts
_____ butter
_____ sugar
_____ brown sugar
_____ eggs, slightly beaten
1 teaspoon vanilla extract

EXAMPLE: STUDENT A: How much flour do you use for the chocolate chip cookies?
STUDENT B: Two and half cups.

2. Now look at the list of ingredients for apple pie. Answer your partner's questions.

Apple Pie

The Crust	The Filling
2 cups flour	1/3 cup sugar
1 teaspoon salt	1/4 cup flour
2/3 cup shortening	1/2 teaspoon ground cinnamon
5 tablespoons cold water	1/2 teaspoon ground nutmeg
	a pinch of salt
	8 medium-size apples
	2 tablespoons butter

EXAMPLE: STUDENT B: How much flour do you use in the apple pie crust?
STUDENT A: Two cups of flour.

EXERCISE 11: Group Presentation

GROUPS: You are preparing dessert for 50 people. Decide what you will serve and how much. Be specific and include different kinds of desserts. Each student talks about one or two of the desserts. Suggestions: nuts, cheese, fruit, dessert drinks, cakes, cookies, mocha ice cream, and flan.

EXAMPLE: STUDENT A: I'm going to buy a variety of nuts. I'm going to get a pound of salty cashews and a pound of unsalted peanuts. I'm also going to buy some almonds and raisins. I like the combination of a salty and sweet dessert.

STUDENT B: I'm going to bake 30 red velvet cupcakes. I'm going to frost half of them and leave half of them without frosting.

STUDENT C: I'm going to buy fresh fruit. I'm going to buy pears, grapes, and strawberries.

EXERCISE 12: Writing

A | *Describe the desserts your group bought for the party in Exercise 11. Use quantity expressions where possible.*

EXAMPLE: We prepared desserts for 50 people. We served nuts, cakes, cookies, fresh fruit, cheese, and crackers. We brought 3 pounds of mixed nuts. Sonia baked a chocolate cake and Ana made three dozen chocolate chip cookies. Mohammed brought fresh fruit. He brought 2 pounds of pears, apples, and two pineapples. Pierre brought a lot of different kinds of cheese and crackers.

B | *Check your work. Use the Editing Checklist.*

Editing Checklist

Did you . . . ?
- ☐ use quantity expressions correctly
- ☐ check your spelling

1. Look at the list of ingredients for chocolate chip cookies. Answer your partner's questions.

Chocolate Chip Cookies

7 ounces of chocolate chips

2 1/2 cups flour

3 teaspoons baking powder

1 cup chopped walnuts

1 cup butter

3/4 cup sugar

3/4 cup brown sugar

2 eggs, slightly beaten

1 teaspoon vanilla extract

> EXAMPLE: STUDENT A: How much flour do you use for the chocolate chip cookies?
> STUDENT B: Two and a half cups.

2. Now look at the list of ingredients. Then ask your partner questions to find out how much you need of each ingredient to make apple pie. Write the amounts.

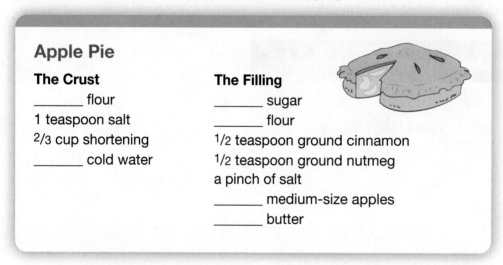

Apple Pie

The Crust

_____ flour

1 teaspoon salt

2/3 cup shortening

_____ cold water

The Filling

_____ sugar

_____ flour

1/2 teaspoon ground cinnamon

1/2 teaspoon ground nutmeg

a pinch of salt

_____ medium-size apples

_____ butter

> EXAMPLE: STUDENT B: How much flour do you use in the apple pie crust?
> STUDENT A: Two cups of flour.

UNIT 28 Review

Check your answers on page UR-6.

Do you need to review anything?

A | *Complete the sentences with* **How many** *or* **How much.**

1. _____ people went to the party?

2. _____ noise was there?

3. _____ servers did they hire?

4. _____ bread did he eat?

5. _____ desserts did they bring?

B | *Write questions with the words in parentheses. Begin with* **How many, How much,** *or* **How often.**

1. _____
   (you / go to the movies)

2. _____
   (close friends / you have)

3. _____
   (time / you spend online)

4. _____
   (people / live in your home)

5. _____
   (you / check email)

C | *Write sentences with the words in parentheses.*

1. _____
   (usually / I / a few times a week / bake)

2. _____
   (in the house / They / have / food / never / enough)

3. _____
   (soccer / we / Every weekend / play / in the park)

4. _____
   (a / He / glass / spilled / of grape juice)

5. _____
   (salt / She / a little / added / to the soup)

D | *Correct the sentences. There are five mistakes.*

1. Never I eat breakfast at home.

2. She once in a while bakes.

3. Do you have milk enough?

4. How much tomatoes did they buy?

5. I rarely don't cook.

Unit 28 Review: *How much / How many,* Quantifiers, *Enough,* Adverbs of Frequency   **333**

Too much / Too many, Too + Adjective
THE RIGHT PLACE TO LIVE

STEP 1 GRAMMAR IN CONTEXT

Before You Read

Does your city or town have any of these problems? Check (✓) them.

- ☐ too much noise or traffic
- ☐ not enough jobs
- ☐ too few parking spaces
- ☐ too much crime
- ☐ too few parks
- ☐ too hot or too cold

Read

Read the online article about three U.S. cities. Which of these cities would you want to live in most?

DREAM LOCATIONS
Home | Lifestyle | Photos

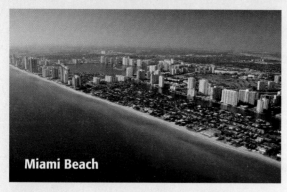

Miami Beach

Some call my town *The American Riviera*. Others say it's the *Latin Hollywood*. For me, it's the best place to live. We have sunny weather, beautiful sandy beaches, and graceful palm trees. From January to March the sky is mostly blue, and the temperature is in the 70s almost every day. There are a lot of water activities, and the night life is great. It is a cosmopolitan area with people from all over the world. But the climate isn't perfect.

In the summer months the weather is **too hot** and **humid**, and storms are common. Public transportation isn't very good. There are **too few busses**, and there isn't a subway, so there's **too much traffic**. It's hard to find a good job. Unemployment is high, and most salaries are low. Some say they pay you here in sunshine. But if you have a job, and you like warm weather, sandy beaches, and a rich nightlife, Miami Beach is a great place to live.

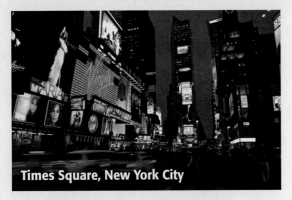

Times Square, New York City

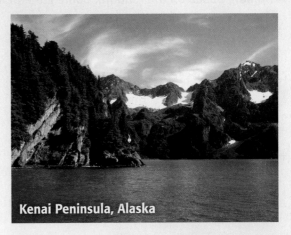

Kenai Peninsula, Alaska

Some say this city is the capital of the world. It has a rich cultural life and offers lots of things to do. There are great theaters, restaurants, museums, sports stadiums, and a wonderful nightlife. There are job opportunities, good health care, and a truly multicultural atmosphere with people from all over the world. It's called the city that never sleeps.

But housing is much **too expensive**. You pay a fortune to live in an apartment the size of a closet. The schools are often **too crowded**. There is a good subway system, but there is **too much traffic**. Still, this is a city of opportunity, and I'd rather live here with 8 million other New Yorkers than any other place on earth.

I find most cities **too busy**, **too dirty** with **too much traffic**, **pollution**, and **crime**. They also have **too many people**, and **too few animals**. That's why I love my town of Kenai in the Kenai Peninsula of Alaska. Here the air is clean, and you can hike and fish and see the stars at night. Of course, it's **too cold** for some people, and there's **too little sunlight** for others. But I'm happy here in this small town far away from the hubbub[1] of big city life.

[1]*hubbub:* confusion

After You Read

A | Practice *PAIRS: Read the article again aloud. Take turns reading each section.*

B | Vocabulary *Complete the sentences with the words from the box.*

| climate | crime | free time | housing | pollution | unemployment |

1. The _____ here is awful. Summers are too hot, and winters are too cold.

2. The _____ from the factories is causing health problems among children in the area.

3. That's a very safe area. There is almost no _____.

4. The government is building _____ for the poor of the city.

5. We're working too much. We have no _____.

6. _____ is low here, so he expects to find a good job soon.

C | Comprehension *Read the statements. Write* **MB** (Miami Beach), **NYC** (New York City), *or* **K** (Kenai), *based on the reading. Some statements are true for more than one place.*

_____ **1.** There's a lot of traffic.

_____ **2.** It has a great nightlife.

_____ **3.** It's great for hiking.

_____ **4.** There are many wild animals.

_____ **5.** Housing is very expensive.

_____ **6.** The transportation system is poor.

_____ **7.** People here feel close to nature.

_____ **8.** This city has a lot of opportunities.

STEP 2 GRAMMAR PRESENTATION

TOO MUCH / TOO MANY / TOO + ADJECTIVE

	Too Many / Too Few	Plural Count Noun
There are	too many	cars.
	too few	parking spaces.

	Too Much / Too Little	Non-count Noun
There is	too much	noise.
	too little	light.

	Too	Adjective
It's	too	hot.
		cold.

GRAMMAR NOTES

1

Too many and **too much** mean "more than the right amount." These words usually have a negative meaning. Use *too many* before plural count nouns. Use *too much* before non-count nouns.

Too few is the opposite of *too many*.
Too little is the opposite of *too much*. Both *too few* and *too little* mean "not enough." These words usually have a negative meaning. Use *too few* with count nouns. Use *too little* with non-count nouns.

- **Too many** students registered for that course. *(There was room for 10 students. Fifteen people registered.)*
- It costs **too much** money. *(We can't afford it.)*

- There were **too few** books. *(There were books for five people, but seven people needed books.)*
- There was **too little** time. *(We couldn't finish.)*

2

Use *too* + **adjective** to say that something has a negative result.

- The water is **too cold**. *(We can't swim here.)*

REFERENCE NOTE

See Unit 35, page 411 for more about *too* + adjective and *very*.

EXERCISE 1: Discover the Grammar

Underline the adjectives that follow **too.** *Circle the nouns that follow* **too much, too many, too few,** *and* **too little.**

1. Housing is too expensive there. Let's not move there.

2. They're building a new school. This school is too crowded.

3. The commute to work was too long. It took two hours each way.

4. There are too many cars on the highway. Let's take a different route.

5. I have too little information about that neighborhood. I don't want to rent a place without more information.

6. There's too much crime in that area.

7. There are too few jobs in that city. People are moving away.

EXERCISE 2: *Too much / Too many*   (Grammar Note 1)

Complete the sentences with **too many** *or* **too much** *and the words from the box.*

crime	noise	pollution	rats	storms	~~unemployment~~

1. Jobs are hard to find. There's _____*too much unemployment*_____ in this town.

2. The climate isn't good. There are

   _____.

3. The streets aren't safe. There's

   _____.

4. It's often hard to breathe here.

   There's _____.

5. There's _____

   in that neighborhood. We won't be able to sleep at night.

6. There are _____ in that area. They should do something to

   get rid of them.

EXERCISE 3: *Too + Adjective*

(Grammar Note 2)

Add **too** *before the adjective in each sentence.*

                  too

1. Homes are expensive in that area. That's why people can't afford to live there.

2. We don't want to move there. The commute is long. It's two hours to downtown.

3. The train is crowded at this time. Let's take a later train.

4. That house is small for you. There are six people in your family. How will you manage?

5. It's not small for us. We love the location. We can manage.

6. I don't like that area. Winters are long.

EXERCISE 4: *Too few / Too little*

(Grammar Note 1)

Complete the conversations. Use **There is, There are,** *or* **There was,** *and* **too few** *or* **too little** *and the ideas in parentheses.*

1. **A:** What's the problem?

   B: _____There are too few doctors_____ in that hospital. The hospital
                   (not enough doctors)
   administration needs to hire more doctors or people's health will suffer.

2. **A:** Why is the grass brown?

   B: _____ this past summer.
               (not enough rain)

3. **A:** Why are so many people moving?

   B: _____ in this area.
               (not enough jobs)

4. **A:** Why are all those people moving so far out?

   B: _____ in the center of town.
           (not enough affordable housing)

5. **A:** _____ this area.
               (not enough schools)

   B: That's true, but the city is planning to build two new schools.

6. **A:** _____ around here.
               (not enough parks)

   B: I agree. The city planners need to build more parks.

EXERCISE 5: *Too much / Too many / Too few / Too little / Too*   (Grammar Notes 1–2)

Complete the conversations with **too, too many, too much, too few,** *or* **too little.**

1. **A:** What's wrong with Middletown?

   B: The climate. It gets _____ *too much* _____ rain and humidity. It's

   damp most of the year.

2. **A:** Why don't you want to move to Rockford?

   B: The climate there is OK, but the health care is terrible. There are

   _____ doctors and hospitals.

3. **A:** How about moving to Newtown?

   B: It's boring. There are _____ things to do.

4. **A:** How was the new restaurant on Spring Street?

   B: It was _____ dark. I wasn't able to read the menu or

   see my food. There was _____ light.

5. **A:** Do you go to that beach?

   B: Not in the summer. There are _____ people at that

   time of year. It's _____ crowded.

6. **A:** Did you take the job?

   B: No. The salary was _____ low, and there were

   _____ holidays and sick days.

7. **A:** Am I _____ late for the talk about the environment?

   B: Yes, it began an hour ago.

8. **A:** Which car did you buy, the Cruiser or the Mercedes?

   B: Neither. The Mercedes was _____ expensive, and the

   Cruiser had _____ problems.

EXERCISE 6: Editing

Correct the conversations. There are seven mistakes. The first mistake is already corrected. Find and correct six more.

1. **A:** I'd like to move to the suburbs. The city is ^too^ noisy for me.

   B: Not me. I think the suburbs are quiet.

2. **A:** What's wrong with that company?

   B: There are too many managers and too little workers.

3. **A:** Did you buy that apartment?

   B: No. It was too money for too few space.

4. **A:** Don't go by bus. It will take too many time. Take the train. It's a lot faster.

   B: Yes, but it's too much expensive. The bus is half the price.

STEP 4 COMMUNICATION PRACTICE

EXERCISE 7: Pronunciation

A *Read and listen to the Pronunciation Note.*

> **Pronunciation Note**
>
> - To pronounce / **t** / as in *time*, touch the upper gum ridge with your tongue.
> - To pronounce / **θ** / as in *three* or / **ð** / as in *this*, place your tongue tip between your upper and lower front teeth.
> - The / **t** / and / **θ** / sounds are not voiced. The vocal cords do not vibrate.
> - The / **ð** / sound is voiced. The vocal cords vibrate.

B *Listen. Then place your hand on your throat and repeat the words.*

/ t / not voiced	/ θ / not voiced	/ ð / voiced
ten		then
tear		there
tease		these
tree	three	
taught	thought	
tin	thin	

C | *Listen and underline the / t / sound. Underline the / θ / sound twice. Circle the / ð / sound.*

1. I thought Ted taught about the environment.

2. There are three trees in front of their house.

3. Is it true that the technician went through the house in only thirty minutes?

D | *Listen again and repeat each sentence.*

EXERCISE 8: Listening

A | *A couple looked at three apartments. Listen to their conversation with a real estate salesperson. Which apartment did the couple like the most? Circle the correct letter.*

    a. the first one   **b.** the second one   **c.** the third one

B | *Listen again and complete the chart.*

	What They Liked	What They Didn't Like
First apartment		
Second apartment		
Third apartment		

EXERCISE 9: Role Play

Act out a situation with a partner. Use **too, too much, too many, too few,** *or* **too little,** *in your conversation.*

Situation 1:

A salesperson is trying to convince a customer to rent a tiny apartment that is far from everything.

Situation 2:

Two friends live in the same big city. One friend wants to move away from the city. The other wants to stay.

    EXAMPLE: **A:** I want to move to Australia for a few years.
                      B: Don't move! It's too far away!

EXERCISE 10: Describe Your City

SMALL GROUPS: Write four good things and four bad things about the city or town you are in. Use **too, too much, too many, too few,** *and* **too little.**

    EXAMPLE: **Good**   **Bad**
                      There's a wonderful concert hall here.   There are too few parking spaces.
                      There isn't much pollution here.   There are too few bicycle paths.

EXERCISE 11: Writing

A | *Write an email to a newspaper. Complain about one aspect of life in your city. Use two of the following:* **too, too much, too many, too few,** *or* **too little.**

> EXAMPLE: Young people are the future of this city, but there are too few jobs for them here. Too many young people have nothing to do. The city needs to help them find jobs. In the past, the city spent too much money on roads and highways and too little on job training. Many young people don't have good workplace skills. The city needs to offer job training and practical skills. The city should offer courses in how to write a resumé, take an interview, and get and keep a job. This newspaper complained that too many young people are getting into trouble. With good jobs, young people will stay out of trouble.

B | *Check your work. Use the Editing Checklist.*

Editing Checklist

Did you . . . ?
- [ ] use **too many**, **too much**, **too little**, **too few**, and **too** correctly
- [ ] check your spelling

A | *Add* **too, too much,** *or* **too many** *to each sentence. Use a ^ symbol.*

1. That movie was long. I didn't enjoy it.

2. We have homework. We can't go to the movies today.

3. I bought milk. Who's going to drink it?

4. There are trucks on that road. Let's take another route.

5. It takes time to get there by bus. Let's take the train.

B | *Complete the sentences with* **too, too much, too many, too little,** *or* **too few.**

1. That desert town is _____ hot, and it gets _____ rain.

2. Unemployment is high in that area. There are _____ jobs.

3. That town is not safe. There is _____ crime.

4. This area has _____ dishonest politicians.

C | *Rewrite the sentences with* **too little** *or* **too few.**

1. There's not enough rain. _____

2. There aren't enough subways. _____

3. There's not enough sunlight. _____

4. There aren't enough traffic lights. _____

5. There isn't enough water. _____

D | *Correct the paragraph. There are five mistakes.*

The climate here is terrible. It gets too much hot in the summer and too cold in the winter. There's too many snow and ice. Winters are to long. There are too little comfortable days with mild temperatures and blue skies. Also, there's too many air pollution from all the traffic on the streets. I want to move.

From Grammar to Writing
A BUSINESS LETTER

1 | *PAIRS: When we write a business letter, we follow a certain style. We use this style for all letters that are not to friends or relatives. Look at the business letter and answer the questions.*

1. Where does your address belong?

_____

_____

2. Where does the date belong?

_____

_____

3. Where does the name and the address of the person you are writing to belong?

_____

_____

4. How do you address the person you are writing to?

_____

_____

Rua Rio de Janeiro 12 **①**
São Paulo, Brasil

March 12, _____ **②**

Lee Spencer, Director **③**
International English Language Institute
Hunter College
New York, New York 10021

Dear Mr. Spencer: **④**

I am interested in attending Hunter College's **⑤**
International English Language Institute in the fall.

Would you please send me an application and a catalog of your courses?

Thank you for your prompt attention to this request. **⑥**

Sincerely yours, **⑦**

João Lima **⑧**
João Lima

5. What do you do in the first sentence?

_____

6. What does the last line of the letter say?

_____

7. How do you end the letter?

_____

8. What do you write last?

_____

2 | *Read the rules we use to write a business letter.*

1. Write your address at the top left of the page.
2. Write the date below your address.
3. Skip at least two lines. Write the name and address of the person you are writing to on the left margin below the date.
4. When you write a letter, it's best to write to a person by name. If you don't know the person's name, you may write "Dear Sir / Madam:" or "To Whom It May Concern:"; be sure to use a colon (:) after the name.
5. In your first sentence, explain what you want.
6. In the last line of your letter, you usually thank the person you are writing to.
7. You may end a letter with "Sincerely yours" or "Yours truly."
8. Finally, write your signature, and write your name below your signature.

3 | *Write one of the following business letters. Follow the rules in Part 2.*

1. Ask for a bulletin of courses and an application for a language program.
2. Ask for a list of moderately priced apartments near the college.

4 | *Exchange letters with a partner. Did your partner follow the directions? Correct any mistakes in grammar and spelling.*

5 | *Talk to your partner. Discuss the mistakes you made. Then rewrite your own paper and make any necessary changes.*

MODALS: REQUESTS, ADVICE, NECESSITY

Advice: *Should, Ought to, Had better*

DOS AND DON'TS OF THE BUSINESS WORLD

Before You Read

PAIRS: Look at the photo of Angelina Jolie and Cambodian Prime Minister Hun Sen. In the United States, a firm handshake is important in business. Is it important in other countries too? Discuss with your partner.

Read

Read the online article about doing business in Chile and Egypt.

BUSINESS NEWS	MONEY MARKETS	POLITICS	SMALL BUSINESS	SEARCH:

Global Business

GLOBAL BUSINESS

It's always a good idea for business people to know the customs of people in the place they are doing business. If you don't know the customs, you might insult someone and lose a business deal. Here is some advice for anyone headed for[1] Chile.

First of all, when **should** you go? Chileans usually take vacations in January and February so you **should not plan** a business trip during those two months. Many offices will be closed for the summer vacation.

Next, how **should** you greet people at business meetings? When attending a business meeting in Chile, you **ought to greet** and **shake hands** with everyone. Later at business dinners and receptions, men sometimes greet other men with hugs. Women often hug and touch cheeks while kissing the air. You **should not be** surprised to get a hug or kiss from a Chilean you know. During a meal, you **should keep** your hands on the table, not in your lap.

In Chile, an open palm upward with the fingers separated means "stupid." You **should avoid** making this gesture. And beware[2]! Slapping your right fist[3] into your left open palm[4] is very impolite. You**'d better not make** that gesture, or you may insult or anger someone.

---

[1] *headed for:* going to
[2] *beware:* be on guard against
[3] *fist:* a hand with fingers closed tightly together
[4] *palm:* the inside of hand

Now in Egypt, you **should not expect** to do business on Fridays. It is the Muslim day of rest. Also, throughout the Arab world, people use the Islamic calendar (also called Muslim calendar or Hijri calendar) and the Western calendar. To avoid confusion, you **should put** two dates on paperwork—the Hijri (Islamic) date and the Gregorian (Western) date.

If you're invited for a meal, you **should eat** with your right hand. In many countries with large Muslim and Hindu populations, people consider the left hand unclean. In Egypt leaving a little food is a sign that you are full, so you **shouldn't eat** everything on your plate. Also, you**'d better not add** salt to your food or you might insult the cook.

What do you know about sitting in Egypt? You **should** never **sit** with legs crossed or **show** the sole[5] of your shoe. In Arab culture, it is a big insult to show the bottom of the foot.

So remember, before you go to another country to do business, learn about the culture. And remember when you're in that country, try and "do as the Romans do."[6]

In the Middle East, it is not polite to cross legs.

---

[5] *sole:* the bottom of foot or shoe
[6] *"do as the Romans do":* copy the people in the place you are visiting

After You Read

A | Practice *PAIRS: Now read the article aloud. Take turns reading each paragraph.*

B | Vocabulary *Complete the sentences with the words from the box.*

business receptions	confusion	consider	customs	insult

1. Business people should know the _____ of the countries they visit.

2. At Chilean _____, men greet other men with hugs.

3. To avoid _____, put the Western and Islamic date on this paperwork.

4. People in the United States _____ a firm handshake is important.

5. It is an _____ to show the bottom of your foot in the Middle East.

C | Comprehension *Write T (True) or F (False).*

_____ **1.** Chileans often take vacations in July and August.

_____ **2.** Offices in Chile are often closed in February.

_____ **3.** When businessmen meet in Chile at dinners, they do not hug.

_____ **4.** When you eat a meal in Chile, you should keep your hands in your lap.

_____ **5.** Egyptians do business on Friday, Saturday, and Sunday.

_____ **6.** You should not use your right hand when you eat in Egypt.

_____ **7.** You should not add salt to your food in an Egyptian home.

MODALS

Should, *Shouldn't*, and *Ought to*

Affirmative Statements			Negative Statements		
Subject	***Should / Ought to***	**Base Form of Verb**	**Subject**	***Should not***	**Base Form of Verb**
I You He She We They	**should ought to**	**go.**	I You He She We They	**should not shouldn't**	**go.**
It	**should ought to**	**happen.**	It	**should not shouldn't**	**happen.**

Yes / No Questions				Short Answers					
Should	**Subject**	**Base Form of Verb**			Affirmative			Negative	
Should	we he they	**wear**	a suit?	Yes,	you he they	**should.**	No,	you he they	**shouldn't.**

Wh- Questions			
***Wh-* Word**	***Should***	**Subject**	**Base Form of Verb**
What	**should**	I	**do?**
When		we	**go?**

Had Better and *Had Better Not*

Affirmative Statements			Negative Statements		
Subject	***Had Better***	**Base Form of Verb**	**Subject**	***Had Better Not***	**Base Form of Verb**
We You	**had better ('d better)**	**go.**	We You	**had better not 'd better not**	**go.**

Contractions	
I had better → **I'd better**	we had better → **we'd better**
you had better → **you'd better**	you had better → **you'd better**
he had better → **he'd better**	they had better → **they'd better**
she had better → **she'd better**	

1	Use *should* to **give advice** or **talk about what is right to do**. Use *should* + the base form of the verb.	• He should **bring** them a gift. Not: He should ~~to bring~~ them a gift. Not: He should ~~brings~~ them a gift.
	Use *should not* for the negative. Use the contraction *shouldn't* in speaking and informal writing.	• We **should not** bring roses. • We **shouldn't** bring roses.
2	We use *should* to talk about the **present** or **future**.	• You **should** do the report **now**. • You **should** turn in the report **tomorrow**.
3	*Ought to* means the same as *should*.	• You **ought to read** that book about Chile. It's very helpful.
4	*Ought to* is not usually used in questions or negatives. We use *should* instead.	• Should I wear a suit? Not: ~~Ought I to wear~~ a suit?
	USAGE NOTE: To sound more polite, use *I think* or *Maybe* before saying, "you should" or "you ought to."	• **I think you should** bring a small gift. • **Maybe you ought to** ask him first.
5	Use *had better* to **give advice**. *Had better* is stronger than *should*. It implies that something bad might happen if you don't follow the advice.	• You had better **call** before you go to the store. *(It may be closed.)*
	Use *had better* + the base form of the verb.	• He **had better send** an email message.
	The negative of *had better* is *had better not*.	• He **had better not** forget his passport.
	We often use the short form *'d better* in speaking and informal writing.	• We**'d better ask** the doctor.
6	*Had better* is used to talk about the **present** or the **future**. (The *had* in *had better* does not refer to the past.)	• I**'d better** finish my report now. • She**'d better not** miss her flight tomorrow.

STEP 3 FOCUSED PRACTICE

EXERCISE 1: Discover the Grammar

Read the questions and answers about using business cards in Japan. Underline **should,**
had better, ought to, *and the base form of the verb.*

1. **Q:** When <u>should</u> I <u>present</u> my business card?

   A: Right after you shake hands or bow.

2. **Q:** Should I translate my card into Japanese?

   A: Yes. It's a good idea to have English on one side and Japanese on the other.

3. **Q:** What should I do when I get my colleague's card?

   A: Read it carefully. You ought to remember the information on it.

4. **Q:** Can we start our business before we exchange business cards?

   A: You'd better not start your business before you exchange business cards.

EXERCISE 2: *Should*: Affirmative and Negative

(Grammar Notes 1–2)

*Some international students are talking about customs in their countries. Complete the
sentences with* **should** *or* **shouldn't** *and the verb in parentheses.*

1. I was in a school cafeteria in the U.S. A guy had a cold. He blew his nose at the table.

   In Korea you _____*shouldn't blow*_____ your nose at the table. It's very impolite.

(blow)

2. In China, you _____ people. Many people feel uncomfortable when

(touch)

   others touch them. Here I notice people touch more often.

3. I think that people in North America don't like silence. Someone always speaks. I

   guess you _____ quiet.

(be)

4. In some cultures, people can clap hands to call a waiter. You _____

   never _____ that here. I think here you _____ until

(do) (wait)

   the waiter looks at you. But sometimes the waiter never looks at you.

5. In North America people often say "We'll have to get together" or "I'll see you later."

   But they don't plan to meet me or see me later. In Poland we don't do that. In my

   opinion, Americans and Canadians _____ that. It's confusing.

(say)

EXERCISE 3: *Should*: Affirmative and Negative

(Grammar Notes 1–2)

Complete the sentences about doing business in Hungary. Use **should** or **shouldn't** and a verb from the box.

| arrive | ~~avoid~~ | be / not | call | keep | pay | surprise / not |

1. You ___should avoid___ taking a business trip to Hungary during July and August and from mid-December to mid-January. These are holiday and vacation periods.

2. You _____ on time in all business matters: You _____ late for appointments.

3. You _____ always _____ bills on time, and you _____ the date you promise for deliveries.

4. You _____ adults by their titles and family names unless they ask you not to.

5. It _____ you to get an invitation to go horseback riding. Horseback riding is a popular sport in Hungary.

EXERCISE 4: *Ought to*

(Grammar Notes 3–4)

Complete the sentences with **ought to** and the verbs from the box.

| ask | become | ~~bring~~ | congratulate | invite | send |

1. We're going to the Chens for dinner tomorrow night. We ___ought to bring___ a gift.

2. We had a wonderful time at their home. We _____ them a thank-you note.

3. I _____ Mr. Chen. His son graduated from law school last week.

4. We _____ them to our home when the Johnsons are here. I think they'd get along well.

5. Judy Chen _____ a party planner. She's so good at giving parties.

6. I _____ the Chens about doing business in Taiwan. I'm going there next month.

EXERCISE 5: *Had better*: Affirmative and Negative

(Grammar Notes 5–6)

Complete the sentences with **'d better** *or* **'d better not.**

1. You _____'d better not_____ show the soles of your feet in Thailand or Saudi Arabia. It is a big insult.

2. In Hindu and Islamic cultures, you _____ eat with your left hand. It's not polite.

3. In the United States, direct eye contact is a sign of honesty, but in other countries it is a sign of disrespect. You _____ understand these differences when you are meeting with people from different parts of the world.

4. We _____ hug them. They might feel uncomfortable. It's not their custom.

5. You _____ find out about gift giving in their country. The wrong gift may cause misunderstanding.

EXERCISE 6: *Had better*

(Grammar Notes 5–6)

Rewrite the sentences with **had better** *or* **had better not** *based on the information.*

1. Be on time when doing business in Germany.

   You had better be on time when doing business in Germany.

2. Don't eat everything on your plate in Cambodia.

   _____

   Leave something to show your host was generous with the food.

3. In China, keep eating while your plate is full to show you like your food.

   _____

4. Do not touch a person's head or show the soles of your feet in Thailand.

   _____

   The head is the most sacred part of the body. The foot is the lowest.

5. Don't keep your hands in your pockets in Turkey. It's a sign of disrespect.

   _____

EXERCISE 7: Editing

A | *Correct the conversations. There are six mistakes. The first mistake is already corrected. Find and correct four more. Add* **should** *or* **shouldn't**.

1. **A:** What should I wear?

   B: You not wear jeans or shorts.

2. **A:** I think I insulted him.

   B: You apologize.

3. **A:** They were really helpful. I send

   them a thank-you note?

   B: That's a good idea.

4. **A:** I take my shoes off?

   B: Yes, please leave them by the door.

5. **A:** When we leave for the business reception?

   B: At 6:15. The invitation is for 6:30, but we don't want to be the first ones there.

B | *Correct five mistakes in the conversations. Add* **'d better** *or* **'d better not**. *The first mistake is already corrected. Find and correct four more.*

1. **A:** I missed the train this morning.

   B: You 'd better leave earlier tomorrow.

2. **A:** You don't fly today. There's a bad hurricane and all flights are late.

   B: Good idea. I'll change my flight for tomorrow.

3. **A:** Can I call John Baker now?

   B: I don't think so. He's on U.S. time. You call him at noon. You won't wake him then.

4. **A:** Is it OK to pay that bill on Friday?

   B: I don't think so. You pay it today.

5. **A:** I told John about my birthday. He doesn't forget about it.

   B: John forgets everyone's birthday except his own.

EXERCISE 8: Pronunciation

A | *Read and listen to the Pronunciation Note.*

> **Pronunciation Note**
>
> When we say ***shouldn't*** followed by a verb, the **/ t /** is not fully heard. ***Shouldn't say*** sounds like **/ ʃʊdən səɪ /** .

B | *Listen and repeat the sentences.*

1. You shouldn't call him.

2. You shouldn't send an email.

3. You shouldn't come early.

4. You shouldn't wear shorts.

5. You shouldn't bring a gift.

EXERCISE 9: Listening

A | *Listen to a conversation between Max and his friends. Then answer the questions.*

1. Where is Max going?   To _____

2. How is he getting there?   By _____

3. What are his questions about? _____

B | *Listen again. Complete the questions. Write the friends' answers.*

1. **MAX:** Should I bow when _____ ?

   ANSWER: _____

2. **MAX:** Should I remove _____ when _____ ?

   ANSWER: _____

3. **MAX:** Should I learn _____ ?

   ANSWER: _____

EXERCISE 10: Discussion: Gift Giving

A | *PAIRS: Ask and answer the questions below. Talk about gift giving in your culture.*

1. Are gifts exchanged in business? When are gifts usually given?
2. Is the way you wrap a gift important? How and when do you present a gift? Do you open a gift right away or do you open it later?
3. Are there gifts that you shouldn't give?
4. What are the most common gifts in business?
5. How do you feel about giving gifts?
6. What kind of gifts do you like to receive?

B | *Discuss gift giving as a class.*

EXERCISE 11: Conversation: Body Language

A | *GROUPS: Body language is a way people speak without words. Use body language: Say something with your, head, hand, shoulders, arms, eyes, nose, or lips. Does your group understand you?*

B | *Talk about body language with your group.*

C | *Present the results of your discussion to the class.*

Advice: *Should, Ought to, Had better* **357**

EXERCISE 12: Writing

A | *Imagine someone wants to do business in a culture you know well. Give the person advice. Use* **should, shouldn't, had better,** *or* **had better not.** *Use a topic from the box or your own idea.*

being on time	eating habits	using business cards
dressing appropriately	tipping	using forms of address

EXAMPLE: **Forms of Address in the United States**

How do you address people when you are doing business in the United States? Do you use their first names or their last names? Do you use titles? And if so, what are the correct titles?

In the United States managers of companies sometimes tell people to call them by their first names. You shouldn't think it means that you are close. It is a part of the culture. In a business relationship, you should first call a person by a title (for example: Dr., Ms., or Mr.) and their last name. Wait for that person to tell you how he or she wants to be addressed. Some people want to be on a first-name basis and others don't. There are no set rules.

B | *Check your work. Use the Editing Checklist.*

Editing Checklist

Did you . . . ?
☐ use **should**, **shouldn't**, **had better**, or **had better not** correctly
☐ check your spelling

UNIT 30 Review

Check your answers on page UR-6.

Do you need to review anything?

A | *Circle the correct words.*

1. You **should to / should** read that book.

2. We **better / had better** call the airline.

3. I **shouldn't not / shouldn't** wear that outfit for a business meeting.

4. We **ought / ought to** buy a small gift.

5. I'd **better no / better not** call her now. She goes to bed early.

B | *Complete the sentences with* **had better** *or* **had better not.**

1. You _____ forget to pay that bill. You don't want to pay a late fee.

2. She _____ buy the gift today. The stores will be closed tomorrow.

3. We _____ wait for them any longer. We'll miss our flight.

4. I _____ go by train. The bus is too slow, and I need to be on time.

C | *Complete the sentences with* **should** *or* **shouldn't.**

1. We _____ take him to the hospital. He seems to be in pain.

2. She _____ work alone. She needs to get help.

3. I _____ talk to a plumber about that problem.

4. You _____ forget your notes. You'll need them.

D | *Correct the sentences. There are seven mistakes.*

1. Where should we meets after work?

2. We better take an umbrella tonight. It's going to rain.

3. Should I to make a reservation now for my flight? I think I outta buy it soon.

4. What I should see during my business trip to Uruguay?

5. Should we leaves Brazil tonight or tomorrow?

6. You ought bring flowers to your hostess to thank her for dinner.

Requests, Desires, and Offers: *Would you, Could you, Can you. . . ?, I'd like . . .*

NEIGHBORS

STEP 1 GRAMMAR IN CONTEXT

Before You Read

A favor is something you do for someone to help him or her. Read these requests for favors. Which ones are OK to ask a neighbor? Check (✓) your opinion.

	OK	Depends	Not OK
Would you please get my mail while I'm on vacation?			
Could you help me move to a new apartment?			
Can you drive me to the airport?			
Can you lend me $500?			

Read

Jade posts a problem on a message board. Luz reads it and posts some advice. Read their posts. Do you agree with Luz?

Jade Last month my neighbor Gina said, "Jade, **can you do** me a favor? **Can you drive me** to the airport tonight? I have a nine o'clock flight."

I said, "**Sure**, Gina. **I'd be glad to. Would you like** me to pick you up at 7:00?"

Then last week Gina said, "Jade, **could you help** me out? I'm going away again for a few days. **Could you water** my plants and walk my dog while I'm away?" Again I said, "**Sure**."

Well, yesterday I needed a favor. I called Gina and said, "Gina, I'm going to paint my bedroom tomorrow afternoon. **Would you lend** me a hand?" She said, "Oh, Jade. **I'd like to help you**, but I'm going to go shopping." I didn't say anything, but I was angry and hurt. What do you think? Was I wrong to feel that way?

Luz0426 No, you were right. Since Gina asks you for favors, she should do favors too. Maybe Gina is a little bit selfish. Maybe she only thinks about herself. Why don't you tell her how you feel? See what she says. Good luck!

After You Read

A | Practice *PAIRS: Now read the posts aloud. Take turns reading each paragraph.*

B | Vocabulary *Match the words and meanings.*

___b___ 1. **lend me a hand**   a. leave

___c___ 2. **post a message**   b. help me

___a___ 3. **go away**   c. write to an online group

___e___ 4. **be hurt**   d. caring only about yourself

___d___ 5. **selfish**   e. feel bad

C | Comprehension *Complete the chart. Who is each sentence about? Check (✓) the correct column.*

	Gina	Jade
1. She would like a ride to the airport.		
2. She offered to pick her neighbor up at 7:00.		
3. She would like her neighbor to water her plants.		
4. She asked her neighbor to help paint her bedroom.		
5. She would like advice.		

STEP 2 GRAMMAR PRESENTATION

REQUESTS, DESIRES, AND OFFERS

Polite Requests				Short Answers	
Would You / Could You / Can You		**Base Form of Verb**		**Affirmative**	**Negative**
Would you				Sure.	Sorry, I can't. I have to work.
Could you	(please)	**help**	me?	Of course.	I'd like to, but I can't. I have a class.
Can you				OK.	Sorry, I'm busy now.

(continued on next page)

Desires			Contractions
Subject	*Would Like*		
I You* He She We They	**would like**	a larger apartment. to move.	I would = **I'd** you would = **you'd** he would = **he'd** she would = **she'd** we would = **we'd** they would = **they'd**

*You is both singular and plural.

Offers				Short Answers	
Would	**Subject**	*Like*		**Affirmative**	**Negative**
Would	you	**like**	some blueberries? to join us?	Yes, thank you. Yes, I would.	No, thanks.

GRAMMAR NOTES

1	*Would you*, *Could you*, and *Can you* are some common ways to make **requests**.	**A: Would you (please)** help me carry these books? **B: Sure**.
	When we agree to a request, we say, *Sure*. *Of course*. *OK*. or *I'd be glad to*.	**A: Could you (please)** help me carry these books? **B: Of course**.
	Can you is the most common and most informal.	**A: Can you (please)** help me? **B: I'd be glad to.** OR **Sorry, I can't. I have to work.**
	When we don't agree to a request, we say *sorry* and **give a reason**.	
2	*Would like* is a polite way of saying *want*.	• The judge **would like** to see you now.
	USAGE NOTE: Use the contraction in speaking and informal writing.	• I**'d like** some advice. • We**'d like** to see you.
	Would like can be followed by **a noun** or **an infinitive**.	NOUN • I'd like **a snack**. INFINITIVE • I'd like **to get** a snack.
3	Use *Would you like* for offers or invitations.	• **Would you like** some help? • **Would you like** to dance?

REFERENCE NOTE
See Unit 7, page 75, for a discussion of requests.

EXERCISE 1: Discover the Grammar

Write **R** (**Request**), **O** (**Offer**), or **D** (**Desire**) for each sentence.

_R_ **1.** Would you give me a ride?

_D_ **2.** We'd like to see you again soon.

_O_ **3.** Would you like some more lemonade?

_R_ **4.** Could you lend me your car?

_D_ **5.** I'd like a shorter workday.

_R_ **6.** Can I see your photos?

_O_ **7.** Would you like another dumpling?

_R_ **8.** Would you call her for me?

EXERCISE 2: Requests, Offers, Desires, and Responses   (Grammar Notes 1–3)

Eun Young and Dae Jung are neighbors. Complete the conversation with the phrases
from the box.

| ~~Could you please~~   I'd like to do ³   I'd love to ⁴   ~~Of course~~   Would you like ⁵ |

EUN YOUNG: Dae Jung, I love to listen to your music, but sometimes I can't get to sleep.

Could you please stop practicing by 11:00 P.M.?
 _1._

DAE JUNG: _Of course_ I'm sorry. Sometimes I forget the time
 _2._

when I practice.

EUN YOUNG: Thanks.

DAE JUNG: Listen, Eun Young, _would you like_ something for you.
 _3._

I would to have dinner together one day next
 _4._

week?

EUN YOUNG: Dinner? Sure. _I w L ove to_ .
 _5._

EXERCISE 3: Responses to Requests and Offers

(Grammar Note 1)

Read the questions. Circle the correct letter.

1. **A:** Would you help me get up?

   B: _____

   a. Sure. *(circled)*   **b.** Yes, thanks.

2. **A:** Could you help me with these bags?

   B: _____

   a. I could.   **b.** Certainly. *(circled)*

3. **A:** Can you get my mail while I'm away?

   B: _____

   a. Sorry, I'm going away too. *(circled)*   **b.** No thanks.

4. **A:** Would you like one of these flyers?

   B: _____

   a. Yes, I want.   **b.** Thanks. *(circled)*

5. **A:** Can you drive me to the supermarket?

   B: _____

   a. I could.   **b.** Of course. *(circled)*

6. **A:** Could you do me a favor and watch my bags? I need to move my car.

   B: _____

   a. I'm sure.   **b.** Sure. *(circled)*

7. **A:** Would you like some of my popcorn?

   B: _____

   a. Thanks. *(circled)*   **b.** Sorry, I don't.

8. **A:** Could you give me some money?

   B: _____

   a. Yes, I would.   **b.** Sorry, I don't have any. *(circled)*

EXERCISE 4: Requests, Offers, Desires

Rewrite the underlined sentences. Change imperative statements to requests with **Could you please,** **Would you please,** *or* **Can you please. . . ?** *Change* **want** *to* **would like.**

ALEXA: The barbecue looks great. Anything we can do to help?

Could you please bring out the drinks?

JAVIER: Sure. ~~Bring out the drinks~~. They're in the cooler.
1.

ALEXA: OK. . . . Here they are. Where should we put them?

Could you please   *Could you please*

JAVIER: Put the lemonade on the table over there. And Roberto, put the juice over here
2.   3.

Can you please

next to the buns. And there's a salad in the refrigerator. Bring it out.
4.

ALEXA: Sure. I'll get it.

would

JAVIER: I think the meat is ready. What do you want—chicken or hamburgers?
5.

ALEXA: Some chicken, please.

would you lik

JAVIER: What about you Roberto? ~~Do you want~~ chicken too?
6.

would lik

ROBERTO: No, I ~~want~~ a burger.
7.

JAVIER: Here you go.

would like

ALEXA: Javier, this chicken is delicious. ~~I want~~ the recipe. *Please*
8.

JAVIER: It's easy to make. I soak it in a honey mustard sauce. Then I grill it.

EXERCISE 5: Editing

Correct the conversations. There are five mistakes. The first mistake is already corrected.
Find and correct four more.

1. **A:** Could you please move my car at 11:00?

    Sorry.

   B: ~~No, I wouldn't~~. I'll be at work at that time.

     would

2. **A:** We like to rent this apartment. Could please you give us an application?

   B: Of course.

          to

3. **A:** Would you like come for dinner?

      Can

   B: Yes, thank you. ~~Would~~ my friend come, too?

4. **A:** Would you help me with these boxes?

     sure

   B: ~~I would~~.

EXERCISE 6: Pronunciation

A | *Read and listen to the Pronunciation Note.*

> **Pronunciation Note**
>
> Do not pronounce the letter *l* in the word **would**. *Would* is pronounced like the word *wood* / **wʊd** / . We pronounce *Would you* / **wʊdʒə** / and *Could you* / **kʊdʒə** / with the / **dʒ** / sound.

B | *Listen and repeat.*

1. Would you like some more lemonade?
2. Could you hold the door open?
3. Would you watch the burgers?
4. Could you hand me a napkin?

EXERCISE 7: Listening

A | *Listen to a telephone conversation beween neighbors. Circle the correct letter.*

Elena asks Ms. Lyons to _____.
   a. watch TV with her
   b. turn off her TV
   c. lower her TV volume

B | *Listen again and answer the questions. Circle the correct letter.*

1. How does Ms. Lyons respond?
   a. She agrees to Elena's request.
   b. She doesn't understand Elena's request.
   c. She doesn't agree to Elena's request.

2. What does Ms. Lyons think?
   a. Her neighbor isn't polite.
   b. Her TV isn't too loud.
   c. The walls in her building are thin.

3. What is Elena doing at this time?
   a. She's studying in medical school.
   b. She's working as a doctor.
   c. She's studying for a test for medical school.

4. Ms. Lyons may have a problem. What is it?
   a. She doesn't see well.
   b. She doesn't hear well.
   c. She doesn't have a kind neighbor.

EXERCISE 8: Survey

A | *GROUPS OF 4: Look at the requests in the list. Talk about these requests. Is it OK for a neighbor, a casual friend, or a close friend or relative to ask them? Is it sometimes OK? If so, when? Would you make these requests?*

Would you lend me your car?   **Could you lend me $50?**

Could you fix my computer?   **Could you walk my dog for two weeks?**

Would you take my picture?   **Could you take me to the hospital?**

> EXAMPLE: **A:** Young Suk, what do you think about the first request, "Would you lend me your car?" Would you make that request?
> **B:** Not for a neighbor, but I might ask a close relative.

B | *Take notes on your group's responses. Then discuss them with the class.*

EXERCISE 9: Making Polite Requests

PAIRS: Read the situations. Take turns making polite requests. Answer the requests.

> EXAMPLE: You're in a restaurant with your neighbor. You want some napkins, which are near your neighbor.
> **A:** Maki, can you please pass the napkins?
> **B:** Here you go.

1. You're in a restaurant with your neighbor. The salt and pepper is in front of your friend. You would like the salt and pepper.

2. It's raining hard and you have to go out. You lost your umbrella. You ask a neighbor to lend you an umbrella.

3. You need to move your sofa. Your neighbor is at your home.

4. You want to hang a painting on the wall. You'd like your neighbor to help you.

5. Your neighbor has parties that keep you up at night. You would like the neighbor to make less noise.

6. Your neighbor borrowed a couple of books a month ago. He still has them.

EXERCISE 10: Extending Invitations

PAIRS: Take turns. Extend invitations to your partner. Your partner can accept or refuse. Use the suggestions from the box or your own ideas

> EXAMPLE: **A:** Would you like to come over for dinner tonight?
> **B:** Sure. What time? OR I'd like to, but I can't. I have too much homework.

go running	go to a concert	see a movie	study calculus together

EXERCISE 11: Role Play

PAIRS: Role-play the situations. You and your partner are neighbors.

Situations:

- Invite your neighbor to a party.
- Ask your neighbor to help you put in a new air conditioner.
- Invite your neighbor to a concert. You have an extra ticket.
- Ask your neighbor for a ride to a store.

> **EXAMPLE:**   **ELENA:** Hey, Pierre, I'm going to have a party tomorrow night. Would you like to come?
>
> **PIERRE:** I'd love to. Is it in your apartment?
>
> **ELENA:** Yes, it is. Please come at around 8:00.
>
> **PIERRE:** OK. I'll be there.

EXERCISE 12: Writing

A | *Write two short email requests to neighbors. Use the situations or your own ideas. Use* **would** *or* **could**.

Situation 1

You are on vacation. You gave your neighbor a key to your home. Ask your neighbor to check your home.

Situation 2

Your neighbor has two teenage sons. They play music at all hours of the night. Ask your neighbor to ask them not to play loud music after 10:00 P.M.

Situation 3

It's winter and the landlord is not giving enough heat. Write to several neighbors and ask them to join you in writing letters of complaint to your landlord.

> **EXAMPLE FOR SITUATION 1:**   Hi John,
> Boris and I are having a great time in Aruba. I read about a storm back home, and I hope all is well. Could you please check our house? We'll be back in a couple of days.
> Irina

B | *Check your work. Use the Editing Checklist.*

Editing Checklist

Did you . . . ?
- [ ] use **would you**, **could you**, or **can you** correctly
- [ ] check your spelling

A | *Circle the correct word or words.*

1. Would you please / (Would you like) another apple?

2. Could you pass / Can you please the salt?

3. (I'd like) / I'll like some more coffee.

4. (We'd like) / We like some more bread, please.

5. (Can you) / Can you to help me?

B | *Read each question. Circle the correct answer.*

1. Would you please help me? (Yes, thanks. / (Of course.))

2. Could you drive me home? ((Sure) / I could.)

3. Would you like another cupcake? (I could. / (Thanks.))

4. Can you lend me your jacket? ((Sorry, I need it) / No, thanks.)

5. Can you show me how the new printer works? ((I'd be glad to.) / I can.)

C | *Complete the sentences with* **I'd like**, **Could you please** *or* **Would you like**.

1. _would_ open the door?

2. _I w_ some more coffee.

3. _3_ drive me to school?

4. _3_ some water?

5. _1_ to go to that concert.

D | *Correct the conversations. There are five mistakes.*

1. **A:** Could please ~~you~~ move my car at 11:00?

   B: No, I ~~wouldn't~~. I'll be at work then. *sorry*

2. **A:** I like to see you this weekend. Would you like to go to the park?

   B: ~~I could.~~ *Sure*

3. **A:** Would you like ~~have~~ some more ice cream? *to*

   B: No, thanks. I'm full.

32 Necessity: *Have to, Don't have to, Must, Mustn't*

RULES AT SCHOOL

STEP 1 GRAMMAR IN CONTEXT

Before You Read

What do you have to do for your English class? Circle the letter of your answers.

a. do homework   **c.** sit in the same seat for each class   **e.** answer questions in class

b. wear a uniform   **d.** take tests   **f.** do class presentations

Read

Read about the requirements for a college history course.

PROFESSOR:	Welcome to American History 102. I'm Rich Anderson. This course covers the period from the American Civil War to the present day.[1] There will be a midterm and a final exam. You **have to score** an average of 65 percent or above on both tests to pass this course. In addition there is a term paper.[2] The term paper **must be** at least 10 pages, and you **have to include** a bibliography.[3] The handout I'm passing out will explain the term paper. Now, are there any questions? . . . Yes?
STUDENT A:	When is the term paper due?

PROFESSOR: You **have to hand** it **in** by the last day of class. That's December 15. It **must not be** late. You should hand in an outline by the fourth week of the term. You can email the outline. My email address is on the board and on your handout. You **don't have to give** me a hard copy of the outline, but I would like a hard copy of your paper. Any other questions? . . . Yes?

STUDENT B:	Last semester, we **didn't have to buy** a textbook. Is there a textbook for this course?
PROFESSOR:	Yes. The textbook is called *American History from the Civil War to Today.*
STUDENT B:	Who's the author?
PROFESSOR:	I am.
STUDENT B:	**Do** we **have to buy** the book?
PROFESSOR:	Only if you want to pass.

---

[1] ***present day:*** today (usually used when talking about history)

[2] ***term paper:*** students' most important written report of the semester

[3] ***bibliography:*** a list of the books and other sources used to write a paper

370   UNIT 32

After You Read

A | Practice *PAIRS: Now read the conversation aloud.*

B | Vocabulary *Complete the sentences with the words from the box.*

average	final	midterm	pass
due	hard copy	outline	percent

1. To _____ this course, you must hand in a paper and do a group presentation.

2. There will be two tests this semester. The _____ will be on October 15, and the _____ will be on December 15.

3. The _____ of 100, 95, 99, and 90 is 96.

4. What _____ of the students finish this program in one year?

5. Do I need to print a _____ or is OK to send it electronically?

6. I can't meet you today. My term paper is _____ tomorrow.

7. I wrote an _____ of each chapter to help me study for the test.

C | Comprehension *Check (✓) what students in Professor Anderson's class **have to do** and **don't have to do.***

	Students have to . . .	Students don't have to . . .
1. take a quiz every week		
2. take a midterm and final exam		
3. give an oral report		
4. hand in an outline		
5. read four books for their term paper		
6. buy the textbook		

MODALS: *HAVE TO* / *DON'T HAVE TO*

Affirmative Statements			
Subject	*Have to / Has to*	**Base Form of Verb**	
I We You They	**have to**	**take**	a history class.
He She	**has to**		
It		**be**	a three-credit class.

Negative Statements				
Subject	*Do Not / Does Not*	*Have to*	**Base Form of Verb**	
I We You They	**don't**	**have to**	**take**	a history class.
He She	**doesn't**			
It			**be**	10 pages long.

Yes / No Questions				
Do / Does	**Subject**	*Have to*	**Base Form of Verb**	
Do	I you we they	**have to**	**study**	tonight?
Does	he she			
	it		**be**	five pages?

Short Answers					
Affirmative			**Negative**		
Yes,	you I you they	do.	No,	you I you they	don't.
	he she it	does.		he she it	doesn't.

MUST AND *MUSTN'T*

Affirmative and Negative Statements			
Subject	*Must*	**Base Form of Verb**	
I You He She It We They	**must** **must not (mustn't)**	**arrive**	early.

Past of *Have to* and *Must*			
Subject	*Had to*	**Base Form of Verb**	
I You He She It We They	**had to**	**leave**	early.

GRAMMAR NOTES

1

Use **have to** and **must** to talk about things that are **necessary**. Both *have to* and *must* are followed by the base form of the verb. *Must* is stronger than *have to*.

USAGE NOTE: We usually use *have to* in speaking and informal writing.

BE CAREFUL! *Have to* is different from the verb *have*.

NOTE: The past of *must* and *have to* is **had to**.

- I **have to take** a test next week.

- Students **must take** a three-credit history course.

- I **have** a psychology class.
- I **have to read** 50 pages for this class.

- Last week I **had to buy** a lot of textbooks.

2

Use **don't have to** or **doesn't have to** when there is no necessity. You have a **choice**.

- I **don't have to sit** in the same seat every day. I can sit wherever I want.
- He **doesn't have to wear** a suit to work. He can wear a shirt and slacks.

3

Must not or the contraction **mustn't** means that you are **not allowed** to do something. You don't have a choice. You can't do it.

- You **must not take** scissors on a plane.

4

Do not repeat *must* or *have to* when you use two verbs or verb phrases with one subject.

- You **must take** a test and **write** a paper.
- He **has to work** and **study**.
  Not: He must take a test and ~~must~~ write a paper.
  Not: He has to work and ~~has to~~ study.

5

BE CAREFUL! Do not use *to* after *must*.

- He **must write** a report.
  Not: He ~~must to write~~ a report.

6

USAGE NOTE: We rarely use *mustn't* in conversation except when talking to small children or telling rules. We use **can't** instead.

- Children, you **mustn't** cross the street when the signal is red.
- You can't park there.
  Not: You ~~mustn't~~ park there.

EXERCISE 1: Discover the Grammar

Read about a special high school for the arts. Underline all forms of **have to, don't have to, must, mustn't,** *and the verb that follows. Circle all examples of the verb* **have.**

New York City has a special high school for music, art, dance, and drama. It's called LaGuardia High School. To be accepted, students have to pass an audition. In addition they must have good grades. The school usually has about 9,000 applicants a year. It accepts about 650 students. All prospective students, even the children of the rich and famous, must audition. They must choose to audition for acting, dance, music, or art. Here are some of the requirements for students interested in art:

1. Each student must submit a portfolio of original artwork. The artwork does not have to be a special size, but all art has to be original. Students mustn't bring in photocopies.

2. Each student must complete three drawing exercises. Students have to bring a pencil and a transcript of their last report card. Students don't have to bring drawing materials. The school has all the necessary drawing supplies for the students.

Madonna with her daughter, Lourdes. Lourdes attends LaGuardia High School.

EXERCISE 2: Have to / Don't have to / Must

(Grammar Notes 1–2)

A | Read LaGuardia High School's audition requirements for dance. Complete the sentences. Use **have to** or **don't have to** and the verbs from the box.

bring	perform
bring / not	take

Dance students

_____ two

1.

classes: a ballet dance class and a modern

dance class. Students who do well in

the classes return for a second audition.

At the second audition, students _____ a one-minute

2.

dance. Students _____ their own music, but they

3.

_____ a CD player. The school has CD players.

4.

B | Complete the audition requirements for music. Use **must** or **don't have to** and the verbs from the box.

bring / not	play	sing	use

To show your musical talent, you _____

1.

a song or _____ an instrument. You

2.

_____ your own instrument if you can carry it. You

3.

_____ a piano or a bass. The school will supply one for

4.

you.

EXERCISE 3: Have / Have to / Had to

(Grammar Note 1)

Complete the conversation with **have, have to,** or **had to.**

A: Would you like to go to the movies this evening?

B: I can't. I _____*have*_____ a test tomorrow. I _____ study this evening.

1.   2.

A: What do you _____ study?

3.

(continued on next page)

B: Grammar. I _____ review the modals *can, could, would, might,* and *must.*
4.

We _____ a test every Thursday.
5.

A: Do you _____ memorize rules?
6.

B: No. We _____ use the grammar to answer questions. We really
7.

_____ understand it.
8.

A: Do you get a lot of tests?

B: Uh-huh. We _____ a quiz after every unit. I don't mind them.
9.

A: I don't like tests. Last year I _____ take a test every week, and I was always
10.

worried.

EXERCISE 4: *Have to / Don't have to* *(Grammar Notes 1–2)*

Complete the sentences with **have to, has to, don't have to,** *or* **doesn't have to** *and the verbs from the box.*

| attend | buy | hand in | listen | pass | pay | say | wear | ~~work~~ |

1. In some classes you almost always ___*have to work*___ in groups.

2. In some high schools, students can wear what they like. They _____ a

uniform.

3. In many high schools students _____ standardized tests or they can't go

on to the next grade.

4. We _____ our term paper by December 15.

5. Hugo says he _____ all classes unless he has a doctor's note.

6. She _____ that book. She can borrow it from the library.

7. My psychology class has many students. I _____ to a lecture and take

notes. I _____ anything in class. I just have to pass the exams.

8. Jay goes to a college near his home, so he _____ for room and board.

EXERCISE 5: *Have to, Must, Must not*

(Grammar Notes 1, 3)

Read the signs. Then explain the rule or warning of each. Begin with **You have to, You must,** *or* **You must not**.

1. No Smoking

You mustn't smoke on the train.

2. I.D. Required

_____

3. Do Not Enter

_____

4. Do not get hairdryer wet

_____

5. Do not drink

_____

6. Do not text when you drive

_____

EXERCISE 6: Editing

Correct the sentences. There are eight mistakes. The first mistake is already corrected.
Find and correct seven more.

1. We ~~has to~~ *have* a lot of new vocabulary words. I can't remember all of them.

2. To learn a new vocabulary word, you must hears it seven times.

3. For me to remember a word, I has to write it down.

4. Avi has a great memory. He just have to hear a word once and he remembers it.

5. Our papers are due next week. I have start working on mine today.

6. We mustn't do any homework today. Tomorrow is a holiday.

7. You mustn't to bring any notes with you to the test.

8. You must to bring a photo ID to the testing center.

STEP 4 COMMUNICATION PRACTICE

EXERCISE 7: Pronunciation

A | *Read and listen to the Pronunciation Note.*

Pronunciation Note

When **have to** or **has to** is followed by a verb, the vowel sound in **to** is unstressed and sounds like / ə / .

EXAMPLE: **A:**   Why is he selling his house?
              B: He has to move.

When **have to** or **has to** is not followed by a verb, there is more stress on **to** and the vowel sounds more like / **u** / .

EXAMPLE: **A:**   Do you need to study tonight?
              B: Yes, I have to.

B | *Listen and repeat.*

1. **A:** Do you want to go there?

   B: No, but I **have to**.

2. **A:** What does she **have to do**?

   B: She **has to write** a paper today.

3. **A:** When do we **have to pay** the tuition?

   B: We **have to pay** it before class begins.

4. **A:** Do you really **have to work** late tonight?

   B: Yes, I **have to**.

C | PAIRS: Follow the directions. Then switch roles.

1. **Partner A:** Tell your partner three things you have to do this week.
2. **Partner B:** Ask your partner, "Do you really have to?"

> EXAMPLE: **A:** This evening I have to study for our test.
> **B:** Do you really have to?
> **A:** Yes, I do. OR No, I don't. I could study tomorrow night.

EXERCISE 8: Listening

A | *Ali is in his second year of college. He is speaking to an advisor about graduate school. Listen to the conversation. What degree is Ali interested in getting?*

_____

B | *Listen again. Write one thing you have to do to get that degree. Write one thing you don't have to do.*

1. _____

2. _____

EXERCISE 9: Discussion

Talk about regulations, management, and teaching methods in schools you know about.
*Use **have to**, **don't have to**, **must**, and **must not**.*

> EXAMPLE: My nephew goes to P.S. 28 in Queens. It's a school for children between the ages of four and eight. Children have to be in school by 8:20. They must come on time for school. There's a school uniform, but they don't have to wear it. Children have to work in pairs and groups. They have to participate in class. They have to take a lot of standardized tests. They must not run in the halls or talk when the teacher is talking. The teachers are great, and the school is beautiful. My nephew loves his school. We're happy he goes there.

EXERCISE 10: Survey

A | *In some schools students try to copy their classmates' answers. Ask five classmates how teachers in their schools prevented cheating during tests.*

> EXAMPLE: **A:** We had to cover our papers.

B | *As a class, make a list of things teachers do to prevent cheating. Use **have to** or **must**.*

> EXAMPLE: Students have to sit in every other seat.
> Students have to leave cell phones at the front of the class.

EXERCISE 11: Writing

A | *Write about an elementary school in the area where you grew up. Use* **have to** *and* **must**.

EXAMPLE:

My Elementary School

by Emiko Shinohara

Children in my elementary school in Japan learn to respect the teachers and take care of the classroom. When the teacher enters the room, children must stand. They say, "Thank you for teaching us." Children have to clean the classroom. They wash the desks and clean the boards. In addition, children have to wear a school uniform. Most children like their school uniform and are proud to wear it.

B | *Check your work. Use the Editing Checklist.*

Editing Checklist
Did you . . . ? ☐ use **have to** and **must** correctly ☐ check your spelling

UNIT 32 Review

Check your answers on page UR-7.
Do you need to review anything?

A | *Circle the correct words to complete the sentences.*

1. You can wear what you want. You **mustn't / don't have to** wear a uniform.

2. It's getting late. We **have to / don't have to** leave.

3. The law says you **must / must not** drive without a license.

4. She can take the test any day this week. She **has to / doesn't have to** take it today.

5. I **have to / mustn't** hand in my term paper tomorrow. I can't go out today.

B | *Complete the sentences with the correct form of* **have, have to, don't have to,** *or* **mustn't.**

1. Children, you _____ cross the street when the light is red.

2. She _____ a lot of homework. She _____ hand in a paper and study for a test.

3. The tickets are good any day this week. We _____ use them today.

4. A doctor _____ fill out a medical form before you can use the gym.

C | *Complete the sentences with* **have to** *and a verb from the box. Use the present or past.*

answer	bring / not	give	read	work

1. He _____ two shifts because two co-workers were out sick.

2. We're busy. We _____ two chapters of our history book and

_____ questions at the end of each chapter. It's due tomorrow.

3. We _____ a presentation in front of the entire school.

4. I _____ my own laptop. They gave me one for my presentation.

D | *Correct the paragraph. There are five mistakes.*

The test starts at 8:10. You must to be in the room at 8:00. You mustn't came late. You have to has two number two pencils and an eraser. You musts brings proper identification, such as a photo ID or a passport. You must leave your cell phone in the front of the room.

PART X

From Grammar to Writing
EXPRESSING AND SUPPORTING AN OPINION

1 | *A fact is something you know to be true; for example, a scientific fact. An opinion is what you believe. Read the sentences. Write* **F** (sentences that express a fact) *or* **O** (sentences that express an opinion).

_____ **1.** I believe that Hollywood actors are not good examples for young people.

_____ **2.** John was in Hollywood last summer.

_____ **3.** The Himalayas are the highest mountains in the world.

_____ **4.** Earth is about 93 million miles from the sun.

_____ **5.** Children shouldn't watch violent movies.

2 | *Study the information about expressing and supporting an opinion.*

<table>
<tr>
<td>**1**</td>
<td>When you express your opinion, you can use expressions such as:
In my opinion
I believe
I think
better than
It's better to . . . than to
should / shouldn't</td>
<td>• **In my opinion**, it's wrong to spank a child.
• **I believe** tests are harmful.
• **I think** tests are helpful.
• Some tests are **better than** others.
• **It's better to** give **than to** receive.
• Parents **shouldn't** spank their children.</td>
</tr>
<tr>
<td>**2**</td>
<td>After you express your opinion, give reasons to support your opinion.</td>
<td>**OPINION**
• In my opinion, it's wrong to spank children.
SUPPORT
• When adults use physical force, children think physical force is OK.</td>
</tr>
</table>

3 | *Read the two paragraphs about Hollywood actors. Circle the sentences that show an opinion. Underline the sentences that support the opinion.*

   I believe that Hollywood actors often set a bad example for young people. Young people look up to them, but these actors show bad values. For example, many stars spend huge amounts of money on homes, cars, and clothes. When young people try to copy their lifestyle, they often buy things they can't afford. Also, most Hollywood actors do not have long-term relationships. They change boyfriends and girlfriends frequently. Finally, many Hollywood actors have cosmetic surgery and go on strict diets, all in order to be more attractive.

In my opinion, some Hollywood stars set a bad example because of their materialism, but others set a good example through their charity. For example, Angelina Jolie and George Clooney are big stars who help others. They give away a lot of their money to help the poor and the sick in different parts of the world. They also encourage others to give to good causes.

4 | *Now write a paragraph on one of the topics. Give your opinion and reasons to support your opinion.*

- Hollywood stars have a right to privacy OR Hollywood stars do not have a right to privacy
- Money can buy happiness OR Money can't buy happiness
- Children shouldn't play violent video games OR Violent video games don't harm children

5 | *Exchange papers with a partner. Did your partner follow the directions? Correct any mistakes in grammar and spelling.*

6 | *Talk to your partner. Discuss the mistakes you made. Then rewrite your own paper and make any necessary changes.*

COMPARISONS

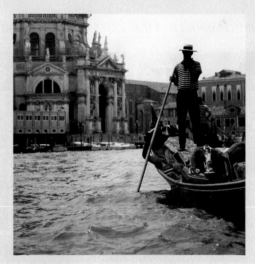

The Comparative
COMPARING CITIES

STEP 1 GRAMMAR IN CONTEXT

This room is larger than the theyone
A   B

a lot { much older / larger / more often / more interesting
X (very) old   older

Before You Read

PAIRS: Discuss. Where would you prefer to live? A big city or a small town? Why?

Read

Read the article about two U.S. cities called Portland. Which Portland would you prefer?

A TALE OF TWO PORTLANDS

Portland, Oregon   Portland, Maine

Liv Tyler played Arwen in three *Lord of the Rings* movies.

Matt Groening, creator of *The Simpsons*, and Liv Tyler, the popular actress, both come from the city of Portland. However, they come from different states in the U.S.

There are two beautiful U.S. cities named Portland. One is in Maine, and the other is in Oregon. Maine is on the East Coast of the United States, while Oregon is on the West Coast. Both Portlands have ports, but Portland, Oregon, is **farther from** the ocean. At 173 feet above sea level, it is also **higher** in elevation. Both cities are not very big, but they are **bigger than** any other city in their states. Portland, Maine, has a population of about 64,000, whereas Portland, Oregon, is much **larger**, with a population of about 540,000. Winter in Oregon is a little **milder than** winter in Maine, but they both have comfortable climates.

Both Portlands offer a nice lifestyle. Portland, Maine, is located on the coast, but the mountains are just 45 minutes away by car. So it's easy to ski in the mountains in the winter or sunbathe on the beaches in the summer. Portland, Oregon, is located on a river. It's a city of different neighborhoods with different personalities. It's much **more diverse**[1] **than** the other Portland.

Portland, Maine (founded in 1632), is a lot **older than** Portland, Oregon (founded in 1845).

[1] *diverse:* have people from different backgrounds

Farther luchicun   further   more

ADJ { - simple   - comp   - superl.
ADV {

A TALE OF TWO PORTLANDS

You may wonder why the two cities have the same name. There's a very good reason. Each of the founders[2] of Portland, Oregon, wanted to name his new city after his hometown. One man came from Boston, Massachusetts. The other came from Portland, Maine. They tossed a coin,[3] and the man from Portland, Maine, won.

[2] **founder:** someone who establishes a business, school, town, etc.
[3] **tossed a coin:** made a decision by throwing a coin (penny, nickel, dime, etc.) in the air and guessing the side it would fall on.

After You Read

A | Practice *PAIRS: Now read the article aloud. Take turns reading sentences.*

B | Vocabulary *Complete the sentences with the words from the box.*

~~coast~~	~~mild~~	~~port~~	~~ski~~
diverse	personality	sea level	are located

1. We drove along the ___coast___ and took some great photos of the ocean and the rocks.

2. The ship picked up the passengers at the ___port___.

3. It was cold yesterday, but today it is ___mild___.

4. We like to ___ski___ in the mountains. We love the snow.

5. The university has a ___diverse___ population. Students come from everywhere.

6. She has a warm ___personality___. That's why everyone likes her.

7. That city is high above ___sea level___.

8. Washington, Oregon, and California ___are located___ on the West Coast of the United States.

C | Comprehension *Check (✓) the correct Portland.*

	Portland, Maine	Portland, Oregon
1. Which Portland has a bigger population?		✓
2. Which Portland is older?	✓	
3. Which Portland has more diverse neighborhoods?		✓
4. Which Portland has warmer winters?		✓

COMPARATIVES

Adjectives

Comparative Forms of Adjectives				
		Comparative Adjective	*Than*	
Portland, Oregon	is	**bigger** **busier** **more crowded**	**than**	Portland, Maine.

Comparative Forms of Irregular Adjectives				
		Irregular Comparative Adjective	*Than*	
My map	is	**better** **worse**	**than**	yours.
My new office		**farther**		my old one.

Questions with *Which*

Which + Noun					*Which*		
Which	**Noun**	**Verb**	**Comparative Adjective**		*Which*	**Verb**	**Comparative Adjective**
Which	city	is	bigger? more expensive?		**Which**	is	bigger? more expensive?

GRAMMAR NOTES

1	Use the **comparative form of an adjective** + *than* to compare two people, places, or things.	• Alaska is **bigger than** Maine.
2	To form the comparative of most **short (one-syllable) adjectives**, add -**er** to the adjective. Add only -r if the adjective ends in *e*. *long—longer* *large—larger* Exceptions: *tired—more tired* *bored—more bored* *fun—more fun*	• The Mississippi River is **longer** than the Hudson River. • For me, the city is **more fun** than the suburbs.

3	To form the comparative of adjectives that end in a **consonant** + *y*, change the *y* to *i* and add *-er*. *busy—**busier*** *easy—**easier*** *heavy—**heavier***	• These days the stores are **busier** than they were two years ago.
4	To form the comparative of most adjectives of **two** or **more syllables**, add *more* before the adjective. *expensive—**more expensive*** *intelligent—**more intelligent*** Exceptions: *quiet—**quieter*** *simple—**simpler***	• The train is **more expensive** than the bus. • Is life in the countryside really **simpler** and **quieter**?
5	Use *less* before an adjective to mean the opposite of *more*.	• A car is **more** expensive than a bicycle. • A bicycle is **less** expensive than a car.
6	The adjectives **good**, **bad**, and **far** have irregular comparative forms. *good—**better*** *bad—**worse*** *far—**farther***	• My new job is **better** than my old one. • The book was bad, but the movie was **worse**. • The bus stop is **farther** than the train station.
7	Use *much* to make comparisons stronger.	• A two-bedroom apartment is **much** more expensive than a one-bedroom apartment. • England is **much** older than New England.
8	**USAGE NOTE:** In formal English, use the subject pronoun after *than*. In informal English, such as casual conversation between friends, you can use the object pronoun after *than*. **BE CAREFUL!** Always compare the same things. **BE CAREFUL!** Do not use two comparative forms together.	SUBJECT PRONOUN • Steve's younger **than she** is. OBJECT PRONOUN • Steve's younger **than her**. • **John's home** is larger than **William's**. OR • **John's home** is larger than **William's home**. Not: John's home is larger than ~~William~~. Not: John's home is ~~more~~ larger than William's.
9	Use *which* to ask about a comparison of **people**, **places**, or **things**.	• **Which city** is larger? • **Which** is larger, **Tokyo** or **Seoul**?

REFERENCE NOTE
See Unit 35, page 411 for a discussion of *not as* + **adjective** + *as*.

EXERCISE 1: Discover the Grammar

A | *Read about two cities in Canada. Underline all comparative adjectives.*

Canada has many beautiful cities. Two of my favorites are Quebec City in eastern Canada and Vancouver in Western Canada. Vancouver is right on the Pacific coast, and it's just 7 feet above sea level. Quebec City is farther from the coast and higher than Vancouver. It overlooks the Saint Lawrence River. When I visited Quebec City, I took

Fairmont Le Château Frontenac, Quebec City

some great photos of the river from the famous hotel Château Frontenac.

Vancouver

Quebec City has the charm of an old historic city. It is a lot older than Vancouver. Vancouver has an old quarter too, but it's younger than Quebec City's. Vancouver, with its milder climate, is better known for its gardens and parks. Stanley Park in Vancouver is bigger than most urban parks, and people visit it all year round, but I think it's more fun to go in the spring or early summer. That's when the flowers are in bloom.

Vancouver has a larger population than Quebec City and is growing each year. These days many films are made in Vancouver because it is less expensive to make them there than in cities like Los Angeles and New York.

In Vancouver most people speak English, while 95 percent of the people in Quebec City speak French. That is because Quebec City was founded by people from France and still has a continental flavor.

All in all, both cities are great places to visit or live in.

B | *Write the base form of the ten adjectives you underlined in Part A.*

1. _____far_____

2. _____

3. _____

4. _____

5. _____

6. _____

7. _____

8. _____

9. _____

10. _____

Fortress, Quebec City

EXERCISE 2: Comparison of Adjectives

(Grammar Notes 1–9)

A | *Complete the conversations with the adjectives in parentheses. Use the comparative form. Add **than** when necessary.*

1. **A:** Which city is _____more expensive_____ to live in, Tokyo or Sydney?
      (expensive)

   B: Tokyo is _____than_____ Sydney.
      (expensive)

2. **A:** Which city is _____more hott_____ in summer, Bangkok or Seoul?
      (hot)

   B: Bangkok summers are _____hott than_____ summers in Seoul.
      (hot)

3. **A:** Which city has a _____high_____ elevation, Bogota or Mexico
      (high)

   City?

   B: Bogota is _____high than_____ Mexico City.
      (high)

4. **A:** Which river is _____long_____, the Nile or the Amazon?
      (long)

   B: The Nile is _____long than_____ the Amazon.
      (long)

5. **A:** Does New York have a _____good boother_____ subway system
      (good)

   _____than_____ Washington, D.C.?

   B: I don't know. The New York subway goes to more places, but the D.C. Metro is

   _____cleaner_____.
      (clean)

(continued on next page)

6. **A:** Is winter in Quebec City _____ *than cold* _____ winter in Vancouver?
       (cold)

   B: Yes, it is.

7. **A:** Is New York a _____ *more popular* _____ tourist destination
       (popular)
       _____ *than* _____ San Francisco?

   B: No, they're both very popular tourist destinations.

8. **A:** Is Miami in summer _____ *more humid* _____ in winter?
       (humid)

   B: Yes, it's much _____ *more humid* _____ in summer
       (humid)
       _____ *than* _____ in winter.

9. **A:** Is Argentina _____ *farter ~~than~~* _____ from the South Pole
       (far)
       _____ *than* _____ Mexico?

   B: No, Argentina is _____ *nearer* _____ to the South Pole.
       (near)

10. **A:** Was the Hudson River _____ *more polluted* _____ 10 years ago
       (polluted)
       _____ *than* _____ it is today?

    B: Yes, it was. It is much _____ *~~much~~ cleaner* _____ today.
       (clean)

11. **A:** Which highway has _____ *heavyer* _____ traffic, the West Highway
       (heavy)
       or the East Highway?

    B: It depends on the time.

B | *Rewrite the sentences. Use **less** and the adjectives in parentheses. Use the comparative form.*

1. Sydney is _____ *less expensive* _____ to live in _____ *than* _____ Tokyo.
       (expensive)

2. Miami is _____ *less humid* _____ in winter _____ *than* _____ in summer.
       (less humid)

3. The Hudson River is _____ *less polluted* _____ today _____ *than* _____ it was
       (less polluted)
   10 years ago.

4. Is the highway _____ *more crowded* _____ between 7:00 and 8:00 _____ *than* _____ it is
       (crowded)
   between 8:00 and 9:00?

5. Is the Eiffel Tower _____ *more famous* _____ than the Egyptian pyramids?
       (famous)

EXERCISE 3: Comparison of Adjectives

(Grammar Notes 1–2, 4, 8)

Write sentences comparing the two cities. Use the information in the chart and the words in parentheses.

	Middletown	Lakeville
number of people	100,000	50,000
average household income	$85,000	$63,000
average rent for a two-bedroom apartment	$1,300	$1,000
cost of a cup of coffee	$2.00	$1.00
percent unemployed	7	9
number of hospitals	5	1
average summer temperature	80°F	68°F

1. (average household income / high)

   The average household income in Middletown is higher than the average household income
   in Lakeville.

2. (two-bedroom apartment / expensive) ~~than~~

   two-bedroom apartment in Middletown
   is more expensive in Lakeville.

3. (a cup of coffee / less expensive)

   a cost of a cup of coffee (in middlehown) is less
   expensive ~~that~~ Lakeville ~~than in middtenoum~~

4. (probably / hard to find work)

   It is Probably harder to find work Lakerits
   then in middletown.

5. (probably / healthcare / bad)

   Hospital's Probabi wells in Lakerville than in
   middletowe

6. (summers / much / warm)

   Summers warmer are in Middletown
   then in Lakeville
        they are

EXERCISE 4: Comparison of Adjectives

(Grammar Notes 1–7)

Complete the paragraph with the adjectives in parentheses. Use the comparative form.

You are choosing between two cities to live in, Los Angeles or Glendale. You aren't sure which is a _____better_____ choice. Los

1. (good)

Angeles is a much _____bigger_____ city than

2. (big)

Glendale, and it has all the problems of big cities. Los Angeles is _____more_____ than

3. (polluted)

Glendale, and traffic is _____badly_____.

4. (bad)

Rodeo Drive, Los Angeles

The streets of downtown Los Angeles are

_____busier_____ too. However, Los Angeles is much _____more exciting_____ than Glendale.

5. (busy)   **6. (exciting)**

Los Angeles has a great night life. Glendale is much _____quieter_____ at night. Both

7. (quiet)

cities have the same great climate. It's hard to compare housing costs. Some parts of Los Angeles are _____more expensive_____ than Glendale

8. (more / expensive)

and other parts are _____less expensive_____. Both

9. (less / expensive)

cities are close, so if you make a mistake, you can always move.

Bicycle trail, Glendale, California

EXERCISE 5: Editing

Correct the sentences. There are seven mistakes. The first one is already corrected. Find and correct six more.

1. Our new apartment is more comfortable than our old one.

2. Florida is more hotter than Maine.

3. Oregon is far north than California.

4. A motorcycle is more fast than a bicycle.

5. Traffic at 8:00 A.M. is more heavy than traffic at 10:00 A.M.

6. The climate in Portland, Oregon, is mild than the climate in Anchorage, Alaska.

7. The location of Jake's apartment is more convenient than his sister's.

EXERCISE 6: Pronunciation

A | *Read and listen to the Pronunciation Note.*

> **Pronunciation Note**
>
> **Than** is unstressed and reduced to / ðn / .
>
> **EXAMPLE:**   Istanbul is a much larger city than Izmír.

B | *Listen and repeat each sentence.*

1. The Nile River is longer than the Amazon River.
2. The Yangtze River is shorter than the Nile.
3. Quebec City is older than Vancouver.
4. The Pacific Ocean is bigger than the Atlantic Ocean.

EXERCISE 7: Listening

A | *Listen to a conversation between two friends. The woman says, "You can thank our mayor." What is the mayor doing to the city?*

_____

B | *Listen again. Circle the correct word or words to complete each sentence.*

1. The downtown area is **livelier** / **less lively**.

2. The seats on the bus are **more comfortable** / **less comfortable**.

3. It's **easier** / **harder** to take the bus.

4. The air is **cleaner** / **dirtier**.

5. It's **easier** / **harder** to park downtown.

6. West Park is **cleaner and safer** / **dirtier and more dangerous**.

7. East Park is **cleaner and safer** / **dirtier and more dangerous**.

EXERCISE 8: Comparing Train Systems

PAIRS: Look at the information about the London Underground and the Moscow Metro. Together write as many comparative questions as you can. Ask other pairs your questions. Answer their questions. Then compare these subways to others you know.

EXAMPLE: **A:** Is the Underground faster than the Moscow Metro?
B: No, it isn't. It's slower.

	London Underground	Moscow Metro
Year opened	1863	1935
Length of tracks	250 miles (400 kilometers)	187.2 miles (301.2 kilometers)
Number of passengers each day	4 million	6.6 million
Hours of operation	5:30 A.M. to 1:15 A.M. (Fri. & Sat. closes at 2:00 A.M.)	5:30 A.M. to 1:00 A.M.
Cost of ride in euros	4 euros for shortest distance	26 rubles = .66 euro
Speed	20.5 mph (33 km / h)	25.82 mph (41.55 km / h)

EXERCISE 9: Discussion: Making Comparisons

PAIRS: Look at the categories in the list. Tell your partner your preferences within each category. Explain why in a sentence with a comparative.

clothes   homes   jobs   travel   vacation places

EXAMPLE: **A:** Do you prefer to travel by bike or by motorcycle?
B: I prefer a motorcycle. It's faster and more exciting. What about you?
A: I prefer a bike. It's safer and better for the environment.

EXERCISE 10: Comparing Cities

Compare cities. Follow the steps.

1. Name a city you know well. (Do not name the city you are in.) Your teacher writes the names everyone suggests on the board.
2. Class: Name adjectives that describe cities, people, and climates. Your teacher writes the adjectives on the board.

EXAMPLES:

Cities	People	Climates
clean	friendly	warm
dangerous	polite	dry
exciting	relaxed	humid

3. Write questions comparing the cities on the board to the city you are in. Use the adjectives on the board or choose your own. Then with a group, ask each other questions comparing the cities.

EXAMPLES: (You are now in San Francisco.)
A: Is Paris cleaner than San Francisco?
B: I don't think so. I think San Francisco is cleaner than Paris.
C: Does Sapporo have a warmer climate than San Francisco?
D: No, it doesn't. Sapporo has a colder climate than San Francisco.

EXERCISE 11: Writing

A | *Compare two ways of travel. Use at least three comparative adjectives.*

EXAMPLE: Most cities have busses and trains, but in San Francisco some people also travel by trolley, and in Venice people sometimes travel by gondola. Both the trolley and the gondola are more fun than the bus or the train. The gondola is more romantic than the trolley, but the trolley is more exciting, especially when you're traveling down one of San Francisco's steep streets.

 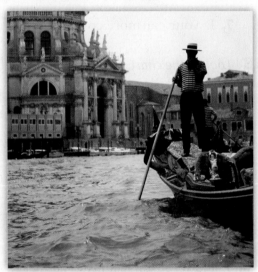

B | *Check your work. Use the Editing Checklist.*

Editing Checklist

Did you . . . ?
☐ use comparative adjectives correctly
☐ check your spelling

UNIT 33 Review

Check your answers on page UR-7.
Do you need to review anything?

A | *Circle the correct words to complete the sentences.*

1. She is **more / much** younger than he is.

2. It is colder **then / than** it was yesterday.

3. This singing group is **more popular / popular more** than the other one.

4. The traffic is **more worse / worse** now than it was an hour ago.

5. Which city has a **high / higher** elevation, Bogota or Mexico City?

6. Which city has a **better / more good** transportation system, Quebec or Vancouver?

7. Is your car more comfortable than your **brother / brother's?**

B | *Look at the chart. Make comparisons. Use the words in parentheses.*

	New City	Sun City
Bus fare	$2.00	$3.00
Cup of coffee	$1.20	$1.50
Average home	$200,000	$300,000
Average income	$65,000	$90,000

1. _____
(bus / expensive)

2. _____
(cup of coffee / cheap)

3. _____
(average home / less / expensive)

4. _The average income is higher in Sun City than New city._
(average income / high)

C | *Correct the paragraph. There are nine mistakes.*

We moved to the countryside, and we're much more happier. Our home is more larger, and the air is cleaner and polluted less. It less expensive than the city too. Fruits and vegetables are more cheap. The people are friendler too. Of course, our commute is more bad; it's much more long, but we listen to Spanish tapes, and our Spanish is more good.

UNIT 34 Adverbs of Manner
PUBLIC SPEAKING

Before You Read

A | PAIRS: List jobs that require speaking in front of large groups. Compare your list with other pairs' lists.

B | How do you feel about giving a speech in front of the following people? Check (✓) your feelings.

How you feel when you speak in front of . . .				
	your classmates?	your friends and relatives?	your bosses?	250 people you don't know?
calm and confident				
nervous but confident				
nervous and not confident				
nervous and miserable				

Read

Read the blog about public speaking.

○ ○ ○

Speaking about . . .

Public Speaking by Michelle Jones

 Like

Last year my boss asked me to give a presentation. It was a bit of a nightmare. I had never spoken in front of a large group before, so I was nervous. Also, I had to prepare **fast**—I had only two days to get ready. The day of the speech came. There were 40 people sitting in the room waiting for me to speak. My manager was there, and my co-workers. I wanted to run out of the room, so I spoke **quickly**, and I didn't look at anyone. Instead I read from my paper. I was afraid to tell a joke. I wanted to sound smart, so in my speech, I gave a lot of facts. I used big words and long sentences. I received polite applause, but I knew my speech was not appreciated. My friend later told me it was a good speech, but that I didn't speak **loudly** enough.

(continued on next page)

The next time I gave a speech, I asked my friend for help. She offered a lot of valuable advice. She helped me to focus on three ideas and to give good examples. In my next speech I spoke **slowly** and **clearly**. I thought **carefully** about everything I wanted to say. I spoke **honestly**, and I gave personal examples. I only said things I really believed. I looked at my audience, and I smiled at the right occasions. This time the applause was long and loud. I connected with the audience, and I felt good. People gave me their time, and I gave them a speech to remember.

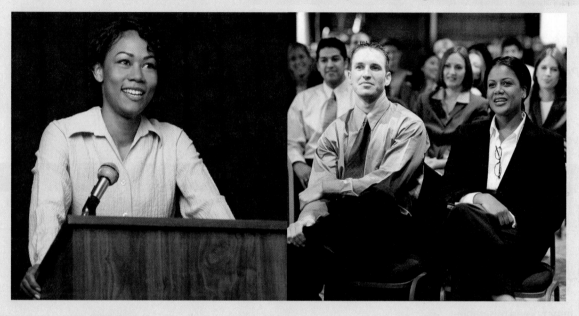

After You Read

A | Practice *PAIRS: Read the blog again aloud. Take turns reading the sentences.*

B | Vocabulary *Circle the letter of the best meaning for the words in blue.*

1. The **audience** was interested in every word he said.

   a. people who write about a performance   **b.** people who watch a performance

2. When he heard the long **applause**, he felt satisfied.

   a. clapping of hands   **b.** stamping of feet

3. Most of his speech was light and funny, but he spoke **seriously** at the end of his talk.

   a. in a way that says something is wrong   **b.** in a way that says something is important

4. He told us many **facts** about his country.

   a. true things   **b.** interesting things

5. We laughed at his **jokes**.

    a. funny stories   **b.** gestures

6. The people clapped to be **polite**, but they didn't really enjoy his talk.

    a. show good manners   **b.** show anger

7. She **appreciated** my help and thanked me many times.

    a. was nervous about   **b.** was grateful for

C | Comprehension *Check (✓) the advice you got from the public speaking blog.*

    ____ **1.** Speak quickly.   ____ **5.** Use humor.

    ____ **2.** Speak slowly.   ____ **6.** Give personal examples.

    ____ **3.** Use big words.   ____ **7.** Have many ideas, not just three or four.

    ____ **4.** Look at audience.   ____ **8.** Speak briefly.

STEP 2 GRAMMAR PRESENTATION

ADVERBS OF MANNER

Subject	Verb	Adverb
He	spoke	well. badly. clearly.

Subject	Verb		Adverb
She	finished	her speech	quickly.

Adverb formed with Adjective + *-ly*		Same Adjective and Adverb Form	
Adjective	**Adverb**	**Adjective**	**Adverb**
bad	badly	early	early
careful	carefully	fast	fast
loud	loudly	late	late
quick	quickly	long	long
quiet	quietly	**Irregular Adverb Form**	
sarcastic	sarcastically	**Adjective**	**Adverb**
slow	slowly	good	well

GRAMMAR NOTES

1	**Adverbs of manner** describe action verbs. They say **how** or the way something happens. The adverb often comes at the end of the sentence.	• She spoke **slowly**. • He walked **fast**.
2	Most adverbs of manner are formed by adding **-ly** to an adjective. **BE CAREFUL!** Some words that end in -ly are adjectives, not adverbs. EXAMPLES: *lively, lovely, ugly, lonely, friendly* These adjectives have no adverb form.	ADJECTIVE • She's a **careful** driver. ADVERB • She drives **carefully**. ADJECTIVE • She's a **friendly** person. • It's a **lonely** job.
3	Some **adverbs** of manner have the **same form as adjectives**.	ADJECTIVE ADVERB • She's a **hard** worker. She works **hard**.
4	*Well* is the adverb for the adjective *good*. *Well* is also an adjective that means "in good health." **USAGE NOTE:** In very informal speaking, when people ask, "How are you?" some people respond, "I'm good."	ADJECTIVE • She's a **good** speaker. ADVERB • She speaks **well**. ADJECTIVE • I feel **well**.
5	**Linking verbs** can connect a subject and an adjective. **Linking verbs** are followed by **adjectives**, not adverbs. Common linking verbs are *appear, be, become, feel, look, seem, smell, sound,* and *taste*.	LINKING VERB ADJECTIVE • The grapes **taste good**. Not: The grapes taste ~~well~~. • She **seems sad**. • It **sounds beautiful**.

EXERCISE 1: Discover the Grammar

Read the paragraph. Underline the adverbs of manner in the paragraph.

A public speaker should remember three things: to entertain, to instruct, and to inspire. Author Bob Rosner likes to say, "It's ha-ha and ah-ha." When you instruct, speak <u>briefly</u> and clearly. Don't speak too long. And don't speak too <u>fast</u>. Use humor. It helps your audience relax. And remember that great speeches inspire and move an audience. Know your audience and touch their emotions.

EXERCISE 2: Adverbs of Manner   *(Grammar Notes 1–4)*

Complete each sentence with the adverb form of the adjectives in parentheses.

1. He spoke _____quickly_____.
   (quick)
2. Sally writes _____well_____.
   (good)
3. They speak Spanish _____fluently_____.
   (fluent)
4. He spoke _____clearly_____.
   (clear)
5. He drove _____fast_____.
   (fast)
6. The audience listened _____careful_____.
   (careful)
7. Did he drive _____dangerously_____.
   (dangerous)
8. Did they sing _____badly_____?
   (bad)
9. The movie began _____slowly_____.
   (slow)
10. It rained _____hard_____ last night.
    (hard)

EXERCISE 3: Adverbs of Manner and Adjectives   *(Grammar Notes 1–5)*

Complete the conversation. Choose from the words in parentheses. Write the correct adjective or adverbs.

1. **A:** How was the debate?

   B: Good. Both sides spoke _____well_____.
   (good / well)

2. **A:** How was the food at the reception after the debate?

   B: It tasted _____good_____.
   (good / well)

(continued on next page)

3. A: There were ___beautiful___ paintings in the room.
(beautiful / beautifully)

    B: The artist is from Colombia.

4. A: How did Roger do in his last debate?

    B: Not ___well___.
(good / well)

5. A: Please drive ___slowly___.
(slow / slowly)

    B: OK.

6. A: How was the talk?

    B: The first part was very ___slow___, but the second part was better.
(slow / slowly)

7. A: How did she sound?

    B: ___Nervous___
(Nervous / Nervously)

EXERCISE 4: Editing

Correct the conversations. There are six mistakes. The first mistake is already corrected.
Find and correct five more.

1. A: How did he do?

    B: He did ~~good~~ well.

2. A: Was the food OK?

    B: Everyone loved it. It really tasted ~~well~~ good.

3. A: Is Harry a good driver?

    B: I don't think so. He drives too slowly.

4. A: How did they do?

    B: They worked hardly and did well.

5. A: Did you hear him?

    B: No, I didn't. He spoke too soft.

6. A: How did she sound?

    B: A little nervously.

EXERCISE 5: Listening

A | *Listen to some tips for giving a speech. Complete the sentences.*

You have a good _____ and _____. You have a couple of good

_____.

B | *Listen again and write the five tips for making a good speech better.*

1. *Look directly at a few people in the audience.*

2. _____

3. _____

4. _____

5. _____

EXERCISE 6: Pronunciation

A | *Read and listen to the Pronunciation Note.*

> **Pronunciation Note**
>
> Sometimes our manner of speaking, our intonation, gives a different meaning to a sentence.
>
> **EXAMPLES:**   Who's he?   Who's he?
>   (questioning)   (angry)

B | *Do you know what the words in boldface mean? If not, use your dictionary. Then listen to the speakers' manner.*

angrily: I love him. He's mine, and you can't have him.

decisively: I love him. I'll love him until I die.

questioningly: Do I love him? Enough to marry him?

sadly: I love him. I miss him so much.

sarcastically: I just love him. His bark wakes me up every day at 5:00 A.M.

C | *Listen again and repeat the sentences.*

D | *PAIRS: Say, "I love him (or her)." Say it angrily, decisively, questioningly, sadly, or sarcastically. Your partner guesses your meaning.*

EXERCISE 7: Writing

A | *PAIRS: Tell about a sports event.*

B | *Write about the event. Use three adverbs of frequency.*

EXAMPLE: It was the final ball game of the season for the Fogville Little League Team. Fogville was up against Lakeville, a very strong team. The score was seven to seven. The bases were loaded. Ron was up at bat. Everyone groaned loudly. Ron never played well. He was the team's worst player. But Ron hit the ball hard. He ran quickly to first base. The man on third ran home. They won. Everyone applauded loudly. It was a great game for everyone, especially Ron.

C | *Check your work. Use the Editing Checklist.*

Editing Checklist

Did you . . . ?
- ☐ use adverbs of manner correctly
- ☐ check your spelling

A | *Complete the sentences with the adjectives in parentheses. Use the adverb form.*

1. He drove _____.
   (quick)
2. She speaks Korean _____.
   (fluent)
3. Did he do _____ on the test?
   (good)
4. Walk _____ and look at the trees.
   (slow)
5. I spoke _____.
   (clear)

B | *Circle the correct word to complete the sentences.*

1. Both sides gave **good / well** arguments.

2. He listened very **careful / carefully**.

3. She sounded a little **nervous / nervously**.

4. He did **bad / badly** on the last test.

5. I can't understand her because she's talking too **quick / quickly**.

C | *Complete the sentences. Choose from the words in the box.*

briefly	clearly	fast	good	honestly

If you want to give a _____ speech, remember these things: Speak
                          1.

_____ and _____. Don't speak too long or swallow your
        2.   3.

words. Don't speak too _____. People need time to understand your
                              4.

ideas. Speak _____. Say only what you mean.
                   5.

D | *Correct the conversation. There are five mistakes.*

A: I think my speech went good.

B: Did they appreciate your jokes?

A: They laughed polite, but I'm not sure they laughed sincere.

B: It's hard to be funny.

A: I hard worked, and I prepared carefully, but I was nervously.

Enough, Too / Very, As + Adjective + As, Same / Different

PROMS AND PARTIES

STEP 1 GRAMMAR IN CONTEXT

Before You Read

A prom is a formal school dance. It usually takes place at the end of the senior year of high school. In the United States, proms can include dinner and dancing. Couples often come in limousines. Are there special parties or dances in your country? When are they? What are they like?

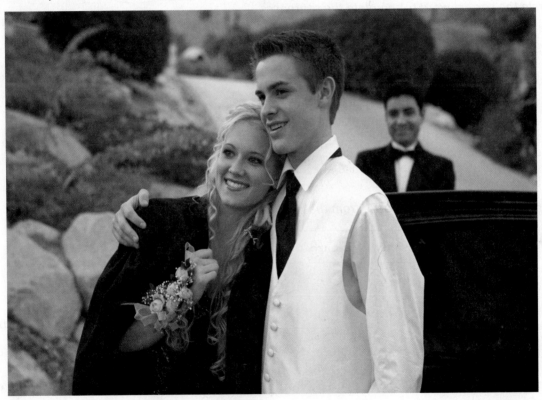

Read

Read a conversation between two high school students, Emily and Haley.

EMILY:	So Haley—what did you decide? Who's your date for the prom?
HALEY:	I don't have one. I'm not going.
EMILY:	What do you mean? You know so many cool guys. . . . How about Mike?
HALEY:	No—he's **too talkative**. When he's around, no one can get a word in edgewise.
EMILY:	Oh. He *does* talk a lot. Well . . . how about David? He likes you.

HALEY: David? He's **way too young** for me. *(Adv Adv Adj handwritten above)*

EMILY: He's in **the same** grade **as** we are. What are you talking about?

HALEY: No, Emily. He's a *sophomore*. He's in our Spanish class because he lived in Spain for a while. I can't go with him. People will say I'm a loser if I go with him.

EMILY: Well how about Jake? He's **old enough**, and he's **very** cute. *(Adj Adv handwritten above)*

HALEY: He dresses funny.[1] *(Adj handwritten above)*

EMILY: Oh, come on, Haley, Jake doesn't dress funny. You're just making excuses.

HALEY: OK, OK. But Jake is **too good looking** and **too popular**. I'm not his type.

EMILY: That's not true. My brother says Jake thinks you're awesome.

HALEY: Really? All right. I'll tell you the real reason. I can't dance. I'm a klutz.[2] I look like an idiot on the dance floor. So . . . I'm not going to make a fool of myself.

EMILY: Not a problem. Jake is sort of a klutz too. He broke his foot in art class.

HALEY: What? In *art class*?

EMILY: He tripped over a can of paint. So it'll be perfect. You can go with him and watch the rest of us dance. I'll talk to my brother. Then Jake will ask you. Don't say no. *(Adj handwritten above "perfect")*

---

[1] **He dresses funny:** (very informal) He dresses strangely, badly.

[2] **klutz:** a clumsy person

After You Read

(handwritten: "ain't" / "isn't")

A | Practice *PAIRS: Now practice the conversation aloud.*

B | Vocabulary *Circle the letter of the best meaning for the words in blue.*

1. "When he's around, **no one can get a word in edgewise**," means _____.
   a. he never says what he means
   (b.) he does all the talking

2. "People will say **I'm a loser**" means _____.
   (a.) I'm unpopular
   b. I get bad grades

3. "You're just **making excuses**," means _____.
   a. you're sorry about something
   (b.) you aren't telling the truth

4. "**I'm not his type**," means _____.
   a. He's too old for me
   (b.) He's different from me

5. "**I'm not going to make a fool of myself**," means _____.
   (a.) I won't do anything that makes me look bad
   b. I'm not stupid

C | Comprehension *Write* **T** *(True) or* **F** *(False) for each statement.*

_____ **1.** Mike is too young for Haley.

_____ **2.** Emily and Haley are sophomores.

_____ **3.** David likes Haley.

_____ **4.** Haley and Emily are in the same Spanish class.

_____ **5.** Haley thinks Jake likes her.

_____ **6.** Haley can't dance well.

_____ **7.** Jake hurt himself in art class.

STEP 2 GRAMMAR PRESENTATION

ENOUGH, TOO / VERY, AS + ADJECTIVE + AS, SAME / DIFFERENT

Adjective + *Enough*

	Adjective	**Enough**	**(Infinitive)**
The room was	**big**	**enough**	to hold all the students.
It wasn't	**warm**		to go without a jacket.

Very + Adjective

	Very	**Adjective**
The prom was	**very**	**expensive.**

Too + Adjective

	Too	**Adjective**	**(Infinitive)**	
His father's tuxedo was	**too**	big	(for him)	to wear.

As + Adjective + *As*

	As	**Adjective**	**As**	
Jake is	**as**	**tall**	**as**	his dad.
He isn't		**heavy**		his dad is.

The Same As

My first name is	**the same as**	yours.
My initials are		his.

Different From

Her dress is	**different from**	mine.
These books are		those.

The Same + Noun (Noun Phrase) + *As*

	The Same	**Noun**	**As**	
My eyes are	**the same**	**color**	**as**	my brother's. yours.
Max has		**last name**		James.
Jim likes		**kind of food**		I do.

GRAMMAR NOTES

1	***Enough*** means that you have the amount you need. It has a positive meaning. Use *enough* after an adjective.	**ADJECTIVE** • He's **old enough** to drive.
	Use *enough* before a noun.	**NOUN** • There are **enough chairs**.
2	***Too*** means "more than necessary." It has a negative meaning. Use *too* before an adjective. ***Much too*** or ***way too*** makes the meaning stronger. **USAGE NOTE:** We use *way too* in informal speaking and writing.	• The coffee is **too hot**. I burned my tongue. • The suit was **much too big** for him. • The prom was **way too short**. I didn't want to go home.
3	An **infinitive** can follow **adjective** + ***enough***. An **infinitive** can follow ***too*** + **adjective**.	**INFINITIVE** • He's **old enough to drive**. • She's **too tired to drive**.
4	***Very*** makes the meaning of an adjective stronger. *Very* comes before an adjective. **BE CAREFUL!** *Too* has a negative meaning, but *very* doesn't.	• He's **very tall**. • He's **very young**. (*He's really young. He's 16, and the other students are 18.*) • He's **too young**. (*He's too young to do something—to drive, to work, etc.*)
5	Use ***as*** + **adjective** + ***as*** to show how two people, places, or things are alike. Use ***not as*** + **adjective** + ***as*** to show how two people, places, or things are not alike.	• Sally is **as tall as** Paula. They're the same height. • Sally is **not as tall as** Mike. Mike is taller.
6	Use ***the same as*** for things that are alike. Use ***different from*** for things that are not alike.	• His family name is **the same as** hers. (*He's Robert Lee, and she's Jennifer Lee.*) • My book is **different from** yours. (*I have a new edition.*)

EXERCISE 1: Discover the Grammar

A | *Circle the adjectives in the sentences. Then underline* **too, as . . . as, enough** *and* **very**. *Draw arrows from the adjectives to the nouns they go with.*

1. Mr. Jones isn't as old as he looks.

2. The food wasn't spicy enough for him.

3. His dress shoes were too tight.

4. Her prom dress was very beautiful.

5. That tuxedo was too expensive.

6. The car wasn't big enough for all of us.

B | *Underline* **the same . . . as** *and* **different from** *in the sentences.*

1. Serena wore the same dress as Jasmin.

2. He has the same voice as his father. It's confusing when I call his home.

3. He's different from his brother. His brother loves to go to parties.

4. Adam Rusk has the same initials as Ali Rogers.

EXERCISE 2: *Enough, Too*   *(Grammar Notes 1–2)*

Haley is talking to her aunt about the prom. Complete their conversation with **enough** *or* **too** *and the words from the box.*

~~hot~~	ice	salty	seats	sweet

AUNT ANNE: So, Haley. How was the prom?

HALEY: I had a great time, but there were a few problems with the place. The air

conditioner didn't work well, so it was _____too hot_____ in the room.
                                                    1.

AUNT ANNE: It was a warm night. I feel bad for the guys in those tuxedos. How was the

music?

HALEY: Good, but the refreshments were so-so. The chips were ___to salty___,
                                                                        2.

and the desserts were ___to sweet___. And there wasn't ___enough ice___
                             3.   **4.**

for the drinks, so the drinks were warm.

AUNT ANNE: That's pretty bad.

HALEY: Also, there weren't ___enough seats___. All but a few of us had to stand. Since
5.
Jake hurt his foot, we were able to sit. But I'm really glad I went. Jake's a nice

guy, and we have a lot in common.

AUNT ANNE: I'm glad. Your mom sent me your picture. You looked very beautiful in that

dress.

HALEY: Thanks.

She isn't old enough to work.
She is too smart to believe him.

EXERCISE 3: Word Order Practice; *Enough, Too . . . To*   *(Grammar Notes 1–3)*

Write sentences with the words given.

enough ——— NP
enough enough
Adj
a lot too tough

1. to vote / She isn't / enough / old

   She isn't old enough to vote.

2. warm / that dress / to wear / It isn't / enough

   It isn't warn enough to wear that dress.

3. too / This steak / is / to eat / tough / much

   This steak much too tough to eat.

4. to call / him / I'm / busy / too / right now

   I'm busy to call him right now.

5. weren't / the sofa / They / enough / strong / to move

   They weren't enough strong the sofe to more.

6. much / restaurant / too / That / expensive / is

   That restaurant too much expensive

7. too / was / to miss / That class / important

   That class was too important to miss

8. before the movie / have / don't / time / enough / We / to eat

   We don't have enough time to eat before the morie

9. clear / wasn't / to read / His address / enough

   His address wasn't clear enough to read.

much too Adj, Adv   too much N
too much N   too man N

Enough, Too / Very, As + Adjective + As, Same / Different **413**

EXERCISE 4: *Too* + Adjective / *The Same . . . As*

(Grammar Notes 2, 6)

A | *Russ Tran, Jean Philippe, and Robert Trent are friends and co-workers. They take turns driving to work. Complete the sentences with the words from the box.*

too carelessly	too fast	too slowly

1. Russ thinks Jean drives _____ too fast _____. He thinks Jean will get a

   speeding ticket.

2. Jean thinks Russ and Robert drive _____ too slowly _____. He complains

   that they drive under the speed limit.

3. Russ thinks Robert drives _____ too carelessly _____. He eats, drinks, and

   answers phone calls while driving.

B | *Look at the three licenses. Use the information from the licenses to write similarities among the people. Use* **has***, the words in parentheses, and* **as***.*

1. **(the same height)** _____

   Jean Philippe is the same height as

   Robert Trent.

2. **(the same color eyes)** JP is

   _____ the same color eyes as Russ.

3. **(the same initials)** Russ is

   _____.

4. **(the same weight)** JP is

   _____ as RT _____.

NEVADA

DRIVER LICENSE

DOB: 06-09-88
SEX: M   **EYES:** BR   **HT:** 6-0
ISSUED: 06-01-11
EXPIRATION: 06-09-17

Russ Tran
8278 Sonoma View Court,
Las Vegas NV 89139
Plainville, NV 10677

Russ Tran

Texas — DRIVER LICENSE

EXPIRES: 06/09/11
Jean Philippe
7807 Maple Brook Lane
Houston, TX 77095

SEX	WEIGHT	HEIGHT	EYES
M	185	5-10	Brown

ISSUE DATE: 080911   **BIRTH DATE:** 060984

Jean Philippe

Texas — DRIVER LICENSE

EXPIRES: 04/08/17
Robert Trent
6103 Martel Avenue
Dallas, TX 75214

SEX	WEIGHT	HEIGHT	EYES
M	185	5-10	Green

ISSUE DATE: 040110   **BIRTH DATE:** 040884

Robert Trent

EXERCISE 5: *Too / Very*

Complete the sentences with too or very.

1. Some people think that a black dress is _____ *too* _____
dark to wear to a prom, but I think it's _____ *very* _____
fashionable.

2. Don't buy those shoes. They're _____ *very* _____ pretty, but
the heels are _____ *too* _____ high. They will hurt your
feet.

3. Jake called _____ *too* _____ late to order a limousine, so
he picked up Haley in his car.

4. He can't reach the shelf. He's _____ *too* _____ short. Ask Ali. He's
_____ *very* _____ tall.

5. Your composition is _____ *very* _____ well written. You did a great job.

6. I can't lift the box. It's _____ *too* _____ heavy. I'll ask Barry. He's _____ *very* _____
strong.

7. It's _____ *very* _____ windy outside. Put on a jacket. It's _____ *too* _____ cold to
go outside without one.

8. It's _____ *very* _____ difficult to get into that school. His grades are
_____ *too* _____ low. He probably won't get in.

9. This jacket doesn't fit. It's _____ *too* _____ tight in the shoulders.

10. It's _____ *too* _____ early to go to the party. We don't want to be the first to arrive.

11. We had a _____ *very* _____ good time at Joel's graduation party, but there were
_____ *too* _____ many guests, so it was crowded.

EXERCISE 6: As + Adjective + As, The Same + Noun + As (Grammar Note 5)

Read the conversation between Jake and Haley. Jake applied to an art school but did not get in. Complete the sentences with the phrases from the box.

~~as hard as she does~~	the same art camp as she did
as serious an artist as she is	the same grades as she did
as well as she does	

as small as student as he is

HALEY: Jake, what's wrong?

JAKE: I'm really angry. Maya got into BCA Art Institute, and I didn't. I work

_____ *just as hard as she does* _____.
         1.

HALEY: And you're really talented.

JAKE: Thanks. I think I'm _____ *the same art camp as she did* _____
                                    2.

HALEY: Yes, you work very hard on your drawings and paintings.

JAKE: And I hand in every project on time. I draw _____ *as serious an artist as she is* _____.
                                                          3.

HALEY: Why do you think she got into BCA Art Institute then?

JAKE: I don't know. I got _____. We had the same art
                              4.

teachers. I even went to _____. Maybe she got in
                              5.

because she knows someone at BCA?

HALEY: That happens sometimes.

EXERCISE 7: Editing

Correct the sentences. There are eight mistakes. The first mistake is already corrected.
Find and correct seven more.

                 enough
1. He doesn't have money ~~enough~~ to pay for the limousine.

2. His girlfriend isn't as nice ~~than~~ *as* his old one.

3. She's very different ~~than~~ her sister.

4. We're very young to vote. You have to be 18 years old. We're 17.

5. She has the same dress ~~than~~ *as* I do.

6. I'm as ~~taller~~ *tall* as my father.

7. Dan's weight is the same as his brother's.

8. Is your new book bag enough big for all your books?

EXERCISE 8: Pronunciation

A | *Read and listen to the Pronunciation Note.*

> **Pronunciation Note**
>
> When an adjective appears between *as . . . as*, stress the adjective and not *as*. **As** is unstressed and reduced to / əz / .
>
> **EXAMPLE:**   She's as cold as ice.

B | *Listen. Complete the sentences with the words you hear.*

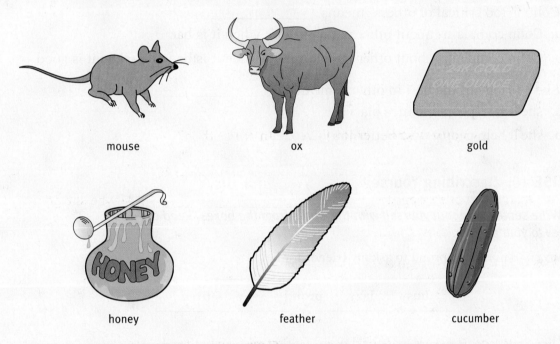

mouse   ox   gold

honey   feather   cucumber

1. She's bright, but she never says a word. She just sits and smiles. She's as quiet as a _____*mouse*_____ .

2. I'm sorry I bought that chair. You have to be as strong as an ____OX____ to lift it.

3. He never shows his feelings. He's as cool as a ___cucumber___ .

4. Her sister is nasty, but she's as sweet as ___honey___ .

5. She doesn't weigh much at all. She's as light as a ___feather___ .

6. I was very upset when she didn't keep her promise. I thought her word was as good as _____gold_____ . trust 100%.

C | *Now listen and repeat each sentence. Remember not to stress the word* **as.**

EXERCISE 9: Listening

A | *Listen to the conversation. Two managers are talking about two young employees, Colin and Maria. Complete the sentence. Circle the correct letter.*

The managers _____.

a. are planning to promote both people

b. promoted one person and didn't promote the other

B | *Listen again. Then complete the sentences. Circle the correct letter.*

1. "Maria's word is good as gold" means _____.
   a. she does what she says she will
   b. she usually says nice things to others

2. "Colin is too critical of others" means _____.
   a. Colin complains about other people's work when it is bad
   b. Colin complains about other people's work when it is bad *and* when it is good

3. "She'll bring out the best in others" means _____.
   a. she'll take people to nice places
   b. she'll help people do a better job

EXERCISE 10: Describing Yourself

PAIRS: Write sentences about yourself with the words from the boxes. Read the sentences to your partner.

EXAMPLE: I'm not too proud to ask my friends for help.

busy	lazy	proud	shy	tired

I'm too _____ to _____.

I'm not too _____ to _____.

old	smart	strong	tall	young

I'm _____ enough to _____.

I'm not _____ enough to _____.

EXERCISE 11: Similarities

Take five minutes. Walk around your classroom. Find classmates who are like you in some way. Use the chart for suggestions. Take notes. Report to the class. The person who finds the most similarities wins.

EXAMPLES: Cecilia and I were born in the same month.
Julio and I have the same color eyes.
Ming and I like the same kind of movies.
Pierre and I have the same number of sisters.
Jasmine and I have the same lucky number.

Suggestions				
Born	**Looks**	**Likes**	**Families**	**Your Ideas**
same month same day	same color eyes same color hair same height	same kind of movies, music, sports	same number of brothers or sisters	

EXERCISE 12: Writing

A | *Write about two friends or two events. Use three of these structures:* **very, too, as . . . as, the same as,** *and* **different from.** *Underline the examples in your paragraph.*

EXAMPLE: I'm a sophomore in college. I went to two parties this year. I liked the first party. The people were very cool. There were lots of different kinds of students: musicians, artists, but also athletes. Everyone was friendly. The second party was not as good as the first party. The people were not the same—this group wasn't friendly. No one talked to me. The music was too loud.

B | *Check your work. Use the Editing Checklist.*

Editing Checklist
Did you . . . ? ☐ use ***very, too, as . . . as, the same as,*** and ***different from*** correctly ☐ check your spelling

Check your answers on page UR-7.

Do you need to review anything?

A | *Circle the words to complete the sentences.*

1. Is that limousine (**big enough** / **enough big**) for us to fit in it?

2. His car is the same kind (**as** / **than**) mine.

3. He's (**very** / **too**) young to get a (driver's license). He can't drive legally.

4. He's not as young (**from** / **as**) he looks.

5. The new driving test is different **as** / (**from**) the old one.

B | *Complete the sentences. Use **very**, **enough**, or **too** and the words from the box.*

~~busy~~	good	~~late~~	short	time	~~warm~~

1. The water isn't ___warm___ ___enough___ for swimming.

2. She's taking a taxi because she's ___very___ ___late___.

3. I had a lot of work. I was ___too___ ___busy___ to go to the party.

4. I don't like my hair. The hairdresser cut it ___too___ ___short___.

5. We don't have ___enough___ ___time___ to go out after the prom.

6. He looks ___very___ ___good___ in his Dad's tuxedo.

C | *Correct the paragraph. There are nine mistakes.*

   I didn't like the prom this year as much than last year. I usually like parties, but the
music at the prom was much very loud. Also, my dress was same as Julia! That was a
too big shock. Also, the dinner portions weren't enough large and the servers this year
were very rude. Then we tried to dance, but there was no enough room and the room
was too much hot. The music was also not good as last year. We had a ~~more~~ better
time last year.

(handwritten annotations: as; too; the 's; very; too much coffee; much too + Adj hot)

The Superlative
PENGUINS

Before You Read

What do you know about penguins? Write **T** (**True**) *or* **F** (**False**) *for each statement.*

_____ **1.** They only live in very cold climates.

_____ **2.** They mostly live south of the equator.

_____ **3.** They can weigh up to 90 pounds.

_____ **4.** English explorers named them.

Read

Read the online article about penguins.

wild nature

WILD NATURE   Animals Home | Animal Facts | Animal Photos | Animal Quizzes | Wild TV

THE PENGUIN

The penguin is one of **the easiest** birds to recognize. Penguins have black backs and white bellies.[1] They look fat. They stand upright, and they waddle.[2] Unlike other birds, most penguins can't fly, but they can swim very fast.

In 1519 Spanish explorers under Ferdinand Magellan saw penguins when they sailed around South America. They thought this type of bird was one of **the strangest** birds in the world. To them, the penguins looked like another strange bird, the Great Auk of Greenland and Iceland. The Great Auk was a large black and white bird that did not fly. The Spanish word for

Fairy Penguin

Great Auk is *pinguis* which means "fat." And that's how penguins got their name.

There are 17 kinds of penguins. They all live below the equator, but they don't only live in very cold climates. Some, like the Little Blue Penguins, (sometimes called Fairy Penguins) live in warmer climates. The Little Blue Penguins are **the smallest** of all. They are 16 inches (about 41 centimeters) tall and weigh only 2.2 pounds (about 1 kilogram). They got their name because of their blue feathers. These penguins live in the warm waters off southern Australia and New Zealand.

---

[1] *belly:* stomach
[2] *waddle:* to walk from side to side like a duck

(*continued on next page*)

The largest penguins are the Emperor Penguins. They are almost 4 feet (about 1.2 meters) tall and weigh from 70 to 90 pounds (about 32 to 41 kilograms). They live on the ice around the Antarctic continent. This is **the coldest** climate on earth.

Of the 17 different species of penguins, the Macaroni Penguins have **the biggest population**, while the Galapagos Penguins have

Emperor Penguin

the smallest. In fact, some scientists worry that the Galapagos Penguins may become extinct.

People say penguins are **the cutest**, **the funniest**, and **the most loved** birds. They also say they're **the most formal**. Do you know why? It's because they look as if they're wearing tuxedos.[3]

---

[3] *tuxedo:* a formal suit worn at weddings or other very formal occasions

After You Read

A | Practice *PAIRS: Now read the article aloud. Take turns reading each paragraph.*

B | Vocabulary *Complete the sentences with the words from the box.*

centimeters	⁶extinct	~~inches~~	pounds
⁸explorer	⁷feathers	kilogram	⁵ species

1. One centimeter is equal to .4 _____inch_____ .

2. 1 millimeter is the same as 0.1 _Centimere_ .

3. In the United States people usually measure their weight in

   _____Pounds_____ .

4. One _____ is the same as 2.2 pounds.

5. There are 17 different _____ of penguins.

6. Some scientists worry that oil spills and global warming may

   cause penguins to become _____ .

7. Most penguins' _____ are white and black.

8. The Magellanic Penguin was named after the _____

   Ferdinand Magellan.

millimeter

inch

centimeter

C | Comprehension *Complete the information with the words from the box.*

> | 3 the Antarctic | 5 Galapagos Penguins | 2 Little Blue Penguins |
> |---|---|---|
> | 1 Emperor Penguins | 4 Greenland and Iceland | |

1. The biggest penguins: _____ Em _____

2. The smallest penguins: _____

3. The coldest place on earth: _____

4. Home of the Great Auk: _____

5. Penguin species with the smallest number: _____

The puffin is descended from the Great Auk.

STEP 2 GRAMMAR PRESENTATION

SUPERLATIVE FORMS OF ADJECTIVES

Superlative Forms of Adjectives			
		Superlative Adjective	
The Emperor Penguin		**the biggest**	of all the penguins.
That photo	is	**the funniest**	of all.
That program		**the most interesting**	one on TV.

Superlative Forms of Irregular Adjectives			
		Superlative Adjective	
This	is	**the best**	photo of all.
We	had	**the worst**	weather on Saturday.
Her home	is	**the farthest**	of all.

The Superlative   **423**

GRAMMAR NOTES

1	Use the **superlative** form of adjectives to compare three or more people, places, or things.	• The Dead Sea is **the lowest** place on earth.
2	To form the superlative of **short (one-syllable) adjectives**, add *the* before the adjective and *-est* to the adjective. 　*fast—**the fastest*** 　*long—**the longest*** If the adjective ends in *e*, add *-st*. 　*large—**the largest***	• The cheetah is **the fastest** animal on earth. • Alaska is **the largest** state in the United States.
3	To form the superlative of **two-syllable adjectives that end in -y**, add *the* before the adjective, then drop the *-y* and add *-iest* to the adjective. 　*funny—**the funniest***	• The penguin is **the funniest** bird in the zoo.
4	To form the superlative of **long adjectives**, use *the most* before the adjective. 　*interesting—**the most interesting*** 　*dangerous—**the most dangerous***	• The bird section was **the most interesting** part of the zoo.
5	These adjectives have **irregular comparative** and **superlative** forms:	• It is **the best** time of year for bird watching. • That was **the worst** time to visit the zoo. • The Birdhouse is **the farthest** section from the entrance.

ADJECTIVE	COMPARATIVE FORM	SUPERLATIVE FORM
good	better (than)	**the best**
bad	worse (than)	**the worst**
far	farther (than)	**the farthest**

6	After the superlative, we often use a **prepositional phrase** to identify the group we are talking about.	• The giraffe is the tallest animal **in the zoo**. • The rhinoceros beetle is the strongest **of all the animals**.
7	*One of the* often comes before a **superlative adjective**. The adjective is followed by a **plural noun**.	• It is **one of the largest animals** in the world. • It is **one of the most intelligent animals** of all. Not: It is one of the largest ~~animal~~.
8	**BE CAREFUL!** Do not use two superlative forms together.	• It's the biggest. Not: It's the **most** biggest. • It's the most important. Not: It's the most ~~importantest~~.

EXERCISE 1: Discover the Grammar

A | *Underline the superlative adjective forms.*

1. Cockroaches are probably the most disliked insect in the world.

2. Cockroaches live everywhere, even in the cleanest kitchens.

3. The world's heaviest cockroach is the Australian Giant Burrowing Cockroach.

4. The best way to kill a cockroach is with boric acid.

5. The most famous cockroach was in a story by Franz Kafka. In it, a man turns into a

   cockroach.

(handwritten: poss Adj His most famous story the)

B | *Write the adjectives used in the superlatives in Part A.*

1. _____disliked_____   3. _____   5. _____

2. _____   4. _____

C | *Find three more prepositional phrases that go with superlative statements in Part A.*

   in the world, _____

EXERCISE 2: Superlative Form of Adjectives   *(Grammar Notes 1–2, 4)*

Complete the sentences with the words in parentheses. Use the superlative adjective
form. Then guess the animal from the choices in the box. Write the correct letter.

a. the African elephant	c. the hummingbird	e. the Macaroni Penguin
b. ~~the blue whale~~	d. the giraffe	f. the sailfish

_b_ **1.** It is both _____the biggest_____ and _____loud_____ animal in the world.
                        (big)   **(loud)**

_a_ **2.** It is _____largest_____ land animal.
              (large)

_c_ **3.** It is _____tallest_____ animal today.
              (tall)

_c_ **4.** It is _____smallest_____ bird. It is as small as 2.5 inches (6.2 centimeters) long
              (small)
      and weighs only .06 ounces (1.6 grams).

_f_ **5.** It is _____fastes_____ fish. It swims up to 68 miles per hour (110 kilometers
              (fast)
      per hour).

_e_ **6.** It is _____ of all the penguins. It has bright yellow feathers on its
              (colorful)
      head.

EXERCISE 3: Superlative Form of Adjectives

(Grammar Notes 1–4, 7)

Complete the paragraph about two deadly animals: snakes and jellyfish. Use the adjectives in parentheses and the superlative form.

Which snakes are ___the most dangerous___?
1. (dangerous)

Which snakes are ___the deadlyest___?
2. (deadly)

The country with ___the highest___
3. (high)

percentage of deadly snakes is Australia, but

only three or four people die of snake bites

in Australia each year. The country with

___largest___ number of fatal snake bites
4. (large)

is India, and ___the scariest___ snake in India
5. (scary)

is the king cobra.

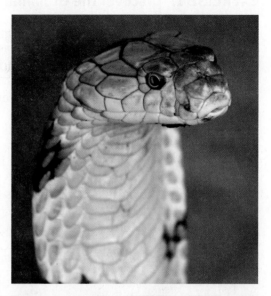

Do you know ___the oldest___ creature
6. (old)

on earth? It's the jellyfish. Jellyfish were around

more than 650 million years ago. They are one of

___the most___ sea creatures. There are
7. (frightening)

over 2,000 different kinds of jellyfish. Some are

tiny, and others are big. ___heaviest___
8. (heavy)

weigh over 450 pounds (204 kilograms), and

___longest___ are 120 feet (40 meters).
9. (long)

The ___deadliest___ jellyfish are the
10. (deadly)

tiny Irukandji jellyfish, which live in the waters off

Australia.

EXERCISE 4: *One of the* + Superlative Adjectives

Complete the conversations with **one of the** and the words in parentheses. Use the superlative form of the adjectives and plural form of the nouns.

1. **A:** I'm going to be in San Diego. Is the San Diego Zoo a good place to go?

   B: I think so. It's ___one of the most popular zoos___ in the United States.
   (popular / zoo)

2. **A:** I think the peacock is

   ___one of the most___ in the world.
   (beautiful / bird)

   B: I agree.

3. **A:** Can an octopus open a jar?

   B: Yes, it can. It's ___smartest___
   (smart / animal)

   of its type.

4. **A:** Are there any good nature shows on TV?

   B: Yes. ___bestes___ is at 8:00 P.M. tonight on the Discovery
   (good / nature show)

   Channel. I saw the show last month.

5. **A:** Are you laughing at that gorilla?

   B: Yes. He's ___funniest___ in the zoo.
   (funny / animal)

6. **A:** My son loves dinosaurs. Where can you see

   dinosaur bones?

   B: The Museum of Natural History in New York

   City has ___bestes___ of
   (good / collection)

   dinosaur bones in the world.

EXERCISE 5: Comparative and Superlative

Complete the sentences with the adjectives in parentheses. Use the comparative or superlative form.

1. African elephants are different from Asian elephants. Asian elephants have

   ___smaller___ ears and ___shorter___ tusks than African ones. The African
   (small)   (short)

   elephants are ___larger___ and ___taller___.
   (large)   (tall)

2. Bear's milk is ___the richest___ of all milk from animals. It is 46 percent fat. This
   (rich)

   rich milk allows the tiny bear cub to grow very fast.

(continued on next page)

The Superlative   **427**

3. <u>The smallest</u> snake in the world is the blind snake. It reaches just slightly more
   (small)

than 5 inches (13 centimeters) in length and weighs less than 0.1 ounce (less than

2 grams).

4. <u>The largest</u> snakes are the anaconda and the python. They grow as long as
   (large)

33 feet (about 10 meters) and can weigh up to 550 pounds (about 250 kilograms).

5. Most female snakes are _____<u>larger</u>_____ than male snakes.
   (large)

6. A snake's body temperature is about the same as the temperature outside. When

the temperature warms up, snakes are <u>more active</u>, and when it gets
   (active)

_____<u>colder</u>_____, they are less active.
   (cold)

7. Many people think the great white shark is <u>the most dangerous</u> of all sharks. Studies
   (dangerous)

show that it's not true. White sharks mostly attack when they confuse humans with

seals or sea lions.

EXERCISE 6: Editing

Correct the sentences. There are seven mistakes. The first mistake is already corrected.
Find and correct six more.

1. The Berlin Zoological Garden is the ~~most old~~ oldest zoo in Germany. It opened in 1844.

2. It is one of the most popular zoo*s* in the world.

3. The zoo has *the* biggest collection of different species in the world.

4. The zoo is very crowded Sunday afternoons. That is the ~~most bad~~ *west* time to visit.

5. The pandas are the most popular resident*s* of the Berlin Zoological Garden.

6. The Birdhouse is one *of* the most modern bird houses in Europe. There are more than

500 species of birds, many of them quite rare.

7. The most good time to visit the zoo is in the spring or the fall.

EXERCISE 7: Pronunciation

A | *Read and listen to the Pronunciation Note.*

Pronunciation Note
Be sure to pronounce the **-est** ending of the superlative, but do not stress the ending. **EXAMPLE:**   Longest

B | *Listen and repeat the sentences.*

1. The biggest is not always the strongest.
2. The loudest is not always the wisest.
3. The funniest is sometimes the saddest.
4. The quietest is sometimes the deepest.

C | *Now listen and repeat the questions.*

1. Is the biggest the best?
2. Is the youngest the fastest?
3. Is the fattest the warmest?
4. Is the slowest the heaviest?

EXERCISE 8: Listening

A | *Listen to a quiz show. Read the questions. Circle the letter of the correct answer.*

1. The first question asks, "Which animal has the longest gestation period?" A gestation period is _____.

   a. the time the baby is carried in its mother   **b.** the time the baby learns to walk

2. The second question asks, "Which animal is _____?"

   a. the fattest   **b.** the fastest

3. The third question asks, "Which animal is _____?"

   a. the loudest   **b.** the proudest

4. The last question asks, "Which animal is _____?"

   a. the deadliest   **b.** the most dangerous

1. What were the answers to the four questions in the quiz show? Choose from the words in the box.

ant	cockroach	horse	mosquito
bear	cow	lion	peacock
cheetah	elephant	monkey	tiger

Answer one: the Asian _____

Answer two: the _____

Answer three: the howler _____

Answer four: the _____

2. How much money did Marcia win? She won _____ dollars.

EXERCISE 9: Survey

A | *Write questions in the superlative. Use the words from the list.*

good / pet to have   interesting / animal to look at

smart / animal you know   beautiful animal / you know

B | *Ask four classmates the questions in Part A. Then ask each student a reason why he or she thinks so. Report results to the class.*

EXAMPLE: **A:** Florian, what's the best pet to have?
            B: Fish.
            A: Why? (. . .)
            (Reporting to class)
            A: According to Florian, fish make the best pets. They're the quietest, the most colorful, and the easiest to take care of, especially for a student who lives in an apartment.

EXERCISE 10: Discussion

PAIRS: Talk about animals or insects that are pests—for example, cockroaches, ants, mice, raccoons, squirrels, deer, or bears.

1. What's the worst pest in your area? Why?

2. What's the best way to handle this pest?

EXAMPLE: **A:** I think one of the biggest problems around here is bears.
            B: Bears? I disagree. There are a lot of bears, and they are big and scary, but they rarely bother people. I think that raccoons are our worst problem. Last summer a raccoon climbed in my attic and made a home there. It was hard to get rid of her.
            A: What did you do?

EXERCISE 11: Game

A | *Make a list from A to Z of as many animals as you can. On the board, write the names of all the animals.*

> **EXAMPLE:**   A = Auk
> B = bear

B | *GROUPS: Students take turns. Each student asks a question using a superlative about one of the animals on the board.*

> **EXAMPLES:**   Which animal has the best memory?
> Which animal is the busiest?

C | *GROUPS: Students write their answers. Compare answers.*

> **EXAMPLE:**   Ten students think that elephants have the best memory. Three students think that dolphins do.

EXERCISE 12: Writing

A | *Write about one or more animals in the zoo, in books, or in movies. Use a superlative and **one of** plus a superlative in your writing.*

> **EXAMPLE:**   Last August I visited the Bronx Zoo. This zoo is one of the best zoos in the world. It covers 265 acres and is home to over 6,000 animals. I enjoyed the Butterfly Zone and the World of Birds, but the most interesting part was the Congo Gorilla Forest. I saw a rain forest and a lot of gorillas. The funniest gorilla imitated one of the visitors. The people laughed a lot. I started to laugh but stopped when I realized I was the one he was imitating!

B | *Check your work. Use the Editing Checklist.*

Editing Checklist

Did you . . . ?
☐ use superlatives correctly
☐ check your spelling

Check your answers on page UR-8.

Do you need to review anything?

A | *Complete the sentences with the adjectives in parentheses. Use the superlative form.*

1. Who was ___*funniest*___ monkey in the cage?
   (funny)

2. What is the name of ___*biggest*___ whale?
   (big)

3. What is ___*betterst*___ nature show on TV?
   (good)

4. ___*The larger*___ sharks are not ___*the moust dangerous*___
   (large)   **(dangerous)**

B | *Complete the sentences with the superlative.*

1. It's 101 degrees. It's ___*hot is day*___ of the year.
   (hot / day)

2. She's 112 years old. She's ___*The old wemn*___ in town.
   (old / woman)

3. The day after Thanksgiving is _____ of the year.
   (busy / shopping day)

4. It was _____ on TV last month.
   (interesting / show)

5. The pandas are ___*onoos the moust*___ at the zoo.
   (popular / animal) *Popular animals*

C | *Complete the sentences with **one of** and the words in parentheses. Use the superlative form of the adjectives and the plural form of the nouns.*

1. The dolphin is _____ in the world.
   (one of the / intelligent / animal) s

2. The Bronx Zoo is ___*best*___ in the world.
   (one of the / good / zoo) s

3. He has ___*west*___ in the stadium.
   (one of the / bad / seat) s

4. It was ___*longer*___ of the year.
   (one of the / long / day) s

5. That was ___*most*___ in the guidebook.
   (one of the / expensive / trip) s

D | *Correct the conversations. There are five mistakes.*

1. **A:** What is the most good way to get to park?

   B: The shortest route is also the ~~complicated~~ *eter*. I'll give you the most direct way.

2. **A:** What's the ~~most~~ hardest part of your job here at the zoo?

   B: Well, the ~~nicer~~ *Nicest* part is taking care of the animals. The ~~most~~ worst part is telling

   people not to feed the animals or bother them.

From Grammar to Writing

THE ORDER OF ADJECTIVES BEFORE NOUNS

1 | *Complete the sentences with the words in parentheses.*

1. I saw a _____ on Main Street.
   (funny / monkey / brown / little)

2. Maria wore a _____.
   (red / dress / beautiful / silk)

2 | *Study this information about the order of adjectives before nouns. When you use adjectives, write them in this order.*

	1. opinion	2. size	3. shape	4. age	5. color	6. origin	7. material	8. noun
1	beautiful	big	square	new	red	French	silk	scarf

2	We use adjectives to describe nouns. Descriptions make writing more lively. They also help the reader form mental pictures. When **several adjectives** come before a noun, they follow a **special order**. • I saw a **beautiful young** woman. NOT: I saw a ~~young beautiful~~ woman.
3	Use **and** to connect adjectives from the same category. • The shirt was *cotton* **and** *polyester.* • The blouse was *red* **and** *white.*

3 | *Complete the sentences with the words in parentheses. Use the correct order.*

1. He ate a(n) _____ pear.
   (brown / big / Asian)

2. His cashmere coat was not as expensive as her _____
   (Italian / new / leather / black)
   _____ jacket.

3. They bought three _____ bowls.
   (silver / beautiful / Mexican)

Detective Work

Several years ago I was walking down the street when I saw my father's brand new shiny blue car. I expected to see my father, but to my surprise a young woman with short, curly bright red hair was behind the wheel of the car. I saw an empty taxi nearby, and I got in quickly. I said dramatically to the driver, "Follow that new blue car." And I told the driver why.

The taxi driver had a cell phone, and I told him to call the police. Soon we heard the siren of the patrol car and a loudspeaker. The police told the woman to pull over. We pulled over too. I immediately said to the woman, "That's not your car. It's my father's."

The woman smiled calmly and said, "Oh. You're Mr. Abbot's younger son. I recognize you from your picture."

Before I could say another word, the woman explained that she was my father's new assistant. My father had asked her to take his computer to the main office to get it fixed. He lent her his car. We called my father, and he confirmed her story. The police laughed, and the taxi driver laughed. I was too embarrassed to laugh. That was the beginning and the end of my career as a detective.

5 | *Exchange papers with a partner. Did your partner follow the directions? Correct any mistakes in grammar and spelling.*

6 | *Talk to your partner. Discuss the mistakes you made. Then rewrite your own paper and make any necessary changes.*

APPENDICES

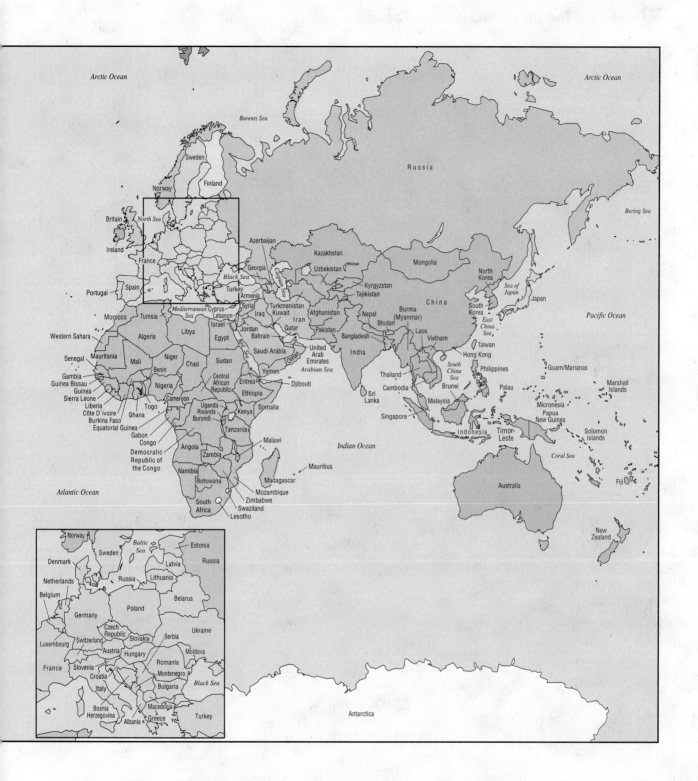

Arctic Ocean   Arctic Ocean

Barents Sea

Sweden   Russia   Bering Sea

Norway   Finland   Sea of
                                                                    Japan
Britain   North Sea   North
                                                        Korea   Japan
Ireland   Azerbaijan   South
                       Georgia   Kazakhstan   Mongolia   Korea   Pacific Ocean
France   East
Portugal   Spain   Black Sea   Caspian Sea   Uzbekistan   China
                       Turkey   Kyrgyzstan   China   Sea
                       Armenia   Tajikistan
                    Cyprus Syria   Turkmenistan Afghanistan Nepal South   Taiwan
           Tunisia Mediterranean Lebanon   Iraq Kuwait   Iran Bhutan Korea
Morocco   Sea   Israel   Qatar   Pakistan   Hong Kong
                           Jordan Bahrain   India Bangladesh Laos
Western Sahara   Algeria Libya   Egypt   Saudi Arabia   Burma   Vietnam Guam/Marianas
                                          United   (Myanmar)
Senegal   Mauritania Mali Niger Chad Sudan   Arab   Arabian Sea   Philippines Marshall
                          Benin   Emirates Yemen   Thailand   Islands
Gambia   Nigeria Central   Eritrea   Cambodia Brunei Micronesia
Guinea Bissau   Cameroon African   Djibouti   Sri   Malaysia Papua
Guinea   Republic Ethiopia   Lanka   Singapore New Guinea
Sierra Leone   South
Liberia   Ghana   Togo   Uganda Kenya Somalia   China   Indonesia Timor- Solomon
Côte D'ivoire   Rwanda   Sea   Leste   Islands
Burkina Faso   Burundi Tanzania   Indian Ocean
Equatorial Guinea   Malawi
Gabon   Coral Sea
Congo   Angola   Zambia   Australia
Democratic   Mauritius
Republic of   Madagascar
the Congo Namibia
Atlantic Ocean   Botswana Mozambique   New
                         Zimbabwe   Zealand
           South   Swaziland
           Africa Lesotho

Norway   Baltic   Estonia
          Sea
Denmark   Sweden   Russia
Netherlands   Russia Latvia
Belgium   Lithuania
          Germany Poland Belarus
Luxembourg Czech
Switzerland Republic Slovakia Ukraine
France Austria Hungary Serbia Moldova
       Slovenia   Romania
       Croatia Montenegro
       Italy Bulgaria Black Sea
       Bosnia Macedonia
       Herzegovina Greece   Turkey
       Albania

Antarctica

A-1

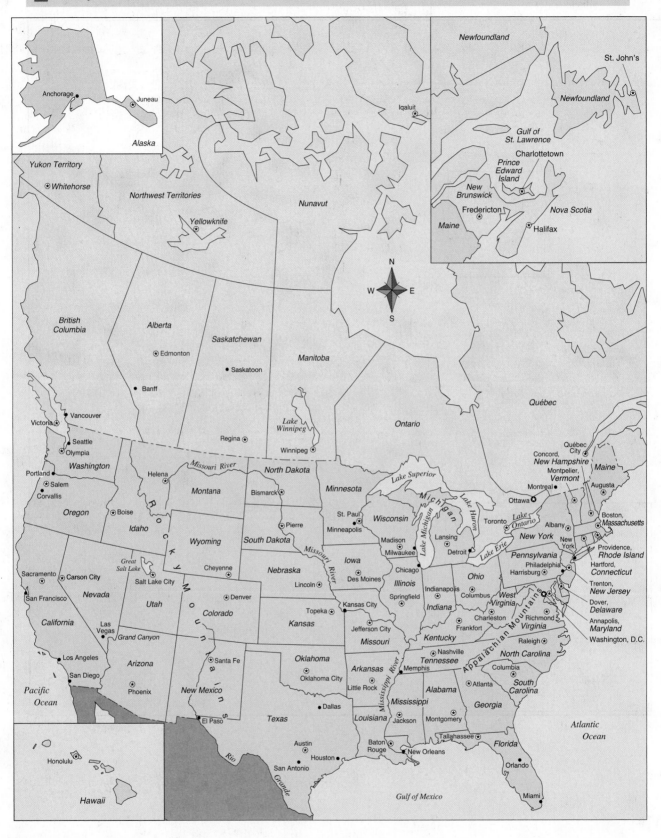

CARDINAL NUMBERS

1 = one	11 = eleven	21 = twenty-one
2 = two	12 = twelve	30 = thirty
3 = three	13 = thirteen	40 = forty
4 = four	14 = fourteen	50 = fifty
5 = five	15 = fifteen	60 = sixty
6 = six	16 = sixteen	70 = seventy
7 = seven	17 = seventeen	80 = eighty
8 = eight	18 = eighteen	90 = ninety
9 = nine	19 = nineteen	100 = one hundred
10 = ten	20 = twenty	101 = one hundred and one
		200 = two hundred
		1,000 = one thousand
		1,000,000 = one million
		10,000,000 = ten million

EXAMPLES

That building has **seventy-seven** pages.
There are **thirty** days in April.
There are **six** rows in the room.
She is **twelve** years old.
He has **four** children.

ORDINAL NUMBERS

1st = first	11th = eleventh	21st = twenty-first
2nd = second	12th = twelfth	30th = thirtieth
3rd = third	13th = thirteenth	40th = fortieth
4th = fourth	14th = fourteenth	50th = fiftieth
5th = fifth	15th = fifteenth	60th = sixtieth
6th = sixth	16th = sixteenth	70th = seventieth
7th = seventh	17th = seventeenth	80th = eightieth
8th = eighth	18th = eighteenth	90th = ninetieth
9th = ninth	19th = nineteenth	100th = one hundredth
10th = tenth	20th = twentieth	101st = one hundred and first
		200th = two hundredth
		1,000th = one thousandth
		1,000,000th = one millionth
		10,000,000th = ten millionth

EXAMPLES

He works on the **seventy-seventh** floor.
It's April **thirtieth**.
He's in the **sixth** row.
It's her **twelfth** birthday.
Bob is his **first** child. Mary is his **second**. John is his **third**, and Sue is his **fourth**.

TEMPERATURE

We measure the temperature in degrees (°).

Changing from degrees Fahrenheit to degrees Celsius:

$$(°F - 32) \times 5/9 = °C$$

Changing from degrees Celsius to degrees Fahrenheit:

$$(9/5 \times °C) + 32 = °F$$

DAYS OF THE WEEK

Weekdays	Weekend
Monday	Saturday
Tuesday	Sunday
Wednesday	
Thursday	
Friday	

MONTHS OF THE YEAR

MONTH	ABBREVIATION	NUMBER OF DAYS
January	Jan.	31
February	Feb.	28*
March	Mar.	31
April	Apr.	30
May	May	31
June	Jun.	30
July	Jul.	31
August	Aug.	31
September	Sept.	30
October	Oct.	31
November	Nov.	30
December	Dec.	31

*February has 29 days in a leap year, every four years.

(continued on next page)

THE SEASONS

NORTHERN HEMISPHERE

Spring: March 21–June 20

Summer: June 21–September 20

Autumn or Fall: September 21–December 20

Winter: December 21–March 20

SOUTHERN HEMISPHERE

Spring: September 21–December 20

Summer: December 21–March 20

Autumn or Fall: March 21–June 20

Winter: June 21–September 20

TITLES

Mr. (Mister)	/ mɪstər /	unmarried or married man
Ms.	/ mɪz /	unmarried or married woman
Miss	/ mɪs /	unmarried woman
Mrs.	/ mɪsɪz /	married woman
Dr. (Doctor)	/ dɑktər /	doctor (medical doctor or Ph.D.)

4 Time

It's one o'clock.
(It's 1:00.)

It's five after one.
(It's 1:05.)

It's one-ten.
It's ten after one.
(It's 1:10.)

It's one-fifteen.
It's a quarter after one.
(It's 1:15.)

It's one twenty-five.
It's twenty-five after one.
(It's 1:25.)

It's one-thirty.
It's half past one.
(It's 1:30.)

It's one forty-five.
It's a quarter to two.
(It's 1:45.)

It's one-fifty.
It's ten to two.
(It's 1:50.)

TALKING ABOUT TIME

1	You can talk about time this way:	**A: What time is it?** **B:** It's one o'clock.
2	**A.M.** means before noon (the hours between midnight and noon). **P.M.** means after noon (the hours between noon and midnight). **BE CAREFUL!** When people say 12:00 A.M., they mean midnight. When people say 12:00 P.M., they mean noon.	It's 10:00 A.M. It's 10:00 P.M.
3	We often write time with numbers.	It's one o'clock. = It's **1:00**. It's two-twenty. = It's **2:20**.

5 Plural Nouns: Spelling and Pronunciation Rules

PLURAL NOUNS: SPELLING RULES

1	Add **-s** to form the plural of most nouns.	student chief picture	student**s** chief**s** picture**s**
2	Add **-es** to form the plural of nouns that end in **ss**, **ch**, **sh**, and **x**. (This ending adds another syllable.)	class watch dish box	class**es** watch**es** dish**es** box**es**
3	Add **-es** to form the plural of nouns that end in **o** preceded by a consonant. **EXCEPTION:** Add **-s** to plural nouns ending in **o** that refer to music.	potato piano soprano	potato**es** piano**s** soprano**s**
4	Add **-s** to form the plural of nouns that end in **o** preceded by a vowel.	radio	radio**s**
5	To form the plural of words that end in a consonant + **y**, change the **y** to **i** and add **-es**.	dictionary fly	dictionar**ies** fl**ies**
6	To form the plural of words that end in a vowel + **y**, add **-s**.	boy day	boy**s** day**s**
7	To form the plural of certain nouns that end in **f** or **fe**, change the **f** to **v** and add **-es**.	half loaf knife wife	hal**ves** loa**ves** kni**ves** wi**ves**
8	Some plural nouns are **irregular**.	woman child person mother-in-law man foot tooth	women children people mothers-in-law men feet teeth
9	Some nouns **do not have a singular form**.	(eye) glasses clothes pants scissors	
10	Some plural nouns are the same as the singular noun.	Chinese fish sheep	Chinese fish sheep

🔊 PLURAL NOUNS: PRONUNCIATION RULES

1	The **final sounds** for regular plural nouns are / s /, / z /, and / ɪz /.	boots	boys	horses
2	The plural is pronounced / s / **after** the **voiceless sounds** / p /, / t /, / k /, / f /, and / θ /.	cups hats works	cuffs myths	
3	The plural is pronounced / z / **after** the **voiced sounds** / b /, / d /, / g /, / v /, / m /, / n /, / ŋ /, / l /, / r /, and / ð /.	crabs cards rugs	doves drums fans	rings girls stores
4	The plural *s* is pronounced / z / **after** all **vowel sounds**.	day toe	days toes	
5	The plural *s* is pronounced / ɪz / **after** the **sounds** / s /, / z /, / ʃ /, / tʃ /, and / dʒ /. (This adds another syllable to the word.)	races causes dishes	churches judges	

6 The Simple Present: Spelling and Pronunciation Rules

THE THIRD-PERSON SINGULAR AFFIRMATIVE: SPELLING RULES

1	Add **-s** to form the third-person singular of most verbs. Add **-es** to words that end in *ch*, *s*, *sh*, *x*, or *z*.	Pete works. I work too. Doug wears sweatshirts. I wear shirts. Norma teaches Spanish. I teach English. Lulu washes her clothes on Tuesday. Elenore and Pete wash their clothes on Sunday.
2	When a base-form verb ends in a **consonant** + *y*, change the *y* to *i* and add **-es**. Do not change the *y* when the base form ends in a **vowel** + *y*. Add **-s**.	I study at home. Carol studies at the library. Dan plays tennis. I play tennis too.
3	*Have*, *do*, and *go* have **irregular forms** for the third-person singular.	I have. He **has**. I do. She **does**. I go. It **goes**.

1	The **final sound** for the third-person singular form of the simple present is pronounced / s /, / z /, or / ɪz /. The final sounds of the third-person singular are the same as the final sounds of plural nouns. See Appendix 9 on pages A-8 and A-9.	/ s / talk**s**	/ z / love**s**	/ ɪz / dan**ces**
2	**Do** and **say** have a change in vowel sound.	I say. / se**ɪ** / I do. / d**u** /	He say**s**. / s**ɛ**z / He doe**s**. / d**ʌ**z /	

7 Possessive Nouns

1	Add **'s** to form the possessive of singular nouns.	Lulu**'s** last name is Winston.
2	To form the possessive of plural nouns ending in **s**, add only an **apostrophe (')**.	The girl**s'** gym is on this floor. The boy**s'** locker room is across the hall.
3	In hyphenated words (*mother-in-law*, *father-in-law*, etc.) and in phrases showing joint possession, only the last word is possessive in form.	My sister-in-law**'s** apartment is big. Elenore and Pete**'s** apartment is comfortable.
4	To form the possessive of plural nouns that do not end in **s**, add **'s**.	The men**'s** room is next to the water fountain.
5	To form the possessive of one-syllable singular nouns that end in **s**, add **'s**. To form the possessive of words of more than one syllable that end in **s**, add an **'** or an **'s**.	**James's** apartment is beautiful. **McCullers'** novels are interesting. OR **McCullers's** novels are interesting.
6	**BE CAREFUL!** Don't confuse possessive nouns with the contraction of the verb **be**.	**Carol's** a student. = **Carol is** a student. **Carol's** book is open. = **Her** book is open.

8 The Present Progressive: Spelling Rules

1	Add -*ing* to the base form of the verb.	drink see eat	drink**ing** see**ing** eat**ing**
2	If a verb ends in a silent **e**, drop the final **e** and add -*ing*.	smil**e**	smil**ing**
3	If a one-syllable verb ends in a consonant, a vowel, and a consonant (**CVC**), double the last consonant before adding -*ing*. However, do not double the last consonant if it is a **w**, **x**, or **y**.	**CVC** sit run sew mix play	 si**tt**ing ru**nn**ing se**w**ing mi**x**ing pla**y**ing
4	In words with two or more syllables that end in a consonant, a vowel, and a consonant (**CVC**), double the last consonant only if the last syllable is stressed.	admit´ whisper´	admi**tt**ing *(stressed)* whispe**r**ing *(not stressed)*

9 Direct and Indirect Objects

Group One

Subject	Verb	Direct Object	To	Indirect Object	Subject	Verb	Indirect Object	Direct Object
She	sent	a gift it	to	us.	She	sent	us	a gift.

Group Two

Subject	Verb	Direct Object	For	Indirect Object	Subject	Verb	Indirect Object	Direct Object
They	found	a towel it	for	him.	They	found	him	a towel.

Group Three

Subject	Verb	Direct Object	To	Indirect Object
He	repeated	the question	to	the class.

Group Four

Subject	Verb	Direct Object	For	Indirect Object
He	fixed	the shelves	for	me.

Group One Verbs (to)		Group Two Verbs (for)	Group Three Verbs (to)	Group Four Verbs (for)
email	sell	build	explain	cash
give	send	buy	prove	close
hand	show	find	repeat	fix
lend	teach	get	say	pronounce
owe	tell	make	whisper	translate
pass	throw			
read	write			

RULES FOR DIRECT AND INDIRECT OBJECTS

1 With **Group One** and **Group Two verbs**, there are **two** possible **sentence patterns** if the **direct object** is a **noun**.

	DIRECT OBJECT	TO/FOR	INDIRECT OBJECT	
I gave the	**money**	**to**	**him**.	=

	INDIRECT OBJECT	DIRECT OBJECT
I gave	**him**	**the money**.

	DIRECT OBJECT	TO/FOR	INDIRECT OBJECT	
We bought	**the book**	**for**	**him**.	=

	INDIRECT OBJECT	DIRECT OBJECT
We bought	**him**	**the book**.

If the **direct object** is a **pronoun**, it always comes **before the indirect object**.

	DIRECT OBJECT	TO/FOR	INDIRECT OBJECT
I gave	**it**	**to**	**him**.
Please get	**them**	**for**	**me**.

Not: I gave ~~him it~~.
Not: Please get ~~me them~~.

2 With **Group Three** and **Group Four verbs**, the **direct object** always comes **before the indirect object**.

	DIRECT OBJECT	TO/FOR	INDIRECT OBJECT
Explain	**the sentence**	**to**	**John**.
She translated	**the letter**	**for**	**us**.

Not: Explain ~~John the sentence~~.
Not: She translated ~~us the letter~~.

THE SIMPLE PAST: SPELLING RULES

1	If the verb **ends in an e**, add **-d**.	arrive like	arrive**d** like**d**
2	If the verb **ends in a consonant**, add **-ed**.	rain help	rain**ed** help**ed**
3	If a **one-syllable verb** ends in a consonant, a vowel, and a consonant (**CVC**), double the last consonant and add **-ed**. However, do not double the last consonant if it is a **w**, **x**, or **y**.	**CVC** hug rub bow mix play	 hu**gged** ru**bbed** bow**ed** mix**ed** play**ed**
4	If a **two-syllable verb** ends in a consonant, a vowel, and a consonant (**CVC**), double the last consonant only if the last syllable is stressed.	refer enter	refe**rr**ed *(stressed)* ent**er**ed *(not stressed)*
5	If the verb ends in a **consonant + y**, change the **y** to **i** and add **-ed**.	worry carry	worr**ied** carr**ied**
6	If the verb ends in a **vowel + y**, do not change the **y** to **i**. Add **-ed**. There are **exceptions** to this rule.	play annoy pay lay say	play**ed** annoy**ed** **paid** **laid** **said**

THE SIMPLE PAST: PRONUNCIATION RULES

1	The **final sounds** for regular verbs in the simple past are / **t** /, / **d** /, and / **ɪd** /.	walk**ed**	plann**ed**	wait**ed**
2	The final sound is pronounced / **t** / **after** the **voiceless sounds** / **f** /, / **k** /, / **p** /, / **s** /, / **tʃ** /, and / **ʃ** /.	laugh**ed** lick**ed**	si**pped** mi**ssed**	wa**tched** wi**shed**
3	The final sound is pronounced / **d** / **after** the **voiced sounds** / **b** /, / **g** /, / **dʒ** /, / **l** /, / **m** /, / **n** /, / **r** /, / **ŋ** /, / **ð** /, / **ʒ** /, / **v** /, and / **z** /.	ru**bbed** hu**gged** ju**dged** pu**lled**	hu**mmed** ba**nned** occu**rred** ba**nged**	ba**thed** massa**ged** li**ved** surpri**sed**
4	The final sound is pronounced / **d** / **after vowel sounds**.	pl**ayed** sk**ied**	t**ied** sn**owed**	arg**ued**
5	The final sound is pronounced / **ɪd** / after / **t** / and / **d** /. / **ɪd** / adds a syllable.	want instruct rest attend	wan**ted** instruc**ted** res**ted** atten**ded**	

11 Base Forms and Past Forms of Common Irregular Verbs

Base Form	Past Form	Base Form	Past Form	Base Form	Past Form
become	became	give	gave	say	said
begin	began	go	went	see	saw
bite	bit	grow	grew	send	sent
blow	blew	hang	hung	shake	shook
break	broke	have	had	shoot	shot
bring	brought	hear	heard	shut	shut
build	built	hide	hid	sing	sang
buy	bought	hit	hit	sit	sat
catch	caught	hold	held	sleep	slept
choose	chose	hurt	hurt	speak	spoke
come	came	keep	kept	spend	spent
cost	cost	know	knew	stand	stood
do	did	lead	led	steal	stole
draw	drew	leave	left	swim	swam
drink	drank	lend	lent	take	took
drive	drove	lose	lost	teach	taught
eat	ate	make	made	tear	tore
fall	fell	meet	met	tell	told
feed	fed	pay	paid	think	thought
feel	felt	put	put	throw	threw
fight	fought	quit	quit	understand	understood
find	found	read*	read*	wake	woke
fly	flew	ride	rode	wear	wore
forget	forgot	ring	rang	win	won
get	got	run	ran	write	wrote

*Pronounce the base form / rid /. Pronounce the past form / rɛd /

COMMON NON-COUNT NOUNS*

Liquids

milk	soda
coffee	water
oil	beer
juice	

Food

bread	ketchup
cheese	jam
lettuce	jelly
broccoli	fish
ice cream	meat
butter	sour cream
mayonnaise	soup

Too Small to Count

sugar	baking powder
salt	cereal
pepper	spaghetti
cinnamon	wheat
rice	corn
sand	

School Subjects

math	biology
history	chemistry
geography	music

City Problems

traffic
pollution
crime

Weather

snow
rain
ice
fog

Gases

oxygen
carbon dioxide
nitrogen
air

Abstract Ideas

love	advice
beauty	help
happiness	noise
luck	time

Others

money	jewelry
mail	garbage
furniture	toothpaste
homework	paper
information	

*Some nouns can be either count or non-count nouns.

I'd like some **chicken**. (non-count)   Did you eat any **cake**? (non-count)
There were three **chickens** in the yard. (count)   I bought a **cake** at the bakery. (count)

QUANTIFIERS: CONTAINERS, MEASURE WORDS, AND PORTIONS

a bottle of (milk, soda, ketchup)	a pair of (pants, skis, gloves)
a bowl of (cereal, soup, rice)	a piece of (paper, cake, pie)
a can of (soda, beans, tuna fish)	a pint of (ice cream, cream)
a cup of (hot chocolate, coffee, tea)	a quart of (milk)
a foot of (snow, water)	a roll of (film, toilet paper, paper towels)
a gallon of (juice, gas, paint)	a slice of (toast, cheese, meat)
a head of (lettuce)	a tablespoon of (flour, sugar, baking soda)
an inch of (snow, rain)	a teaspoon of (sugar, salt, pepper)
a loaf of (bread)	a tube of (toothpaste, glue)

METRIC CONVERSION

1 liter	= .26 gallons or 1.8 pints	1 mile	= 1.6 kilometers	1 ounce	= 28 grams
1 gallon	= 3.8 liters	1 kilometer	= .62 mile	1 gram	= .04 ounce
		1 foot	= .30 meter or 30 centimeters	1 pound	= .45 kilogram
		1 meter	= 3.3 feet	1 kilogram	= 2.2 pounds
		1 inch	= 2.54 centimeters		

These are the pronunciation symbols used in this text. Listen to the pronunciation of the key words.

VOWELS

Symbol	Key Word
i	beat, feed
ɪ	bit, did
eɪ	date, paid
ɛ	bet, bed
æ	bat, bad
ɑ	box, odd, father
ɔ	bought, dog
oʊ	boat, road
ʊ	book, good
u	boot, food, student
ʌ	but, mud, mother
ə	banana, among
ɚ	shirt, murder
aɪ	bite, cry, buy, eye
aʊ	about, how
ɔɪ	voice, boy
ɪr	ear, beer
ɛr	bare
ɑr	bar
ɔr	door
ʊr	tour

CONSONANTS

Symbol	Key Word	Symbol	Key Word
p	pack, happy	ʃ	ship, machine, station, special, discussion
b	back, rubber	ʒ	measure, vision
t	tie	h	hot, who
d	die	m	men
k	came, key, quick	n	sun, know, pneumonia
g	game, guest	ŋ	sung, ringing
tʃ	church, nature, watch	w	wet, white
dʒ	judge, general, major	l	light, long
f	fan, photograph	r	right, wrong
v	van	y	yes, use, music
θ	thing, breath	t̬	butter, bottle
ð	then, breathe		
s	sip, city, psychology		
z	zip, please, goes		

GLOSSARY OF GRAMMAR TERMS

action verb A verb that describes an action. It can be used in the progressive.
- *Sachiko **is planning** a big party.*

adjective A word that describes (or modifies) a noun or pronoun.
- *That's a **great** idea.*

adverb A word that describes (or modifies) an action verb, an adverb, an adjective, or a sentence.
- *She drives **slowly**.*

adverb of frequency A word that tells the frequency of something.
- *We **usually** eat lunch at noon.*

adverb of manner A word that describes a verb. It usually answers the question *how*.
- *She speaks **clearly**.*

affirmative statement A sentence that does not use a negative verb form (*not*).
- *I **have a car**.*

apostrophe A punctuation mark used to show possession and to write a short form (contraction).
- *He**'s** in my father**'s** car.*

base form The simple form of the verb without any ending such as *-ing*, *-ed*, or *-s*. It is the same as the infinitive without *to*.
- *Arnold will **come** at 8:00. We should **eat** then.*

be going to future A verb form used to make predictions, express general facts in the future, or talk about definite plans that were made before now.
- *Mei-Ling says it**'s going to be** cold, so she**'s going to take** a coat.*

capital letter The big form of a letter of the alphabet. Sentences start with a capital letter.
- ***A**, **B**, **C**, etc.*

comma Punctuation used to separate single things in a list or parts of a sentence.
- *We went to a restaurant**,** and we ate chicken**,** potatoes**,** and broccoli.*

common noun A noun for a person, place, or thing. It is not capitalized.
- *The **man** got a **book** at the **library**.*

comparative form An adjective or adverb ending in *-er* or following *more*. It is used in comparing two things.
- *My sister is **older** and **more intelligent** than my brother.*
- *But he studies **harder** and **more carefully**.*

consonant The letters *b, c, d, f, g, h, j, k, l, m, n, p, q, r, s, t, v, w, x, y, z*.

contraction A short form of two words. An apostrophe (') replaces the missing letter.
- ***It is** late and **I am** tired. I **should not** stay up so late.*
- ***It's** late and **I'm** tired. I **shouldn't** stay up so late.*

count noun A noun you can count. It usually has a singular and a plural form.
- *In the **park**, there was a **man** with two **children** and a **dog**.*

definite article *The*; It makes a noun specific.
- *We saw a movie. **The** movie starred Sean Penn.*

demonstrative adjective An adjective used to identify the noun that follows.
- ***This** man is resting, but **those** men are busy.*

demonstrative pronoun A pronoun used in place of a demonstrative adjective and the noun that follows.
- ***This** is our classroom, and **these** are my students.*

direct object A noun or pronoun used to receive the action of a verb.
- *She sold a **car**. He bought **it**.*

exclamation point A punctuation mark (!) used at the end of a statement. It shows strong emotion.
- *Help**!** Call the police**!***

formal language Language we usually use in business settings, academic settings, and with people we don't know.
- ***Good morning, ladies** and **gentlemen**. **May** we begin?*

gerund   The *-ing* form of a verb. It is used as a noun.
- *Skiing is fun, but we also enjoy swimming.*

imperative   A sentence used to give an instruction, a direction, a command, or a suggestion. It uses the base form of the verb. The subject (you) is not a part of the sentence.
- *Turn right at the corner. Drive to the end of the street. Stop!*

indefinite article   *A* and *an*; used before singular, nonspecific non-count nouns.
- *Jaime brought a sandwich and an apple for lunch.*

infinitive   *To* + the base form of a verb.
- *To travel is my dream. I want to see the world.*

informal language   The language we usually use with family and friends, in email messages, and in other informal settings.
- *Hey, Doug, what's up?*

inseparable phrasal verb   A phrasal verb that cannot have an object between the verb and the particle.
- *She ran into John.*

irregular verb   A verb that does not form the simple past by adding *-d* or *-ed*.
- *They ate a fancy meal last night. The boss came to dinner.*

modal   A word that comes before the main verb. Modals can express ability, possibility, obligation, and necessity.
- *You can come early, but you mustn't be late, and you should wear a tie.*

negative statement   A statement with a negative verb form.
- *He didn't study. He wasn't ready for the test.*

non-action verb   A verb that does not describe an action. It can describe an emotion, a state, a sense, or a mental thought. We usually don't use non-action verbs in the progressive.
- *I like that actor. He is very famous, and I believe he won an Oscar.*

non-count noun   A noun we usually do not count. We don't put *a*, *an*, or a number before a non-count noun.
- *All you'll need is rice, water, salt, and butter.*

noun   A word that refers to a person, animal, place, thing, or idea.
- *Paula has a friend at the library. She gave me a book about birds.*

noun phrase   A phrase formed by a noun and words that describe (modify) it.
- *It was a dark brown leather jacket.*

object   A noun or pronoun following an action verb. It receives the action of the verb.
- *I sent a letter. He read it.*

object pronoun   A pronoun following a verb or a preposition.
- *We asked him to show the photos to them.*

period   A punctuation mark (.) used at the end of a statement.
- *I'd like you to call on Saturday. We need to talk.*

phrasal verb   A two-part (or three-part) verb that combines a verb and a particle. The meaning of the parts together is often different from the meaning of the verb alone.
- *We put on our gloves and picked up our umbrellas.*

phrase   A group of words that can form a grammatical unit.
- *She lost a red hat. He found it under the table.*

plural   The form that means more than one.
- *We sat in our chairs reading our books.*

possessive   An adjective, noun, or pronoun that shows possession.
- *Her book is in John's car. Mine is at the office.*

preposition   A small word that goes before a noun or pronoun object. A preposition often shows time or place.
- *Maria saw it on the table at two o'clock.*

prepositional phrase   A phrase that consists of a preposition followed by a noun or a noun phrase.
- *Chong-Dae saw it under the black wooden table.*

present progressive   A verb form that shows an action happening now or planned for the future.
- *I'm working hard now, but I'm taking a vacation soon.*

pronoun   A word that replaces a noun or a noun phrase. There are subject pronouns, object pronouns, possessive pronouns, and demonstrative pronouns.

- *He is a friend—I know **him** well. **This** is his coat; **mine** is black.*

proper noun   The actual name of a person, place, or thing. A proper noun begins with a capital letter.

- ***Tom** is living in **New York**. He is studying **Russian** at **Columbia University**.*

quantifier   A word or phrase that comes before a noun and expresses an amount of that noun.

- *Jeannette used **a little** sugar, **some** flour, **four** eggs, and **a liter of** milk.*

question mark   A punctuation mark (?) used at the end of a question.

- *Where are you going**?** When will you be back**?***

quotation marks   Punctuation marks (" . . .") used before and after the actual words a person says.

- *I said, **"Where are you going?"** and **"When will you be back?"***

regular verb   A verb that forms the simple past by adding -d or -ed.

- *We **lived** in France. My mother **visited** us there.*

sentence   A group of words with a subject and a verb.

- ***We opened the window.***
- ***Did they paint the house?***

separable phrasal verb   A phrasal verb that can have an object between the verb and the particle.

- *She **put on** her coat. She **put** it **on** before he **put** his coat **on**.*

simple past   A verb form used to show a completed action or idea in the past.

- *The plane **landed** at 9:00. We **caught** a bus to the hotel.*

simple present   A verb form used to show habitual actions or states, general facts, or conditions that are true now.

- *Kemal **loves** to ski, and it **snows** a lot in his area, so he**'s** very happy.*

singular   The form that means only one.

- *I put on my **hat** and **coat** and closed the **door**.*

small letter   The small form of a letter of the alphabet. We use small letters for most words except for proper nouns and the word that starts a sentence.

- ***a, b, c**, etc.*

subject   The person, place, or thing that a sentence is about.

- ***The children** ate at the mall.*

subject pronoun   A pronoun used to replace a subject noun.

- *Irene works hard. **She** loves her work.*

superlative form   An adjective or adverb ending in -est or following most. It is used in comparing three or more things.

- *We climbed the **highest** mountain by the **most dangerous** route.*
- *She drives the **fastest** and the **most carelessly** of all the drivers.*

syllable   A group of letters with one vowel sound. Words are made up of one or more syllables.

- *One syllable—**win***
- *Two syllables—**ta ble***
- *Three syllables—**im por tant***

verb   A word used to describe an action, a fact, or a state.

- *He **drives** to work now. He **has** a new car, and he **is** a careful driver.*

vowel   The letters a, e, i, o, or u, and sometimes y.

wh- question   A question that asks for information. It begins with what, when, where, why, which, who, whose, or how.

- ***What**'s your name?*
- ***Where** are you from?*
- ***How** do you feel?*

will future   A verb form used to make predictions, to talk about facts in the future, to make promises, to offer something, or to state a decision to do something at the time of speaking.

- *It **will** probably rain, so I'**ll take** an umbrella. I'**ll give** you my extra one.*

yes/no question   A question that has a yes or a no answer.

- ***Did you arrive on time?** Yes, I did.*
- ***Are you from Uruguay?** No, I'm not.*
- ***Can you swim well?** Yes, I can.*

UNIT REVIEW ANSWER KEY

Note: In this answer key, where a short or contracted form is given, the full or long form is also correct (unless the purpose of the exercise is to practice the short or contracted forms).

UNIT 1

A 1. are   3. am   5. are
   2. is   4. is

B 1. 'm   3. 're   5. 're
   2. 's   4. 's

C 1. He isn't (He's not)   3. We aren't (We're not)
   2. They're   4. She's

D My father and mother are from India, but they're in Canada now. My parents are doctors.

My father ~~is~~ a sports doctor and my mother ~~she~~ is a foot doctor. My parents and I love sports. My

father ~~are~~ *is* a soccer fan, and my mother ~~_~~ *is* a baseball

fan. I'm a soccer fan. My father and I ~~am~~ *are* fans of

Lionel Messi and Nuno Gomes. My sister ~~no is~~ *isn't* good at sports. She's not a sports fan. She loves movies.

UNIT 2

A 1. Where's   3. What's   5. Is
   2. How's   4. Are

B 1. I am
   2. it isn't (it's not)
   3. they aren't (they're not)
   4. we are
   5. you aren't (you're not)

C 1. What's today's date?
   2. Where's the men's room?
   3. Why is he absent? (Why's he absent?)
   4. When's your first class?
   5. Who's your teacher?

D 1. ~~She~~ *Is she* your teacher?
   2. What *is* your name?
   3. Where *is* your class?
   4. ~~Is~~ *Are* Bob and Molly good friends?
   5. Why *are* you late?

UNIT 3

A 1. was   3. Were   5. Was
   2. was   4. were

B 1. c   3. d
   2. b   4. a

C 1. was   5. were
   2. was   6. wasn't
   3. Were   7. was
   4. was

D John ~~is~~ *was* at a job interview yesterday. It ~~were~~ *was* for a

job at a bank. The questions ~~no were~~ *weren't* easy, but

John's answers were good. He was happy. It ~~_~~ *was* a good day for John.

UNIT 4

A 1. a   3. Ø   5. Ø
   2. an   4. Ø

B 1. cities   3. clothes   5. people
   2. watches   4. fish or fishes

C lin = Lin   london = London
   ali = Ali   thanksgiving = Thanksgiving

D Melanie Einzig is *an* artist and ~~an~~ *a* photographer. She was born in Minnesota, but lives in

New ~~york~~ *York*. Einzig captures moments in time.

Her ~~photograph~~ *photographs* are striking. They are in ~~museum~~ *museums*

in San ~~francisco~~ *Francisco*, Chicago, and Princeton.

UNIT 5

A 1. a   3. Ø   5. Ø
   2. Ø   4. an

B 1. c   3. b   5. b
   2. a   4. c

C 1. I'm at the new museum.
   2. It is full of interesting things to see.
   3. It has unusual bowls from long ago.
   4. It has beautiful carpets too.
   5. The museum is a great place to visit.

D The Grand Canyon National Park in Arizona is ~~a~~ *an* awesome place to visit. Almost five million people

visit this ~~park unusual~~ *unusual park* each year. The weather

is good in the late spring and summer, but it *is* crowded ~~x~~ during those months. There are seven

~~differents~~ *different* places to stay in the park. I like El Tovar.

It is ~~a~~ *an* old hotel with a great view.

UNIT 6

A 1. on   3. behind   5. in front of
   2. under   4. next to

B 1. at   3. at, on the
   2. at

C

D A: Is Jon at ~~the~~ school?

B: No. He's ~~in~~ ^{at} home.

A: Where does he live?

B: He lives ~~at~~ ^{on} Oak Street, between First and

Second Avenue ~~at~~ ⁱⁿ Lakeville.

A: Does he live in an apartment?

B: Yes. He lives ~~in~~ ^{on} the third floor.

UNIT 7

A 1. Let's get   4. Let's not meet
   2. Why don't we invite   5. Don't touch
   3. Don't buy

B 1. Wear   4. Don't bring
   2. Don't wear   5. pay
   3. Bring

C 1. Let's go to the gym.
   2. Let's watch a movie this afternoon.
   3. Why don't we take a trip together?
   4. Why don't we hang out with Pietro this
     weekend?

D 1. Why ~~you~~ ^{you} don't ask Andrij for help?

   2. You look really tired. ^{Why don't you} ~~You~~ take a short nap[?].

   3. Let's ~~to~~ walk to work. Let's not drive.

   4. Don't ask Boris to fix the car. ^{Ask} ~~Asks~~ Mickey.

   5. I'm on a diet, so buy yogurt at the store. Don't
     ~~to~~ buy sour cream.

UNIT 8

A 1. shops   3. don't like   5. has
   2. likes   4. go

B 1. don't need   3. play
   2. need   4. doesn't like

C 1. is   3. wears   5. are
   2. works   4. don't wear

D 1. My son doesn't ~~has~~ ^{have} a suit.

   2. He always ~~wear~~ ^{wears} jeans, T-shirts, and hoodies.

   3. He ~~need~~ ^{needs} a suit for my brother's wedding.

4. Suits ~~is~~ ^{are} expensive and my son ~~don't~~ ^{doesn't} like to
   wear them.

5. We ~~wants~~ ^{want} to rent or borrow a suit for him.

UNIT 9

A 1. Do   3. Does   5. Am
   2. Is   4. Are

B 1. Do / have   3. Does / watch   5. Are
   2. Does / speak   4. Is

C 1. Are the neighbors noisy?
   2. Does the apartment building have an elevator?
   3. Is the apartment near trains or buses?
   4. Does the bedroom have two closets?
   5. Is the bedroom big?

D 1. A: Does he have a big TV in his room?
     B: Yes, he ~~has~~. ^{does.}

   2. A: Does she ~~needs~~ ^{need} help?
     B: No, she ~~don't~~. ^{doesn't}

   3. A: ~~Do you are~~ ^{Are you} friends?
     B: Yes, we ~~aren't~~. ^{are} (OR No, we aren't.)

UNIT 10

A 1. Why   3. Who   5. Where
   2. When   4. How

B 1. Who snores in your family?
   2. What do you dream about?
   3. What time does your mother get up?
   4. What time do you go to bed?
   5. Where does your brother sleep?

C 1. Who meets his uncle at the diner (on
     Saturdays)?
   2. Who does John meet at the diner (on
     Saturdays)?
   3. Where does John meet his uncle (on
     Saturdays)?
   4. When does John meet his uncle at the diner?

D 1. Where ^{do} you live and who ^{do} you live with?

   2. Why ^{does} he daydream in class?

   3. When does she ~~gets~~ ^{get} up?

   4. How ^{do} they feel about sleeping pills?

   5. Who ~~does~~ ^{do} you dream about?

UNIT 11

A 1. A: Are there   B: there are
   2. A: Are there   B: there aren't
   3. A: Is she   B: she is

4. A: Are they   **B:** they aren't
5. A: Is there   **B:** there isn't

B 1. There's / It's
  2. There are / They're
  3. There's / She's

C Visit the new Shopper's Mall on Route 290.
  There are
  ~~There's~~ over 100 stores. ~~There~~ *There's* a movie theater,
  there
  and ~~they~~ are ten great places to eat. Come early.

  Every morning at 10:30 ~~there are~~ *there's* a free show for
  children. The mall is three miles from the Tappan
  Bridge on Route 290.

UNIT 12

A 1. Their   **3.** Its   **5.** Her
  2. His   **4.** Their

B 1. A: mine   **B:** yours   **A:** your
  2. A: Whose   **B:** Ali's
  3. My / Its
  4. A: Her / yours   **B:** Mine

C A: ~~Who's~~ *Whose* bag is that on the floor?
  B: I think it's ~~Maria~~ *Maria's*.
  A: No. Her bag is on her arm.
  mine (OR my bag)   *Rita's*
  B: Well, it's not ~~mine bag~~. Maybe it's ~~Rita~~.
  yours (OR your bag)
  A: Rita, is that ~~bag your~~?

UNIT 13

A 1. couldn't understand / can understand
  2. can't run / could run
  3. couldn't drive / can drive

B 1. A: Can   **B:** can
  2. A: Could   **B:** couldn't / can
  3. A: Can   **B:** can

C A: Can you ~~x~~ get online?
  get
  B: No, I can't ~~x~~. I couldn't ~~got~~ online last night
  either.
  A: My brother is good with computers. Maybe he
  help
  can ~~helps~~.
  can't
  B: Great. I ~~can no~~ figure out what's wrong.
  can't
  A: I ~~no can~~ reach him now, but I can ~~x~~ call him
  after 6 P.M.

UNIT 14

A 1. may eat   **4.** may not use
  2. can't eat   **5.** may drink
  3. can have

B 1. When can I return to work?
  2. When can I take a shower?

3. Can I go to the gym?
4. Can I ride my bike?

C 1. You may not eat. (You may not bring food.)
  2. You may not use a pencil.
  3. You may not make phone calls.
  4. You may bring a bottle of water.
  5. You may use a black or blue pen.
  6. You may use a dictionary.

D A: May I ~~sees~~ *see* a menu?
  Sure.
  B: ~~Sure, you might~~. Here you go.
  A: And can we ~~x~~ have some water?
  B: I'll be right back with the water. . . . Ready?
  A: Yes. I want the chicken with mushroom sauce.
  have
  But may I ~~has~~ the sauce on the side?
  I'm sorry.
  B: ~~You may not~~. We cook the chicken in the
  sauce.
  A: Oh? Well, then I'll have grilled chicken with
  rice.

UNIT 15

A 1. 'm not getting   **4.** 're doing
  2. 're preparing   **5.** 's feeling
  3. isn't playing

B 1. is listening to
  2. are standing and talking
  3. are running
  4. is driving
  5. is carrying

C 1. is texting / isn't ('s not) calling
  2. are working / aren't giving up
  3. is swimming / 's trying

D My classmates and I ~~am~~ *are* sitting in a computer lab.
  is
  One student writing a composition. Two students
  checking   *helping*
  are ~~check~~ their email. A teacher is ~~helps~~ a student.
  The other students are surfing the Internet.

UNIT 16

A 1. A: Are / watching   **B:** they are
  2. A: are / doing   **B:** 'm listening
  3. A: 's happening   **B:** is putting

B 1. Are you working?
  2. Is he buying tickets online?
  3. Are they watching a mystery?
  4. Is she enjoying the movie?

C 1. Where are they going?
  2. What music group is performing?
  3. Where are they playing?
  4. Why is Bob staying home?

D 1. A: Is ~~it's~~ *it* raining outside?
  B: Yes. I hope it stops.

2. A: Are they playing soccer?

 B: No, they*'re* not. They're playing rugby.

3. A: *Are you* ~~You~~ watching a good movie?

 B: It's OK.

4. A: What *are* they doing?

 B: They're fixing the cabinets.

UNIT 17

A 1. don't own   4. needs
  2. doesn't like   5. want
  3. has

B 1. is using   3. 's getting   5. wants
  2. is surfing   4. has

C 1. is / doing   4. don't know
  2. 's trying   5. Does / need
  3. 's

D 1. **A:** Where *are* you calling from?

  B: Downtown. *I'm walking* ~~I walk~~ along Second Street.

 2. **A:** Is she *playing* ~~play~~ tennis at West Park?

  B: No, she's not. She *doesn't* ~~no~~ like those courts.

 3. **A:** Does he *understand* ~~understands~~ Greek?

  B: Yes, he does. He was in Greece for a year.

UNIT 18

A 1. watched   4. Last night
  2. visited   5. didn't land
  3. an hour ago

B 1. helped   4. didn't ask
  2. stayed   5. didn't want
  3. didn't snow

C 1. canceled   4. played
  2. didn't stay   5. didn't enjoy
  3. didn't rain

D Hello from London. Our friends ~~did~~ invited us here for a week. We're having a great time.

 Yesterday we *visited* ~~visit~~ Big Ben, and we *toured* ~~tour~~ the Royal Palace. This morning we *watched* ~~watch~~ the Changing of the Guard. We wanted to shop this afternoon, but we didn't. The prices were high, but we ~~are~~ enjoyed looking at the store windows.

UNIT 19

A 1. saw   3. tried
  2. was / wanted   4. got / didn't want

B A lucky man **found** a pot of gold. He **kept** the pot of gold in a hole in the ground of his garden. A jealous worker **stole** the gold from the man.

The man **became** upset. But a neighbor laughed because the man **didn't use** the gold. He just enjoyed counting it.

C 1. didn't stay   3. ran   5. took
  2. lost   4. didn't see

D 1. William Sidney Porter *was* born in North Carolina in 1862.

 2. He was a famous American short story writer. He wrote under different names, but he ~~did~~ became best known as O. Henry.

 3. His stories ~~were~~ had surprise endings.

 4. O. Henry had many talents, but he ~~did get~~ *got* into trouble and spent time in prison.

UNIT 20

A 1. Did they go to the theater?
  2. Did she get there by bus?
  3. Did you have good seats?
  4. Did he understand everything?
  5. Did we miss the beginning?
  6. Did it have a happy ending?

B 1. What play did you see?
  2. Where did you see it?
  3. How long was the show?
  4. Did you enjoy the performance?
  5. Who were the stars?
  6. Did you go out after the show?
  7. Where did you go?
  8. What did you order?

C 1. Where *did he* ~~he did~~ go last night?

 2. What *did he see* ~~saw he~~?

 3. Did he *enjoy* ~~enjoyed~~ it?

 4. Who *did* he *meet* ~~met~~?

 5. When *did* they go?

 6. Who ~~did pay~~ *paid* for it?

UNIT 21

A 1. was born   5. started
  2. grew up   6. became
  3. attended   7. expanded
  4. went

B 1. When did she go to college?
  2. Who did they meet?
  3. Where did he study?
  4. How long did they live in Canada?

C 1. Were   3. Was   5. Did
  2. Did   4. Did

D Steve Paul Jobs ~~did start~~ *started* college in 1970, but he ~~no did~~ *didn't* finish it. In 1976 Jobs and his friend ~~begin~~ *began* to make their own computers. They worked in the Jobs' garage. That was the beginning of Apple® Computers. Their company ~~become~~ *became* a big success. Apple® changed the field of computers, and by the age of 30, Jobs was a multimillionaire.

A
1. starting
2. to sell
3. to return
4. to become
5. flying / seeing
6. to help

B
1. to work
2. to change
3. quitting / going
4. to study
5. doing

C Carol volunteers at a hospital. She enjoys ~~to take~~ *taking* care of patients. Some patients refuse ~~do~~ *to* exercise, but Carol keeps ~~to push~~ *pushing* them. Carol intends *to* study physical therapy in college. She needs ~~taking~~ *to take* a lot of science courses. She expects to ~~went~~ *go* to college next fall. She hopes *to* get a degree in physical therapy in five years. She prefers ~~to~~ working with teenagers, but she will work with adults too.

A
1. is taking
2. make
3. made
4. likes

B
1. invented
2. didn't work
3. wanted
4. became
5. started
6. use
7. are sewing

C
1. Where did you go last weekend?
2. How did you get there?
3. What did you see at the museum?
4. How was the museum?
5. Do you go there often?

D
1. Last night I ~~did watch~~ *watched* a movie about fish.
2. I thought the fish were beautiful, and I ~~enjoy~~ *enjoyed* the movie.
3. My brother is watching the movie now, but he ~~don't~~ *doesn't* like it.
4. He ~~is only liking~~ *only likes* action films.

A
1. is going to build
2. 's going to cost
3. 's going to have
4. are going to be
5. isn't going to begin

B
1. are not going to increase
2. aren't going to play
3. 're going to visit
4. 's going to retire
5. 'm not going to do

C
1. **Q:** When is she going to the dentist? **A:** On Monday at 5:30.
2. **Q:** Where is she meeting Yu Chen? **A:** At Pappa Pizza.
3. **Q:** Is she meeting Yu Chen on Monday? **A:** No, she isn't.

D This city *is* going to change under our new mayor. ~~People's~~ *People are* going to ride bikes and they're ~~gonna~~ *going to* use public transportation. They're ~~no~~ *not* going to drive big cars. There are probably going to be higher tolls on bridges and more bike paths on the roads.

A
1. Where will people travel in twenty years?
2. Will people fly to the moon?
3. How will they get around?
4. Will the climate change?
5. Will people look different?

B
1. won't
2. won't
3. will
4. will
5. won't

C
1. Will / be hot
2. Will / have a test
3. Will / be a storm
4. Will / rain
5. Will / work late

D I usually bring my lunch to work, but tomorrow I ~~no will~~ *won't* bring it because it's my birthday. My co-workers will ~~takes~~ *take* me out to a restaurant. We'll ~~to~~ order a few different dishes, and we'll share them. They'll ~~singing~~ *sing* "Happy Birthday," and they'll give me a small gift. I'm sure it will ~~is~~ *be* a lot of fun.

A
1. go
2. buy
3. might not
4. may
5. Will

B
1. may (might) snow
2. may (might) not get
3. may (might) need
4. may (might) not see
5. may (might) stay

C 1. There may (or There might) be a restroom in the library.
2. He may (or might) be the director.
3. The plane might (or may) be late.
4. They may (or might) be cousins.
5. It might (or may) be his coat.

D 1. He might ~~goes~~ *go* on vacation next week.
2. He may ~~works~~ *work* late tomorrow.
3. They might ~~to~~ visit him tomorrow. Are you free?
4. I might not help him. I might ~~to~~ help her instead.
5. She ~~maybe~~ *may* take a yoga class.

UNIT 27

A 1. a few   3. an
    2. the   4. any

B 1. many   3. a little
    2. much   4. a few

C 1. a   4. the
    2. a   5. a
    3. the   6. a

D 1. **A:** What are you looking for?
      B: I need a ~~little~~ *few* stamps. I wrote ~~any~~ *some* postcards, and I want to mail them.
2. **A:** There isn't ~~some~~ *much* yogurt in the refrigerator. There's only half a container.
      B: There ~~isn't much~~ *aren't many* eggs either. We need to go shopping, but we don't have ~~many~~ *much* time.

UNIT 28

A 1. How many   4. How much
    2. How much   5. How many
    3. How many

B 1. How often do you go to the movies?
2. How many close friends do you have?
3. How much time do you spend online?
4. How many people live in your home?
5. How often do you check email?

C 1. I usually bake a few times a week.
2. They never have enough food in the house.
3. Every weekend we play soccer in the park.
4. He spilled a glass of grape juice.
5. She added a little salt to the soup.

D 1. ~~Never~~ *never* I eat breakfast at home.
2. ~~She once in a while~~ *Once in a while she* bakes.
3. Do you have ~~milk enough~~ *enough milk*?
4. How ~~much~~ *many* tomatoes did they buy?
5. I rarely ~~don't~~ cook.

UNIT 29

A 1. too long
2. too much homework
3. too much milk
4. too many trucks
5. too much time

B 1. too / too little
2. too few
3. too much
4. too many

C 1. There's too little rain.
2. There are too few subways.
3. There's too little sunlight.
4. There are too few traffic lights.
5. There is too little water.

D The climate here is terrible. It gets too ~~much~~ hot in the summer and too cold in the winter. There's too ~~many~~ *much* snow and ice. Winters are ~~to~~ *too* long. There are too ~~little~~ *few* comfortable days with mild temperatures and blue skies. Also, there's too ~~many~~ *much* air pollution from all the traffic on the streets. I want to move.

UNIT 30

A 1. should   4. ought to
    2. had better   5. better not
    3. shouldn't

B 1. had better not   3. had better not
    2. had better   4. had better

C 1. should   3. should
    2. shouldn't   4. shouldn't

D 1. Where should we ~~meets~~ *meet* after work?
2. We ~~'d~~ better take an umbrella tonight. It's going to rain.
3. Should I ~~to~~ make a reservation now for my flight? I think I ~~outta~~ *ought to* buy it soon.
4. What ~~I should~~ *should I* see during my business trip to Uruguay?
5. Should we ~~leaves~~ *leave* Brazil tonight or tomorrow?
6. You ought *to* bring flowers to your hostess to thank her for dinner.

UNIT 31

A 1. Would you like   4. We'd like
    2. Could you pass   5. Can you
    3. I'd like

B 1. Of course.   4. Sorry, I need it.
    2. Sure.   5. I'd be glad to.
    3. Thanks.

C 1. Could you please
2. I'd like
3. Could you please
4. Would you like
5. I'd like

D 1. A: Could ~~please~~ you *please* move my car at 11:00?

   B: ~~No, I wouldn't.~~ *Sorry.* I'll be at work then.

2. A: ~~I like~~ *I'd like* to see you this weekend. Would you like to go to the park?

   B: ~~I could.~~ *Yes, I would.*

3. A: Would you like ~~have~~ some more ice cream?

   B: No, thanks. I'm full.

UNIT 32

A 1. don't have to
2. have to
3. must not
4. doesn't have to
5. have to

B 1. mustn't
2. has / has to
3. don't have to
4. has to

C 1. had to work
2. have to read / answer
3. had to give OR have to give
4. didn't have to bring

D The test starts at 8:10. You must ~~to~~ be in the room at 8:00. You mustn't ~~came~~ *come* late. You have to ~~has~~ *have* two number two pencils and an eraser. You ~~musts~~ *must* ~~brings~~ *bring* proper identification, such as a photo ID or a passport. You must leave your cell phone in the front of the room.

UNIT 33

A 1. much
2. than
3. more popular
4. worse
5. higher
6. better
7. brother's

B 1. A bus ride is more expensive in Sun City than in New City.
2. A cup of coffee is cheaper in New City than in Sun City.
3. The average home is less expensive in New City than in Sun City.
4. The average income is higher in Sun City than in New City.

C We moved to the countryside, and we're much ~~more~~ happier. Our home is ~~more~~ larger, and the air is cleaner and polluted ~~less~~ *less*. It less

expensive than the city too. Fruits and vegetables are ~~more cheap~~ *cheaper*. The people are ~~friendlier~~ *friendlier*. Of course our commute is ~~more bad~~ *worse*; it's much ~~more long~~ *longer*, but we listen to Spanish tapes, and our Spanish is ~~more good~~ *better*.

UNIT 34

A 1. quickly
2. fluently
3. well
4. slowly
5. clearly

B 1. good
2. carefully
3. nervous
4. badly
5. quickly

C 1. good
2. briefly (clearly)
3. clearly (briefly)
4. fast
5. honestly

D A: I think my speech went ~~good~~ *well*.

   B: Did they appreciate your jokes?

   A: They laughed ~~polite~~ *politely*, but I'm not sure they laughed ~~sincere~~ *sincerely*.

   B: It's hard to be funny.

   A: I ~~hard worked~~ *worked hard*, and I prepared carefully, but I was ~~nervously~~ *nervous*.

UNIT 35

A 1. big enough
2. as
3. too
4. as
5. from

B 1. warm enough
2. very late
3. too busy
4. too short
5. enough time
6. very good

C I didn't like the prom this year as much ~~than~~ *as* last year. I usually like parties, but the music at the prom was much ~~very~~ *too* loud. Also, my dress was the same as ~~Julia~~ *Julia's*! That was a ~~too~~ *very* big shock. Also, the dinner portions weren't ~~enough large~~ *large enough* and the servers this year were very rude. Then we tried to dance, but there was ~~no~~ *not* enough room and the room was ~~too much~~ *much too* hot. The music was also not as good as last year. We had a ~~more~~ better time last year.

A 1. the funniest
  2. the biggest
  3. the best
  4. The largest / the most dangerous

B 1. the hottest day
  2. the oldest woman
  3. the busiest shopping day
  4. the most interesting show
  5. the most popular animals

C 1. one of the most intelligent animals
  2. one of the best zoos
  3. one of the worst seats
  4. one of the longest days
  5. one of the most expensive trips

D **1. A:** What is the ~~most good~~ *best* way to get to the park?

  B: The shortest route is also the *most* ^complicated. I'll give you the most direct ^way.

  2. A: What's the ~~most~~ hardest part of your job here at the zoo?

  B: Well, the ~~nicer~~ *nicest* part is taking care of the animals. The ~~most~~ worst part is telling people not to feed the animals or bother them.

CREDITS

INDEX

This index is for the full and split editions. All entries are in the full book. Entries for Volume A of the split edition are in black. Entries for Volume B are in red.